# THE
# SMALLER
# ACADEMIC LIBRARY

# The
# Smaller
# Academic Library

## A MANAGEMENT HANDBOOK

EDITED BY

## Gerard B. McCabe

**THE GREENWOOD LIBRARY MANAGEMENT COLLECTION**

Greenwood Press
NEW YORK • WESTPORT, CONNECTICUT • LONDON

**Library of Congress Cataloging-in-Publication Data**

The Smaller academic library.

(The Greenwood library management collection,
ISSN 0894-2986)
Bibliography: p.
Includes index.
1. Libraries, University and college—Administration
—Handbooks, manuals, etc.   2. Small libraries—
Administration—Handbooks, manuals, etc.   I. McCabe,
Gerard B.   II. Series.
Z675.U5S57   1988        027.7        87-23655
ISBN 0-313-25027-8 (lib. bdg. : alk. paper)

British Library Cataloguing in Publication Data is available.

Library of Congress Catalog Card Number: 87-23655
ISBN: 0-313-25027-8
ISSN: 0894-2986

First published in 1988

Greenwood Press, Inc.
88 Post Road West, Westport, Connecticut 06881

Printed in the United States of America

The paper used in this book complies with the
Permanent Paper Standard issued by the National
Information Standards Organization (Z39.48-1984).

10   9   8   7   6   5   4   3   2   1

# Contents

## PART VI: TECHNICAL SERVICES

## PART VII: PHYSICAL PLANT

# Preface

This book is for librarians who work or plan to work in smaller academic libraries that serve institutions with average enrollments ranging from a few hundred to about 7,500 students. The publisher and I perceived a need for a reference handbook for the managers and staffs of these libraries. The result is a volume of chapters written by peers from smaller academic libraries (with only three exceptions) that describes ideas for coping with contemporary problems. I hope that the solutions presented in this handbook can serve as starting points for the development of solutions in the libraries where its readers serve. The contributors offer a wide range of experience. Two of them (Jean Johnson and George Libbey) work in larger libraries, but their writings are applicable to certain situations affecting smaller libraries. The author of the bibliographic essay that completes this volume (Rashelle Karp) is a faculty member of a college of library science.

I divided the book into parts so that related chapters could be read as a group. The largest section, that on user programs and services, has seven chapters, while most of the others have four chapters. The last part on the physical plant has three chapters followed by a concluding bibliographic essay. The book can be read in sequence, if the reader wishes to do so, or, as a reference book, according to the reader's need at some particular moment.

Nearly all of the contributors supply references or a bibliography. The bibliographic essay provides further assistance.

This book, covering a wide range of topics, suggests ideas, notes trends, and above all strives to stimulate thinking to help readers arrive at solutions to their library's problems, resolve questions, and find new and better ways to provide library service.

# Acknowledgments

I want to express my sincere thanks and gratitude to Peggy Postlewait, Carlson Library's administrative secretary, who reviewed each chapter for technical form and offered many helpful suggestions. Her help made the preparation of this book much easier. I also appreciate the help of the Greenwood Press editors who provided guidance during this preparation.

# PART I

# General Administration

# 1

# Administrative Styles

## Fred M. Heath

In a remarkable article in the *Journal of Academic Librarianship*, Anne Roberts demonstrated that the demands on the academic library director have changed fundamentally over time. During the nineteenth century, she observed, there existed a climate that demanded and rewarded a *leader*. The world of knowledge at that time was more finite and self-contained. "Academic librarians," she noted, "were allied with a subject discipline and connected with a department, often teaching courses while also running the libraries" (1985: 14). In this capacity, they were not only leaders in the academic community but were scholars with an affinity for the humanities. This characterization, however, changed steadily and inexorably with the transformation of the college and university library during the emerging decades of the twentieth century. As Guy Lyle wrote in his classic treatise on library administration, there were several factors at work that forced a transformation in the nature of the library director. During the first decades of this century, the curriculum expanded rapidly as the frontiers of knowledge advanced on all fronts with astonishing speed. Publication rates soared, and the library was transformed through new features such as reserve book reading and independent honors sessions. The rise of accrediting societies, which placed new emphasis on the libraries, and the rapid increase in enrollments, which placed additional stresses on existing facilities, also created new demands on libraries and added to the sense of their centrality in the educational scheme of things (1974: 1–7).

As the pressures mounted, the twentieth-century library director was compelled to become a manager in the scientific sense. As Roberts wrote, "whereas the nineteenth-century academic librarian was a humanist, the twentieth-century academic librarian has become a specialist" (1985: 15–16). To cope with the rapid change, library administrators have had to abandon their concern with the humanities and to occupy themselves with the scientific management of increasingly complex organizations. In the library schools, the writings of Frederick Taylor and Henri Fayol were discovered and applied to the business of library management. Although the classic textbooks on library administration still placed a value on "the man himself" as recently as fifteen years ago and suggested that "intelligence, judgment, and personality will, in the end, be of more importance than his formal training and experience," there is a growing recognition of the unimportance of gender and the prerequisite for command of an important set of management skills if one is to succeed in the business of library administration (Rogers and Weber 1971: 26).

## CHALLENGES FACING THE LIBRARY ADMINISTRATOR

A modern academic library faces many challenges to its mission: the support of the instructional, research, and public-service functions of the university. Some of these challenges are common to all aspects of higher education. Among the issues that pervade the campus are the continuing erosion of public confidence in the efficacy of higher education, the declining size of the applicant pool of those of traditional college age, and the steady rise in fixed costs at rates that persistently outstrip hard-fought gains in local budgets. In addition, library administrators must address concerns that impact more narrowly on libraries, such as the rapidly changing face of library technology and the continuing requirements for staff and organizational development.

Libraries are sometimes removed from the center of academic decision-making, and it is often difficult to communicate the needs of libraries to those making resource-allocation decisions. To make those needs known, the administrator must be an effective communicator. For a member of the university administrative team, an understanding of higher education issues and of the place of the library in the university is vital. For the chief administrative officer of one of the largest and most costly units in the university, the ability to communicate clearly the requirements of the library is an obvious prerequisite. Equally important is an ability to communicate effectively with the staff of the library. Here, the administrator serves as the connecting link between the external decision-making apparatus and the library organization.

Maintenance of academic excellence in times of scarce resources and competing demands requires careful planning. To be successful, library planning should be strategic in outlook and comprehensive in its involvement of the staff. It is the responsibility of the chief library administrator to be acutely aware of the trends that affect higher education in the nation and the state, to be fully conversant with all aspects of institutional academic planning, and to involve all levels of the university library staff in the planning process. With staff involvement and a careful study of trends at every level, there are fewer surprises, fewer exigencies that call for that staple of library administration: crisis management.

Budgeting is one aspect of planning in which the chief library administrator must excel. As fixed costs rise and programs proliferate, resource-allocation decisions on all university campuses are becoming more complex. In the midst of the fiscal problems universally afflicting higher education, libraries are in the first years of the full bloom of library technology. Participating in that revolution and harnessing technology to the service mission of the library while maintaining the performance indices of other measures of library quality require considerable skills. They demand, on the one hand, that the library administrator enjoy the confidence of campus planners who must make tough budgetary decisions. They require, on the other hand, an understanding of alternative funding sources and a willingness to work hard to secure external funds to support the development of library programs.

Inescapably, the demands of the time place a premium on productivity and efficiency. Libraries and universities that place staff development and staff welfare as very high priorities are more likely to be successful in the pursuit of their missions than those that do not. It is a major goal of the chief administrator to create that kind of open environment within which work can take place and to establish the high standards that connote the professional nature of the undertaking. Staff development that allows the staff to keep abreast of the dizzying developments in libraries, to upgrade their skills, or to contribute to the corpus of knowledge through publication or presentation of papers is another important aspect of the director's personnel role.

The chief library administrator must be a change agent, able to create a library that is responsive to the many disparate demands made upon it. Organizational skills require an understanding of library systems, and the impact of changes in one component upon all other components. Indeed, the ability to serve as an effective change agent and to overcome inertia without disrupting the purposes of the system is one of the most demanding jobs of the chief administrator.

Finally, the chief administrator is inescapably the chief public relations officer of the library. As much as the services themselves, the attitudes with which the staff delivers those services color the public's perception of a library. On the one hand, the chief administrator must convey clearly to the staff the public nature of library service, insisting upon high standards for the delivery of those services. On the other hand, the library director must work effectively with faculty and campus groups, such as the academic senate and the student-government association. An ability to work with external groups, such as state governing boards and professional associations, is also essential.

An effective administrator of an academic library is an individual who understands higher education in all of its aspects, is fully aware of contemporary developments in librarianship, and capably handles the public relations responsibilities of the office. The administrator displaying these traits while competently discharging the various planning, organizing, communicating, and budgeting duties that the job demands would be a welcome addition to any campus administrative team. The development of such an administrator is a challenge faced by the library schools, institutional staff-development programs, and individuals alike. The panaceas that have been embraced over time are myriad.

## SCHOOLS OF MANAGEMENT THOUGHT: A REVIEW

Since the days of Frederick Taylor and Henri Fayol, librarians have been quick to attempt to adapt innovative principles of management to their discipline. In search of the universally applicable management style, management problems have been analyzed by a seemingly unending parade of sociologists, psychologists, sociometricists, economists, and others, creating what Harold Koontz has called the "Management Theory Jungle" (Koontz 1972: 8–17). From the Hawthorne experiments to Theory Z, practitioners have been quick to digest innovative new concepts and apply them to their disciplines (Roethlisberger and Dickson 1939; Ouchi 1981). In his own classification of the various schools of thought that have emerged to guide the manager through administrative responsibilities in today's complex organizations, Koontz identified six ideologies.

Among the first to evolve was the school known as the *management process school*, pioneered by Fayol (1949) and Taylor (1967). As the name implies, this approach views management as a process that can best be dissected by analyzing the role of the manager in an organization and breaking down management responsibilities into component parts. A second approach, popular especially among schools of business administration today, is referred to by Koontz as the *empirical school*. Essentially, this is a case-study approach, which assumes that through the study of examples of successful approaches to business problems and business management, one can learn the techniques and processes that produce success, generalize them, and transfer them universally to other situations and contexts.

Librarianship has shown a special partiality over time to the *human relations school*, whose basic tenet is that business is a process of getting things done through people. The adherents of this school cover a broad spectrum; their unifying characteristic is their focus on human relations and a certain tendency to equate management with motivational leadership. This school has a dominating concern with group dynamics and interpersonal relationships and includes people such as Douglas McGregor and popular new concepts such as "quality circles."

Somewhat more abstract in concept, but closely allied, is the so-called *social system school*, which emerged from the works of Chester Barnard (1938) and was further developed by Herbert Simon (1946). In many ways, this sociological approach has helped all organizations understand themselves better, although it has not improved the quality of individual managers. As Koontz pointed out, the social system approach has allowed practitioners to recognize that a corporate or other organized structure is a *social* organization that responds in certain predictable ways to internal dynamics and the external environment.

Other models, which are newer, include the *decision theory school* and the *mathematical school*. Although an occasional article will surface in the field literature, these works have not yet carved out a broad niche in librarianship. The former school grows out of the field of economics, out of the concepts of marginal utility and consumer theory. The focus is on the alternatives that present themselves to the manager in the process of decision-making. The decision and the decision process are thus elevated to a dominant place in the field of management. The latter school perhaps should not be singled out as a separate school, for mathematics is properly a tool for many aspects of the management process. Koontz, however, used the term to aggregate those theorists who suggest that the logical processes of management can be expressed as mathematical relationships and reduced to models that can be analyzed objectively and transferred generally among different types of organizations (1972: 9–13).

For every school, and for virtually every concept that emerges in the field of management, there soon emerge popularizers prepared to transfer the idea from its field of origin to their own discipline. Elizabeth Stone quoted another educator as stating that ''I do wish that when a principle has been worked out, say in ethics, it didn't have to be discovered all over again in psychology, in economics, in government, in business, in biology, and in sociology. It's such a waste of time!'' (1967: 21). Librarianship is no exception. It is unnecessary to demonstrate here that each of the schools discussed by Koontz has had its adherents in librarianship. An article published twenty years ago by Tai Keun Oh adequately treated the applications of management theory to librarianship up to that time (1966: 431–38). Other writers, such as Charles Martell and Donald Morton, have been quick to transfer emergent ideas to the field of library administration (Martell and Tyson 1983: 285–87; Morton 1975: 302–7).

## EFFECTIVE ADMINISTRATIVE STYLES

While grounded in the ideas of the human relations school, this chapter is predicated on a contingency approach to the concept of effective administrative styles in the library environment. Just as there are different approaches to planning and budgeting in the not-for-profit sector, there are different administrative styles that can be used to direct the organization. Building on the overview of the challenges facing the library administrator and the review of the different schools of management thought, it is possible to isolate some particularly important traits that contribute to an effective ''style'' of management. This section attempts to discuss those traits in a manner that will be useful to the practitioner and perhaps transferable to another context.

Both the large number of schools of management thought coexisting at any time and a brief look at history should be sufficient justification for the contingency or eclectic approach taken here. Clearly, different administrative styles are variously effective when applied to different tasks in different environments. For example, Richard Nixon—generally acknowledged to be one of the shrewder managers to occupy the chief executive's office—was at the end of his tenure the subject of a *Fortune* article that lambasted the Watergate crisis as a classic case of mismanagement (Ways 1973: 109). Thirteen years later, in an era of good feeling, the same periodical would feature an article praising the managerial talents of another chief executive whom many regard as "a good old Irish actor who stumbled onto the right set" (Dowd 1986: 34).

It is ironic that the central tenet of the Reagan philosophy is the very characteristic that got his predecessor into so much trouble: "surround yourself with the best people you can find, delegate authority, and don't interfere as long as the policy you've decided upon is being carried out" (Dowd 1986: 34). Whatever the fallacies of a management style that permits subordinates to operate with insufficient supervision, the president's philosophy echoes the central theme of twentieth-century management thought: the ability to work with people is the key to the development of any successful management style. As mentioned in the literature review above, one of the earliest efforts to deal with the management of people was described in the pioneering work of Frederick W. Taylor (1967), who undertook to make management a science.

Taylor's work, developed to increase the productivity of large-scale industry, has as its end goal an efficient organization with enhanced production that is mutually beneficial to employer and employee alike. His views were quickly adopted by a wide spectrum of enterprises, and his work remained the pervasively dominant management theory during the first decades of the century (Burkel 1984: 26). Whereas Taylor's work introduced into production principles a concern for the welfare of the worker as a unit of production, the Hawthorne experiments conducted by Elton Mayo for General Electric in the late 1920s and early 1930s introduced even more fundamental changes in management-employee relationships (Roethlisberger and Dickson 1939). For the first time, questions were raised about the applicability of Taylor's principles when the experiments appeared to show that social factors were often more influential in affecting worker productivity than were physical conditions.

The Hawthorne experiments opened the way for the human relations school, which began to see the worker as more than just a unit of production. Among the proponents of the human relations school have been luminaries such as Douglas McGregor, Rensis Likert, Frederick Herzberg, and Peter Drucker. The central tenets of this school are neatly encapsulated in the ideas of McGregor, who popularized the Theory Y concept. To develop this concept, he characterized the pervading theory of management as "Theory X." That more rigid perspective suggested that the average worker was by nature a lazy person who worked as little as possible, who avoided responsibility, and who was without ambition. The average worker was seen as self-centered, opposed to change, and indifferent to organizational needs. Management of this human resource required strong external controls (1968: 213–14).

In opposition to this orthodox view, McGregor suggested that the individual finds the expenditure of energy on work to be as natural as play or rest. Individuals, he contended, will exercise self-direction in the service of organizational directives when properly motivated and that strong external controls *are not* the only means of ensuring compliance. Workers will commit to organizational objectives to the extent to which they find the rewards for their achievement to be meaningful, according to Theory Y, and satisfaction of ego and self-actualization are more important as motivators of employees than certain lower-level needs. The work force was underused in the modern industrial world, and managers needed to take advantage of the creativity, innovation, and ingenuity that were far more widely distributed in the work force than they realized (1960: 47). Theory Y suggests that well-motivated people do not resist organizational requirements, have a capacity for assuming responsibility, and have an ability to direct their efforts toward the goals of the organization. "It is a responsibility of management to make it possible for people to recognize and develop these human characteristics for themselves" (1968: 214).

As it developed, the human relations school stressed the positive contributions of workers, given responsibility and freedom. Frederick Herzberg took those ideas of a highly motivated staff to a new level with his further development of those "lower-level" or "hygiene" factors, which he distinguished from the motivating factors in a working environment (1968: 53–62). *Hygiene factors* are those things whose absence can create a disgruntled, unmotivated staff. They are essentially the lower level needs of A. H. Maslow's hierarchy (1943: 370–96). In Herzberg's determination, they include things such as salary levels, working conditions, relationships with peers, company policies and administration, and security. Presence of these factors, he maintained, is insufficient to ensure a staff with a high level of job satisfaction. Only the *motivational* factors are sufficient to develop employee satisfaction. Those factors include achievement, recognition, responsibility, opportunity for growth and advancement, and the quality of the work itself (Herzberg 1968: 57; Burkel 1984: 26).

From the concepts of Herzberg, it is a short step to the rise of the participatory management school. Although today it has many branches and proponents, the founder of the school may be said to be Rensis Likert, whose influential ideas were laid out in works such as *The Human Organization* (1967: 63). In his work, Likert created a range of organizational modes ranging from the undesirable authoritarian system at one end of the spectrum to the most desirable participative scheme at the other end (Burkel 1984: 25). High performance of employees, noted Likert, required an effective organization with high levels of performance by employee and administrator alike. Performance goals of staff generally reflect those of management. In a departure from the ideas of McGregor, there is the suggestion that employees generally *will not* set high goals for themselves if management does not have such aspirations. Likert concluded that this is best achieved in a participatory setting: "A superior with high performance goals and excellent job organization is much more likely to have subordinates who set high goals for themselves and organize their work well when he uses group methods of supervision and applies the principles of supportive relationships than when he does not" (1967: 63).

## MANAGEMENT STYLES IN THE ACADEMIC LIBRARY

It is not surprising that before long the human relations school, and the participative mode in particular, found its adherents in the library field. Perhaps one attraction has been the mechanical aspects of the participatory idea, a belief that it is something that can be easily "imposed" upon an organization by a single manager who believes in the concept. As such, it may be viewed by ailing organizations as a quick solution to administrative difficulties. It is also an attractive concept to library professionals in an academic setting, where the faculty governance structure provides ample evidence of effective collegial and participative structures (Burkel 1984: 25).

One of the leading popularizers of the participatory idea in libraries has been Maurice Marchant (1976), whose works are a continuing outgrowth of his doctoral research. Marchant concluded in his research that participatory management permits decision-making to flow to the most logical level of the organization, where the information most suited to resolution is available. Decentralization of decision-making, meanwhile, frees the director for a myriad of other, external, responsibilities, and according to some researchers, a direct relationship can be shown between the presence of a participatory management style in an organization and high staff morale (Burkel 1984: 27).

In its own work, the ARL Office of Management Studies staff has looked at the participatory style and has cataloged a number of advantages over more orthodox structures. In addition to improved staff-management relations, these advantages include better service to clients as a by-product of improved morale and enhanced relations with the central administration as an outgrowth of increased productivity (Webster and Gardner 1975: 13). During the past few years, the concept has been embraced by many library administrators, including those at Duke University, the University of California at Los Angeles, the California State University at San Diego, Dickinson College, and the University of Guelph (Burkel 1984: 30; Dunlap 1976: 402).

For all of its popularity, however, the participatory approach is not without its detractors. Just as the school has its roots in the literature of human relations and the recognition that group cohesiveness can lead to increased productivity, so, too, are the objections grounded in the same research. Lost in the enthusiasm for the positive aspects of the human relations ideas were the cautions of follow-up studies to the Hawthorne experiments suggesting that some of the lessons drawn from that study had been oversimplified and that group cohesiveness in some situations can have the opposite effect: restrictions on output, declining productivity, and resistance to management (Sayles 1958; Seashore 1955). In the words of one researcher:

It would be a mistake . . . to assume that all group standards are consistent with the objectives of the larger organization. We have stressed the positive aspects because so much of the literature only emphasizes the negative results of the group effort. But many times groups do urge their members to produce less than they might otherwise accomplish, do try to reject new assignments because they do not approve of the work, and do even coalesce in opposing a new supervisor. (Sayles and Strauss 1960: 93)

In the library world, authors have emphasized a more particular objection to the participatory approach: that the committee time librarians spend in a participatory setting necessarily leaves less time for professional work (Burkel 1984: 30). James Govan has suggested that in a time of diminishing resources, when libraries must be concerned about the erosion of the level of service to clients, the time and money spent on making a participatory structure work is particularly hard to justify (1977: 259).

In addition, as William G. Ouchi has pointed out, the participatory concept works best in organizations in which there is a well-understood organizational philosophy that fosters a sense of group ownership. Academic libraries are part of larger organizations, whose chief academic officers and others have a large part in establishing the organizational philosophy. Also, library directors are all too often transient people, and the constant turnover mitigates against a permanent organizational philosophy. In addition, the participatory structure is most effective when there is long-term employment and good opportunity for advancement within. Libraries do not always satisfy these characteristics. Finally, the complexities of library organization, requiring highly specialized skills at each position, make the job rotation needed to develop a broad organizational perspective difficult to achieve in a library setting. For these reasons, it may be difficult to achieve decentralized decision-making in a library environment (Lewis 1986: 344).

In concluding his study of the applicability of the participatory approach to library governance, Nicholas Burkel noted the intensity of the claims and counterclaims of its effectiveness and offered his hope that in some unfolding of the Hegelian dialectic it will be possible to arrive at some synthesis upon which all librarians can agree (1984: 32). While we await the organizational miracle that the dialectical process may offer, it may be possible to find some refuge in the theories of Henry Mintzberg, who suggested that social structures are unique and must seek their own organizational "fit." He suggested that an organization must determine the type of structure whose characteristics are best for its own environment and suits its particular functions. "When these characteristics are mismatched—when the wrong ones are put together—the organization does not function effectively, does not achieve a natural harmony. If managers are to design effective organizations, they need to pay attention to the fit" (1981: 104).

Although it is perhaps unfair to leave the field practitioner with a sense of incompleteness, it is the thesis of this chapter that a flexible, eclectic approach to administrative responsibilities remains the most advisable strategy. Clearly, one must remain abreast of the trends in the management literature and must remain sensitive to major developments such as the trend toward participatory styles. Yet the administrator must not forget the responsibilities of management to provide a sound organization structure. As Chris Argyris pointed out, employees suffer when there is no clear organization. "Some human relations researchers . . . have unfortunately given the impression that formal structures are 'bad' and that the needs of the individual participants should be paramount in creating and administering an organization. A recent analysis of the existing research, however, points up quite clearly that the importance of the organization is being recognized by those who in the past have focused largely upon the individual'' (1957: 7). Even Maurice Marchant has observed that ''abdicating the leadership role and allowing staff members to do whatever they wish is no more permissible under participative management than it is under an authoritarian style'' (1976: 7).

Some writers have suggested that variants of what Henry Mintzberg called the ''professional bureaucracy'' might work well in libraries. As he defined this concept, Mintzberg described an organization that relies heavily on trained professionals with specialized skills for its work. The skills of the individuals are more important than the work processes or assembly line, and thus the organizations that adopt the model are likely to differ considerably from large-scale industry. Because the organization must depend on the skills of the individuals, they are given a large measure of autonomy in their work. Mintzberg named hospitals, accounting firms, and universities among such organizations. In this type of organization, decision-making and power are decentralized, often following down to the operating level, where the skills exist to make the correct decision (1981: 109).

David Lewis has adapted Mintzberg's concept to libraries and has suggested that a modified version of it would work effectively in most contexts (1986: 348–49). In his model, middle-management levels would be trimmed as much as feasible. The widest possible span of control should be established, creating an environment in which communications would flow effectively. Because most first-line administrators would also be line professionals, decision-making would take place at the proper level, with top management being brought closer to the operating core. There would be a deliberate focus on the group in the organizational structure, which would preserve some of the best aspects of the participatory concept, but management would not abandon its responsibilities for control (1986: 348–49). Although it is not a pretty name, Lewis's ''modified professional bureaucratic configuration'' does appear to be a good ''fit'' for most academic libraries. It emerges out of the mainstream of the human relations school and the participatory ideas. The final section of this chapter offers a brief look at how the library administrator can balance the concepts of concern for productivity and staff participation.

## THE MANAGERIAL GRID®

Some years ago, Robert Blake and Jane Srygley Mouton developed a conceptual device that, given a specific organizational context, is especially helpful to a manager attempting to devise an administrative style appropriate to the tasks at hand (Blake and Mouton 1964). This chapter has suggested that the most effective organizational context for the library administrator is a decentralized bureaucracy in which librarians operate with a high degree of autonomy. Within that rather democratic environment, the library administrator seeks to maximize the organization's productivity. That is the usefulness of the Blake and Mouton concept of the managerial grid. Given an understanding of the literature of management science and in particular the human relations school, the administrator can apply the grid concepts to a local context in an effort to maximize the productivity of the organization.

Blake and Mouton began by suggesting that all organizations are characterized by three universal characteristics: purpose, people, and hierarchy, In the most general terms, they suggested that production, in some measurable output of goods or services, is the purpose of most organizations. Similarly, the need for people working together in some fashion to achieve production is another condition of organization. Finally, hierarchy is the third attribute: "The process of achieving organization purpose . . . through the efforts of people . . . results in some people attaining authority to set direction and coordinate effort; that is, to exercise the responsibility for the activities of others" (Blake and Mouton 1985: 9).

As shown in figure 1, the managerial grid depicts the interactions between a concern for production and a concern for people. The horizontal scale is the axis for production; the vertical axis depicts the concern for staff and their welfare. Each is expressed as a nine-point scale of concern. A low level of concern is indicated by a one, an intermediate degree of concern by a five, and a high level of concern by a nine. The grid permits eighty-one combinations of concern from 1.1 to 9.9. The concept is easy to grasp and to apply and has been applied by the authors and others to various applications such as sales, supervision, media, and marriage (Blake and Mouton 1970, 1975; Mouton and Blake 1971; Miller 1974). It is proof of Elizabeth Stone's dictum that the concept was eventually applied to libraries.

An orientation to managerial styles can be obtained from a look at the corners of the grid. The lower right corner will produce a 9.1 manager with a driving concern for services but little concern for employees or staff welfare. At the opposite diagonal is the 1.9 manager, whose style is characterized by a compassionate concern for staff with little concern for productivity. It is a managerial style that assumes staff members will respond productively when "warm, supportive, nondirective and nonjudgmental supervision is provided" (Blake, Mouton and Tapper, 1981: 3). It is, perhaps, reflective of the position taken by some of the more naive proponents of the participatory management idea and is certainly the position that the opponents of participatory management have in mind in their criticisms.

In the lower left-hand corner of the grid is a laissez-faire 1.1 strategy of supervision. To the extent that it exists at all, it is largely a position of non-management, with little concern for either productivity or staff. The upper right corner of the managerial grid produces the 9.9 manager, combining a high degree of concern for staff welfare with an equally great concern for productivity. It is the most difficult management level to achieve. Generally, it can be demonstrated

**Figure 1**
**The Managerial Grid®**

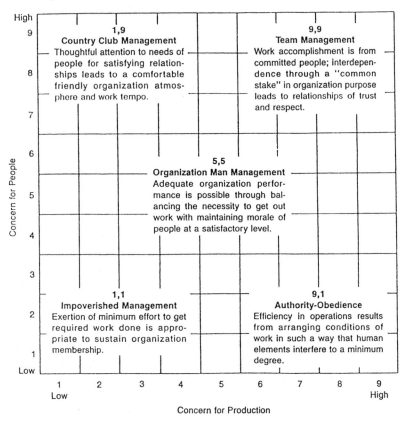

that an administrative style as depicted on the grid can be stable over time, but
in keeping with the eclectic, contingency approach advocated in this chapter, it
also shifts over time to respond to local exigencies. According to the authors of
this concept, almost all administrators have a backup style. In their view, ''a
person's backup style becomes evident when it is difficult or impossible to apply
the dominant or most characteristic grid style. It is the style reverted to when a
person is under pressure, tension, or strain, frustrated, or in situations of conflict
that cannot be solved in his or her characteristic way'' (Blake, Mouton and
Tapper, 1981: 3).

Adapting the grid to a library context, one would suggest that the 9.1 manager
exhibits a concern for the delivery of services over the welfare of staff. There
would likely be considerable stress placed on form, with emphasis on established

policies and procedures. In this circumstance, the focus is likely to be on the quantifiable, and there is likely to be considerable pressure on staff to produce steadily improving indices on numerical measures of performance, such as reference questions answered, instruction sessions offered, and books purchased or circulated. Considerable emphasis is likely to be placed on contact with patrons because that is viewed as a primary role, but the contact is likely to be "by the book," formal, and routine. In contrast, in the 1.9 management style interactions with faculty and students are likely to be sincere and warm; close relationships are likely to be built with individual staff members and patrons. Interactions, however, are likely to be undirected. Little attention will be paid to policies and procedures, and some librarians are likely to offer assistance without regard to established procedures. Written communications, reporting, and other control mechanisms are likely to be pushed to the background since meeting student and faculty needs is considered to be the primary responsibility of staff, and all other duties are considered to be secondary (Miller 1974: 7).

As mentioned previously, the 1.1 position is one of abdication, with little concern for services or staff. Contacts with the academic community are avoided, and faculty and students must force relationships and must take the initiative to secure use of library facilities and equipment. Written policies and procedures, if they exist, are outmoded. There is no innovation or growth. If development of library programs and facilities occurs at all, it is from the outside.

The style that is considered the most enviable is the 9.9 management style. There is an attempt to ensure an effective overall service profile, developed through deep interaction with faculty and students. Indeed, the ability to identify and meet the needs of the academic community is the foundation of the library program. In the 9.9 style there is a caring relationship between the administrator and staff. Procedures, policies, and collections are carefully and meticulously maintained, reviewed, and revised as required. Innovation flows from the effective interaction of administration, professionals at the operational level, and the community (Miller 1974: 9).

With the 9.9 administrator, concern for optimal efficiency joins a similar concern with people. In the other grid patterns, the two concerns are seen as mutually exclusive: to some degree concern for either personnel or productivity predominates at the expense of the other (Blake, Mouton and Tapper, 1981: 84). The 9.9 orientation, to be maintained, requires greater leadership skills and more effective group process than is evident in the other styles. The following concerns, which typify the 9.9 manager, are in keeping with the mainstream ideas of the human relations school:

1. The employee finds fulfillment through contributions made in the workplace; in Herzberg's terms the work is meaningful in itself.

2. Respect and trust are prerequisite to productive human relationships; there is a high level of trust between the administrator and the employee, permitting high performance goals to be set by each.

3. Communications that promote communications are effective and in a professional bureaucratic hierarchy are probably best achieved by a flattened administrative hierarchy that brings top management as close to the operational core as possible.

4. There is prompt and effective conflict resolution; the cumbersome decision-making structure that some opponents of the participatory management idea oppose is largely absent.

5. In the best sense of Mintzberg's idea of the professional bureaucracy, there is sufficient freedom and autonomy to promote innovation and to cultivate a sense of personal responsibility for one's actions.

Although it is an artificial device, it is useful to the administrator wanting to assess managerial styles in an organization and to set the stage for further organizational development activities (Blake, Mouton, and Tapper, 1981: 85).

## SUMMARY

This chapter has traced the evolution of management thought from the early works of Taylor and others through the rise of the human relations school to the emergence of currently popular concepts such as participatory management and Theory Z. Recognizing the central place that the concern for staff has in essentially professional organizations such as libraries, close attention has been given to those administrative styles that have grown out of the human relations school. However, the argument is advanced that no single organizational pattern or administrative style is universally applicable to any institution. The argument is made in favor of an eclectic approach to administration. Within that context, it is suggested that a modified professional bureaucratic configuration, as proposed by Lewis, is a generally workable model. The concepts of the managerial grid as developed by Blake and Mouton were introduced to assist in evaluating different administrative styles. If there is a final word to be offered, it is a note of caution. Management science is a literature of fashion. New ideas and new concepts come into vogue regularly. Each year some new concept dominates the literature and the best-seller charts as it flashes into general popularity and is then applied inexorably to the various disciplines until it has worked its way into all occupations. Whether the ideas are management by objectives (MBO), zero-base budgeting (ZBB), quality circles, or Theory Z, in time they all make their way into the library literature. The field administrator needs only to remember that these new ideas are merely tools; they are never panaceas. A broad understanding of the human relations literature and a commitment to one's staff and to the purposes of the organization are the prerequisites to a sound administrative style. The concepts discussed in the literature of management and library science are James Govan's "better mousetraps," which each manager should evaluate and employ as best fits the local situation.

# REFERENCES

Argyris, Chris. 1957. "The Individual and Organizations: Some Problems of Mutual Adjustment." *Administrative Science Quarterly* 2 (June): 1–23.

Barnard, Chester. 1938. *The Functions of the Executive*. Cambridge, Mass.: Harvard University Press.

Blake, Robert R., and Jane Srygley Mouton. 1964. *The Managerial Grid: Key Orientations for Achieving Production through People*. Houston: Gulf Publishing Company.

———. 1970. *The Grid for Sales Excellence: Benchmarks for Effective Salesmanship*. New York: McGraw-Hill.

———. 1975. *The Grid for Supervisory Effectiveness*. Austin: Scientific Methods.

———. 1985. *The Managerial Grid III: The Key to Leadership Excellence*. Houston: Gulf Publishing Company.

Blake, Robert R., Jane Srygley Mouton, and Mildred Tapper. 1981. *Grid Approaches for Managerial Leadership in Nursing*. St. Louis: C. V. Mosby Company.

Burkel, Nicholas. 1984. "Participatory Management in Academic Libraries: A Review." *College and Research Libraries* 45 (January): 25–34.

Dowd, Ann Reilly. 1986. "What Managers Can Learn from Manager Reagan." *Fortune* 114 (September 15): 32–35.

Dunlap, Connie. 1976. "Organizational Patterns in Academic Libraries, 1876–1976," *College and Research Libraries* 37 (September): 395–407.

Fayol, Henri. 1949. *General and Industrial Management*. Translated by Constance Storrs. New York: Pitman Publishing.

Govan, James F. 1977. "The Better Mousetrap: External Accountability and Staff Participation." *Library Trends* 26 (Fall): 255–68.

Herzberg, Frederick. 1968. "One More Time: How Do You Motivate Employees?" *Harvard Business Review* 46 (January-February): 53–62.

Koontz, Harold. 1972. "The Management Theory Jungle." In *Management: A Book of Readings*. Edited by Harold Koontz and Cyril O'Donnell. New York: McGraw-Hill.

Lewis, David W. 1986. "Organizational Paradigm for Effective Academic Libraries." *College and Research Libraries* 47 (July): 337–53.

Likert, Rensis. 1967. *The Human Organization*. New York: McGraw-Hill.

Lyle, Guy R. 1974. *The Administration of the College Library*. 4th ed. New York: H. W. Wilson.

McGregor, Douglas M. 1960. *The Human Side of Enterprise*. New York: McGraw-Hill.

———. 1968. *Leadership and Motivation*. Cambridge, Mass.: MIT Press. Reprinted in P. Wasserman and M. Bundy. *Reader in Library Administration*. Washington, D.C.: NCR Microcard Editions, 1968, pp. 213–14.

Marchant, Maurice P. 1976. *Participative Management in Academic Libraries*. Westport, Conn.: Greenwood Press.

Martell, Charles and John Tyson. 1983. "QWL Strategies: Quality Circles." *Journal of Academic Librarianship* 9: 285–87.

Maslow, A. H. 1943. "A Theory of Human Motivation." *Psychological Review* 50: 370–96.

Miller, Thomas E. 1974. "The Media-Management Grid—A Tool for Introspection." *Audiovisual Instruction* (April): 7–8.

Mintzberg, Henry. 1981. "Organizational Design: Fashion or Fit." *Harvard Business Review* 59 (January): 103–16.

Morton, Donald J. 1975. "Applying Theory Y to Library Management." *College and Research Libraries* 36 (July): 302–7.

Mouton, Jane Srygley, and Robert R. Blake. 1971. *The Marriage Grid*. New York: McGraw-Hill.

Oh, Tai Keun. 1966. "New Dimensions of Management Theory." *College and Research Libraries* 27 (November): 431–38.

Ouchi, William G. 1981. *Theory Z: How American Business Can Meet the Japanese Challenge*. New York: Avon.

Roberts, Anne F. 1985. "The Academic Librarian as Leader or Manager." *Journal of Academic Librarianship* 11 (March): 14–18.

Roethlisberger, F. J., and William J. Dickson. 1939. *Management and the Worker*. Cambridge, Mass.: Harvard University Press.

Rogers, Rutherford D., and David C. Weber. 1971. *University Library Administration*. New York: H. W. Wilson.

Sayles, Leonard R. 1958. *Behavior of Industrial Work Groups: Prediction and Control*. New York: Wiley.

Sayles, Leonard, and George Strauss. 1960. *Human Behavior in Organizations*. Englewood Cliffs, N.J.: Prentice-Hall.

Seashore, Stanley E. 1955. *Group Cohesiveness in the Industrial Work Group*. Ann Arbor, Mich.: Institute for Social Research, Survey Research Center.

Simon, Herbert. 1946. "The Proverbs of Administration." *Public Administration Review* 6 (Winter): 53–67.

Stone, Elizabeth. 1967. *Training for the Improvement of Library Administration*. Urbana: University of Illinois.

Taylor, Frederick Winslow. 1967. *The Principles of Scientific Management*. New York: W. W. Norton. Reprint.

Ways, Max. 1973. "Watergate as a Case Study in Management." *Fortune* 88 (November): 109–12.

Webster, Duane, and J. J. Gardner. 1975. "Strategies for Improving the Performance of Academic Libraries." *Journal of Academic Librarianship*. 1 (May): 13–18.

# 2

# The Small-College Library Director

## Herbert D. Safford

### THE AMERICAN SMALL COLLEGE

It would be whimsical to suggest precisely which institutions of higher education are really "small colleges" and why, given that such schools are as diverse in size and character as Amherst and Avila, Middlebury and Milligan, or Williams and Westmar, but in the aggregate their relatively small enrollments and their emphasis on undergraduate, arts and sciences education distinguish them from other institutions of higher learning in the United States, both the principal universities and the specialized schools focusing on a single subject or on the trades.

The American Association of University Professors in its annual statistical issue of *Academe*, basing its definition on that of the National Center for Educational Statistics, characterized Category IIB (General Baccalaureate Institutions)

by their primary emphasis on general undergraduate baccalaureate-level education. Included are institutions which are not considered as specialized and in which the number of post-baccalaureate degrees granted is fewer than thirty or in which fewer than three post-baccalaureate-level programs are offered and which either (a) grant baccalaureate degrees in three or more program areas, or (b) offer a baccalaureate program in interdisciplinary studies.

For the most part, these IIB schools are America's small colleges. Many of the observations in this chapter are based on my survey of about 300 small-college library directors and the persons to whom they report administratively.

### THE SMALL-COLLEGE LIBRARY

Libraries of small colleges share stringent limits of budget, collection size, staff, and often facilities. They share, in general, the charge to support an intellectually broad undergraduate curriculum by developing resources and services directly pertinent to classroom teaching. The dilemma of the small-college library is that of reconciling significant limits with a charge so general in scope. This dilemma is also the challenge that the small-college library director accepts. This chapter focuses on those aspects of this challenge to small-college library directors that, at least in part, distinguish their jobs from those of their colleagues in other kinds of institutions.

## THE SMALL-COLLEGE LIBRARY DIRECTOR

Small-college library directors must develop and oversee the programmatic exploitation of limited resources in order to support the teaching of the undergraduate curriculum. The director must balance various investments in materials, facilities, staff, and programs so that the library serves best the particular nature of its institution's commitment to enhancing the capacity of students to do intellectual work. This balance involves policy and planning, budgeting and fund raising, staffing, and representation of the library to power structures outside of the library itself. It is this set of tasks that we term *administrative*.

The director's share of the library's work is in essence administrative. This is not to suggest the pejorative notion that the director should lose sight of the special character of intellect that attaches to the library's centricity in learning. Nor is it to suggest that library administration is of necessity at odds with collegial and collegiate values. It is rather to state that administrative action is necessary for this character to emerge and for these values to be sustained within a library and that the director is perforce the embodiment of this action. Administration requires a special kind of attention to a coherent set of matters that affect the capacity of the library to sustain service to its patrons over time, and it is the director who must accept the principal responsibility for these matters. This is the nature of the job, not a side benefit or an entangling irritant.

## ADMINISTRATION AND SCALE

A significant problem for the very small college libraries is that it must be determined in each case the extent to which the library can afford a librarian whose full attention can be devoted to conducting the library's administrative business. Each library director must decide the extent to which he or she should be involved in library duties that are not administrative, whether to fulfill the practical necessities of getting other kinds of library work done, to ensure that the director will not become isolated from the working realities of the library for which he or she is making decisions, or to remain vital in the profession. Usually, the larger the library, the more likely it is that administrative duties will usurp time available for other library tasks, but there is no easy answer to just how many professionals permit one person to be only a director in the administrative sense. What is important is the recognition that even in the one-professional college library some significant part of the director's time should be devoted to administrative responsibilities. A very common error is the director's view that he or she cannot afford time for "administrivia." It is rather the case that the director neglects administration at the library's peril. Too often all administration seems merely trivia to the librarian who really prefers reference work or cataloging or some other aspect of librarianship for which the director has talent. The individual who cannot appreciate the necessity of commitment to management activities should not consider a directorship under any circumstances.

Does this mean that libraries that can afford to devote one or more person's time to administration are better libraries than those that cannot? No. It does mean that the chances of understanding and achieving a patterned set of goals through resource development within a library increase to the extent that administration is taken seriously and is well performed, whether by a full-time administrative director or as a portion of an individual's responsibilities. Unfortunately, little in the literature of librarianship in higher education reflects the difficulty of this *forced* commitment to library management, since much of the literature is written by librarians in larger institutions (who have time to write) and is devoted to a directorial sphere in which the director has the prerogative to select a portion of the administrative agenda and to allocate other portions among staff middle managers. Even one-professional libraries can work smoothly with a certain degree of sharing of managerial responsibility, but the pressure to accept personal responsibility for administrative decisions and their consequences is much closer to the bone in small college libraries.

## FOUR LEVERS OF MANAGEMENT

Given that the small-college library director's particular task is library management, we might well ask what leverage the director has to implement action, to construct a future for the library that best meets institutional curricular needs. In broad terms, we may consider four levers for enhancing the director's capacity to act.

### Budget

The library budget is a principal lever to implement action. It should never be regarded passively, as a given, but should be considered a point of departure. It is particularly important to understand thoroughly both the ratio of expenditures as a whole for the library relative to the general institutional operating budget and the ratios for internal categories that the director may find useful (or mandated). Colloquially, it is important to know both how big the budgetary pie is (relative to other elements of institutional expenditure) and how the portions of pie are served. Both of these matters are absolutely subject to consideration, negotiation, change, and improvement over time.

College administrators are likely to have heard repeatedly the plight of the library in seeking new dollars. Too often librarians adopt a whining, backward-looking tone that reinforces college administrators' notion that the library is a bottomless pit into which to pour institutional resources. This is especially true if requests for dollars have always been for increased materials funding only. It is important to construe the budget to the administration in two ways.

First, if the college is spending less than about 5 percent of its operating budget on the library, it clearly has decided, albeit implicitly, that academic excellence is less important than other institutional criteria for survival. This point needs to be made emphatically. Few administrators are willing to accept this idea over the long term, however crass they may appear with respect to pleas for enhanced funding. To the level of 5 percent of the operating budget, the administration will usually yield funding to the library, however slowly this may happen.

Second, college administrations respond much more positively to funding for projects than they do to a general request for a budgetary increase, even when such a project request is for enhancement to a particular portion of the collection (e.g., to increase reference resources). It is important to have always in front of the persons who grant funding an array of requests for funding at a variety of levels and for a variety of projects, ranging from the very small (perhaps a computer for $2,500) to the very large (perhaps a building for $3 million). Administrators may take a fancy to one sort of project while being dead set against other kinds of requests. The administration should always *have the opportunity to appear to be cooperating* by helping make choices from this array given the year's particular fiscal circumstances. The nature of the small college is that funding does vary from year to year, campaign to campaign, or bequest to bequest, and the library should have a record of aggressive, forward-looking requests before the administration to take advantage of the good years that will come.

Internally, once the 5 percent (or, one hopes, higher) figure for the overall library budget has been achieved, it is important to determine what budgetary elements are eroding the capacity of the director to move in the direction that seems appropriate. As a general matter (and the exceptions are as important and as interesting as the general case), libraries are badly underfunded for capital expenditures and are overfunded for personnel. That is, it is highly likely that the library is spending too much on salaries and benefits and too little on materials and equipment. The true yield on salaries in the aggregate is likely to be disproportionately small compared to that in other kinds of institutions, even given small-library salaries. This distorts the meaning and impact of the hoped-for 5 percent of the institution's operating budget.

The director should set, at least in mind and in a planning document, a minimum percentage for materials expenditures and should adhere to that minimum, regardless of the implications for personal popularity. Furthermore, contemporary libraries, even small ones, are and should be equipment intensive. People require interpretive devices; books and microforms require shelving; patrons must have places to sit and study. Increasingly, it will be possible for very small college libraries to have access to collections unheard of a few years ago as compact and optical disk storage gather their market share, but these things require capital investment. The director should consider seriously cutting or keeping staff spending to the barest of minimums, hiring and retaining only the best, most dedicated, most effective, and most efficient people in what is, after all, a buyer's market in higher education. Some reflection on the quality of library employees may confirm that it is better for much of the small-college library work to have top-notch paraprofessionals working full time than an equal number of mediocre professional faculty whose notion of recompense is weighted by a sense that they are and should be competing for salary and benefits with members of the Chemistry Department. Lest this seem unfair to the profession, the director should think clearly about which library tasks really require the professional degree and may reflect further on whether it is as unfair to the profession that the library budget support more than a core of the very best professionals if those professionals will have no collections to catalog, classify, and interpret because the money is gone.

Although many directors spend agonizing hours on the matter, the problem of allocation of the materials budget among the various constituencies of the library, usually the departments, can be set aside as trivial in comparison with the two matters treated here, the size of the pie and the principal divisions of the pie into capital and noncapital categories. Many directors go to great lengths to justify their division of book monies, but as a general matter, allocation formulas should yield to the good judgment and experience of the director and involved collection development and acquisitions staff, and the commitment to a bigger pie and to a bigger slice for materials as a whole usually makes the matter of cross-departmental rivalry for funds moot. The complexities of formula budgeting are so great as to render this process more cumbersome than helpful. The director must be willing to exercise judgment that takes into account more considerations than could or should possibly be written into a formula. It *is* very useful to document actual amounts spent for various constituencies over time to demonstrate that as the library "pie" increases, so does money for each department, whatever the ratio of the materials budget allocated to each department.

## Personnel

The discussion of budget has by implication led to the importance of library personnel as a second lever for directorial action. The small-college director, having few persons with whom to work in the library, professional and non-professional, will need to recognize just how important every individual is to the success of the library in achieving its mission. Having said that the library budget should minimize personnel costs, let it be said furthermore that the director should maximize personnel effectiveness. The director can start by determining how many professional librarians are absolutely necessary to run an effective library program. Having cut that number to the minimum, the director should ask how many support staff are similarly necessary. *Minimum* and *necessary* here can be given some bite by considering beneath which levels of staffing the director should go elsewhere just because staff size is too small to run a respectable library program. However, the director must take into account the variety of considerations related to this matter: number of service points, hours the library is open, the possibility of depending upon well-trained student help, elimination of redundant and cumbersome tasks from the work flow, and so forth. But too often directors will not consider that staff size may be excessive given total institutional dollars available for investment in the library.

Once possible staffing minimums are considered, the director should set out to put these minimums into effect. Two principal matters govern in this process: people leaving and people joining the staff. Too often a person's leaving a staff is seen as a problem (who will do "x" now?) rather than as a rare opportunity. But the job pool is often very good, better than it has been for many years, and the likelihood of improvement in staff effectiveness through new hiring is actually very high once one discounts the initial investment in training time. Often we hire too quickly, not having considered a reconfiguration of our staffing pattern or not having taken the precious time needed to find the person who will maximize our personnel expenditure (in absolute dollars and in training, attention, and general personal energy). It is critical to bear in mind that a dedicated staff with quality people working within a properly configured organizational structure, clear about what they are up to and committed to achieving the library's programmatic goals, will exceed—in the capacity to serve—a staff larger by perhaps a factor of four or five to one. In sum, it is possible to do justice to the matter of library personnel without focusing too much on sheer numbers by considering effectiveness within the percentage of the budget reasonably allocated to people costs. The number of well-run one-professional libraries in small colleges testifies to the fact that sheer numbers of master's degrees do not provide a good measure of quality library service.

## Extralibrary Relationships

The third lever for library managerial success is that of the set of extralibrary relationships developed within and without the college community. This set includes the perceptual and active commitment of administration, faculty, students, and all others to the library as a central academic enterprise within the college.

Of these commitments, any one can forge new directions for the library. For example, many libraries have found alumni and friends of the library instrumental in achieving certain levels of service. Clearly, a supportive, involved faculty is healthy and helpful. Here, it should be said that the set of perceptions most amenable to change and to exploitation for the general good is that of the college administration. This is true for two reasons.

First, the director has generally built into the college organization chart a clear reporting relationship with the vice-president for academic affairs (dean, provost) and perhaps the president. This relationship can and should be integral to matters such as budget and personnel, our first two levers of management. The success of this reporting relationship requires work on the director's part, but that the relationship exists to be exploited is generally not arguable.

Second, the administration has real power with respect to the library's welfare and is therefore worth exploiting. Here, *exploitation* is used in the political sense of mutual aggrandizement, not with any pejorative moralistic tone. The director who falls into the trap of aligning the library against the evil centrists in the administration has probably lost the most effective tool for achieving ends in view for the library being managed. Where, after all, does the director think that funds for the budget, our first management lever, will be coming from? The number of dollars of increased library support arising from the expressed indignation of the faculty is really very small. It is interesting that so often in interviews for the position of library director is voiced the administrative complaint that the previous director has not understood that the administration has done all it can to help the library help the institution at large. Whether this is or is not a fact, it is not particularly interesting that a sense of enmity exists. But it is valuable to know that librarians are so maladroit as to have been perceived to be at odds with what is in many respects their sole source of support.

It is, then, very important that a library director understand the college administration, its personalities, its quandaries, its ambitions, its limitations. It is important that the director sit with administrative colleagues as often as possible and contribute as much as possible to the general success of administration ambition. Social contact, lunch for example, is often useful in enhancing good feeling in the workplace. These kinds of liaisons having been established, the director almost inevitably will find the proper channels for influence open and waiting for development along lines the director will determine. It is not by any means a case of "know your enemy," as so often seems to be assumed. It is a case of recognizing and working within a Balkanized, politicized environment in which real people are achieving personal and institutional destinies. Lest the director think the library is above this kind of machination, let it be recognized that the human animal is in essence political. It is not a matter of deciding to be or not to be a participant in the arena of administrative politics. It is a matter of whether or not to be successful within this environment.

## Planning and an Orientation to the Future

Administrative action can be either intuitive or planned. For those library directors who act on behalf of their libraries intuitively with grace and style over long periods, all the best. Most of us will require a long-range plan, the fourth lever of management.

A long-range plan will have, in general, three parts. First will be a set of perhaps ten or so goals specifying the general charge to the library within the institutional environment provided by the college and the curricula (e.g., to acquire, house, preserve, and make physically and bibliographically accessible to "Whimsical College" students a collection of print and nonbook materials sufficient to support the curricula of the college; furthermore, to acquire in-depth collections of materials to support faculty research, as this is possible; furthermore, to provide for "Whimsical College" students and faculty such supplemental collections as are required to satisfy leisure reading interests).

Second will be sets of objectives, specified year by year on a timetable of no more than five years. Objectives will be written to fit the context of the statement of goals but will be time bound; that is, they will be able to be accomplished at definable points in time. One might be "to initiate a library-orientation program and provide appropriate materials for new 'Whimsical College' faculty in order to familiarize them with library facilities, personnel, resources, and procedures."

Finally, a long-range plan will have a strategy, including budget projections and sources of support, personnel and organizational changes, and principal projects that bear on the anticipated level of service of the library to the college (e.g., expanded facilities, automated systems). The strategy should be oriented to accomplishing the objectives within the framework of the library's goals for support of the curricula within the college.

A long-range plan may be developed for the director's own personal guidance, may well serve as a document for eliciting staff viewpoints and focusing staff action or as a vehicle for faculty library committee and administrative discussion, and may eventually be published after appropriate sharing within the college at large as a "white paper" to guide the library's development over time. It will thus be useful to elicit ideas, focus energies, reach consensus, and provide a way of measuring success.

However it is used, it is also subject to update and revision and should always be a plan, a guide, and not serve to inhibit creative new action as times, persons, technologies, and so forth change. As a new year begins, as a new proposal for direction is made, the plan should be reviewed for currency and rewritten as necessary in light of the best current thinking that is to be embodied in the plan. Action and strategy, goals and objectives, and future and past traditions should be made to mesh in a manner that gives the best sense of continuity and fit while yielding first place for the new when that seems on balance appropriate. However the long-range plan is created, published, consumed, revised, adhered to, or adjusted, the existence of such a plan, mulled over and brought into accord with present realities and new ambitions, is extraordinarily important to give general focus to our plans for budget, for personnel, and for liaison with the extralibrary perceptions that form the framework within which libraries evolve.

It may be seen that these management levers are universal and not peculiar to the administration of small-college libraries. It is the context of these levers that is unique to small-college libraries. That context, as we have seen, embodies commitment to the curricula of the undergraduate arts and sciences program as well as a stringent set of limitations on resources. Each lever might well be examined within this context. As an example, the director's personnel decisions have, in the small-college library, of necessity more personal impact than they would have in a large, corporate environment. Volumes might be written to address the difficulty of hiring (or not hiring) the faculty wife who may or may not be as highly qualified as competitors for a library position. Budgets are small. Although this is a curse, the reciprocal blessing is that even incremental changes can have a dramatic, highly visible effect and can do credit to the library and to its administration. The point is not to lose sight of the value of the context of smallness or to undervalue the uniqueness of commitment to the education of young men and women in the broad methodologies and knowledge of the arts and sciences. It is similarly important to remember that the levers of management, taking into account limited resources and the undergraduate college context, remain management levers, manners of exerting force toward a direction taken with ends in view after a decision-making process. Thus the small-college library director is at once a manager, with all that this implies, and a denizen of the rich, varied, but limited environment he or she has selected as the arena for working out an institutional destiny.

## ENDS IN VIEW: LIBRARIANSHIP WITH A PURPOSE

Library directors adroit enough to develop appropriate schemes for budgeting, for personnel, for enhanced extralibrary perception, and for the future may occasionally need to remind themselves what it is about libraries in particular that sets their management tasks apart from those of other persons acting administratively. At least three "ends in view" are particular to librarianship, and they should not be lost sight of in any striving for managerial and institutional success.

### Collection Development

The heart of the library is the collection of materials or resources that serve the intellectual needs of the college constituency. No action should be taken that impinges in the long term on the healthy growth of resources for patrons.

### Collection Organization

An unorganized group of materials is not a library. It is the organization of these materials into a collection that permits ready access to them for patrons and that distinguishes a library from a warehouse. Organization by appropriate schema, classifications, groupings, is critical to librarianship, and every management decision should take this clearly into account.

### Collection Interpretation

An organized group of materials is a library but a minimal one without trained personnel who at the least assist in the development of the skills of using the collection and, furthermore, actually find materials for patrons who want that service. (The distinction here between training to find and finding is one that must be a matter of local policy.) Whether one calls this generic activity "reference," "bibliographic instruction," or another name or set of names, it is essentially an interpretive rather than an acquisitive or categorical activity and also is fundamental to librarianship.

Lest these three categories—collection development, collection organization, and collection interpretation—seem overly simplistic, let it be noted that it is very easy in the library director's new challenge to emphasize the management of change to lose sight of the fundamental principals of the profession, and it is thus particularly important to remind ourselves what it is we are managing. Management principals may apply to supermarkets, gas stations, and libraries, but library fundamentals distinguish the tone and tenor of library management. The director will do well to bear the three ends in mind as he or she emphasizes the levers of management: budget, personnel, external perceptions, and planning.

## WHAT KIND OF FOOL AM I? THE STYLE OF DIRECTORSHIP

Archimedes said in reference to the lever, "Give me where to stand, and I will move the earth." If there are levers of management, where should one stand to exert force through those levers? The director must stand on "style," on the director's approach to people and problems as that approach embodies the director's unique character.

Although much has been written about styles of management, very little is revealed about what will guarantee effectiveness and whether it is genuinely possible to change one's style over time even if one wishes to do so. Perhaps good advice is to bear in mind as one exerts the levers of management the very real interpersonal consequences of any action, however tangential to the main course it may appear, when that action emanates from a person in authority. This suggests that on the one hand the director has the opportunity to exert hierarchical pressure on situations to force those situations to a conclusion that the director finds satisfactory, but it also suggests that it is necessary to exert such pressure with care and on appropriately important occasions lest the director come to be perceived as tyrannical and arbitrary.

The style of directorship to be commended is the one with which the director feels most true to himself or herself. A limiting principal on the comfort one feels with oneself, however, is that any style wears thin in a small-college environment if it comes to be seen as a cloak for either indecision or caprice. Generally, then, the best guide for the director is an openness to criticism, to ideas contradictory to the director's immediate impulse, and the strength of character to follow over time a course of action that, upon due and continuing reflection, seems not safe but best. This ''where to stand'' may seem treacherous, but it is the choosing of this place and the exerting of leverage with this foundation for which library directors are paid.

## SUMMARY

Small-college library directors are, in essence, managers of change, of activity over time, toward a variety of purposes within an environment characterized by a commitment to undergraduate teaching and constrained by limited resources. Once dedicated to this proposition and to this context, they may recognize several tools or levers for exerting the forces of change in a direction commensurate with their best thinking. The nature of libraries constrains the managerial environment in which administrative action is taken and should be borne in mind so that management is never an end in itself but a way to achieve the library's ends in view. Each director will have successes and failures, but an understanding of how he or she acts and is perceived to act over time along with the will to be successful by being true to oneself as a decision maker will optimize the director's chances for institutional success and a rewarding career.

# 3

# Community Relations

## *John K. Amrhein*

Few would quarrel with the proposition that academic libraries exist primarily to serve their institutions' students, faculty, staff, and administrators. At the same time, it would be a very unusual academic library mission statement that did not include some degree of commitment to community service. The balance between these potentially conflicting objectives can be delicate, and it can take many forms.

*Community relations* can refer to any of a spectrum of familiar activities: service to local residents, multitype library cooperation, Friends' groups, arrangements with business and industry, and so forth. That these relationships vary in degree as well as in kind is not a recent phenomenon. Some of the closest town and gown library ventures on record occurred in the first decade of the twentieth century: In 1908 a new building was dedicated to house the unified academic and public library in Oberlin, Ohio (Tucker 1983: 73). Under a contract that has been in force since 1907, the University of New Hampshire Library serves as the official public library for the town of Durham, in exchange for an annual appropriation (Josey 1967: 187).

There are many factors external to the library itself that can influence its policies. Communities vary in their size, location, values, and resources. Colleges and universities also differ in these ways, as well as in their ownership and governance. Institutional motives are generally a mixture of altruism, self-interest, and, some would add, cynicism:

In no case has the researcher determined that an academic library was provided funds to provide services outside the college community, although lip service is often paid to such service. Lyle, Rogers and Weber, Wilson and Tauber, each the author of a basic book on academic library administration, devote less than a chapter, usually only a few pages, to the problem of the community user of the academic library. . . . The tone is one of obvious tolerance of a troublesome aspect of service that is to be endured but not encouraged. (Duhrsen 1981: 9)

In 1975 the Association of College and Research Libraries (ACRL) adopted a set of guidelines intended to assist academic libraries in "codifying their policies with respect to access by persons other than their respective primary clientele" (1975: 322). Significantly, these guidelines studiously avoid prescribing specific formulas for community access. The whole point of the guidelines is each library's need to analyze institutional characteristics and environmental forces to arrive at clear and explicit policies that are appropriate to the situation. Although access to academic library collections by nonaffiliated persons is only one aspect of community relations, the policy-making approach suggested by ACRL is applicable to other aspects of the issue as well.

## PROBLEMS AND OPPORTUNITIES IN COMMUNITY RELATIONS

Each academic library's problems and opportunities in community relations arise from a unique combination of institutional characteristics and environmental forces. The following sections list some of the important factors that influence the development of typical programs.

### Institutional Characteristics

#### Ownership and Support

Is the parent institution private or public? Libraries that are part of publicly owned institutions often feel some degree of obligation to provide services to residents of the states or local community. Sometimes the "obligation" is legal; more often it is considered to be a moral obligation or just politically wise. On the other hand, library administrators at some publicly owned colleges and universities are concerned that an extreme open-door policy on their part could be a disincentive to public library development, as well as a serious drain on resources intended to support the teaching and research objectives of their parent institutions.

Public *support* can be just as significant as public *ownership*. Particularly in the eastern part of the United States, there are state-aided institutions that are not technically state owned. There are many private institutions that receive public support for certain academic programs. Library policy must take into account the degree of legal, moral, or political "obligation" that public support implies. For example, any library that is designated a federal depository is required to make its federal documents collection available to everyone. At the very minimum, this requirement implies physical access to the depository collection; in practice, it will probably involve access to other collections in the library building and demands for reference service from nonaffiliated users.

## *Institutional Mission*

To what extent does the institution as a whole identify with the community? Institutional mission, aspirations, or traditions can be powerful forces influencing an academic library's community relations policies. The library of a regional state university will feel this type of motivation. So will the library of any institution that emphasizes local fund raising or that is the dominant cultural presence in a relatively small college town. In most areas, both the mission and the support of community colleges is primarily a local matter, and their libraries are expected to respond to this reality in some way.

## *Available Resources*

Does the academic library have resources that would be especially useful to the community? Can the community's needs be met without adversely affecting the academic library's primary constituency? Could the academic library benefit from resources that the community can provide? Perceptions in the administration building or city hall are not always realistic. Sometimes the only honest answer to one or more of these questions is no. Honest answers are not always appreciated, but healthy relationships cannot thrive for long if they are based upon false hopes.

# Environmental Forces

## *Community Size and Location*

More than any other single factor, the relative size and isolation of the local population influences the approach that an academic library is likely to take to community relations. An urban setting provides more opportunities for multitype library cooperation and relationships with business and industry, but service to individuals in the same urban setting will probably be restricted, because of the sheer numbers of nonaffiliated potential users (Judd and Scheele 1984: 129). In a small town with no large city nearby, the academic library is likely to adopt more relaxed policies toward serving nonaffiliated persons, and the library faces less competition for local philanthropic support.

## *Community Library Resources*

The variety and adequacy of other local library resources is an environmental factor that is not always directly proportional to the size of the community. Sharing can be mutually beneficial only when both parties have something to share. Although large university libraries have been particularly sensitive to the effects of one-sided "cooperation," the following sentiments would be echoed by administrators of some smaller academic libraries:

In the more affluent sixties and early seventies, "resource sharing" with smaller libraries and with individuals in the local community often represented, in practice, a donation of services by the resource library to these other groups. Difficulties arise when attempts are made to introduce a situation in which the costs of providing access to resources are shared by the parties in question, rather than given by the one to the other. (Piternick 1979: 153)

### Socioeconomic Factors

In a relatively affluent community with traditions that emphasize educational and cultural values—the very type of place that is likely to have other relatively strong library resources—there will be more demands for service to local residents. The academic library so located can expect to be "adopted" by students home from other colleges, people in professional occupations, academically motivated high school students, and adults involved in continuing-education activities. Excessive pressure for service to an upscale community can be a problem for the academic library, but there are usually compensating opportunities. Here, there is potential for genuine resource sharing and for significant local support through a Friends of the Library group.

## Patterns in Community Relations

In the following discussion we shift our perspective from tendencies to outcomes, from institutional characteristics and environmental forces to the typical relationships that develop under the influence of these factors.

### Service to High School Students

From the early 1960s to the present the dominant issue in discussions of community access to academic libraries has been service to high school students. There is no comparably sized group of nonaffiliated persons that has a greater need to use academic libraries. Because of their numbers, high school students can aggravate equipment shortages and overcrowding of facilities. Because they generally have no opportunity for group instruction in the use of advanced research tools, high school students can consume an excessive share of reference librarians' time. Their numbers also magnify their potential impact on the collection, parts of which can be temporarily exhausted or permanently damaged as a result of inappropriate assignments or theft. In a discussion of ACRL's 1965–1966 national survey of community use of academic libraries, it was remarked that "the community group that appears closest to being genuinely unwelcome in American college and university libraries is the high school student segment. Barely restrained emotions on the part of many respondents to our question on high school students indicate a substantial distaste for service to this group" (Josey 1967: 187–88). It must be remembered, however, that many colleges and universities depend upon area high schools for a large percentage of their own future enrollment. The interests of such institutions are not well served by librarians who can offer nothing better than "distaste for service to this group."

In practice, most academic libraries allow some use by high school students. Few can offer unlimited access to all high school students. Realistic limitations, coupled with proactive measures to head off problems, can benefit the interests of all concerned. Once an academic library has determined what kinds of services it is able and willing to provide for what kinds of high school students, it is important to work out appropriate arrangements with the schools and the public libraries that serve the region.

A study funded by the Council of Library Resources concluded that "far and away the most successful high school/research library cooperation is found where direct service links exist between a college and its surrounding local and regional high school communities. Frequently, cooperation includes regular orientation and bibliographic instruction" (LeClercq 1986: 16). Although the service model proposed by this study was developed in the context of an urban university enrolling more than 20,000 students, smaller institutions have also offered ambitious programs of bibliographic instruction for high school students (Boisse 1979: 6–7).

A referral system can be an effective means of identifying the academically superior student with legitimate needs for college-level resources. Several versions of this approach have been successfully implemented. Basically, a referral system requires the student to go first to the high school library (and sometimes also the public library), consult the librarian concerning resources available there, and obtain a statement attesting to the student's unmet needs. In some plans, referrals are available only to high school students who are enrolled in advanced placement or honors courses.

If impact on the collection is perceived to be the main problem, referral forms may be required only for borrowing (Schwartz 1970: 16). If demands on staff time are also a concern, high school students may also be required to present referral forms when requesting assistance (Craig and Perrine 1962: 478). To separate high school students with research needs from those who come to the academic library to socialize, the library might even reserve admission to the building to those with referral forms (Farber and Shore 1964: 164–66).

A referral system that is carefully thought out in consultation with local school and public librarians is certainly a more constructive approach toward the needs of the youth of the community than grudging endurance of unsolved problems. It may also be more constructive than unrestricted access, which can be counterproductive if it undermines support for adequate school and public libraries (Deale 1964: 1696). Referral systems avoid this pitfall, without completely withholding academic library service from the high school students who can most benefit from it. School and public librarians generally respond very positively to referral systems, which emphasize the community's primary responsibility to provide the library resources that its high school students need.

## Students of Other Colleges and Universities

Students who commute long distances between home, work, and campus are likely to give more consideration to convenience of location than institutional affiliation when seeking library resources. Some instructors make assignments without knowing that the necessary titles are unavailable in their campus libraries; others deliberately encourage research that requires their students to use the collections of neighboring institutions. Often direct use is faster (for the student) and more economical (for the libraries) than interlibrary loan. Whether or not there are consortial ties among the parent institutions, academic libraries often recognize the needs of these students through mutual-use agreements. Obviously, such arrangements work best for institutions with comparable enrollments and library collections with strengths that offset each others' weaknesses. Large research libraries that are besieged by many students from have-not institutions are apt to charge substantial fees or impose other restrictions.

### Service to Other Local Residents

Most academic libraries make some provision for service to nonaffiliated adult members of the community, but the degree of openness varies considerably. A comparatively restrictive policy would provide only in-building use of materials and limited reference service for local teachers, clergy, and other professionals with demonstrable research needs. At the other extreme, some libraries extend borrowing privileges and other services to any adult resident upon request. Factors that are often associated with more restrictive policies are urban location and private ownership and support.

Athletic events, the fine and performing arts, and libraries are the chief attractions on most campuses for the general public. Whether it is urban or rural, public or private, an institution whose mission or aspirations emphasize community ties will expect its library to do its part. This can be a powerful influence for openness, even when there are shortages of space, staff time, or library materials. At such an "outer-directed" institution, the farsighted library director will find ways to provide community services that do not unduly strain the library's resources.

### Library Cooperation and Networking

In the preceding sections, which have ostensibly dealt with academic library services to unaffiliated *individuals* from the local community, a recurring point has been the importance of relationships with other *agencies* in the community. The academic library that overlooks the resources of other information providers in the area or that inadvertently undermines support for them by usurping their functions is serving nobody's long-term interests. To avoid pitfalls of this kind, we've emphasized bilateral arrangements to facilitate cooperation with area high schools, public libraries, or academic libraries.

A logical extension of this approach is the multitype library network, which is designed to enhance the effectiveness of *all* participating libraries in a geographic area. Multitype networks facilitate sharing of resources through any of a number of typical joint ventures: union lists or catalogs, interlibrary-loan clearinghouses, interlibrary delivery, reference-referral centers, storage centers, and in-service workshops. Cooperative acquisitions programs in multitype networks have been only moderately successful.

It has been suggested that to achieve its maximum potential, a multitype network must avoid defining "information provider" too narrowly:

A first step is to explore the information universe that exists in any community. It includes more than libraries. It is comprised of government agencies, special interest groups, voluntary organizations, and even commercial ventures. Health information, especially, is disseminated from a variety of public and private agencies with little coordination of effort. Although informal networks of information referral exist in any metropolitan area, academic and public librarians generally have little knowledge of the information resources in the community, unless a formal community information and referral program has been established. . . . A university library's prestige will increase the political power of such a network and its leadership will assure that the arrangements made are in its best interest. (French 1979: 287)

The academic library and community agencies can also profit from sharing professional expertise. Examples are plentiful: An academic librarian with a track record in grant writing provides free consultant services to area public libraries. A community college library assists local agencies and associations who are trying to organize their own information resources. The specialized knowledge and skills represented on any university library's staff are obviously of potential value to other agencies, but it is important to remember that this can be a two-way street: Community college and school librarians often are more experienced in working with nonprint media than librarians from four-year institutions. The college librarian who is charged with developing a campus archive could receive valuable advice at the county historical society. The person who is likely to know the most about nearby facilities that could be used for freeze-drying of wet books almost certainly does not possess an MLS.

## Service to Business and Industry

Corporate use of campus library collections and services is on the increase, but most of this activity is confined to large research libraries. However, a smaller institution with strong graduate programs in science and technology will also have the type of library collections and subject specialists that may attract potential "customers" from business and industry. Rice University has established a separate organization within its campus library to market various information services to the private sector; in return, the library receives support for certain subscriptions (McDonald 1985: 85). The Lehigh University Libraries established a comprehensive fee-based information service for local industry in 1981, and it is still going strong in 1988:

The general benefits every subscriber receives include corporate borrowing privileges, a copy of the Libraries' serial lists, staff-prepared bibliographies and guides to the literature, monthly new acquisitions lists from Linderman and Mart, and a tour of the libraries for company personnel. Use of computer search, reference, document delivery, and other specific services is charged against the subscriber's deposit account at current rates. The annual subscription fee is $1,000, of which 40 percent is earmarked for general benefits and 60 percent for services charged against the deposit account. (Cady and Richards 1982: 175)

Academic libraries that are considering services of this kind should be aware of some potential problems. A library's fee-for-service program may conflict with campus fund-raising efforts if corporate donors to the institution expect special treatment by the library. On the other hand, with a little imaginative cooperation, the library and the development office might be able to transform this problem into a mutual opportunity.

Academic libraries have traditionally protected the confidentiality of the individual user's research interests. It seems natural enough to adopt similar safeguards to protect the corporate user against industrial espionage. Circulation records, photocopy requests, interlibrary-loan requests, records of on-line searches performed, and other information about a client's interests should be confidential—for *all* clients. But what about limiting access to materials that the library has accepted on condition that they be restricted to certain classes of users? The values of the business world and of academe do not always coincide. The corporation views confidentiality as a defense of its property rights; the academic library employs confidentiality in defense of intellectual freedom. An academic library that becomes preoccupied with corporate values runs the risk of compromising its own dedication to the free exchange of ideas. Dependence upon corporate funding can be an unhealthy influence on collection development as well, if the library lacks a clear sense of its primary objectives (McDonald 1985: 85).

## Local History

There is a natural overlap between an ambitious local history collection-development program and community relations activities. One illustration of this overlap is Allegany Community College Library's oral history project in Cumberland, Maryland, for which the library received the John Cotton Dana Public Relations Award (Eldredge 1983: 189). Another example is provided by the University of Wisconsin-Parkside, whose University Archives and Area Research Center (a division of the Library/Learning Center)

works extensively with area groups in gathering historical material on the development of Kenosha and Racine counties. The staff attends meetings of governmental bodies, labor groups, and ethnic organizations. With funds provided by the National Historical Publications and Records Commission, staff members are also conducting inventories of the noncurrent records of many area businesses. Slowly we are creating an ''Archives of the Industrial Society'' which will serve both the needs of serious researchers and of faculty who want to involve their students in studying the development of the area. (Boisse 1979: 7)

## Fund Raising: Friends' Groups

It is rare for an academic library to receive institutional funding to support service to the community, but libraries with established off-campus ties have the opportunity to use these contacts in their own fund-raising efforts. An informal community advisory group can be very helpful in identifying prospects (Eaton 1971: 355.) The Friends of the Library group is one way of combining fund raising with social and cultural events that bring town and gown together. Obviously, the potential appeal of a Friends' group will depend to a great extent on socioeconomic characteristics of the community itself, which we discussed earlier as one of the "environmental forces" that must be considered.

Although large private universities might seem to present the most promising opportunities for groups of this kind, "there seems to be no relationship between the size of the university and the size of the Friends" (*Friends of Libraries Sourcebook* 1980: 37). An outstanding example of what a Friends' group can accomplish for a publicly supported academic library is provided by Cuesta College, a community college that enrolls 6,000 students in San Luis Obispo County in the central coastal region of California. Within four years, this Friends group—which began with three active members—grew to include ninety people who raised more than $66,000. "But dollars haven't been the only benefit. Foremost is staff morale. Sharing successes and knowing everyone's energies are required creates good feelings, a team spirit, and pride in being part of the library" (Wilhelm 1984: 31).

## PLANNING FOR SUCCESSFUL COMMUNITY RELATIONS

It would be pointless to try to lay out a blueprint for a model community relations program, precisely because the success of all such programs depends entirely upon how well they respond to unique situations. We have been emphasizing the components of those unique situations—the factors that are catalysts or obstacles to various types of academic library-community interaction. But a healthy relationship does not simply happen as the inevitable result of the interplay of these factors. On the contrary, without clear-cut objectives and decisive action to solve problems and seize opportunities, misunderstanding and frustration are guaranteed.

An analysis of institutional characteristics and environmental forces is the first step in a process of planning, communication, experimentation, and evaluation, through which the library seeks to manage—rather than simply endure—its future.

## REFERENCES

Association of College and Research Libraries, Committee on Community Use of Academic Libraries. 1975. "Access Policy Guidelines." *College and Research Libraries News*, no. 10 (November): 322–23.

Boisse, Joseph. 1979. "A Total Responsibility for Service." *LJ Special Report*, no. 9: 5–7.

Cady, Susan A., and Berry G. Richards. 1982. "The One-Thousand-Dollar Alternative." *American Libraries* 13 (March): 175–77.

Craig, Hardin, and Richard H. Perrine. 1962. "Problems of Urban Universities: Library Services for the High School Student." *Library Trends* 10 (April): 469–81.

Deale, H. Vail. 1964. "Campus vs. Community." *Library Journal* 89 (April 15): 1695–97.

Duhrsen, Lowell R. 1981. "Use of the New Mexico State University Library by High School Students in Las Cruces, New Mexico." DLS diss., University of Southern California.

Eaton, Andrew J. 1971. "Fund Raising for Academic Libraries." *College and Research Libraries* 32 (September): 355.

Eldredge, Jon. 1983. "A Special Public Relations Opportunity for Academic Libraries." *College and Research Libraries News*, no. 6 (June): 188–90.

Farber, Evan, and Philip Shore. 1964. "High School Students and the College Library." *Library Occurrent* 21 (September): 164–66.

French, Beverlee A. 1979. "The Fourth Generation: Research Libraries and Community Information." In Association of College and Research Libraries. *New Horizons for Academic Libraries*. New York: Saur, 1979.

*Friends of Libraries Sourcebook*. 1980. Chicago: American Library Association.

Josey, E. J., moderator. 1967. "Community Use of Academic Libraries: A Symposium." *College and Research Libraries* 28 (May): 184–202.

Judd, Blanche, and Barbara Scheele. 1984. "Community Use of Public Academic Libraries in New York State: A SUNY/CUNY Survey." *The Bookmark* 42 (Winter): 126–34.

LeClercq, Angie. 1986. "The Academic Library/High School Library Connection." *The Journal of Academic Librarianship* 12 (March): 12–18.

McDonald, Ellen. 1985. "University/Industry Partnerships: Premonitions for Academic Libraries." *The Journal of Academic Librarianship* 11 (May): 82–87.

Piternick, Anne B. 1979. "Problems of Resource Sharing with the Community." *The Journal of Academic Librarianship* 5 (July): 153–58.

Schwartz, Philip J. 1970. "The High School Student and the College Library." *PNLA Quarterly* 34 (July): 15–18.

Tucker, John M. 1983. "Librarianship as a Community Service: Azariah Smith Root at Oberlin College." Ph.D. diss., University of Illinois at Urbana-Champaign.

Wilhelm, Mary Lou. 1984. "Fund Raising: The Cuesta College Library Experience." *Community & Junior College Libraries* 2 (Summer): 25–31.

## SELECTED BIBLIOGRAPHY

Cory, John M. "The Network in a Major Metropolitan Center (METRO, New York)." *The Library Quarterly* 39 (January 1969): 90–98.

Goeddecke, Ann Bernard, Sister. "College Library Public Relations." *Catholic Library World* 46 (February 1975): 286–89.

Henderson, Mary Emma. "The Role of the Georgia Public Junior College Library in the Community." Ph.D. diss., Florida State University, 1985.

Josey, E. J. "Community Use of Academic Libraries." *Library Trends* 18 (July 1969): 66–74.

"UC-Santa Cruz Committed to Community Service." *Library Journal* 110 (July 1985): 14.

Varnet, Harvey. "Community Services: An Overview of the Role of a Library/Learning Resources Center." *Community & Junior College Libraries* 1 (Fall 1982): 21–24.

# 4

# Statistics and Record Keeping

## Ronnie W. Faulkner

Every library administrator is familiar with the copious data available in even the smallest academic library. The possibilities for data collection are so alluring that many libraries maintain statistics to excess without serious regard for any potential use of the raw data. "Librarians are great compilers of statistical data," concluded Australian librarian Geoffrey G. Allen, "but exhibit poor abilities in its interpretation, manipulation or use" (Allen 1985: 211). Hence much of the meticulously collected data go unused or misused. This fact led Russell Shank of the University of California, Los Angeles, to conclude that often "administrative behavior seems to be based on a sample of one—preferably apocryphal incident" (1983: 9).

The purpose of this chapter is to outline the various types of data maintained by smaller academic libraries, the reasons such data are collected, and the methods for effective collection and record maintenance. It is hoped that readers will be prompted to consider appropriate administrative uses for library data in their respective libraries. The word *statistics* is used in the general sense of data unless otherwise indicated. At present, the methodologies and even the definitions used to describe items to be counted are so diverse that comparisons between libraries are frequently invalid. Even responses to the Higher Education General Information Survey, the only nationwide data collection for academic libraries, may vary according to the interpretation of a given respondent. A study conducted by Mary Jo Lynch for the National Center for Education Statistics, concluded in 1984: "Valid, reliable, and timely statistics about libraries collected and disseminated by a respected federal agency are essential if our nation is to plan effectively for the utilization and development of that vast learning resource" (1984: 3).

This is why it is important to rely on sources such as Mary Jo Lynch's work, Helen M. Eckard's *Library Data Collection Handbook* (1981), and the American National Standards Institute's (ANSI's) *Standard for Library Statistics, Z39.7)* (1983) when establishing the nature of what is counted. Eckard and ANSI's work provide clear definitions of library terms—definitions essential to proper record maintenance. The ANSI standard states that it was designed "to provide a pool of defined statistical data items about libraries, from which various surveys and studies may be designed by selecting the information most valuable to collect for their purposes" (1983: 7). Until such a standard is adhered to nationwide, many comparative library statistical studies will lack reliability. Nonetheless, examination of *Sources of Library Statistics* reveals a listing and description of the college and library statistics currently available for possible comparative analysis (Lynch 1983: 12–17). Information derived from the sources noted must be used with caution.

## WHY COLLECT LIBRARY DATA?

There are many valid reasons for the collection of library statistics. They may be divided into five categories:

1. The requirements of state and federal law
2. The requirements imposed by surveys of various government agencies or private organizations
3. The requirements imposed by the academic institution
4. The need for information in internal management decisions
5. The need for information to justify library requests or present the value of existing services

The validity of the above items hardly needs comment. State and federal law require the maintenance of accurate records for audits and a variety of other activities. The HEGIS report of the National Center for Education Statistics, surveys conducted by state library agencies (Samore 1984: 348–56), and studies and standards of the American Library Association all require the maintenance of specific types of records. Unlike the university library standards, the college standards are highly quantitative (College Library Standards Committee 1986; Stubbs 1981: 527–38). Regional and national accrediting agencies have established standards that require the availability of certain data for evaluation and accreditation purposes (Wallace 1972: 31–38). Similarly, the administration of the academic institution itself will require the collection of certain data for purposes of local reporting.

Library statistics are basically of two types: enumerative statistics and sampling statistics. Most library data are of the former type (circulation count, reference questions asked, number entering the library, and so on). Although there are times when sampling is necessary, Paul B. Kantor has pointed out that a totally random sample using random number tables is seldom practical in the typical academic library because it would involve a major and obtrusive interference in staff and patron activity. Library sampling must rely on "the joint requirements of representativeness and convenience" (Kantor 1984: 18). For library purposes

**Table 1**
**Sample-Size Table**

| Pop. Size | Sample Size | Pop. Size | Sample Size | Pop. Size | Sample Size |
|-----------|-------------|-----------|-------------|-----------|-------------|
| 10 | 9 | 2600 | 334 | 6000 | 361 |
| 100 | 79 | 3000 | 340 | 7000 | 364 |
| 500 | 217 | 3500 | 346 | 8000 | 365 |
| 1000 | 277 | 4000 | 350 | 9000 | 366 |
| 1500 | 305 | 4500 | 354 | 10000 | 368 |
| 2000 | 322 | 5000 | 356 | 20000 | 376 |

Confidence level is 95 percent with a reliability of ± 5 percent. Percentage in population is assumed to be 50 percent.

*Source*: Hall (1985: 120).

sampling usually involves simply drawing on a part of a larger group for the purpose of making inferences (Hamburg 1978: 34). A simple sample-size table can often be used to determine the probable accuracy of a given sample. As table 1 illustrates, the return for increasing the size of the sample diminishes as the population being studied increases. Hence a random sample of 376 out of a population of 20,000 is as statistically accurate as a sample of 9 out of 10.

The library manager should not forget cost analysis of any data collection or sampling study. Before starting the collection or study it should be determined if the benefits to be obtained justify the costs in labor and materials. The diminishing returns from increased sample size must be considered in any cost analysis.

The library director must remember that data and information are not the same thing. *Data* consist of coded messages distinct from use by an individual, whereas *information* is the result of interpretive and largely subjective analysis of data by an individual. It is the interpretation of data and its conversion into information that guides the decision-making process (Boland 1983: 10). Finally, the administrator must consider the problems posited by Allen:

The failure of library statistics to solve all the problems that library management would have them solve may not . . . be entirely the fault of the statistics. A number of questions may reasonably be asked. Do libraries collect the appropriate statistics? Are the statistics collected either accurate or compatible among similar libraries? Do we ask valid questions of the data? And above all, do we know how to manipulate and interpret statistical information? (Allen 1985: 212)

Although often the answer is no to the above questions, more and more library managers are realizing that the answer must be yes if data collection is to be of any real value in administrative decision-making.

Both sampling and enumeration are discussed in the following section, which covers statistics and record keeping as it relates primarily to administrative activity and public services, with lesser attention devoted to technical services. Nonprint media services, although often staffed separately from the rest of the library, are generally understood to be a part of public services.

## ADMINISTRATIVE SERVICES

Administrative services are specifically those services that relate directly to the functions of the library manager. All other areas of the library are relevant to the functions of the administrator. In an analysis of the needs of library managers for data for internal decision-making and external communication, Lynch and Eckard concluded that seven classes of data should be collected by libraries:

1. The institutional identity of the library
2. The target group to be served
3. The collection resources
4. The financial resources
5. The personnel resources
6. The facilities resources
7. The programmatic functions—What a library *does*

(Lynch and Eckard 1981: 17)

The discussion that follows treats primarily resources and programmatic functions as they relate to library management.

Certain types of data collection and record-keeping activity clearly fall within the library director's primary domain. Budgeting, staffing, and related data are needed for the appropriate functioning of administrative services and for reporting purposes (Strain 1982: 165–72). Usually, library directors must prepare an annual report for the campus administration. Such a report should have a variety of statistical components in addition to a narrative explanation. An annual report should be used as a public relations tool as well as an instrument for the provision of factual data about the library's activities. In writing reports and conducting studies, administrators will find much of value in Ray Carpenter and Ellen Storey Vasu's *Statistical Methods for Librarians* (1978) and John Martyn and F. Wilfrid Lancaster's *Investigative Methods in Library and Information Science* (1981). The latter book deals with vital matters such as how to prepare questionnaires, do performance evaluations, and do cost analysis. The Association of Research Libraries' *Use of Annual Reports in ARL Libraries, SPEC Kit 49* (1978) outlines the fundamental elements of a library annual report and contains examples from twenty libraries.

Managers know the importance of budget data. In fact, budget justification is one of the most common uses of library statistics (Allen 1985: 211). Most academic libraries use the line-item method of budgeting (Gillespie 1980: iv); yet most administrators do not know the budget status at a given time because academic accounting units are generally separate from the library. Reports provided by that unit may be weeks or even months behind. This problem should be dealt with by maintaining complete internal files of invoices or a manual ledger system or by means of an automated ledger system using a microcomputer. It is often difficult to obtain flexible ledger software appropriate for library applications. This may prompt development of one's own system as was done at the University of California at Berkeley (Brownrigg 1983: 160). Although small libraries seldom have adequate programming expertise to develop their own programs from scratch, they may find that spreadsheet programs like Multiplan and Lotus 1–2–3 or data-base management software such as dBase III have the flexibility for application to library record keeping. The dBase III software has an especially wide range of library uses including acquisitions, budgeting, and in-house indexing. Library administrators should consult sources such as the American Library Association's (ALA's) *Library Technology Reports* and Meckler Publishing's *Library Software Review*, *Micro Software Reports*, and *Small Computers in Libraries* for information on software with library applications. Also, a series of guides on the requirements and techniques for evaluation of automated library applications—including automation's relationship to the generation of statistics—has been published by James E. Rush Associates and is entitled *Library Systems Evaluation Guides* (1983–1985).

Morris Hamburg has written: "In the library managerial decisions can be wisely made only in the light of knowledge of present library use and through the aid of careful estimates of future use" (Hamburg 1978: 33). It is up to the administrator to see that library departments maintain records or conduct studies appropriate to the decision-making process. Statistical data collection and analysis should tie in directly to library and institutional goals and objectives. At the same time data needed for reporting purposes must be maintained. For example, statistics on hours, staffing, expenditures, collections, interlibrary loans, and public services are required for accurate completion of the HEGIS report. The HEGIS form provides an explanation of how to count items as well as the appropriate method for making estimates. Libraries must follow the directions if the data are to have value for comparative purposes. Methodology in all areas of record keeping should be a direct concern of the library manager. The manager should take care in evaluating data, especially when comparing current trends to past activity, keeping in mind the statement of Geoffrey Allen:

"The nature of library outputs is such that there is almost bound to be considerable variation in the reliability of the statistics that purport to measure them" (1985: 213).

## PUBLIC SERVICES

According to the ANSI standard, public services or user services include "those activities related to the provision of services directly to users" (1983: 31). Public services is understood to include reference and information service, circulation services, interlibrary loan, media services, and service for government publications, microforms, reserve, and other special collections. Included are reprographic and computer services that support the noted functions.

Reference and information services are among the most difficult to quantify in terms of effectiveness. As Samuel Rothstein wrote more than two decades ago: "A harsh fact of library life seems to be if it cannot be counted, it does not count" (1964: 468). Terrence Brooks (1982) has established that reference statistics do not correlate with other library counts. This makes the maintenance of some type of independent reference data essential. In most libraries a variety of data are collected and special studies are periodically performed to measure the reference function. For purposes of the HEGIS report, a library *must* maintain a count of reference and directional transactions at all public service desks. *Reference transactions* are those contacts involving the use, recommendation, interpretation, or instruction in the use of one or more information sources. *Directional transactions* involve contacts that facilitate the use of library facilities without resort to information sources (American National Standards Institute 1983: 21, 28). For example, explaining the use of the card catalog is a reference transaction, but telling a patron on which floor audiovisual materials are located is a directional transaction. Statistics on these two types of contacts can be maintained at the service desks on weekly tally sheets broken down by type of transaction, hour, and day, a simple hash mark indicating each transaction.

Keeping a record of the fill rate for reference transactions is more difficult and time consuming. The *fill rate* is the number of reference questions divided by the number successfully answered. It is advisable to use sample weeks throughout the year to obtain an accurate reflection of the fill rate. This basic method was suggested by Douglas Zweizig and Eleanor Jo Rodger for public libraries but could be adapted to the academic terms of a college library (1982: 45–49). This method would generally depend upon reference staff reporting on tally sheets indicating if the queries of patrons are completed accurately (Chait 1978: 83).

The library administrator may use either an obtrusive or unobtrusive approach in evaluating reference. Studies have indicated that if librarians are given a set of questions with knowledge that there is an evaluation, they perform better than when questions are asked by unidentified surrogates (Weech and Goldhor 1982: 305–24). In both types of studies, however, it is better to evaluate a librarian's actual performance than to use only patron perceptions of performance. Objective performance measures, as pointed out by Paul Kantor, are preferable to subjective measures that may represent client prejudices (1984: 2).

Circulation statistics are frequently used to demonstrate the level of library use and are needed to complete the HEGIS report accurately. Academic libraries often maintain circulation figures broken down by Dewey or Library of Congress classes and also by type of user (faculty, students, nonaffiliated users) and format. Automated circulation makes the maintenance of such data fairly simple, but many smaller academic libraries will have to rely on manual tabulation of data. Reserve statistics are a form of circulation statistics maintained for items with restricted checkout periods. They should be tabulated separately for HEGIS. Internal media circulation records should be maintained by format as well as subject. These circulation data are often the responsibility of a separate media desk. For sample circulation statistics forms, see Elizabeth J. Futas's *Library Acquisition Policies and Procedures* (1984: 145–53).

Subject, author, and title fill-rate studies conducted in one-week periods by means of questionnaires distributed to patrons are an indication of how well the collection meets user needs. In such studies unsuccessful telephone requests should also be noted. Telephone requests that are positive would bring the user to the library to complete a survey sheet in person (Zweizig and Rodger 1982: 53–59). Fill-rate studies can answer questions about weaknesses in the collection and are a better indication of collection-development requirements than are faculty and librarian perceptions.

Shelving studies are often conducted to reveal in-house use of materials. In-house studies, which frequently correlate with circulation, are needed to respond to HEGIS. It is simpler to use typical weeks, weeks in which the library maintains its regular hours, as a basis for measurement than to attempt comprehensive records for every day (Brooks 1982: 341–53; American National Standards Institute 1983: 31). Shelving data for the regular collection should be kept by the appropriate call-number categories. Sheets appropriately organized by call number and marked by student shelvers are usually adequate. If periodicals are cataloged, the data can be collected in the same fashion as for the general collection. That, however, is seldom the case, meaning that data must be maintained by title. An entire listing by title is cumbersome, making a sheet with space for writing in the title followed by hash marks more appropriate. An accurate method for conducting a periodical shelving study over a period of time is described by Blaine Hall in the *Collection Assessment Manual for College and University Libraries* (1985: 66–68) and another method by Julia Long in *Quantitative Measurement and Dynamic Library Service* (1978: 95–102).

Interlibrary loan is a valuable avenue for obtaining materials not held, and most libraries maintain data on the number of items borrowed and loaned, often broken down further by type of material (article, book and so on). It is also wise to collect data on the subjects borrowed since this information can aid in collection development. Such information when compared with circulation and acquisitions data can be useful in guiding library purchasing (Allen 1985: 214; Del Frate 1980: 247–53; Byrd, Thomas, and Hughes 1982: 1–9).

Statistics should be collected relative to bibliographic instruction sessions, including the classes, times, instructors, and number of students. It is wise to keep data on a general library-orientation program separate from that for specialized subject presentations. Likewise, similar information should be maintained relative to class use of media facilities.

The above areas of data collection do not preclude specialized studies that may from time to time be needed for internal public service purposes. Surveys of patron views may be especially appropriate in indicating the need for improved public relations or the need for modifications in certain areas of service. User studies are among the most important of library activities for they reveal most accurately how one might best meet user needs (Bentley 1979: 151).

## TECHNICAL SERVICES

Technical services include those activities related to the acquisition, organization, and preparation of materials. This area of library activity commonly encompasses acquisitions services; serials control services; cataloging services; catalog maintenance and production services; binding, rebinding, and preparation-for-binding services; and conservation and computer services in support of the noted functions (American National Standards Institute 1983: 31). All of these functions are vital to the library, but this is seldom recognized by the average patron.

Unlike reference activity, technical service activity is likely to generate a significant amount of easily quantifiable data for administrative analysis. Because the vast majority of academic libraries participate in the Online Computer Library Center (OCLC), they should obtain a number of reports on their technical processing activities. Data on costs and number of items processed in cataloging is relatively easy to obtain and maintain. If a library uses the acquisitions, interlibrary loan, and serials subsystems, it will receive additional data for those areas of usage. Likewise, if engaged in the retrospective conversion of records to machine-readable format, the library will be the recipient of data on that activity. The OCLC and regional networks are generally glad to supply information that will help the library administrator make cost projections about any number of technical processing activities.

Typical technical services data will include things such as volumes added to the collection, periodicals added, volumes retrospectively converted, volumes requiring original cataloging, and gifts received by the library. The volume information is generally broken down by call-number classes on a weekly or monthly basis to indicate the flow of processing activity.

Acquisitions is a very important service in any academic library. It is the one area of technical services that will arouse considerable faculty interest. Every library should maintain some type of acquisition file indicating the status of orders. Automated acquisitions can often provide printouts by requestor, title, call number, or a variety of other avenues. An acquisitions system that can keep up with allocations and expenditures is an especially valuable source of data on book-collection activity. The recent institution of an automated acquisition system at a small-college library using dBase III and an IBM PC not only increased the information available to faculty relative to book orders but also resulted in a significant upsurge in faculty ordering (Faulkner 1986: 129–34).

There are a variety of data that are relevant to acquisitions and book-selection activity. Statistics on circulation, interlibrary loan, in-house use, enrollment by discipline, number of faculty, number of degree programs, and so on are all fundamental to appropriate collection development. User studies and curricular needs are especially useful in collection development. "It does not matter how many millions of volumes a library has," wrote Stella Bentley, "if that one volume which the user requires is not available" (1979: 151). George S. Bonn has identified a number of avenues of data collection that can be used to guide collection-development activity (1974: 267–74). Statistics in this area must not be overlooked.

Because administrators most often come from the ranks of public services personnel, they must be sure to use appropriately the input of technical services staff to interpret technical services data. Also, they must realize that the performance of technical processing often determines whether public service workers will be able to provide for user needs.

## CONCLUSION

As Allen has stated, statistics must never become the sole reason for management decisions or there could be "a tyranny that would destroy the essence of professional judgment" (1985: 217). Nonetheless, statistics and records are a vital part of administrative activity in the smaller academic library. Library managers must learn to collect and analyze the available data to make timely decisions about budgeting, staffing, hours, and a variety of internal library activities. One does not need to be a statistician, with all that implies both negatively and positively. One needs, however, to be proficient in the interpretation and use of the data collected. Statistics can be expected to become ever more vital in future efforts to maintain the level of service in the face of budget retrenchment and declining enrollments. Hence the modern library manager must be able to combine the humanistic with the statistical to be an effective administrator. Turning data into information is one of the responsibilities of every director.

## REFERENCES

Allen, Geoffrey G. 1985. "The Management Use of Library Statistics." *IFLA Journal* 11:211–22.
American National Standards Institute. 1983. *American National Standard for Library*

*and Information Sciences and Related Publishing Practices—Library Statistics, Z39.7.* New York

Association of Research Libraries. 1978. *The Use of Annual Reports in ARL Libraries, SPEC Kit 49.* Washington, D.C.: Office of Management Studies.

Bentley, Stella. 1979. "Academic Library Statistics: A Search for a Meaningful Evaluative Tool." *Library Research* 1:143–52.

Boland, Richard J., Jr. 1983. "Tutorial on Management Information Systems." In *Automation as a Source of Management Information.* Edited by F. Wilfrid Lancaster. Urbana: University of Illinois.

Bonn, George S. 1974. "Evaluation of the Collection." *Library Trends* 22:265–304.

Brooks, Terrence. 1982. "The Systematic Nature of Library Output Statistics." *Library Research* 4:341–53.

Brownrigg, Edwin B. 1983. "An Online General Ledger System." In *Automation as a Source of Management Information.* Edited by F. Wilfrid Lancaster. Urbana: University of Illinois.

Byrd, Gary D., D. A. Thomas, and Katherine E. Hughes. 1982. "Collection Development Using Inter-library Borrowing and Acquisition Statistics." *Bulletin of the Medical Library Association* 70:1–9.

Carpenter, Ray L., and Ellen Storey Vasu. 1978. *Statistical Methods for Librarians.* Chicago: American Library Association.

Chait, Melissa. 1978. "Quantification of Reference Services at the Wayland, Mass., Public Library." In *Quantification Measurements and Dynamic Library Service.* Edited by Ching-Chih Chen. Phoenix: Oryx Press.

College Library Standards Committee. 1986. "Standards for College Libraries, 1986." *College and Research Libraries News* 47:189–200.

Del Frate, Adelaide C. 1980. "Use Statistics: A Planetary View." *Library Acquisitions: Practice and Theory* 4:247–53.

Faulkner, Ronnie W. 1986. "The Glenville State College dbase III Acquisitions System." *Library Acquisitions: Practice and Theory* 10:129–34.

Futas, Elizabeth J., ed. 1984. *Library Acquisition Policies and Practice.* 2d ed. Phoenix: Oryx Press.

Gillespie, David M. 1980. "A Survey of Business Managers and Library Directors to Identify the Variables Affecting the Final Decision on Library Budgets . . . " Ph.D. diss., School of Library Science, Florida State University.

Hall, Blaine H. 1985. *Collection Assessment Manual for College and University Libraries.* Phoenix: Oryx Press.

Hamburg, Morris. 1978. Statistical Methods for Library Management. In *Quantitative Measurement and Dynamic Library Service.* Edited by Ching-Chih Chen. Phoenix: Oryx Press.

Kantor, Paul B. 1984. *Objective Performance Measures for Academic and Research Libraries.* Washington, D.C.: Association of Research Libraries.

Long, Julia L. 1978. "Journal Use Study in a VA Hospital." In *Quantitative Measurement and Dynamic Library Service.* Edited by Ching-Chih Chen. Phoenix: Oryx Press.

Lynch, Mary Jo. 1983. *Sources of Library Statistics, 1972–1982.* Chicago: American Library Association.

———. 1984. *Analysis of Library Data Collection and Development Plans for the Future: Final Report.* 3 vols. Washington, D.C.: National Center for Education Statistics.

Lynch, Mary Jo, and Helen M. Eckard. 1981. *Library Data Collection Handbook.* Washington, D.C.: National Center for Education Statistics.

Martyn, John, and F. Wilfrid Lancaster. 1981. *Investigative Methods in Library and Information Science: An Introduction.* Arlington, Va.: Information Resources Press.

Rothstein, Samuel. 1964. "The Measurement and Evaluation of Reference Service." *Library Trends* 12:456–72.

Rush Associates, James E. 1983–1985. *Library Systems Evaluation Guides.* 8 vols. Powell, Ohio: James E. Rush Associates.

Samore, Theodore. 1984. "An Inventory of Statistical Surveys by State Library Agencies." In *The Bowker Annual of Library and Book Trade Information, 1984.* 29th ed. New York: R. R. Bowker.

Shank, Russell. 1983. "Management Information and the Organization: Homily from the Experience of the Data Rich but Information Poor." In *Automation as a Source of Management Information.* Edited by F. Wilfrid Lancaster. Urbana: University of Illinois.

Strain, Paula M. 1982. "Evaluation by the Numbers." *Special Libraries* 4:341–53.

Stubbs, Kendon. 1981. "University Libraries: Standards and Statistics." *College and Research Libraries* 42:527–38.

Wallace, James O. 1972. "The Practical Meaning of Library Standards." In *Quantitative Methods in Librarianship Standards, Research, Management.* Edited by Irene B. Hoadley and Alice S. Clark. Westport, Conn.: Greenwood Press.

Weech, Terry L., and Herbert Goldhor, 1982. "Obtrusive versus Unobtrusive Evaluation of Reference Service in Five Illinois Public Libraries: A Pilot Study." *Library Quarterly* 52:305–24.

Zweizig, Douglas, and Eleanor J. Rodger. 1982. *Output Measures for Public Libraries: A Manual of Standardized Procedures.* Chicago: American Library Association.

# PART II

# Personnel

# 5

# Personnel Management in the Library

## David R. Dowell

Very few library administrators have experienced the opportunity I confronted in 1981 when I was asked to help the Illinois Institute of Technology (IIT) take operational control of its own library system. For the previous nineteen years the library system of the university had been operated on a contract basis by the John Crerar Library. The first major task I embarked upon was to organize the personnel system. I did little else for the first six weeks, and this activity took up a major portion of my time in the ensuing months. Almost six years later our personnel system is still not fully mature.

Even though many may think that it would be easier to design a library personnel system from scratch than it would be to live with the system that one inherited, my experience on other campuses convinces me that it is possible to modify even well-entrenched systems if one is willing to work to document needs and to convince the university administration that change is needed.

Personnel costs in libraries are usually the highest cost component in the budget—often totaling more than all other costs combined. Therefore it is important that the library be managed so that all human resources are contributing to the accomplishment of the library's mission. The role of the personnel function of the parent institution and the management role of the library should be interactive and mutually supportive. Both parties must operate with mutual respect to achieve the overall goal: effective deployment of human resources to provide service to the clients of the parent institution.

## GOVERNMENT REGULATIONS

In this quest one is assisted and constrained by federal and state law and regulations that were designed to protect the interest of individuals. These regulations include equal opportunity requirements and the regulations of the Department of Labor, which define the difference between exempt and nonexempt staff. *Exempt staff* are professional, administrative, and supervisory staff who occupy positions that have met the criteria for exemption from the wages and hours provisions of the Fair Labor Standards Act. Legally, exempt employees are hired to do a specific job and are not hired to work a specific number of hours. *Nonexempt staff* are hired to work a certain number of hours. Strict documentation must be maintained as to the actual hours worked. Employers must not require or allow nonexempt staff members to work more than the maximum hours per week without paying overtime.

One of the most troublesome aspects of administering these regulations is how coffee-break time and meal-break time are accounted for. According to federal regulations if the employer decides to allow breaks of five to twenty minutes to reduce worker fatigue, this time is counted as time worked for pay purposes. Breaks of thirty minutes or longer are to be considered an interruption in the workday, and this time is not counted as time worked for pay purposes. Employees are not required to take coffee breaks. On the other hand, two such breaks cannot be batched to take a longer break once a day. In addition, they cannot be skipped to allow the staff member to come to work late or to leave early or to take an extralong lunch period. In addition, some states mandate that a meal break of at least thirty minutes must be taken by each employee. It is not in the interest of the library or the employee to adopt a strict, inflexible, legalistic interpretation of these regulations. However, if an institution is ever audited by the Department of Labor and found to be in violation, the monetary penalties can be severe.

In addition, one is assisted and constrained by institutional policy. This policy will interpret how federal and state laws and regulations will be implemented. For example, if the campus adopts a standard work week of less than forty hours a week, the policy must clearly state whether hours worked greater than the standard week but less than forty hours are to be compensated at the regular wage rate or at the rate of time and a half. Institutional policy should be designed to balance rights of individual staff members and the responsibility of managers to achieve the mission of the institution. If an institutional policy does not seem to achieve this balance, one should work with other managers to change the policy or one's understanding of it.

## UNIONS

If one is managing on a unionized campus, one should not passively accept the current work rules and terms of employment if they are not conducive to delivery of high-quality services to library clientele. Remember that everything got to be the way it is through negotiation. Therefore, those work rules and terms of employment that unduly restrict effective management can be up for discussion the next time the contract is up for renewal. If such changes would benefit a campus, one should share concerns with other managers and the labor-relations staff of the institution well in advance of the beginning of the next round of actual contract negotiations.

On some campuses unions have had the positive benefit of forcing haphazard administrative practices to be improved. If a staff is unionized it is probably in the interest of the library for some of them to be involved actively in the leadership of the union. Then issues of interest to the library staff will have to be considered by the union when it chooses its bargaining issues. If the union decides to support the concept of comparable worth, this has the potential of being one of the most effective means of raising the salaries of all library workers. Women librarians earn considerably less than men librarians, and men librarians earn only 60 percent of what other men with comparable education earn.

## STAFFING STRUCTURE

Librarians, support staff, and student assistants each require somewhat different approaches in an effective personnel system. The appropriate number of librarians and support staff for a particular academic library are suggested by the *Standards for College Libraries, 1986* (Association of College and Research Libraries 1986).

One of the first steps in designing a library personnel structure is to articulate carefully the distinction between librarians and supporting personnel. Many activities may be performed by both groups. Some overlap is inevitable and desirable. With the supporting staff an activity is an end in itself. For the librarian the same activity should serve other ends as well—such as evaluating the activity to see if it is the best way to provide access to information for the library's clients. This distinction is made in "Library Education and Personnel Utilization":

The title "Librarian" carries with it the connotation of "professional" in the sense that professional tasks are those which require a special background and education on the basis of which library needs are identified, problems are analyzed, goals are set, and original and creative solutions are formulated for them, integrating theory into practice, and planning, organizing, communicating, and [carrying out] successful programs of service to users of the library's materials and services. In defining services to users, the professional person recognizes potential users as well as current ones, and designs services which will reach all who could benefit from them.

The title "Librarian" therefore should be used only to designate positions in libraries which utilize the qualifications and impose the responsibilities suggested above. Positions which are primarily devoted to the routine application of established rules and techniques, however useful and essential to the effective operation of a library's ongoing services, should not carry the word "Librarian" in the job title.

The objective of the master's program in librarianship should be to prepare librarians capable of anticipating and engineering the change and improvement required to move the profession constantly forward. The curriculum and teaching methods should be designed to serve this kind of education for the future rather than to train for the practice of the present. (American Library Association 1970)

Position descriptions are the foundation upon which an effective personnel system is built. In addition to listing the major responsibilities or tasks, the descriptions should carefully define the knowledge, skills, and other abilities that are required to perform a job successfully. One should make sure that the statements that are made are carefully defined. For example, the statement "uses a computer terminal to process library materials" is of very limited value. What is important is the knowledge the staff members must have in their heads as they push the keys of the computer terminal. How many sources of information must the person integrate in making decisions? Do the fingers merely transfer to the screen what the eyes see in front of them? An example of the variety of different levels of knowledge that may be required for different tasks in one functional area—cataloging—may be useful to illustrate this point (A. Dowell 1976:23–29). If this activity is done well, the investment of effort will be useful in a number of subsequent components of personnel administration.

Once the individual positions are defined, it is necessary to arrange them in a systematic way so that pay ranges may be assigned to each position that takes into account different levels of responsibility. Normally, the campus personnel office will have the final word on placing a position into a pay grade. For that reason the descriptions should be relatively free of "library jargon." The statements "catalogs audiovisual materials," "revises the filing of student assistants," and "responsible for stack maintenance" do not adequately and accurately describe to a nonlibrarian what the activities involve. The "Library Education and Personnel Utilization" statement provides a framework for organizing positions (American Library Association 1970). This statement does not pretend to cover every variation that might conceivably occur. However, the basic categories described there cover almost any generic grouping of related positions that may be needed in libraries along with the educational requirements that may be appropriate.

## SALARY ADMINISTRATION

Although the campus personnel office will be responsible for conducting periodic salary surveys, the library will want to have some activity in this area. It is likely that the campus salary monitoring will not explicitly collect information on the salaries paid to library staff members. What is more likely is that the personnel office will collect information on what employers in the same geographic area are paying for certain bench-mark positions that are likely to be present in many kinds of organizations (e.g., secretary, data-entry operator, custodian, electrician). A pay scale will then be constructed using these salaries as reality checks. Other (i.e., nonsurveyed) positions will be assigned a salary range that is a ratio of these bench-mark positions. This ratio is established on the basis of points assigned to each position category. On some campuses this system is used to rank every nonfaculty position from "a pair of hands requiring no thought" to vice-president.

## Factors Used to Evaluate Positions

The following factors are used in one private institution to achieve internal equity among positions based on the responsibilities of the incumbent.

### Complexity of Duties

How many activities are involved in the position? How diverse are they from one another to the extent that they call for different knowledge or skills? How many sources of information must the person consult to make decisions? Are these sources of information likely to give contradictory information?

### Educational Requirements

What is the minimum amount of education required for entry to this position?

### Experience

What is the minimum amount of related work experience required for entry to this position?

### Latitude

To what extent do routine procedures, precedents, and rules guide decisions? To what extent do decisions made by the incumbent become policy to guide others in the university or the department? How much must the staff member operate without having a supervisor nearby to check with or to refer problems to?

### Accuracy

How many checks are there on the work of the incumbent? What is the likelihood that errors will be undetected? To what extent will undetected errors damage the ability of the institution to achieve its mission?

### Contacts

Who, outside the work group, does the incumbent come in contact with in the normal course of business? What is their status (e.g., faculty, vendors, trustees, potential donors)? How frequent are these contacts, and what is their purpose (e.g., to relay information, to negotiate, to persuade, to solicit gift collections)? This category should also recognize the potential for emotion-charged contacts such as dealing with irate students to negotiate fines.

### Physical Application

The lowest level is a good mix of sitting, standing, and walking. Extreme amounts of any of the three may be weighted more heavily. Lifting, carrying, and other strenuous activities are rewarded the most.

## Job Conditions

Normal office conditions receive the lowest weight. Outdoor work in extreme weather conditions or work in hazardous laboratory conditions are examples of conditions that receive more weight.

## Supervision of Others

Most scales of this kind recognize two levels of supervision. *Functional supervision* is being responsible for training and checking the work of others. This level receives only very minimal weight. On the other hand, administrative supervision receives considerable weight. *Administrative supervision* involves being responsible for initiating recommendations for hiring, evaluating, rewarding, disciplining, promoting, and, if necessary, terminating other staff members. Even administrative supervision of less than four or five clerical staff members may not be very well recognized—which is often a sore point for the supervisors of small units. However, the diversity of the duties of the supervisees is often taken into account. So is the level of the staff being supervised. Responsibility for one other librarian may be valued as much or more than responsibility for a half-dozen supporting staff or twenty students.

Listed in table 1 are the possible points in each category and the points that a wage and salary analyst from the campus personnel office assigned to two librarian positions at that institution. The points assigned by the analyst do not represent my opinion and are offered only as an illustration. In fact, librarians were shortly thereafter removed from this classification scheme.

It would be well worth the time to attempt to secure a copy of the point scale that is used by the campus personnel office to assign positions to pay levels. In most cases the personnel office will be reluctant to give out that information. At least two reasons account for this hesitation. First, wage and salary specialists do not want to get into a situation in which they are forced to justify the number of points assigned in each of the above categories to a given job. They believe this would lead to endless quibbling and would unreasonably complicate their jobs. The second reason is related to the first. The application of this point system constitutes one of the main professional activities of their positions. If the mystique of it were removed by making the formula widely available, their very professionalism might be threatened because then everyone would believe themselves to be competent to assign jobs to pay grades. If a personnel office is unwilling to make the entire classification plan available, one should request a list of the criteria that are applied to each position. Even if one does not know the maximum number of points that can be assigned to each category or the point spreads for each pay grade, one can make sure that each position description sent out for review contains a statement or phrase that addresses all of the criteria that the personnel staff will be applying during its analysis. The key is to make the campus system work for the library without having to make exaggerated claims that damage one's credibility.

**Table 1**
**Professional Position Review**

| Factors | Possible Points | Reference Librarian | Catalog Librarian |
|---|---|---|---|
| Complexity of Duties: | 150 | 60 | 60 |
| Educational Requirements: | 125 | 80 | 80 |
| Experience: | 150 | 80 | 80 |
| Latitude: | 100 | 60 | 60 |
| Accuracy: | 100 | 40 | 40 |
| Contacts: | 100 | 20 | 20 |
| Physical Application: | 15 | 5 | 5 |
| Job Conditions: | 20 | 5 | 5 |
| Supervision of Others: | 100 | 0 | 10 |

| Point Range/Level | | Point Range/Level | | Point Range/Level | |
|---|---|---|---|---|---|
| Under 100 | 1 | 280 to 300 | 9 | 480 to 500 | 17 |
| 105 to 125 | 2 | 305 to 325 | 10 | 505 to 525 | 18 |
| 130 to 150 | 3 | 330 to 350 | 11 | 530 to 550 | 19 |
| 155 to 175 | 4 | 355 to 375 | 12 | 555 to 575 | 20 |
| 180 to 200 | 5 | 380 to 400 | 13 | 580 to 600 | 21 |
| 205 to 225 | 6 | 405 to 425 | 14 | 605 to 625 | 22 |
| 230 to 250 | 7 | 430 to 450 | 15 | 630 to 650 | 23 |
| 255 to 275 | 8 | 455 to 475 | 16 | 655 to 675 | 24 |
| | | | | 680 to 700 | 25 |

It is not my intention to discuss fully whether librarians should have faculty status and rank. However, it is my observation that such arrangements may be more appropriate in a college where emphasis is on quality teaching than they are at research universities where original research is valued more highly. The best of all possible worlds may be an academic model that is similar to the faculty model but not tied directly to it. For persons interested in exploring a professional structure somewhere between the civil service approach described above and the faculty model, a paradigm can be found in ''The Four Stages of Professional Careers'' (Dalton, Thompson, and Price 1977; Thompson, Baker, and Smallwood 1986).

## RECRUITING

Carefully constructed position descriptions serve as a reliable underpinning to support recruiting to fill an open position:

Before even advertising a position opening, the supervisor should list the areas of competency that a fully functioning staff member is required to master for that position. Then the supervisor should decide which of these competencies can reasonably be learned in the context of the work environment. All other competencies should become minimum qualifications for that position, that is, pass/fail requirements that *must* be met before the candidate can be seriously considered. The competencies that could reasonably be gained on the job become desirable qualifications to be sought in candidates who have met the minimum qualifications. Theoretically, the best qualified candidate is the one who has demonstrated all the minimum qualifications and offers more optional competencies than any other. Other factors, such as demonstrated learning ability, may also be a legitimate consideration. (D. Dowell 1979:62–64)

The job market for librarians is national. To build a good staff of librarians it is necessary to recruit nationally. Although some good candidates for librarian positions may already be located in one's local geographic area, in most cases better candidates are available if the search is wider. Those seeking advancement in any profession look for challenging jobs in that profession wherever they may be located. In all but the largest metropolitan areas, the job may have to take precedence over the locality. Local candidates, particularly those on your staff, should not be ignored; however, they should not be the only source of candidates. Even if there were no such thing as affirmative action, it would make good sense for managers to locate as many good candidates for themselves as they could expeditiously so do. Spot shortages have already occurred in some specialties within librarianship. The number graduating from the American Library Association (ALA) accredited programs of library education has declined steadily since 1974. With the closing of several schools in the past few years, the job market can only tilt more in favor of the job seekers as we enter the 1990s. This will require even more aggressive recruiting on the part of those institutions that are committed to acquire and retain first-rate professional staff members. It also means that the salary and benefits offered to librarians will have to be monitored regularly to ensure that an institution is remaining competitive in a changing marketplace.

In recruiting for librarian positions, the library director is generally expected to take the lead. If this is the case the campus personnel office will play a supplementary and monitoring role in the process. No matter which party takes the more active role, the library manager must take responsibility for knowing where the job should be advertised. An academic librarian position should be advertised in one or more of the following publications to ensure the broadest possible applicant pool: *American Libraries, Chronicle of Higher Education, College and Research Library News*, or *Library Journal*. Other publications such as the *Journal of Academic Librarianship* and *LJ Hotline* can be useful, but they generally are not read by many of the librarians one would like to attract. In addition, various journals that are targeted at specialized subgroups of librarians such as the *Special Libraries* and *Journal of the American Society for Information Science* may be useful for attracting librarians interested in various subspecializations within librarianship. These latter publications, however, should supplement rather than replace the primary announcement vehicle. If one is particularly interested in attracting recent library-school graduates, one should consider sending job announcements to all accredited library schools in the local geographic region if not the nation. Lists of the currently accredited library schools are available from the Committee on Accreditation, American Library Association. Some library schools either publish a list of job announcements for the benefit of their alumni or selectively notify alumni of jobs about which they might be interested. One also may want to list the job with one or more of the telephone joblines. A list of such joblines is published monthly in the "Career Leads" section of *American Libraries*. The latest vehicle for listing library jobs is the electronic bulletin board. One example is Grapevine, a weekly on-line job alert that is accessible through ALANET, the electronic-mail service sponsored by the American Library Association. Many of these journals and services will accept a job advertisement over the telephone. All publish or change their listings on a regular basis. One can check with those of interest so as not to miss the deadline and thus unduly delay the search. The wider one advertises the position, the more likely one is to attract a strong applicant pool, but each listing has some cost that will have to be weighed against the potential benefit.

When building an applicant pool in January or late June, one should consider listing the opening with the placement service operated during the American Library Association midwinter and annual conferences. Listing forms and other information are available from the Office for Library Personnel Resources, American Library Association. These and other professional association meetings that offer placement services enable one to conduct brief screening interviews with several candidates at a much lower cost than it would take to bring them to campus for a full-scale interview. The few best candidates can then be brought to campus for follow-up sessions during which one can more thoroughly explore the candidate as a potential employee and the candidate can more thoroughly examine the library as a potential employer.

If the applications are received by the library, each of them should be logged in at the time of receipt. It is a thoughtful touch to notify the applicants that their application has been received. If it is clear that some of the applicants do not meet the minimum qualifications and cannot be considered, it is better to notify them of this at this time in a gentle manner. The log sheet that one uses should have a column to list a brief job-related reason why the decision was made not to interview or not to offer the job to those to whom no job offer is extended. If a job offer is rejected or an applicant withdraws from consideration, that should be noted on the applicant log. Finally, the log should contain a brief statement of the job-related reasons why the person to whom an offer was made is the best qualified in terms of the selection criteria that were established before the beginning of the search. If these steps are followed, one should have satisfied equal opportunity regulations, and more importantly, one should have satisfied oneself that the person hired is most likely to be successful in the job and required only the minimum amount of on-the-job training.

The applicant logs and the letters of application and resumes of all applicants would be retained together for at least three years unless an institution requires that they be retained longer. Although it is unlikely that an applicant will challenge this decision, good business practice dictates that one be prepared. It is more likely that one will want to refer back to a candidate in the pool at a later time when one is again seeking to fill a position.

Recruiting candidates for support-staff positions is usually the responsibility of the campus personnel office. The applicant pool is generally local, and the personnel office should have the expertise to know how to go about attracting candidates. It may be useful to supplement this applicant pool by sending paraprofessional job notices to schools that have associate's or bachelor's degree programs in library science. Typically, the personnel office will have a budget for advertising in local newspapers and will list openings with the state employment agency. However, there is a less clear pattern whether they will have a budget line to cover the fee if a candidate is referred by a private employment agency. One should clarify this point before opening the search to determine how to respond if one is called directly by a private personnel agency. The campus personnel office should have the capacity to test applicants for selection criteria such as typing ability and otherwise to screen out candidates who do not meet the minimum criteria for consideration.

Recruiting for student assistants is a joint responsibility of the library, the student financial aid office, and sometimes another placement office for students who are not on financial aid. It is beneficial to attract students who are eligible to receive work-study funds. Such students cost the budget only a fraction of what a nonwork-study student would cost. Good relations with the financial aid office can result in actual savings if it will refer work-study students. It is also helpful to post a conspicuous sign near the entrance of the library just before the beginning of each semester or quarter and at any other time when entering freshmen or transfer students are on the campus for orientation. The signs should announce that the library is accepting applications from students eligible for work-study awards. In addition, if the campus has a separate orientation session for entering freshmen on financial aid, one should ask if it would be possible to have a few minutes on the program to explain employment opportunities in the library. If one can get them when they are freshmen and keep them, they can be very valuable employees by the time they graduate.

One of the main problems with work-study students is that they often are awarded too small a work-study subsidy for them to work a reasonable number of hours throughout the academic year. Generally, students have to quit working when their work-study awards are exhausted because, at least in theory, their financial need has been met. Often students who are on financial aid but do not have work-study awards or who have small work-study awards can negotiate with the financial aid office to change the composition of their aid package. This is particularly true if loans make up a significant part of the package. By converting loans to work-study arrangements, the students may be able to work enough hours throughout the year to justify the training time that the library must invest in student employees. At the same time, the students benefit by not having as much debt to repay after graduation.

## STAFFING AND TRAINING[1]

My experience indicates that there are two key elements in getting work done through people. The first is to select the right person for each position and the second is to give each staff member the training needed to do the job well. I believe supervisors should be evaluated on and held accountable for the degree to which their units contribute to the achievement of organizational objectives.

My conviction that staffing and training are the two most important elements in successful supervision was, until recently, based only on intuitive feelings. Now, however, empirical data have been collected in support of this conclusion. ... In a 1976 dissertation, Alan Bare studied the relationship between the performance of forty-three work groups [in the Rutgers University Library] and the participation of the groups' supervisors in the following activities: (1) counseling and team building, (2) coordination, (3) staffing, (4) formalizing, (5) training, (6) external representation, (7) communication and feedback, and (8) performance-reward contingency management. ... The supervisory activities with the most significant relationship to group performance were staffing and training. ... Bare measured the supervisors' staffing activities by examining the extent to which raters agreed or disagreed with the following statements:

S/he hires the most competent people available;
S/he hires people who fit well with job requirements,

S/he makes sure the group has the talents it needs;

S/he has good ideas;

S/he tries new ways of doing things; and

S/he defines jobs in a way that makes good use of the talents we have.

In measuring a supervisor's training competency Bare asked raters to indicate whether they agreed with the following statements:

S/he provides opportunities to learn on the job;

S/he encourages participation in formal training programs;

S/he encourages self-development; and

S/he delegates challenging assignments.

## EVALUATION AND APPRAISAL

Once one has hired the right people and given them good training, periodic evaluation is essential. Evaluation and appraisal activities have two primary objectives that often are at odds with each other. The first is a backward look at the "review period" to record what has already happened. The purpose is to justify rewards and punishments. The campus personnel office is more likely to emphasize this form of evaluation because the results can be used to justify raises, promotions, disciplinary action, and other personnel actions. It is important that such evaluations be meaningful and related to job performance rather than to personal traits. Appraising performance is probably the most difficult thing supervisors are asked to do. Often the employee is only interested in how big a raise will result from the process. All too often supervisors inflate the ratings of borderline performers because they do not want to deal with the hassle of discussing an honest rating with the employee. If, at a later date, it is decided that that level of performance can no longer be tolerated, it is difficult to take any kind of action because the employee has several satisfactory evaluations in the file. At the other extreme, it is difficult to recognize the truly outstanding contributors because the inflated ratings of others leave little room for differentiation.

The second objective of a good appraisal system is to initiate a dialogue concerning where performance is today and where it needs to be going in the next "review period." This form of appraisal is more likely to lead to improved performance than is the form focused on rewards and punishment. If this dialogue can be carried out when the employee's focus is not on how big the raise will be, the discussion will not be as emotion charged and will have much more chance for success.

If the campus-mandated evaluation process does not channel energy toward how future performance will be improved, it may be necessary to supplement it. Such a mechanism can be set in motion by a form that calls for one short list and asks four very simple open-ended questions:

1. List the *most important responsibilities* associated with this position:

2. To what extent are *job knowledge and other skills* sufficient to perform each of these responsibilities satisfactorily?

3. To what extent has the *quantity* and *quality* of work produced in each of these areas been satisfactory?

4. Has work been performed in a *manner that facilitates* good performance on the part of coworkers, subordinates, and superiors?

5. To help move the library ahead in the coming year, what can the employee do to *improve performance* and what will you do to assist?

## DISCIPLINARY ACTIONS

A disciplinary procedure is also necessary in an effective personnel system. It is important that the supervisor keep in mind that the purpose of disciplinary action is to encourage an employee to become productive. This should always be stated to the employee when it is necessary to take disciplinary action. The purpose is not to punish.

If it should become necessary to take disciplinary action, one should check with the campus personnel office if one is not fully conversant with the institutional procedure. It never hurts to consult with the personnel staff to make sure that neither one is undercutting the other. One never knows when the employee may decide to consult with the personnel staff. If they are in the dark, they cannot be as fully supportive as one might want them to be. Particularly in a disciplinary action, it is important not to take any steps that the personnel office is not prepared to back.

Most disciplinary processes follow the following steps: oral warning, written warning, suspension, and termination. The steps must be taken in this sequence. The suspension step is not always considered to be appropriate at some institutions for some problems. For example, it might seem to be counterproductive to suspend staff members whose transgressions were that they did not come to work. This would not send them the signal that the library was depending on them to be present and carry their share of the load. The only other exception to the above sequence would be for extremely serious offenses for which one offense would be grounds for immediate termination. Such offenses occur rarely, and most personnel offices should have a list of them as part of the campus personnel policies. In general, the violation would be one in which the continued presence of the staff member would threaten the safety of others.

One should document thoroughly any action taken and solicit the cooperation of the staff member in cooperating to correct the situation. One should also explain how important it is that all staff members carry their fair share of the load and how library service is being affected, set a specific time limit for the behavior to be improved, and state what the consequences will be if the behavior continues.

## PROBLEM SOLVING

When staff members report a personnel problem, they probably are not looking for logical responses. They believe that something unfair has happened to them. They do not want someone to rationalize why the situation occurred. They are feeling wronged, and they want someone to fix it. This was one of the lessons that it took me the longest to learn in my own personnel experience. The first thing one should do is to acknowledge that they feel an injustice has been done. Once their feelings have been acknowledged, it will be more profitable to try to resolve the logical and rational aspects of the problem.

When I was in graduate school my advisor said: ''People say they go into personnel work because they like to deal with people. But look around you. Personnel people build rules and regulations so that they will not have to deal with people.'' I have found this to be an extremely useful reality check to help me monitor what I do in personnel activities. Am I dealing with people or am I trying to insulate myself from having to deal with people?

Personnel work can be very rewarding, and it also can drain one's emotions. In all personnel activities, as with other management tasks, one should keep in mind that the real objective is to enrich the curriculum for the students and to make the faculty more efficient in its information gathering.

## NOTE

1. The section ''Staffing and Training'' has been reprinted, with permission, from ''The Role of the Supervisor in Training and Developing Staff'' (D. Dowell 1979: 57–59).

## REFERENCES

American Library Association. 1970. ''Library Education and Personnel Utilization.'' A Statement of Policy Adopted by the Council of the American Library Association, June 30, 1970, 8 pp. (Copies are available from the Office for Library Personnel Resources, 50 E. Huron Street, Chicago, IL 60611.)

Association of College and Research Libraries. 1986. ''Standards for College Libraries, 1986.'' *College and Research Libraries News* (March): 189–200.

Dalton, Gene W., Paul H. Thompson, and Raymond Price. 1977. ''The Four Stages of Professional Careers: A New Look at Performance by Professionals.'' *Organizational Dynamics* (Summer): 19–42.

Dowell, Arlene Taylor. 1976. *Cataloging with Copy*. Littleton, Colo.: Libraries Unlimited.

Dowell, David R. 1979. ''The Role of the Supervisor in Training and Developing Staff.'' In *Supervision of Employees in Libraries*. Edited by Rolland E. Stevens, pp. 57–68. Urbana-Champaign: University of Illinois Graduate School of Library Science.

Thompson, Paul H., Robin Zenger Baker, and Norman Smallwood. 1986. ''Improving Professional Development by Applying the Four-Stage Career Model.'' *Organizational Dynamics* (Autumn): 49–62.

# 6

## Staff and Unions

### *George H. Libbey*

This chapter examines the issues raised by unionization in academic libraries and stresses the role of management in a union setting. The extent of union representation and the library employees' status within a bargaining unit may vary considerably, as may the nature of the union or unions representing the employees. The combination of these factors in a library, along with other institutional factors, will help to determine how management can do its job in a collective-bargaining environment.

An issue of some importance as librarians looked toward unionization was the distinction between professional organizations and unions. Because they are in an adversarial role, unions can deal with local issues such as compensation and working conditions, challenging the library administration over issues that might not be taken up by professional organizations. Librarians' organizations have traditionally included all levels of librarians and have tended to advise rather than challenge on local issues (Biblarz et al. 1975: 123ff.).

A recent chapter by Frederick Duda (1981), "Labor Relations," describes the development of union representation in a library, beginning with the reasons for unionization, continuing through negotiation of the first contract, and ending with the necessary building of bridges between management and the staff who now sit on opposite sides of the table. This is important reading for any library administrator faced with the need to deal with a collective-bargaining agent. Most of the remarks below deal with operations in an existing union setting rather than the initial period of organization. Professional and support staff unions are stressed, since their members deal with actual library operations.

## THE LIBRARY WORKING ENVIRONMENT

In this section *library staff* refers to librarians, paraprofessional and technical employees, and clerical employees; security and maintenance employees are excluded unless specifically mentioned. *Library administration* includes the director; associate, assistant, or deputy director; and personnel officers. Depending on local practice, library department heads may be either professional staff or library administration.

Library staff and administration share many goals and concerns, but in the end there is a division that separates staff from administration. The magnitude of this division and the factors that contribute to it will determine the nature of union representation desired by the library employees. In general, the concerns expressed by library employees involve salary; fringe benefits such as sick leave, vacation, and insurance; and working conditions such as work space, supplies, and building temperature (Seidman, London, and Karsh 1951: 76–79). Among librarians, issues may include governance and professional concerns (Guyton 1975: 2).

Local circumstances will vary, but the request for a collective-bargaining election must be initiated by employees. The impetus for this may come from within, or it may be the result of a union's effort to expand by representing the library staff. The specific union that wins the collective-bargaining election will vary widely. The American Federation of State, County, and Municipal Employees (AFSCME); the American Association of University Professors (AAUP); the National Education Association (NEA); the American Federation of Teachers (AFT); and their affiliates are active in many educational institutions. The library staff, however, has been organized by other labor unions ranging from the Teamsters Union to the National Union of Hospital ánd Health Care Employees.

Whatever the local conditions, it is clear that a successful effort to hold an election reflects some desire on the part of at least some members of the library staff to improve their working conditions—in the broadest sense—by means of collective bargaining. Although the focus of this chapter is the library that already employs unionized staff members, it is essential for library administrators to examine the period before and during an election to understand better the motives for initiating collective bargaining. In addition, records of grievances filed by the library staff can be a quick means of identifying supervisory and general management problems.

Frederick Duda noted that there are both positive and negative implications in collective bargaining (1981: 176–80). Most significant for most library administrators is the abridgement of some of the rights formerly held solely by management. It is important for administrators to understand why management's rights were weakened. While running the library and therefore administering at least some aspects of the labor agreement, further limitation of management rights may be avoided if one is aware of past management actions that may have driven, or encouraged, the staff to seek representation. Library administrators will probably find that day-to-day library operations are the same in union and nonunion institutions but that personnel actions—hirings, evaluations, discipline, and termination—are slowed.

Unions also bring opportunities for resolution of problems and encourage standardization of employment policies. In the former case the grievance procedure can provide a forum for improving human relations, even though it is an adversarial setting. Standardization may result from legislation as much as from a union agreement, since both look to procedures that ensure equal opportunities (Duda 1981: 178); since the union contract is a local product, it may be the more important force toward standardization within a single institution.

Finally, a brief defense of the union is in order. There are institutions in which library workers are very poorly compensated or have little job security or poor working conditions. When appeals for change within the institution go unanswered, collective bargaining may be the only satisfactory way to win improvements. Union contract demands often sound strident and unreasonable, but in the end the union needs the institution to ensure its own survival. Inflated demands and strong rhetoric are part of labor negotiations. Both must be taken with a grain of salt.

## THE LIBRARYWIDE UNION

For many years academic libraries have had staff associations, usually a combination of a social group, professional association, and representative of staff concerns about the library. Some libraries developed bargaining agents from these associations, often "company unions" not affiliated with any labor organizations. In general, such associations had little power to negotiate but did give library staff members an opportunity to discuss working conditions and to be informed of administrative problems and activities in a nonhierarchical way. By becoming "company unions" staff associations introduced some libraries to the practice of collective bargaining and served as steps on the way to affiliation with formal external labor organizations.

A staff association informally turned bargaining agent may have only the powers granted to it by the library administration; but if it wins a collective-bargaining election it has the same right to negotiate as does any other union. If it remains isolated, not affiliated with any regional or national labor organization, its power is likely to remain circumscribed; the local union cannot call on the financial resources or expertise of a parent organization.

The academic library that has a local union may find little changed from its nonunion days, except that negotiations of all kinds are in the hands of the library staff and administration, who may be too close to the new situation to deal with it realistically. Negotiated settlements apply to both parties; if protracted or hard-fought, these settlements may have repercussions that would be less severe if negotiators did not work together on a daily basis. Conversely, working together on a daily basis may be the key factor in fashioning workable compromises.

## THE SUPPORT-STAFF UNION

In general, library support-staff members are more likely to unionize than are their professional coworkers. A good parallel to a library might be a hospital, where the nurses, technicians, and clerical and maintenance staff are unionized—

in several different organizations—and doctors and administrators remain without representation. On a college campus the similarity in duties of library clerks and clerical workers in academic and administrative departments is a strong argument for inclusion in the same bargaining unit (*Collective Bargaining Agreement . . .*, 1981). Although there is no firm guideline, since bargaining agents are recognized by both state and federal law, it is common for the governing agency to seek to identify all similar positions for inclusion in a bargaining unit. Thus the situation noted above—a merger of all clerical workers—is fairly standard.

A support-staff union presents some complications in supervision, but they can be viewed as challenges and opportunities rather than problems. Job descriptions, position ranks, and salary grades probably existed before election of a bargaining agent but tended to become more rigid in a union setting. Supervision of members of one's own bargaining unit is a matter of concern for many first-line supervisors; in practice it can work reasonably well, but the potential for disciplinary actions and grievances can be very stressful for first-line supervisors.

One potential advantage of a support-staff union is that it may require the professional staff to be more closely involved in the work of the support staff. This can lead to higher quality work and a better-informed staff at all levels and at the same time reduce or eliminate the problems of supervision noted above.

## PHYSICAL PLANT OR SECURITY UNIONS

The origins of unionism is among blue-collar workers, so it may be expected that the physical plant and security workers would be the first to organize. In a college setting it is fairly common for these workers to be organized campuswide even if supervision of such a staff is not centralized.

Dealings with a union such as this will probably be highly structured. Because of the nature of the work performed, which can be readily timed or otherwise quantified, there may be greater emphasis on rigid job descriptions and work rules to govern behavior and performance. In academic institutions it is common for maintenance and security to be the responsibility of a central office, which provides service to the library and other units.

The effect of blue-collar unions on libraries can still be substantial. The rigidity in job duties is difficult to understand in a library where job duties often overlap. The library may find its building maintenance and security needs in conflict with work schedules and what may appear on the surface to be an arbitrary division of tasks among several craft classifications, such as plumber, electrician, carpenter, and locksmith.

## THE PROFESSIONAL UNION

The movement toward unionization among librarians started during the 1960s and was firmly established by the 1970s. In general, public librarians joined with other professional workers in municipalities and states, school librarians joined with teachers, and academic librarians joined with faculty members and other academic professionals (Weinberg 1979: 364–65). Clearly, in all of these groups librarians constitute a small minority.

One difficult part of unionization for librarians is related to another issue that has been debated for many years. Librarians and others have both confirmed and denied that librarianship is a profession. Becoming part of a bargaining unit with other clearly professional groups is confirmation for some librarians and discomfiting for others who believe that their jobs are more "clerical" or more "administrative." Regardless of the potential gains in voting for a union, librarians may find their position within a bargaining unit to be lower than desired. Within a faculty bargaining unit librarians may or may not have faculty status and the benefits that belong to that status. As a small group within the unit, librarians may find that their issues are given less attention than those of faculty members who constitute the majority of the unit. In this case the librarians may have a boost in prestige by their affiliation with the faculty but reap few additional benefits.

Although the professional union may exist in any library, it is more likely that it will develop in a library where there is a support-staff union. As noted elsewhere, although the issues may be different, relations with the various collective bargaining agents are essentially the same, governed by legislation and the specific contract.

## ADMINISTRATION IN A UNION SETTING

The library administrator in a unionized library faces the same challenges— sometimes intensified—as does a colleague in a nonunionized institution. In addition, the director faces some problems that are local and union related. A collective-bargaining agreement usually abridges some rights once held exclusively by management; often the unchanged rights are broadly defined in a "management rights" clause. Those rights, given to or shared with the collective-bargaining agent, are carefully defined and usually comprise most of the contract.

Although the concerns expressed by professional and support-staff unions may differ considerably, the method of dealing with them is the same if they reach the point of becoming a formal grievance (Duda 1981: 119–20). In most labor contracts the grievance procedure is an item of great concern to both parties. A procedure for considering employee complaints may exist in a nonunion library, but it usually is a process established—and therefore subject to elimination or alteration—by management. The negotiated grievance procedure has the force of law, assuming that it does not violate current statutes, and can be changed only by mutual consent of the parties.

## THE GRIEVANCE PROCESS

A formal grievance usually has three or four steps, beginning with the supervisor or department head, progressing to the director, and then going to the director's superior or a campus personnel office dealing with labor relations. The grievance may be resolved to both parties' satisfaction at any of these steps. If there is a campus officer who deals with grievance hearings it is important to consult with him or her to understand the procedure and the impact of any formal resolution on future grievances.

Although local conditions will vary, the following example outlines some of the general procedures and problems encountered in a grievance:

Roger Smith, a library paraprofessional, has worked in the library for three years. He is in a level-one position, the lowest of three. Smith is a good worker, whose output in the cataloging department is of high quality and greater quantity than three other paraprofessionals who occupy similar positions. Two have worked in the library for ten years. Because of the union pay scale all earn the same salary. No merit pay is possible under the contract, and rank is tied to position rather than to person (librarians will more likely have personal rank equal or similar to faculty members).

Smith asks his supervisor, Janice Johnson, who is head of cataloging, to either upgrade his position or give him a pay increase based on his level of productivity. Johnson sympathizes with him but can do neither, since his duties are unchanged and there is no possibility for merit pay in his bargaining unit. Unsatisfied with this, Smith files a grievance through his union asking for an increase in pay or that his position be upgraded; the union opposes merit pay in principle and will not ask for individual consideration for any member, but it does agree to grieve that Smith's position is improperly graded.

Step one of the grievance goes to Johnson, who denies it because Smith still has the same job, which she believes is graded appropriately. An additional consideration for Johnson is that Smith's three colleagues would also have to be upgraded should his request be granted. Normally, there is a five- to ten-day time limit to respond, but had Johnson not given a timely response, the grievance would automatically have moved to step two.

Step two moves the grievance to the library director, who also has a five- to ten day period in which to respond. The director may overturn the decision of his department head and agree to review the position, but he has even more positions to consider as he looks at the implications for the entire paraprofessional staff. Assuming that the director concurs with the department head, the grievance moves to its final step, outside the library, but the procedure remains essentially the same.

At step three the grievance is heard by upper level administrators, a personnel officer, or a combination of these two. The library administration in this case provides the expertise upon which the college or university administration bases its decision. In practice very few grievance decisions are changed at this level, although it is always possible for institutional politics to intervene or for contract negotiations to influence decisions. Assuming that the final step affirms the earlier denials, there may remain one step—arbitration.

If voluntary binding arbitration is part of the negotiated procedure, the final outcome of the grievance will be decided by a neutral party outside the institution. Arbitration is costly in time as well as money; the financial costs are normally shared by the institution and the union. The arbitrator bases his decision on the cases presented by the parties and the negotiated collective-bargaining agreement. The arbitrator's decision is final. In practice few grievances reach arbitration, partially because of the costs incurred and partially because both sides stand to lose future cases that will very likely cite the arbitrator's decision. Arbitration can have far-reaching effects.

What, then, are the possible results of grievance hearings? There are some obvious negatives that may drive the parties apart. Preparation for hearings is time-consuming; usually, the aggrieved party and his delegate are granted some work time to prepare, and the management representatives also need to spend time getting their responses ready. The formality of the process also has its drawbacks. Although grievance procedures are never so rigid as to prevent withdrawal of a grievance, the fact of filing a complaint supposes a willingness to follow through at least to the final grievance step if not to arbitration. Finally, another result of the formal process is the establishment of precedents and the likelihood that other staff members will see part of their own working situations in the proceedings.

In the example above the grievance procedure seems both intrusive and cumbersome. If it were the only way of resolving problems, library administrators might find a great deal of their time spent in opposition to their staff members rather than directing and working with them. In the example, Johnson's refusal of Smith's request before formal filing need not have led to a formal grievance. Among the options available, Smith may have found some satisfaction and the grievance could have been avoided altogether, or an agreement could have been reached at step one or two. Library administrators can provide job counseling or mentoring, can offer opportunities for job enrichment, can redesign jobs and revise work flow, and can in various ways show that they appreciate the work done by their staff members.

## UNION RELATIONS DAY TO DAY

Whereas grievance procedure is the most formal encounter of union and management—except for contract negotiations—there are daily encounters between union and management. Most of them are simple daily working interactions on which the fact of unionization has no impact. But there are aspects of day-to-day administration that are affected or even determined by the collective-bargaining agreement. Two examples illustrate some of the areas in which unionization plays an important role: work rules and pay scales.

If not specifically described in the contract, work rules are often grouped in the general category of management rights. Regardless of how work rules are established, the collective-bargaining agreement by its very existence heightens awareness of rules that govern work activities. Management always has rules to look to in evaluating the performance of employees; work rules govern work activities and may establish corrective measures such as formal warnings and suspensions. To the union these measures may seem harsh or counterproductive. To promote good working relations within the library, management needs to be aware of the work rules and ensure that they are enforced equitably.

Pay scales can be another frequent point of contact between union and management. Many union contracts, especially for support staff, establish single salaries for each pay scale or allow a very limited salary range. In addition, many contracts call for across-the-board percentage increases and do not allow merit pay for superior job performance. This can be frustrating for managers who want to reward superior employees and for employees who feel they should be compensated for superior performance. Related to pay scales are overtime and extra payments for working certain shifts or days. These matters, too, are usually regulated by contract and often limit the flexibility in scheduling desired by management and limit the employees' choice of work hours or of earning compensatory time for future use instead of earning money.

Although unions do impact library operations, generally, they do not disrupt activities. Operating procedures may change, but end results remain the same with or without collective bargaining.

## REFERENCES

Biblarz, Dora, et al. 1975. "Professional Associations and Unions: Future Impact of Today's Decisions." *College and Research Libraries* 36:121–28.

*Collective Bargaining Agreement between Temple University of the Commonwealth System of Higher Education and the Guild of Professional, Technical, and Clerical Employees, a Division of the National Union of Hospital and Health Care Employees, AFL-CIO and Its Affiliate District 1199C.* 1981. Philadelphia.

Duda, Frederick. 1981. "Labor Relations." In *Personnel Administration in Libraries.* Edited by Sheila Creth and Frederick Duda, pp. 119–99. New York: Neal-Schuman.

Guyton, Theodore L. 1975. *Unionization: The Viewpoint of Librarians.* Chicago: American Library Association.

Seidman, Joel, Jack London, and Bernard Karsh. 1951. "Why Workers Join Unions." *Annals of the American Academy of Political and Social Sciences* 274:75–84.

Weinberg, William M. 1979. "Collective Bargaining and Librarians." In *Recurring Library Issues.* Edited by Caroline M. Coughlin, pp. 362–78. Metuchen, N.J.: Scarecrow Press.

## SELECTED BIBLIOGRAPHY

American Library Association/Office for Library Personnel Resources. *Unionization and Collective Bargaining.* T.I.P. Kit #1 (Topics in Personnel). Chicago, 1982.

Branscomb, Lewis C., ed. *The Case for Faculty Status for Academic Librarians.* Chicago: American Library Association, 1970.

Cruzat, Gwendolyn S. "Issues and Strategies for Academic Librarians." In *Collective*

*Bargaining in Higher Education.* Edited by Millicent D. Abell, pp. 91–107. Chicago: American Library Association, 1976.

Kusack, James M. *Unions for Academic Library Support Staff.* Westport, Conn.: Greenwood Press, 1986.

Lynden, Fred C. ed. *Unionization in ARL Libraries* (SPEC Kit 118). Washington, D.C.: Association of Research Libraries/Systems and Procedures Exchange Center, 1985.

Marchant, Maurice P. *Participative Management in Academic Libraries.* Westport, Conn.: Greenwood Press, 1976.

Massman, Virgil F. *Faculty Status for Librarians.* Metuchen, N.J.: Scarecrow Press, 1972.

Schlipf, Frederick A. *Collective Bargaining in Libraries.* Urbana-Champaign: University of Illinois, 1975.

Todd, Katherine. "Librarians in Labor Unions." *Journal of Collective Negotiations* 14, no. 3 (1985):255–67.

Weatherford, John W. *Collective Bargaining and the Academic Librarian.* Metuchen, N.J.: Scarecrow Press, 1976.

# 7

# Staff Development and Continuing Education in Smaller Academic Libraries

## Kenneth G. Walter

### DEFINITIONS

There is a difference between *staff development* and *continuing education*, although most people use the terms synonymously. Elizabeth Stone said that the individual is the basis for continuing education whereas the group is the basis for staff development (Stone, Sheahan, and Hardy 1979: 303–4). She described continuing education as follows: "Planned learning experiences utilized by individuals following their preparatory education necessary for entrance into the field . . . implies . . . lifelong learning . . . includes staff development as one of its elements. Similarly, inservice training and orientation are subsets under staff development." Many do not distinguish between the terms. Stone preferred to use "professional development" (Stone 1969: 21).

The National Commission on Libraries and Information Science's (NCLIS's) report puts people as the keys to continuing education (Stone, Patrick, and Conroy 1974: 1–2). People connect the need for information with the resources for it. NCLIS's survey, done by Stone and others, found that 88 percent of all respondents thought developmental activities should be definitely provided for libraries' professional and support staffs (Stone, Patrick and Conroy 1974: 2–3). Among the reasons were a basic need, technological impact, obsolescence, benefits of economy, committed leaders, libraries' potential, a matter of survival, good opportunities, and because other groups have their own professional development (Stone, Patrick, and Conroy 1974: 2–9).

### BACKGROUND APPLICABLE TO SMALLER ACADEMIC LIBRARIES[1]

It is generally agreed that Malcolm Knowles is the father of modern continuing education. In the same way, the work of Rensis Likert, Douglas M. McGregor, Chris Argyris, and Frederick Herzberg have formed the basis for staff development, a subfield of the former concept (Snyder and Sanders 1978: 144). In librarianship, Elizabeth Stone's 1969 study and her work for the 1974 NCLIS report, as well as Barbara Conroy's study (Conroy 1974) and that of the Western Interstate Commission for Higher Education (WICHE), had perhaps the greatest impact on library continuing education.

The first American Library Association (ALA) workshop on this was held at the June 1970 ALA convention the year after the Council of Library Resources began its Fellowship Program for midcareer librarians and its Library Management Intern Program for development of skilled academic library managers. NCLIS's 1974 report recommended the establishment of the Continuing Library Education Network Exchange (CLENE). Also in the early 1970s, Indiana University began systematically to implement a staff-development plan under a personnel librarian. In 1975 some librarians from the Association of Research Libraries (ARL) began to meet in San Francisco on staff development and later held a one-day workshop at the 1977 ALA Midwinter Conference. Also in 1975 the Council on Library Resources (CLR) started its Advanced Study Program to help librarians take full-time graduate courses. Next followed surveys by WICHE and the Southwest Library Interstate Cooperation Endeavor (SLICE). The former also cosponsored an institute for training in the principles of staff development. In 1976 ARL sponsored three Management Review and Analysis Programs within the same spirit and cosponsored several ongoing programs for supervisory and administrative development. The CLR then began the Academic Library Development Program for smaller academic libraries, and simultaneously a few academic libraries experimented with job exchanges. These same activities extended to 1978 also, along with various state and regional meetings on the new copyright law, AACR–2, and closings of public catalogs.

Funding and staff cutbacks became more frequent in 1979, 1980, and 1981 and affected the availability of continuing-education programs at most academic libraries except the wealthiest. In 1981 the San Francisco ALA convention emphasized staff development with a number of programs and special handouts.

The years 1981 and 1982 saw microcomputers and new technologies rapidly develop library applications, with a number of workshops being given on them, but there was an overall decrease in total staff-development offerings. In 1983 King Research was asked by the U.S. Department of Education to determine professional competencies so as to guide future library-school curricula. Next, CLR, the Medical Library Association, and three ALA divisions began to put stronger emphasis on management and planning issues for continuing-education offerings. The ALA's regional institute series started with more than fourteen programs on aspects of those areas in 1984. With the shift starting from centralized to decentralized organizational structure about then, there were offerings on negotiation, assertiveness, persuasiveness, and decision-making, which seemed to be some strong directions for the future.

In 1986 the Association of College and Research Libraries began more preconference courses under its chapters, library schools, and so on. It also redesigned course formats for 75–100 participants each to keep costs low for the smaller libraries.

## PURPOSES AND FACTORS AFFECTING PROGRAMS

Thorough staff-development programs, based on the group, are generally difficult for all but well-funded academic libraries to afford. Continuing-educational workshops, however, are easier to budget for individuals because fewer attendees than at staff-development meetings mean fewer scheduling problems. Both types of programs are important, though, so that staff members can keep up with current developments in their particular areas.

Marie Gorecki, writing about library automation, gave five administrative areas for developmental programs: (1) establishment of objectives, (2) software education, (3) learning of skills to retrain staff, (4) area of responsibility, and (5) teaching methods used (1985: 473–75). The programs' success depends on meeting the participants' needs in these areas and on effective reinforcement to ensure change and learning (Kruger and May 1985: 70–71). Improved productivity should be the end result. Both internal and external programs provide the means of improvement.

It is imperative for library staff members in smaller academic libraries to keep up with current developments, because if low funding allows no money for continuing education, the staff could stagnate professionally. Consequently, growth, continual library and institutional changes, avoidance of stagnation, and up-to-date patron programs assume greater importance at smaller libraries if services are to continue to meet patron needs with new technology. These aims must be supported both philosophically and budgetarily by the library director and the college administration. Janet Flowers pointed out that there should be "a continuum of refresher courses, workshops, programs, and conferences" (1980: 199). She recommended in-house offerings because of audience familiarity, ability to meet specific needs, and ease of program coordination. In return for allowing the staff member time off to participate in them, the library has the right to expect improved performance, Flowers believes.

For smaller academic libraries, "since libraries are not typically overburdened with resources to launch full-blown staff development programs with their own trainers . . . , careful planning is a must . . . [and] supervisory levels should be able to identify educational needs in their departments that can be met externally . . . for the individual learner" (Nelson 1979: 355).

One must note, however, that that which benefits the individual does not necessarily help the library and vice versa, hence the need always to keep the purpose, size, and context of the organization in mind when considering staff training (Martell and Dougherty 1978: 153). Robert Means said an individual's readiness is the key part in continuing education (1978: 490).

## STAFF ATTITUDES NEEDED FOR SUCCESS

### Openness to Change

Inherent in the scope of continuing education and staff development is change that leads to improvement of library services. It is a view shared by James Neal (1980: 128) and Margaret Monroe (1967: 276–77). Monroe said, "The first task of continuing education should be that of reducing the resistance to change," agreeing with Sarah Reed that necessity overrode " 'role' assignment, and the importance of continuing education for librarians is, thus, established." This outlook must begin in each individual before the organization can benefit. In a teaching context, Forrest Parkay specified four assumptions about change: (1) it must start with determining how the teaching-learning process is conducted; (2) it must be a process of gradual growth; (3) it should result in new teacher-student [or librarian-patron] relationships; and (4) its acceptance is best in two-way, face-to-face communication (1986: 386). He argued that "one-shot" staff-development workshops do not work. *Ongoing*, coordinated professional growth and learning is effective, however, when the recipient understands it and how and why to apply its findings. The focus of staff development is inquiry, and inquiry promotes change and improvement.

### Creativity

Another aspect of continuing education's acceptance is staff-member creativity. Eugene Raudsepp said that "creativity, properly encouraged and directed, can be . . . greatest asset. A flexible attitude . . . is key" (1985: 38, 40). He added that it should be used more because it is connected closely with productivity and quality improvement in that it raises the quality of solutions, helps innovations, motivates higher productivity, improves personal skills, and sparks teamwork. Smaller academic libraries should encourage staff creativity to achieve goals, not perpetuate yesterday's roles, so that people can have something to work toward, to feel self-fulfillment, and to give the latest in library services.

### Motivation

If change is toward upgrading of personal skills and library progams and if creativity is the means by which it is done, motivating factors must be present. Among them are the chance to learn new technologies, to give better service, to improve work flow, and to enable the staff to give better service. Stone said that "the administrator planning professional improvement activities [should] give top priority to those sources of encouragement" to optimize results (1969: 201).

## Planning

For continuing education and staff development to succeed in any size academic library, Gerald Hodges emphasized systematic planning. In his work with the National Council on Quality Continuing Education for Information, Library, Media Personnel, he believed six steps were important: (1) assessment of the client group's needs; (2) relating learning objectives to those needs for attitude changes, mastering new knowledge, or revising outdated concepts; (3) identification of the method and locating personnel and means for the program; (4) timeliness of program content; (5) systematic promotion of the educational offering; and (6) evaluation of the activities based on the original objectives (1981: 30–33).

## PROBLEMS FOR SMALL ACADEMIC LIBRARIES TO OVERCOME

Compared with large research university libraries, fewer reports were found of successful staff-development programs in the smaller libraries. One reason is the lack of staff to conduct them. I have seen several aspects of that situation: (1) insufficient staff trained to produce programs, (2) too small a staff both to cover services and to allow release time regularly for attendance at in-house programs, (3) scheduling problems, (4) lack of proper facilities, (5) some supervisors discouraging staff development, (6) unsatisfactory delivery system, (7) lack of reinforcement or rewards for program participants, and (8) lack of funds.

Very pertinent to sparse staff development in smaller academic libraries is insufficient funding. According to Stella Bentley, "few administrators have the money . . . [for] staff to attend expensive workshops or courses. And with most of us receiving salaries that are less than generous, few librarians are able to finance the registration fees as well as the other expenses" (1980: 164). She added that a good alternative to programs that are very expensive or too superficial to be useful is formal college courses to attain the depth of knowledge needed. Robert Goehlert, though, suggested that continuing education focus more on mutual workshops between associations and job exchanges to obtain ideas from outside sources (1981: 286). In any case, small academic libraries cannot design programs for future needs if funds for workshops on them are unavailable. The result is a stagnant library.

Darlene Weingand proposed several means for making payment of tuition if college courses are elected: (1) reimbursement by the employer, (2) payment by the student-participant, (3) grant or scholarship, or (4) tax-supported aid (1985: 223–25). Two more reasons come to mind also. The library could give a release to the librarian for attendance but not fees; thus the librarian might qualify for a tax deduction if inquiry were made. Also, the librarian might be eligible for one of the competitive Fund for the Improvement of Post-Secondary Education grants, or those like them in other specialty areas, and use that to defray tuition expenses. However financed, librarians must ultimately keep up with rapid technical advances in their field in any way possible if their patrons are to be served well regardless of their libraries' sizes. If not, information specialists or computer personnel may take charge.

## EFFECTIVE PROGRAMS AND DELIVERY SYSTEMS

### Basic Principles

Although, as previously noted, library continuing education is sparse at smaller academic libraries compared with that at ARL libraries, I believe there are several ways the former can take part in development programs: (1) cosponsorship of them with nearby libraries; (2) cooperation with the state library association to give workshops at a central location; (3) presentation of workshops by a regional Association of College and Research Libraries (ACRL) chapter or regional library association (those of the Southeastern Library Association are noted for their timeliness); (4) sending staff to one of the regional automation networks' workshops dealing with computerized operations; the New England Library Network (NELINET) 113 for fiscal year 1987 is one of the most thorough of any consortia's series (NELINET 1986); or (5) encouraging librarians to attend the many ALA conference and nonconference continuing education meetings and workshops.

For effective development of staff capabilities, I believe there must be an ongoing commitment to this professional training by staff, supervisors, and administrators in smaller libraries. For recognizable effects, however, programs must be regular, applicable, and at times repetitious to reinforce learning, and all librarians should regularly participate in accordance with their assignments. Programs must be in parallel with long-range library goals (Stone 1969: 212), and their purposes and subjects should be clearly defined (Mitchell 1973: 147). If goals for staff development have not been articulated, a committee should draft them to provide direction for the library's departments and staff.

Locations for continuing-education programs ideally should be easily accessible to participants, maximizing the number and minimizing the costs. Hands-on practice should be built into the format as well as into the theory and rationale of the workshops; otherwise lasting effects will be minimal. Ronald Fingerson noted that librarians should not expect library schools to bear most of the burdens, though, for they "are neither equipped nor inclined to offer more than a brief, theoretical introduction to . . . skills required at the career level" (1977: 35). James Groark and Mark Yerburgh recommended, in view of decreasing funding, that "staff development activities should be initiated more intensively within the unique environment of each individual library" (1979: 144–45). In their opinion, programs should follow systematically and developmentally the following four steps and not be one-shot programs: (1) assessment of learning needs, (2) identification of strategy and resources, (3) implementation of the learning program, and (4) evaluation of the learning program. For optimal results, they recommended that the program be segmented into small, manageable units and be tailored so that librarians' needs are matched to an appropriate methodology. At the program's conclusion an analysis of its effects should be conducted.

## Successful Approaches of Other Libraries

Community-college-library continuing-education needs were analyzed in Illinois by Robert Means (1978: 490–97). A questionnaire was developed first to identify interests, background, present staff developmental activities, and obstacles. The interests found were used to (1) develop abilities for needed changes; (2) improve communication, planning, and conflict resolution; (3) improve staff knowledge of their principal patrons; (4) develop adult learning experiences; and (5) develop technical skills in various services. Among factors bearing on program success were the differences in types of personnel and their ages; types of libraries; amount of prior continuing education; availability; the education formats preferred; location, length, content, and accessibility of programs; amount of subsidization of participation; and an incentive and reward system. The study report advised the reader to become familiar with potential obstacles so that recommendations for the planners of programs would be sound.

Writing from Westchester Community College, New York, Marilyn Menack and Rosanne Kalick (1983: 220–21) observed that before anything is done with either services or staff development, librarians must participate in their institutional environment fully as faculty. From that perspective, they should openly communicate with other faculty about institution needs from their collective standpoints, for then a better concept of librarians' training needs can be developed. Library staff assignments are critical at community colleges because more mature and more part-time students are encountered whose needs differ from those of traditional, resident undergraduates. Menack and Kalick viewed the librarians there as needing to help patrons become the self-directed learners they wish to be. It is implied that their librarians are far more involved in communicating and using interpersonal skills, with entrepreneurial approaches to services.

Joyce Ball and Stefan Moses (1979: 177–78), writing about staff development at the Reno campus of the University of Nevada, found the pressures of managing staff development required familiarity with management work within the environment of the library. They discovered a weekend MBA degree program that fit those needs and promoted it to the library-management personnel as having both present usefulness and future utility. Among the subjects included were society, regulatory effects of affirmative action, copyright law, communication, principles of management, and a practical applications workshop.

The City University of New York is composed of a number of separate, smaller units with their own identities and libraries. James Neal (1980: 132) studied their attitudes and experiences toward continuing education and found some interesting variables applicable to other small academic libraries that encourage continuing education. They were (1) that their librarians preferred interacting with colleagues at conferences, (2) that they liked self-study programs, (3) that continuing education was very popular with the forty to forty-nine age group and with mid-career librarians, (4) that younger librarians were more interested in subject approaches, and (5) that there was greater interest in continuing education for those librarians with higher career aspirations. No connection was found between continuing education and sex, job security, type of college, or additional degrees. A close relationship found between experience and attitude suggested that median age- and experience-group librarians would benefit more from the training and that probably continuing education should best be structured for them. Automation was one area of high interest, and the subjects of data-base operations, nonbook materials, and systems design and analysis were most preferred within it. He found that two-year college librarians in CUNY were interested in practical work applications, with library automation, data-base operation, nonbook and audiovisual materials, and remedial instruction of best benefit.

Georgia Southern College began annual in-house orientation programs for a new staff in December 1975 (Barbour, 1986). This consisted of two weeks of orientation sessions from one to three hours each day right after final exams were over. The first week consisted of library departmental tours with presentations, questions, and discussion, and it was for both librarians and clerks. The second week was primarily for clerks and dealt with basic librarianship needed for working in library departments. Evaluations were positive, sometimes with as many as 10 percent repeaters. In 1978 its Library Staff Association began a series of quarterly luncheon meetings with invited speakers. Topics included subjects such as the University of South Carolina Library's Movietone News Collection and the material in the Georgia Collection of the University of Georgia. At times supervisors gave programs on automation of acquisitions, on-line database searching, and award-winning audiovisual programs from the library's Georgia Endowment for the Humanities Collection.

A smaller professional academic library, the Moody Medical Library of the University of Texas Medical Branch at Galveston (Eaton 1981: 317–21), has had a regular staff-development program for all of its staff since 1976. It covers specific services, interrelationships of the library's various areas, teamwork, and job pride, among other subjects. Its staff teaches the material in-house, and effectiveness ratings have been over 90 percent most of the time. Courses are developed also and are offered quarterly, with seventeen topics now available. The subjects are all work related and include topics such as accounting for libraries, computer-terminal operation, copyright regulations, extension program, MEDLINE, Mini-German for library work, and serials procedures. Each instructor has sole responsibility for presentation of the material, and the only guidelines from the library administration for each course were to have a final quiz for reinforcement and for the attendees to fill out an evaluation form on it. Measured results showed that the staff was better able to deal with patrons and developing technology after having the instruction.

A consortium, the Microcomputer Users Group for Libraries in North Carolina, according to the *Library Journal* ("Micro 'Summer Camp' in N.C. Teaches Computing Basics," 1984: 133), sponsored on a statewide basis a three-day workshop-summer camp in 1983 in Durham. This was to give librarians hands-on experience in various aspects of library automation that could include microcomputers; the instructors were mostly staff members from small libraries in the state that could not afford to produce such a meeting locally with their own funds. An introductory session was on the computer language BASIC. The next part split, in closed-loop fashion, into four three-hour tracks, with each librarian able to take part in three of them. Covered in the tracks were data-base management, spreadsheets, word processing, and public access. Comments revealed an interest in additional work at later meetings with the microcomputers. Funded by a Library Services and Construction Act grant, the gross cost was only $6,400 for the entire workshop, and the total cost per person was only $75.

The Council on Library Resources has, since its founding in 1956, been concerned with helping the nation's libraries with various programs, studies, institutes, and other means of support so that they can cope with their problems. Part of its thrust has been in the area of continuing education, believing that, "Well-educated librarians are essential to assure a high level of library performance" (Council on Library Resources 1985: 28). Especially under Fred Cole's leadership ("Newsnotes," 1986: 16), it started new programs designed to improve managerial effectiveness in academic libraries, to provide better undergraduate services, and to build up librarians' skills. Librarians from both smaller and larger academic libraries were eligible to apply, and programs were available such as the Academic Library Management Intern Program, the Library Services Enhancement Program, the College Program, and the Professional Education and Training for Researching Librarianship Program. In fiscal year 1985 a total of twenty-six grants were awarded for professional education projects to academic libraries of all sizes, and eighteen went to individuals or groups of individuals (Council on Library Resources 1985: 29–34).

Although this section has been devoted to what I consider noteworthy with different types of emphasis on continuing education from various institutions, so as to present the reader with a variety of ideas for programs, brief mention is needed of various professional development programs offered regularly by places such as the University of Illinois, the University of Wisconsin, and the University of Denver, as well as ALA itself. A wide range of subjects can be found to fit almost any need and both with and without Continuing Education Units (CEUs) being given. Some are presented annually, whereas others have a common thread running through various different offerings. Some may be subsidized partially or wholly also. Most are either cosponsored or at least given moral support by ALA's CLENE. All exist to aid the librarian in keeping up to date with new developments in librarianship so as to give the best service to local patrons.

If planned on a regular basis, continuing education and staff-development groups can serve smaller libraries as well as larger libraries. Many tend to be one-shot types. Nevertheless, if a needs assessment has singled out certain topics, the staff should be able to attend, as appropriate to their jobs. Contacts made at workshops with persons from other libraries can provide valuable data later when librarians need to plan changes in systems. Goehlert supported cooperation on programs between groups such as the Special Library Association and the American Society for Information Science promote (1981: 286). This cooperation may be aimed at small or large localities. The Central Georgia Associated Libraries and the South Georgia Associated Libraries, for example, have jointly sponsored workshops on the new copyright law, motivation, and OCLC-SOLINET (Online-Computer Library Center—Southeastern Library Network) new ventures, at appropriate times, for both small academic as well as public libraries. Goehlert also recommended that librarians seriously consider job exchanges to areas with some variant library applications, such as the campus computing center, its research institute, a data archive, or the college research and development office (1981: 286).

Delivery systems can vary widely, and preferences may often be dictated by things such as available funding. Travel reimbursements may not be possible in some places or locales. An interesting finding was made by Barbara Smith in writing about effective needs of librarians doing bibliographic instruction in Pennsylvania. In surveying their perceptions about the best continuing-education delivery system for the future, she found 34 percent favored workshops, 33 percent chose credit courses, 21 percent wanted in-service programs (followed by a wide gap), and, at the bottom, a mere 5 percent preferred self-study and 4 percent wanted conferences (Smith 1982: 204). The one-fifth that desired staff development at the home site undoubtedly reflects the awareness that funding is difficult although the training is important enough to require keeping up with new methodologies. Thus they are willing to remain at home to receive the staff development, if need be, instead of being away a day or two. The 33 percent who chose academic course work showed the value still placed in formal training and the willingness to pay for what will meet the participants' needs.

For announcements of programs, Joseph Natale recommended the On-Line Network of Continuing Education (ONCE), funded by the Illinois State Library Advisory Committee in 1983 for Illinois residents (Natale 1984: 35–37). Listings are also available elsewhere in different professional publications, such as *American Libraries* and the *Library Journal*, and in various advertising circulars usually sent to library administrative offices.

## EVALUATION

For best effects and carryover from workshops, there should be ongoing continuing-education and staff-development programs that are timely and are designed for performance improvement. Feedback is important, however. Evaluations need to be conducted on each program right at its conclusion. They should cover subject matter, audience, instructor, setting, presentation, and timing and should be both general and topic specific, with especially the quality being measured.

Gail Trapnell said that the type of evaluation should be based on the program's nature. This should include (1) the environment present, (2) appropriateness and adequacy of the resources, (3) the training process, (4) competencies of the trainees, and (5) the impact the training makes on the organization and its operations (1984: 90–92). She then noted that all evaluations should have "objectives, identification of the data to be collected, standards, procedures, time frames and staff assignments" (p. 92).

Darlene Weingand reported that the National Council on Quality Continuing Education recommended specific evaluations to cover "awareness of client needs; specific, measurable and/or observable learning objectives (attitude and/or skills); systematically designed delivery systems; timeliness; responsible promotional procedures; evaluation; human resources; facilities and materials; budget; and administrative procedures (1984: 210). Also, I believe there should be two parts to an evaluation on the effectiveness of continuing-education and staff-development programs. One should be on the program's success, whether it did what it said it would do and the benefit to the library. Another should be in regard to the amount of professional fulfillment each participant received. Although the evaluation measures a past event, it should be structured to gauge, in summation, the impact and future utility of the program on the library as a result of the staff's participation. An enlightened staff is of the highest importance, but the members' expertise should be improved so that the academic library's service will be the best.

## FUTURE DIRECTIONS

Librarians need to prepare for a completely new information infrastructure by the 1990s. Already rapid advances in linked systems, microtechnology, personal computers, gateways, compact disk storages (especially for full texts), optical disks, chips, telefacsimile transmission, electronics, data-base retrieval, telecommunications, and digital transmissions (replacing the asynchronous), among other things, signal radical changes in library services before A.D. 2000. Goehlert said:

At the same time that librarians learn about the new information technologies, they need to know how . . . to design new . . . arrangements that will change academic libraries into information and research management centers. . . . [L]ibrarians would have to learn new skills of data librarianship. Additionally, the creation of a data center/research library might require the redesigning of institutional arrangements that allow for a variety of individuals, including librarians, computer scientists, etc., who share a combination of skills. (Goehlert 1981: 285–86)

If librarians at smaller institutions learn no new technologies, the 1990s will find them no longer in charge of their collections.

Charles Martell and Richard Dougherty said that "few libraries budget more than 2 percent on staff development related activities" (1978: 155). Most libraries budget far less. For a small academic library with a staff budget of $900,000, for example, this would come to $18,000, but small libraries seldom have anything close to that for professional training. The travel budget of most libraries with that size of personal services budget may have at the most $2,000, and a sizable amount of that is generally set aside in advance for representing the library at required functions. This stresses even more the need for in-house programs instead of continuing-education workshops away from home.

Librarians know that their libraries are the main campus-research data repository. They, therefore, should take advantage of all opportunities to make that material more accessible to patrons by planning for things such as campus dial access, public catalogs on line to faculty offices, on-line data retrieval, and student word processing applications. Staff development and continuing education will provide the librarian at the smaller academic library the knowledge of new technologies, and enthusiasm will promote the new product. Ralph Waldo Emerson said nothing great was ever done without enthusiasm.

## NOTE

1. General source: *The ALA Yearbook*, vols. 1–10, columns entitled "Personnel and Employment: Staff Development."

## REFERENCES

Ball, Joyce, and Stefan Moses. 1979. "Continuing Education-XIV," *College and Research Libraries News* 40, no. 6 (June): 177–78.

Barbour, Wendell A. 1986. Personal communication.

Bentley, Stella. 1980. "Getting Quality for the Price," *College and Research Libraries News* 41, no. 6 (June): 164.

Conroy, Barbara. 1974. *Staff Development and Continuing Education Programs for Library Personnel: Guidelines and Criteria*. Boulder, Colo.: Western Interstate Commission for Higher Education.

Council on Library Resources. 1985. *Twenty-ninth Annual Report*. Washington, D.C., pp. 29–34.

Eaton, Elizabeth K. 1981. "Library Staff Development Course." *Medical Library Association Bulletin* 69, no. 3 (July): 317–21.

Fingerson, Ronald L. 1977. "Competencies to Be Demonstrated." *Journal of Education for Librarianship* 18, no. 1 (Summer): 35.

Flowers, Janet L. 1980. "Role of the Local Professional Association in Continuing Education." *College and Research Libraries News* 42, no. 7 (July): 199.

Goehlert, Robert. 1981. "CE and the Information Environment." *College and Research Libraries News* 42, no. 9 (September): 285–86.

Gorecki, Marie J. 1985. ''Continuing Education for Automation Librarians: Current Issues and Practice.'' *Illinois Libraries* 67, no. 5 (May): 473–75.

Groark, James J., and Mark R. Yerburgh. 1979. ''Staff Development for Academic Libraries: The Art of the Possible.'' *The Bookmark* 38, no. 3 (Spring): 144–45.

Hodges, Gerald G. 1981. ''Continuing Education for Professional Growth.'' *North Carolina Libraries* 39, no. 1 (Spring): 30–33.

Kruger, Michael J., and Gregory D. May. 1985. ''Training: Two Techniques to Ensure That Training Programs Remain Effective.'' *Personnel Journal* 64, no. 10 (October): 70–71.

Martell, Charles R., and Richard M. Dougherty. 1978. ''The Role of Continuing Education and Training in Human Resource Development: An Administrator's Viewpoint.'' *The Journal of Academic Librarianship* 4, no. 3 (July): 153, 155.

Means, Robert. 1978. ''A Study of the Continuing Education Interests of Illinois Community College Library and Learning Resource Center Personnel.'' *Illinois Libraries* 32, no. 5 (May): 490–97.

Menack, Marilyn, and Rosanne Kalick. 1983. ''The Community College Library and Learning Resource Center: A Model for Continuing Education.'' *The Bookmark* 41, no. 4 (Summer): 220–21.

''Micro 'Summer Camp' in N.C. Teaches Computing Basics.'' 1984. *Library Journal* 109, no. 2 (February 1): 133.

Mitchell, Betty Jo. 1973. ''In-House Training of Supervisory Library Assistants in a Large Academic Library.'' *College and Research Libraries* 33, no. 2 (March): 147.

Monroe, Margaret. 1967. ''Variety in Continuing Education.'' *ALA Bulletin* 61, no. 3 (March): 276.

Natale, Joseph A. 1984. ''The Once and Future Data Base.'' *Illinois Libraries* 66, no. 1 (January): 35–37.

Neal, James G. 1980. ''Continuing Education: Attitudes and Experiences of the Academic Librarian.'' *College and Research Libraries News* 41, no. 2 (March): 128, 132.

Nelson, Jim. 1979. ''Continuing Education Investments for Staff Development Benefits.'' *College and Research Libraries News* 41, no. 11 (December): 355.

New England Library Network. 1986. *Training and Program Catalog, FY '87*. Newton, Mass.

''Newsnotes.'' 1986. *The New Library Scene* 5, no. 3 (June): 16.

Parkay, Forrest W. 1986. ''A School/University Partnership That Fosters Inquiry-Oriented Staff Development.'' *Phi Delta Kappan* 67, no. 5 (January): 386.

Raudsepp, Eugene. 1985. ''101 Ways to Spark Your Employees' Creative Potential.'' *Office Administration and Automation* 46, no. 9 (September): 38, 40.

Smith, Barbara J. 1982. ''Background Characteristics and Education Needs of a Group of Instruction Librarians in Pennsylvania.'' *College and Research Libraries* 43, no. 3 (May): 204.

Snyder, Carolyn A., and Nancy P. Sanders. 1978. ''Continuing Education and Staff Development: Needs Assessment, Comprehensive Program Planning, and Evaluation.'' *Journal of Academic Librarianship* 4, no. 3 (July): 144.

Stone, Elizabeth W. 1969. *Factors Related to the Professional Development of Libraries*. Metuchen, N.J.: Scarecrow Press, pp. 21, 201, 212, 217–18.

Stone, Elizabeth W., Ruth J. Patrick, and Barbara Conroy. 1974. *Continuing Library and Information Science Education: Final Report to the National Commission on*

*Libraries and Information Science*. Washington, D.C.: U.S. Government Printing Office, pp. 1–9.

Stone, Elizabeth W., Eileen Sheahan, and Katharine J. Hardy. 1979. *Model Continuing Education Recognition System in Library and Information Science*. New York: K. G. Saur, pp. 303–4.

Trapnell, Gail. 1984. "Putting the Evaluation Puzzle Together." *Training and Development Journal* 38, no. 5 (May): 90–92.

Weingand, Darlene. 1984. "Continuing Education" (column). *Journal of Education for Librarianship* 24, no. 3 (Winter): 210.

———. 1985. "Continuing Education: Who Shall Pay?" *Journal of Education for Librarianship* 25, no. 3 (Winter): 223–25.

# 8

## New Patterns for Managing the Small Staff

### Gerard B. McCabe

The organization of most small academic libraries imitates that of the largest university libraries, progressing even to the point of copying minor procedural details. Departmental structure, staff titles, and responsibilities often are the same with similar internal operating routines. There may be some slight justification for this, but this very structure may inhibit professional staff development and retard better use of human resources, obstructing truly effective staff management and the opportunity for growth. It is time for reconsideration and development of organizational patterns better suited to present circumstances including the size of the library, patterns that will provide new challenges for librarians, and the offering of new opportunities for improving their status both on campus and in the national purview of their rightful role in society.

This chapter postulates that smaller academic libraries should have their own internal organization suited to what they really need and that all academic libraries need not be exactly alike in organization. If there is a common characteristic, it should be the emphasis on service to users; toward that end a unified service pattern or concept should prevail, with a very flexible internal structure. This breaking away from the model of large academic libraries will provide better use of libraries and faster service more in line with the needs of today's library users.

In an important article Allen Veaner (1985) described professional needs for the decade 1985–1995. His two-part paper appeared in *College and Research Libraries* and was instigated by a request from a study group of the Association of College and Research Libraries. Veaner discussed several factors that academic librarians and their administrators must consider and respond to in the next few years, citing other authors in support of academic libraries. The need to respond to Veaner's observations is acute. What has been said is important and should be considered carefully; it can lead to better and more effective employment of librarians and hence better management.

The further imitation of large libraries requires serious reconsideration. When leading librarians like Veaner are doubtful of the future value of their internal structure, there is no security for small libraries in copying them. Veaner expressed his doubt directly by questioning the very heart of larger libraries' internal organization, the infrastructure of departments. How worthwhile is continuing this internal structure for the future and what negative effects on library progress does this structure have are the focus of his concerns (1985:213).

In a small academic library, new concepts of organization can be identified through internal self-study with the assistance of good outside consultation. The Office of Management Studies, Association of Research Libraries, has a management-review and analysis program and a planning program for the small academic library. Both are well known and have been described elsewhere (Webster and Sitts 1982).

Before focusing precisely on specific issues of staff management, some trends in the library profession should be considered. In an earlier article, Veaner summarized some of these trends. He pointed out the continuing movement toward the intellectual aspects of a librarian's work, its variety, and the deemphasis of measureable production in physical units or in time used (1984:623).

In that article he identified a guiding principle for staff management today and perhaps for long after: for management by professional librarians, the characteristics of high-level performance are mandatory; for the management of support staff, the characteristics of specialized technical training are essential. For librarians, Veaner's second sentence illustrates perfectly the two chief characteristics that their work must have today—thinking and variety. The typical organization of today's small academic library stifles those chief characteristics. Why? Veaner elaborated further and used the phrase "institution's *program*" to explain his meaning as applied to librarians, again emphasizing intellectual nonproduction aspects. Before continuing, the support staff must be considered. Veaner described what has occurred by listing a catalog of common tasks once the daily responsibility of librarians and now that of the support staff (1984: 623–24).

It is not uncommon to find a senior library assistant responsible for subject-heading maintenance in a large library's catalog department. All subject headings chosen by a cataloger, professional or nonprofessional, are checked against policy and changed without consultation if inappropriate. On-line searching is performed by library assistants with bachelor's or master's degrees in other disciplines, and some departments have nonprofessional supervisors, and all staff members are nonprofessionals. The department-head position is no longer exclusively reserved for librarians. Universally, this has not happened in small academic libraries. Far too many of their librarians are locked into the production aspects of library work. In his 1985 two-part article in *College and Research Libraries*, Veaner remarked on the incredible management load carried by the head librarian of a smaller academic library (1985:295). Without the advice and support of staff librarians all too overwhelmed by their production duties, the smaller library's head must make almost all decisions, set policy, and guide development. This level of responsibility will require unusual training and considerable experience.

What Veaner is describing in these articles is the direction in which the library profession is moving; in their organizational planning small academic libraries should move also in that direction. In the early stages of development of a new organizational plan, every procedure, every detail of work, especially that of librarians, must be examined for usefulness and appropriateness of assignment. A librarian's working assignment that does not provide for challenging thought and contribute to a variety of such experience must be either reassigned or discarded. Similarly, for the support staff, unneeded assignments should be discarded, and any necessary training should be provided for those tasks that are left or that are transferred from a librarian's former duties. Once called the work simplification concept, it is a means of shifting work responsibilities downward from librarians to the support staff or, as Veaner noted, shifting production activities to the support staff, leaving the librarians free to face the more challenging intellectual demands of the decade he discussed. Again, his remarks relating to larger libraries are pertinent. He commented that librarians in these larger libraries now perform assignments once done only by the highest echelon of library managers and that few production type duties remain (1984: 623). I recall observing librarians counting material order cards as a measure of daily work, and catalog librarians filling in tally sheets for the materials they cataloged with Library of Congress catalog cards, or through original cataloging without any predetermined assistance. This change does not represent the case in many small academic libraries. In many of these libraries, librarians work as circulation librarians, acquisition librarians, and reserve librarians and their work involves counting production, units circulated or processed and acquired. Positive change is clearly in order for these positions, and in all three cases the support staff can assume the practical duties. Some further training and well-written policy statements will provide sufficient guidance for successful performance. The circulation and reserve librarians are freed for bibliographic instruction and reference duties. The acquisition librarian can assume strong collection-management responsibility, working with colleagues and teaching faculty to further collection quality. Even the work of reference librarians should be reviewed for the same reasons. It may be more difficult to conceive of some of their work being of a production nature, but if some fair portion of their time is expended on directional questions, repetitive instruction, or something similar, an obvious need exists for a bibliographic instruction program. There may be other needs that such a study would reveal, including a case for on-line data-base searching, a service for which sufficient time is required for effectiveness. The major management duties may now be shared, and participation in planning for the future becomes a meaningful endeavor.

## ON-LINE SEARCHING AND NEW TECHNOLOGY

On-line data-base searching offers a proven way of assisting students and faculty in finding and identifying bibliographic information. This service has been a major component of larger libraries' reference service for years but has not been emulated very quickly in small libraries. Usually, it has not been adopted for budgetary reasons, but it is a beneficial asset, providing economy of time for students and faculty and, in the case of the latter, helping those with heavy teaching loads maintain their currency of knowledge and productivity of contributions to scholarship. Depending upon the scope of the institution's academic program, each available reference librarian could specialize in retrieval of one or more specific data bases. The more time librarians have for this, or the more librarians are on reference duty, the greater the coverage, and so the better the service. A review of duties and reassignment to the support staff or elimination of those judged unnecessary could provide the required time.

The means of supporting on-line data-base searching in academic libraries has been the subject of considerable debate; each institution has to deal with the issue and find its own best way to provide for the cost, but it cannot be withheld from the library's services without some peril to reputation if nothing else. The managers of libraries lacking this service must overcome any obstacle and have this service provided both for the benefit of users and the intellectual welfare of their librarians.

Vendors offering packaged retrieval systems for periodical references promote them by including either an automatic microfilm bibliography or videodisks containing thousands of citations. When such packages are added to the known potential of on-line searching, the reference service is greatly enhanced, although library textual resources may not be, and dependency on interlibrary loans may increase. In small libraries, assessment of the need for and value of these packages must consider possible cost increases in support areas.

Such systems are expensive, but they appear to offer an opportunity to advance professional services, improving the effectiveness of reference and information librarians. In situations in which the staff increases are not at all possible, they may offer an alternative means of promoting library service, something a library manager cannot overlook.

For a library's audiovisual service component, the reception of foreign and domestic educational and cultural television programs and of statistical data transmitted from space satellites offer many possibilities. Some of these are discussed in a later chapter. The opportunity to improve language study and cultural exposure and to promote research through such capability is becoming a strong reality as equipment costs decrease and space satellites increase.

Lower equipment costs and technical advances are making local or regionally shared on-line catalogs a real possibility for smaller libraries. Before beginning such an effort, however, careful study and consideration of a library's individual requirements are necessary; although debate still continues over the real capabilities of on-line catalog systems and their actual fulfillment of what an on-line catalog should be, librarians not engaged in this undertaking, where there is a need for such study, are not realizing their potential for thinking or for using their professional training and knowledge to advance their library's service. Their professional standing in their academic community is indeed threatened or certainly not being advanced.

Librarians overburdened with production responsibilities do not have the time to evaluate fully these advanced offerings made possible by innovative adaptations of technology. Veaner alluded to the transference of production from professional to support staff in both his articles (1984, 1985). But for small libraries this transference is all too slow and must be accelerated. If the necessary transitions to new technology are to happen in small libraries, thinking must happen first. Planning's chief ingredient is simply the time to think through necessary changes and their consequences. Continuing to keep librarians in production positions denigrates their professional standing and deprives the library and the people it serves of the full values of highly trained human resources. The skillful library manager will direct efforts toward providing librarians time for thinking through their library's needs and their own response to them.

## SUBJECT SPECIALIZATION AND COLLECTION DEVELOPMENT

Librarians as collection-development officers, subject librarians, or bibliographers are not common in smaller academic libraries. In contrast to large libraries in which either collection-development departments or large numbers of subject bibliographers exist, the prevailing approach in small libraries is to rely almost exclusively on teaching faculty for recommendations of material to be added to the collections. Librarians, with a lesser role often confined only to items for the reference and bibliography collections, are denied a very challenging and intellectually demanding responsibility. Many other authors have stated that librarians and faculty members should be working together to identify meaningful books and other items that will enhance the collection in terms of curricular support. Material selection is precisely the sort of intellectual challenge that brings us to Veaner's characteristics for professional work noted earlier, thinking and variety. As we move further into the decade of Veaner's other article (1985), subject proficiency of librarians in small academic libraries can be a tool ensuring both the acquisition of worthwhile materials and the furtherance of the librarians' stature as professionals. Depending upon available numbers, each librarian could have specific subject assignments, coordinating recommendations with those of teaching faculty. If numbers permit, one librarian could serve in the role of coordinator for collection development and management.

The smaller the library's complement of librarians, the broader this responsibility must become. Such efforts ensure the wisest use of limited funds. Present circumstances of scholarly publishing, especially limited printings, demand this consideration also.

In his 1984 article, Veaner raised the question of technical proficiency required of catalog librarians in view of the almost universal availability of on-line bibliographic utilities. In the larger libraries, support staff are taught the rules of cataloging and apply them to most of the items being processed (1984: 624). Each library will make its own decision in this matter, but for successful performance, whether there is only one or several catalog librarians, subject proficiency cannot be overlooked. To achieve this proficiency in or among librarians, more support staff should be trained to do most of the routine cataloging.

Advertisements for professional openings in academic libraries may assist in identifying current thinking about the requirements librarians must meet for employment or advancement. To clarify this idea, advertisements for fifty-seven opportunities in the December 1985 issue of *American Libraries* were reviewed. Of these fifty-seven jobs, twenty-eight required subject expertise, only nine required knowledge of a foreign language, and forty-eight required experience with an appropriate on-line system. Forty-one of them were considered broadly as public service positions and of them, twenty-five required a subject background, and thirty-three required experience with an on-line system; only five required knowledge of a foreign language. Specific reasons for these requirements in each case may vary, even allowing for their use as screening devices, but following the majority trend, it is clear that subject backgrounds and experience with an appropriate—for the job—on-line system are important. College training at the baccalaureate level will provide the basis for a subject background that can be developed by actual working experience in an academic library. The opportunities for librarians today to develop a subject background other than that gained through undergraduate or graduate-level work by means of on-the-job experience seem limited but, in a small academic library, may be the only way to provide a librarian with a background in the humanities or the social sciences with a science background. Larger academic libraries can recruit scarce reference librarians with science backgrounds more readily than smaller libraries can. As a function of the marketplace, training may be necessary. Training in library school for on-line systems may cover fundamentals, and the real experience may be gained after employment in a library. Applicants for openings that indicate advancement will have no difficulty if their present employment provided that experience.

If this small sampling has any validity, it clearly shows emphasis on requirements that meet Veaner's characteristics of thinking and variety. Assuming that a subject background and on-line system experience will assist in daily performance of duties, intellectual exercise of a high order can be anticipated.

The library manager must lead the way in promoting the significant changes Veaner called for or assumed is the current case. Clearly, smaller academic libraries trail their larger counterparts in conversion of production duties from professional to support staff. They must provide their own initiative, drop the imitation role, and find the organization for service best suited to their own local need. This is a time for innovation not for emulation of organizations whose management may be successful at the larger level but is stifling at the smaller.

## NOTE

This paper is based on an earlier paper, "Managing the Smaller Academic Library Staff in Austerity," in *Nos Ressources Humaines: la Clé d'un Bon Service* (Personnel: Key to Successful Public Service). Textes des communications de départ pour les ateliers au 16e Congres de la C.B.P.Q., du 23 au 26 Mai 1985 a l'Auberge du Mont Gabriel. Edited by Rejean Savard. Montreal: Corporation des Bibliothecaires Professionnels du Québec, 1985, 168 pp.

## REFERENCES

*American Libraries*. 1985. Vol. 16, no. 11 (December): 785. Seminary library openings were excluded as were advertisements for administrative staff, assistant directors, or the equivalent and higher. No distinctions were made for varying sizes of academic libraries. Appropriate on-line systems for public service jobs included on-line data-base searching, interlibrary loan, and circulation systems; for technical service openings on-line systems included those of the major bibliographic utilities.

Veaner, Allen B. 1984. "Librarians: The Next Generation." *Library Journal* 109, no. 6 (April 1): 623–25.

———. 1985. "1985 to 1995: The Next Decade in Academic Librarianship." *College and Research Libraries* 46 (May): 209–29; (July): 295–308.

Webster, Duane E., and Maxine K. Sitts. 1982. "A Planning Program for the Small Academic Library: The PPSAL." In *Planning for Library Services*. Edited by Charles R. McClure. pp. 128–44. New York: Haworth Press. (Also published as *The Journal of Library Administration* 2, nos. 2/3/4 [1982, summer, fall, winter].)

# PART III

# Budgets and Finance

# 9

# Budgets in the Smaller Academic Libraries

*Murray S. Martin*

The basic budgetary needs of all libraries are similar. The allotted budget must cover the costs of the resources and services needed to meet library goals. These costs commonly fall into three categories: personnel, library materials, and operating costs.

By and large these three initial divisions are satisfactory, but an even more basic approach is the division into time and things. This may seem like a vast oversimplification, but reflection will show that all activities are composed of these two elements.

## BUDGETARY STYLES

The traditional line budget separates elements that are intimately connected. Other strategies such as program budgeting have been used to overcome this problem, but they are subject to the difficulty of separating allied activities. A good example is the interlibrary loan. Is this part of reference or lending services, or should it be allied with acquisitions as an alternative means of acquiring materials? (See Dowd, Whaley, and Pankake 1986; N. Martin 1982; Poole and St. Clair 1986.) These kinds of questions cannot be solved by any budgetary strategy. They are political questions, which need to be decided from that perspective. Budgets can answer questions such as how much or how many. They cannot answer why.

In a smaller library many functions are handled by the staff along with other duties, simply because they do not justify being set up as separate departments. The labor of disentangling such costs is time consuming and may not be as justifiable for a small library as for a large one. The aim, therefore, should be to keep the strategy as simple as possible. All libraries cover the same broad range of functions, and they should not be lost sight of, since, no matter how small, they cost money. It is simply a matter of finding the simplest way to account for them.

None of this invalidates the usefulness of the many existing budgetary styles.

(For studies of specific budgetary styles, see Chen 1980 and Young 1976.) All that it implies is that care must be taken in using them. Statistics and budgetary projections tend to take on a life of their own, and it is easy to lose sight of their justification—keeping the library going.

Whether the institution favors line budgets, program budgets, or some variation on the program planning and budgeting system (PPBS), in the long run all are the same—ways of accounting for time and things. For the most part, academic institutions tend to use incremental budgeting, with perhaps a bow to program budgeting when units are asked to propose and cost out new programs. For a library it is seldom a question of new programs but more of extensions of existing ones caused by changes elsewhere. Unfortunately, most libraries must carry on their budgetary preparations at the same time as those units whose decisions will affect library needs. Action to support new programs will therefore tend to be reactive and delayed. When the library itself has a new program to propose, as for example data-base searching or automation, it affects most budget lines so that it may need to be presented separately in order for its full impact to be assessed. Use as creatively as possible the process available to support library needs.

Moreover, libraries are in the midst of massive change, which will, as it develops, affect many aspects of budgeting. (See, for example, Spyers-Duran and Mann 1985, and Lee 1977.) Any plan must be flexible enough to accommodate change but must equally be able to be used as a guide to the present.

## PURPOSE OF A BUDGET

The purpose of a budget is to present the needs of the library to the funding authority for approval and thereafter to be a planning guide, a way of keeping a tag on progress. It sets out in monetary terms the goals and objectives of the library. The document that embodies it should therefore be firmly grounded in those goals, but it should not be seen as cast in concrete. The goals may change, there may be emergencies, or the original expectations may remain unrealized. There are many such possibilities, and accounting systems that insist on exact line matches or the return of unexpended funds from one part, even when there is real need elsewhere, do not recognize this. However, they do surmise that we are all imperfect and may misappropriate the unspent funds. In any case, what happens during a year may totally change budgetary needs, and there has to be a way of responding. Budgets are only guides; people have to use them responsibly.

## FUNCTIONAL ANALYSIS

The first step in preparing a budget is to determine where the library is now (see Riggs 1984). The gradual adoption of rolling budgets and the way in which preparation time has crept forward frequently mean that a librarian will have to start preparing the budget for the year after next before the year is even over. This makes the determination of how successful the present budget was in meeting library needs difficult, but the effort has to be made, or it may be five years before any corrective action can be taken—sometimes for a condition that no longer exists. To meet this difficulty requires something like a snapshot approach—what is happening in the library today? The need is to know what resources are being used for what functions.

## DISTRIBUTION OF TIME

This analysis is different from a time and motion study. It is a time-distribution study, which is then combined with a distribution of things to produce a cost distribution. The first thing is to decide what the separate activities should be. They can be as many or as few as make sense for the library. Some are relatively easy to separate. Circulation and other station-based activities have fairly clear time requirements, such as the number of hours the library is open. Others, such as data-base searching, are entwined with other activities, while processing activities form a kind of whole that may have to be subdivided. The object should be to determine what proportion of library time is devoted to each activity. Studies such as those conducted by Paul Kantor (1985) are beginning to develop appropriate measuring devices for determining the costs and achievements of library programs.

A possible division might look like this:

Administration
Collection development
    Selection
    Weeding
Lending services
    Circulation
    Reserves
    Shelving
    Door guards
Reference services
    Data-base searching
    Interlibrary loan
    Reference
Technical services
    Acquisition
    Cataloging
    Filing

Processing

Serials

When there are branches, each activity may have to be subdivided. If there are specialized activities, such as audiovisual or microform units or government publications, they should be accounted for separately.

Using this relatively simple breakdown, it is possible to convert the time distribution into money since the people involved and their salaries are known. This avoids the costly completion of time studies (although they may be necessary if the unit costs of functions are required) and is probably sufficiently sophisticated for the smaller library. Table 1 shows such a distribution for a hypothetical library.

What is of most interest from the results of such a study, for budget-making purposes, is the distribution of the time between activities. At first glance the results may seem surprising. Do we really spend that much on circulation or on administration? The smaller a library, the greater the proportion of its time that must go into such basic tasks. Circulation desks do, for example, require a staff at all hours when the library is open, and providing guards at a door can be a very expensive activity, one I once calculated as requiring a minimum of $25,000 a year, probably now closer to $30,000.

There are no norms. Each library's mix results from its own distinctive character. Factors such as the design of the building, the teaching timetable, or the academic program combine with historical circumstances to produce a specific mix. Whether it is good or bad, could be improved or changed, is not the issue at this point, which is simply the need to know how the present staff is being used.

## DISTRIBUTION OF THINGS (GOODS AND SERVICES)

The second part of this analysis may be more difficult. Each operation consumes certain things—for example, order slips, catalog cards, Online Computer Library Center (OCLC) services, supplies, overdue notices—and each requires the use of certain equipment—typewriters, filing cabinets, terminals, catalog drawers. Although most of them are not annual purchases, they do carry maintenance costs and have to be replaced or added to at relatively regular intervals, costs that have to be allowed for. (See table 2 for a breakdown of these costs.)

## LIBRARY MATERIALS

One major expenditure on things—library materials—is difficult to assign to functional units, although when appropriate, this should be done. The cost of indexes, abstracts, and so on is an appropriate part of the cost of doing reference business. Equally, it is appropriate to know what proportion of materials ex-

**Table 1**
**Time Distribution: Typical College**

| Unit | Personnel FTE | Cost | % |
|---|---|---|---|
| Administration | 5.25 | $157,000 | 18.2 |
| Collection Development | | | |
|   Selection | 1.5 | $37,000 | |
|   Weeding | 0.75 | $17,000 | |
|     Subtotal | 2.25 | $54,000 | 6.3 |
| Lending Services | | | |
|   General | 0.25 | $6,000 | |
|   Circulation | 8.0 | $124,000 | |
|   Door Guards | 3.0 | $30,000 | |
|   Reserves | 7.0 | $90,000 | |
|   Shelving | 3.0 | $34,000 | |
|     Subtotal | 21.25 | $284,000 | 33.0 |
| Reference Services | | | |
|   General | 0.5 | $14,000 | |
|   Database Searching | 1.0 | $24,000 | |
|   Interlibrary Loan | 2.5 | $35,000 | |
|   Reference | 3.5 | $68,000 | |
|     Subtotal | 7.5 | $141,000 | 16.4 |
| Technical Services | | | |
|   General | 0.0 | -0- | |
|   Acquisitions | 2.0 | $30,000 | |
|   Cataloging | 7.0 | $121,000 | |
|   -Filing | 2.0 | $24,000 | |
|   Processing | 2.0 | $22,000 | |
|   Serials | 2.0 | $28,000 | |
|     Subtotal | 15.0 | $225,000 | 26.1 |
| Total | 51.25 | $861,000 | |

*Note*: This distribution is based on having only one library building. Branches, or added special units, would add more personnel.

To these direct expenditures on salaries would have to be added the costs of any fringe benefits. Since these items are treated differently by different institutions, they are not usually included in statistical reports. Because the rate may vary among classes of employee, its effect would be to change the cost distribution.

Administration includes departmental administration.

**Table 2**
**Distribution of Expenditures on Goods and Services (Things)**

| Unit | Item | Cost | % |
|------|------|------|---|
| Administration | | | |
| | Supplies | $12,000 | |
| | Travel | 10,000 | |
| | Maintenance | 5,000 | |
| | Memberships | 5,000 | |
| | Telephones | 3,000 | |
| | Postage | 3,000 | |
| | Printing | 6,000 | |
| | Repairs | 22,000 | |
| | General | 3,000 | |
| | | $69,000 | 33.3 |
| Collection Development | | | |
| | Supplies | $ 1,000 | |
| | Travel | 1,000 | |
| | Maintenance | 500 | |
| | Telephones | 500 | |
| | General | 500 | 1.7 |
| | | $ 3,500 | |
| Lending Services | | | |
| | Supplies | $ 6,000 | |
| | Forms | 3,000 | |
| | Repairs | 3,000 | |
| | Travel | 2,000 | |
| | Equipment | 2,000 | |
| | Maintenance | 5,000 | |
| | Postage | 2,000 | |
| | Telephones | 3,000 | |
| | General | 1,000 | |
| | | $27,000 | 13.0 |

**Table 2 (*continued*)**

| Unit | Item | Cost | % |
|------|------|------|---|
| Reference Services | | | |
| | Supplies | $ 3,000 | |
| | Printing | 3,000 | |
| | Travel | 6,000 | |
| | Maintenance | 2,000 | |
| | Contracts | 2,000 | |
| | Equipment | 4,000 | |
| | OCLC | 3,000 | |
| | Postage | 1,000 | |
| | Telephones | 2,000 | |
| | General | 2,000 | |
| | | $28,000 | 13.5 |
| Technical Services | Supplies | $15,000 | |
| | Forms | 6,000 | |
| | Travel | 6,000 | |
| | OCLC | 30,000 | |
| | Security Strips | 5,000 | |
| | Maintenance | 6,000 | |
| | Equipment | 4,000 | |
| | Postage | 4,000 | |
| | Telephones | 4,000 | |
| | | $80,000 | 38.6 |
| | | $207,500 | |

**Table 3**
**Distribution of Expenditures on Library Materials**

| Unit | Serials | Books | Other | Total | % |
|------|---------|-------|-------|-------|---|
| General/Inter- disciplinary | $20,000 | $25,000 | $6,000 | $51,000 | 5.6 |
| Reference Bibliography | 85,000 | 20,000 | 3,000 | 108,000 | 11.9 |
| Fine Arts | 10,000 | 20,000 | 5,000 | 35,000 | 3.9 |
| Humanities | 50,000 | 60,000 | 10,000 | 120,000 | 13.3 |
| Social Sci. | 70,000 | 60,000 | 5,000 | 135,000 | 14.9 |
| Sciences | 230,000 | 40,000 | 2,000 | 272,000 | 30.1 |
| Technology | 80,000 | 40,000 | 3,000 | 123,000 | 13.6 |
|  | $545,000 | $265,000 | $34,000 | $844,000 |  |
| Binding | 50,000 | 10,000 | - | 60,000 | 6.6 |
| Totals | $595,000 | $275,000 | $34,000 | $904,000 |  |

penditure is going to any isolated activity such as a branch library. Beyond that, it is good to be aware of what proportion is going to the various academic subdivisions, because the object is always to know where library expenditure is directed. What is needed is a way of relating library expenditure to the academic program. It is not necessary to follow in full detail the distribution adopted by the Resources and Technical Services Division (RTSD) Collection Development Committee but rather to follow a taxonomy that is meaningful within the context of the institution. Others will doubtless suggest themselves, but overelaboration can be distracting. In smaller schools broad subdivisions are most likely to be useful. (Table 3 suggests a possible distribution of this kind.)

The development of a library profile is useful for predicting change, whether in scope or cost. It is also useful for determining how closely the library program matches the academic program. Here one cannot expect exact synchronization because many library materials, for example, indexes and abstracts, are essentially multidisciplinary. Wide departures, as evident from disparities in the proportions of total budget assigned to departments by the college and the library, should be investigated. These departures may result from price differentials, from history, or, in a few cases, from external obligations, as to a consortium for maintaining unique collections. Whatever the reason, they should not develop from inattention.

## INTERPRETATION

By this stage a fairly clear picture of the library should have emerged. It may or may not look like the original expectation. By moving the pieces around, a

**Table 4**
**Total-Cost Distribution**

| Unit | People | G. & S. | Lib. Matls. | Total | % |
|---|---|---|---|---|---|
| Administration | | | | | |
| | $157,000 | $69,000 | $2,000 | $228,000 | 10.6 |
| Collection Development | | | | | |
| | 54,000 | 3,500 | 1,000 | $58,000 | 2.7 |
| General | | | 788,000 | $788,000 | 36.7 |
| Lending Services | | | | | |
| | 284,000 | 27,000 | | $311,000 | 14.5 |
| Reference Services | | | | | |
| | 141,000 | 28,000 | 108,000 | $277,000 | 12.9 |
| Technical Services | | | | | |
| | 225,000 | 80,000 | 5,000 | $310,000 | 14.4 |
| Totals | $861,000 | $207,500 | $904,000 | $1,972,500 | |
| Fringes | 177,200 | | | 177,200 | 8.2 |
| | $1,038,200 | $207,500 | $904,000 | $2,149,700 | |
| % | 48.3 | 9.7 | 42.0 | | |

new pattern has been created. If the process has been carefully carried out, it will provide a new light on the library and enable the planner to look at it from a new perspective. For example, the long-standing proportions 60:30:10 (60 percent people, 30 percent materials, 10 percent operating costs) are good as far as they go, but they do not reveal what is being done with those expenditures. Sherman Hayes suggested that the proportion for "other" is more likely to be 12 percent and to be rising and that much of it is hidden by budgetary conventions (1982: 124–26). The formula can be used as a check to see how far one differs from the norm, but it cannot state whether changes should be made. That can derive only from an examination of what exactly is being purchased with the various combinations of expenditures revealed by the analysis. Table 4 shows a financial analysis and provides the basis for further evaluation of the library.

From the hypothetical example several conclusions may be drawn. First, the expenditure on people appears relatively low in comparison with the standard ratio, particularly in relation to the actual expenditure on library materials. Second, the expenditure on other operating costs, while apparently substantial, is on the edge of adequacy. There is no spare money for new ventures, for any substantial changes, or for unexpected costs. Third, it appears that, over the years, money has been added to the library materials budget without corresponding additions to processing staff or operating costs. Finally, all units are staffed at a bare minimum. Any unexpected vacancies or sicknesses will result in added arrearages or delays.

Our example represents a library that has been developed in accordance with the priorities of earlier times. Any new programs, such as an expanded audiovisual service of any quality, will need new funding. It also suggests an institution not very prepared to listen to requests for new staff or nonbook money. The result is a library with no marginal investment capacity; almost the entire budget is predicated at the beginning of the year. Yet the answer is not to cut money from library materials, since that amount, although large in proportion to other budgetary segments, is not large in relation to the academic program supported by the institution. A way of testing such an assumption is to expand the budget to meet the 60:30:10 rule. If this were done, the library budget would grow to $3 million and comprise: personnel, $1.8 million; library materials, $900,000; and operating costs, $300,000. This is not so unreasonable a budget that savings should be looked for from library materials. It operates on the edge. There is no way to generate internal savings to pay for automation; yet automation is the only way to escape from the constrictions created over time by the parent institution. This kind of pattern is widespread among libraries and indicates the dichotomy that has arisen between the apparent status of libraries and their real status.

## INTERNAL FACTORS

If the analysis has been properly carried out, it is now possible to decide whether the present distribution is appropriate and, if not, what changes should be made. It is also now easier to determine what the effects are on the budget of opening for one more hour each day, of buying 10 percent more books, of providing more reference support, or similar changes. As an example: if 10 percent more items were added, there would need to be a staff increase of 10 percent, a further cost of $22,500 plus benefits. It would also require an increased expenditure on goods and services of $13,000 and one-time costs for furniture. The total cost of such a move would therefore be not the $90,000 for materials themselves but $128,000 in continuing costs and perhaps $5,000 in one-time costs. Similar figures can be derived for any other changes proposed.

There is also the matter of what is not being done. Having the present distribution in front of you makes it easier to fit in any known problems. Are there recurrent arrearages in processing? Are there problems of finding books that are waiting to be reshelved? Are there queues at peak periods in circulation or reserve? Such questions cannot be solved budgetarily in a vacuum. They require knowledge of how they fit into the total budget. What are the trade-offs? Is it possible to shift resources between activities, or will that simply cause other, different problems? It is necessary to be aware of the effects of each change. For example, buying two more encyclopedias at a cost of $2,000 has a totally different processing impact than buying 200 recordings for the same amount of money would have. In the same way, adding clerical staff will cost less than adding professional staff, but the added effects are also different. The analysis provides the underlying support for any such considerations.

Any budget request requires documentation, and that documentation must be in a form that is meaningful to those who see it. By looking at the activities within a library it is possible to show how changes in a budget will affect services and resources.

## EXTERNAL FACTORS

More exacting, and in the long run more necessary, is the projection of change brought about by external factors. Chief among them are inflation, automation, and academic program shifts. The effects of these changes cannot be shown unless there is a clear base from which to project them, hence the importance of the analysis suggested above.

What is the nature of these changes that makes them so important? First, they result in the redistribution of resources, and that needs to be planned. Second, they may require new resources, which may not always fit harmoniously into existing budget categories. Third, they frequently carry significant up-front costs and cannot be introduced gradually. To underline the last point, consider the frustration felt in libraries when academics calmly introduce new programs without providing for library support and offer in justification: now we have the program, they (who?) will have to find the money. It is not possible to be automated partially; you can't buy half a computer. Planning for change is very complex and must begin years before the change is expected to come into effect.

### Inflation

Although inflation has been around for a long time, its differential effects throughout the library have been insufficiently recognized. Although most obvious in the matter of library materials, when it has been recorded in minute detail, it affects all supplies and services and, although we do not think of it in that way, personal services. Simply to stay where we are, that is, buying the same numbers of books, the same numbers of hours of work, and so on, will automatically cost more money (Harvey and Spyers-Duran 1984). Most institutions make some allowance for price increases. It is usually called by some euphemistic name such as an economic adjustment, but what it deals with is inflation.

### Library Materials

In libraries, library materials, for as long as records have been kept, have risen in price at a rate far higher than general inflation (Lynden 1982). If such a rate is not allowed for, the library will have to sacrifice something else to keep up its level of purchasing. Furthermore, within this general rate there are other variations. Periodicals increase in price more quickly than books, and scientific periodicals increase faster than general ones. If this is not recognized the materials expenditure will become, over time, more and more skewed by the operation of these differential rates (M. Martin 1977: 298). This is why it is so important to be completely aware of the distribution of materials purchased by the library. If no action is taken either to increase the amount available or to correct the distribution, these nondecisions become, in a remarkably short time, negative decisions in favor of periodicals and of science, thus dramatically changing the nature of the library.

## Service Contracts

The same process will occur if cost increases for service contracts, for example, OCLC, are not allowed for. Telephone and postage costs illustrate yet another cause of change. By legislative, judicial, or administrative action, governments can and do affect library costs. Some effects are direct. Increased telephone charges and added costs for postage are examples. But they also have indirect effects by adding to the cost of services, for example, data-base searching or the costs passed on by book suppliers. Sometimes this process may last for years and be further changed by legislative action, as was the case with the library rate for postage. Sometimes the cost cannot be estimated in advance, as was the case with telephone rates. In most cases no counteraction can be taken because the expenditures involved are an integral part of the library's function. It is, however, possible to seek alternatives, for example, to AT&T for long-distance charges, but that is a matter usually reserved to the parent institution. That institution, however, will frequently introduce changes of its own without consultation, usually to charge back some central service like overhead to cover the administrative costs of repairs and alterations, and like most overheads, that rate is likely to increase as well. See Hayes (1985) for general discussions of these issues.

## Automation

The impact of automation is a somewhat different matter. When libraries first began to use OCLC for catalog copy, there were expectations that cataloging costs could be cut almost to nothing, that there would be no need of catalogers whose function would be absorbed centrally. Neither of these things happened. What happened instead was a shift of responsibilities, with the support staff taking on more duties and the professional staff at last finding time for the maintenance of quality. Costs did not go down, and even if they did not escalate, their mix changed. Then came the use of data-base searching and interlibrary loan via terminal, and again costs did not drop but were rather transferred from inside the library to outside, and it became necessary to keep a wary eye on the budget line representing outside contracts and services.

In most libraries these electronic services now represent a substantial expenditure, one that, moreover, cannot be reversed. The changes that have come about in staffing are permanent, and the patterns of activity have shifted. For the smaller library there is the real problem that these costs tend to come in large pieces. An OCLC terminal brings with it maintenance and communications costs. To justify these costs the terminal must, in a sense, put in a full work day. If there is not enough cataloging, it must be used for some other purpose, such as reference searching, although that in turn adds cost. What this means is that external partners have crept into the budget-making process, not only OCLC but the local or regional network, and some decisions now have to be made with that in mind.

As automation grows, its effects both on operations and on budget grow also. What is the point at which it becomes realistic to think of a local automated system? A year or two ago such an idea was appropriate only to large libraries. Now the range of systems available makes it possible for any library to contemplate automating, either alone or with a group of libraries. Automation includes not only capital expenditure but a reordering of the operating budget (M. Martin 1983). The effects of such a decision range from changes in staff to the replacement of circulation cards and other supplies, with added costs for system maintenance. This is not the place for an extended discussion of the merits of automation; there are plenty of sources for such information. Not all of them, however, discuss the long-term budgetary changes involved. Most funding authorities are less frightened, paradoxical as it may seem, by capital expenditure than they are by long-term costs, since, particularly in a private institution, they must be funded from tuition. Any consideration of automation must then be accompanied by a clear idea of its future financial effects.

## OPERATING COSTS OF AUTOMATION

These effects are not always additive. Although the annual maintenance charges are certainly new, there can be offsetting savings, for example, the fact that catalog cards are no longer needed nor are their filing costs. Equally, although there will be a need for new skills (time), some existing functions will either cease or be reduced. What this implies, as for any change, is a cost-benefit projection. Indeed, most consultants will recommend that system cost be considered not only to include the actual capital outlay but the annual operating costs for, perhaps, five years, in order to make adequate comparisons between systems (Matthews 1980: 50–52). Unless this is done it will not be possible to make good budget projections.

The effects of automation are not usually confined to technical processes or circulation but tend to require a complete reassessment of the way in which the library operates. If users can access the catalog from outside the library, as is becoming increasingly common, what is the effect? Will personal reserves increase, will there be a demand for a delivery service, will circulation increase, will reference become a kind of information center? The questions are endless but must all be considered as part of the budget-making process. A further question that is becoming increasingly important to colleges facing financial uncertainty is whether the advent of automation will allow them to save on traditional expenditures. Can access to other libraries permit decreased purchasing locally? Can access to electronic article services substitute for costly subscriptions?

As can be seen, such questions lead back to the earlier suggestion that we may have to rethink the boundaries of library accounts (M. Martin 1985). Electronic access and on-demand purchase may enable smaller libraries to support individual faculty research in a way that could not have been contemplated in times when it was necessary to own materials for them to be accessible or to force the faculty to go to the resources. Both are still necessary, but there are now alternatives for materials that are used less but still are not in the category of rare or unusual.

## PROGRAM CHANGES

The issue of faculty support leads to the issue of programmatic change by the institution. As colleges face issues such as a shrinking student pool or declines in state and federal support and the need to contain fee increases, they have to look also at their academic attractiveness. Will the programs offered attract students? Are there new fields into which they should expand? Since research funding is another way of making up a tuition shortfall, we are also witnessing an increased drive for funded research. All such changes can have profound effects on libraries. Any librarian will remember how schools of education have ridden a kind of roller coaster. Can a library afford to reflect entirely such academic fads and fashions? Administrators mostly ignore the fact that the library needs of a program are based not on student numbers but on the fact of its existence. Although it may be reasonable not to emphasize education when it is at a low level, it is irresponsible to ignore it completely, since an upswing later would find the library having to fill in all the gaps.

It is particularly difficult to cope with all the whims of an institution. What does an emphasis on computer literacy or decision-making mean? What happens when this year's favorite idea is superseded? How do you deal with a president who is firmly persuaded that the library of the future will contain no books? How do you persuade a department head to support the purchase of popular materials because the instructors in writing simply assign topics at random without regard to the library's holdings? For a library without any financial reserves, any of these requirements can be devastating. Budget presentations must therefore take them into account not so much by asking for specific funds as by providing a setting in which such effects can be described and understood. This is the importance of annual reports and statistics for libraries. They provide a context in which the specifics of the budget request can be considered.

## OUTSIDE INCOME

There is another side to library budgets—one that is receiving more attention—the creating of income. (See Lee 1984.) For many years libraries have generated minor income from fines and overdues. Occasionally, a library would benefit from a gift or endowment income. On the whole, however, such income formed a minor part of the library's budget. Now with the possibility of income from photocopy machines, from data-base search surcharges, from the sale of reference services or contracts with businesses, the library has become a potential income source for the institution (Ungarelli and Grant 1983). Although the days of federal largesse are over, there are still federal programs that support construction and automation. The National Endowment for the Humanities has had to beg for applicants for its library programs. No coherent philosphy has yet emerged, but there are sufficient examples for any library now to follow. (See Breivik and Gibson 1979; Clark 1986; Talbot 1982.)

In keeping with the institution itself, the library is also becoming more accustomed to the idea that, to support new ventures or capital expenditure, it must itself seek the funding, whether from foundations, alumni, or local corporations (M. Martin 1986). In few cases has it come to the situation now familiar in some colleges in which an academic program may be continued only if it generates enough research income to pay for, perhaps, 25 percent of the faculty. Nevertheless, any librarian must now be ready to look for budget increases from outside funding, and a goal of seeking 5 to 10 percent of the budget from such sources might well be received with delight by the administration. Planning for this sort of venture requires not only the sizing up of possibilities but also the realization that success or failure will each affect the shape of the library. Outside funding cannot, at least initially, be for ongoing needs; it must be sought as substitutional. Donors who give money for renovations or new equipment free up funds that would otherwise have had to go for those purposes. Since donors seldom give money for ongoing operational costs, their donations can be seen as allowing the costs of one-time outlays to be exchanged for outlay on what would otherwise have had to go unfunded. Clearly, one-time gifts cannot be relied on to provide support for permanent staff positions, but they can free money for "unfundable" projects such as rearranging the collection or repainting the catalog room.

## BUDGET PRESENTATION

Given the range of possibilities that have been outlined in the preceding sections, it is clear that any librarian must be prepared to outline the next year's possibilities with sufficient clarity to enable an account-oriented budget to be established. Whatever the changes that are contemplated, the budget must be able to accommodate them. Unless there are clearly understood objectives, this may be very difficult. What are the added staffing requirements? What are the changes between individual budget lines? What are the income expectations? How do these changes relate to the objectives of the parent institution?

## RECONCILING DIFFERENCES

When a budget request is presented, it will be given due consideration, but it is unusual for any request to be honored in full without further discussion; the result tends to be less than requested. This is not done from malice but because all requests must be considered along with other priorities and will therefore take their place in a queue.

When the result is made known, the first need is to determine why the decision was made. It is not usually because any specific library need was rejected, although that may happen. It is mostly because total requests exceeded the amount of funding available, and some selection had to be made. If an actual rejection occurred, the reasons for this rejection have to be determined and counterarguments offered, if allowed. Mostly, however, it will be necessary to set aside that particular initiative. If the reason was lack of funds, the next step is to see whether substitutions or changes in the library's own program are allowed.

When the reasons for the change have been determined, the next step is to reexamine the entire budget to determine what internal changes can be made. The extent of such changes will be determined by the institutional guidelines. If specific positions were disallowed it may not be possible to recreate them using other money. If all that is controlled is the bottom line wider adjustments are possible.

Whatever the rules, the budget must be reconstituted if it is to provide a guide for the next year. It is wise to submit the new proposal to the funding agent to be sure that it will be approved. In doing so pay attention to the message given. It may, for example, state that the institution wants the library to acquire more materials or to spend less on personnel. Going against such indications is unwise. The resulting reconstituted budget must be acceptable to the library *and* to the institution.

## BUDGETARY CONTROL

Once a budget is established there follows the need to adhere to its principles. This does not necessarily mean slavish adherence to line amounts but rather adherence to the goals that were enunciated in establishing the budget. Most institutions will recognize that reality frequently overtakes prediction, but equally, most require that actuality should not depart too far from the predicted actuality. The control of expenditures is as important as their prediction.

Expenditure control is not simply the recording of what happens but a reading of the pattern. For example, many accounting systems predict on a monthly basis what percentage should have been expended, in fact, 8.3 percent per month. Many library expenditures do not follow this pattern. Serial renewals tend to happen in blocks, perhaps in August or September. The result is that the entire amount may be spent long before the year is over without there being any cause for alarm. Similarly, the academic calendar may require that substantial amounts of money be spent for student help in a pattern that does not follow the month-by-month draw-down of permanent salaries. These variations are important in monitoring expenditures (M. Martin 1978: 37–39). In the same manner an annual membership payment may well exhaust a particular budget line early in the year without implying any further impact on annual expenditures. Prediction of expected expenditures enables a library to control the total without preventing the payment of special costs.

## NATURE OF LIBRARY EXPENDITURES

Library expenditures vary significantly from most other institutional expenditures. The principal difference lies in the fact that libraries spend within a continuum. Books may be ordered this month but be published six months from now and supplied (i.e., arrive) a year from now. They may be encumbered when ordered but can be paid for only when supplied. In effect, book ordering operates within a continuum. At the end of each year there will be outstanding orders (i.e., encumbrances) for items ordered but not supplied, and this pattern will be repeated each year. If the attempt is made to match each year's orders with what is supplied each year, the result will be multiple cancellations and multiple reorders. No accounting system should aim to achieve such a result. Systems that try to maintain total control by requiring the cancellation of unfulfilled orders are pursuing a self-defeating course; the same thing applies to those that require libraries to put their standing orders out on bid each year. These are the kinds of differences that librarians must be alert to and explain to their fiscal officers.

Another problem relates to the actual as opposed to the predicted costs of each item. When a book is ordered, the only fact known is its published cost. In fact, in France this is not known, since each retailer is expected to set a price, but in general, the price is public information. To this must be added the cost of mailing and so on, and from it must be deducted any discount allowed by the publisher or dealer. As a result the actual price paid for each item may differ considerably from the previously announced price. These differences are a major problem to any institution that follows an accrual-based accounting system. For this reason, librarians must be careful to explain to their financial officers where library practice differs (for good reason) from standard accounting practice.

## CLOSING THE BUDGET YEAR

Apart from the obvious requirement of settling the accounts, there is the need to understand whether expenditures followed the predictions on which the budget was based.

## Nonprofit and Profit Differences

One of the long-standing differences between nonprofit and profit financing lies in the fact that the former operates within a preset budget, whereas the latter has to earn its money as it goes. The goal of the first thus is to spend money, by this means justifying next year's budget; of the second it is to earn money so that costs will be covered and a profit earned. This is a subtle but profound difference of approach. Having a predetermined budget lessens the drive for efficiency, not that nonprofit institutions are not efficient but they measure it differently by reaching social objectives rather than by expanding sales to maximize profit. Financial exigency in higher education is introducing new factors, particularly in private, tuition-dependent schools. Sigmund Ginsburg set out these factors and their results (1985: 15–22). This change is one reason behind the greater emphasis on outside funding.

## Capital Expenditure

A second major difference is that higher education seldom works with a capital budget. New buildings or major equipment purchases become one-time projects. There is nothing inherently wrong with this, but it tends to separate capital and ongoing expenditures in a way that discourages long-term planning. In the case of minor expenditures for equipment or furniture, a sudden extra need can be balanced by other savings. Major expenditures cannot be met this way. Since library buildings, for example, are very expensive, construction tends to be delayed as long as possible with serious effects on efficiency. (For a survey of such needs see Shirk 1986.) Except in a very few instances, library materials are not regarded as capital, although they are clearly one of the major long-term investments for any institution. Library budgets, therefore, tend to contain both capital and operational portions. Whereas a business would include furniture as a kind of temporary expense, a library budget contains a line for equipment and furniture that, cumulatively, represents significant capital accumulation, without the necessary balancing line for depreciation. In looking over the budget record, capital expenditures of this nature should be set aside and examined separately.

## Salaries

Within any salary line, there will have been savings. Not every position can be filled immediately and may also be filled at a different salary level. The result is some total of lapsed salary money. Some states require that they be returned to the state, and so do some institutions. Others allow the savings to be used for other purposes, provided that the total budget amount is not exceeded. One excellent way of dealing with this situation is to allow the underexpenditure to be transferred to a quasi-capital account for use later on equipment or renovations.

This is possible only when there is no requirement to spend everything within the one budget year.

Whatever can be done with a salary underexpenditure, the question of how it arose must be examined. Is there a pattern such as persistent turnover in a department? Is it a result of the noncompetitive position of the institution or of slow personnel practices? Is one kind of position more affected than others? What have been the effects of the vacancies? Is it possible that the position can be relocated with better results? The answers to such questions lie within each library, but good salary planning is essential for any library (Gherman 1982).

## Use of Savings

If adherence to individual budget lines is required, librarians have no discretion in using unspent funds. (Program budgets do not avoid this problem, since for control purposes they are transformed into line budgets anyway.) If the library does not suffer from any such stricture and is instead required to meet only the requirements of the bottom line, there is a great deal more flexibility.

In such conditions the watch for savings should begin well before the end of the year. Differences begin to show up during the third quarter and by the end of the ninth month it should be clear where expenditures will be over and where under. Although it may be necessary to hold back in one area when expenditures are exceeding the budget, it may be both possible and necessary to use savings from elsewhere to meet the necessary cost of doing business. Savings can also be used to pay in advance for unavoidable costs, perhaps for next year's network dues. Some institutions forbid such a practice. Discounted advance payments are beneficial to the library, but the institution may be more interested in cash flow or in the investment of its current balances. These are legitimate concerns, but most accounting offices are amenable to discussion. Whatever the case, it is essential to remember that the payment is an annual one and has not gone away. Even if it enables the library to redirect what would have been spent for this purpose in the next year, in the year after that it will have to be paid once more. Nevertheless, such action provides one way in which a library can meet unusual one-time costs, such as renovation. In reviewing the budget, remember what was done and why.

## Year-End Money

A different problem accompanies the once-common practice of transferring savings to the library "for books." It still happens in institutions in which it is necessary to balance an underexpenditure in one area with an overexpenditure in another or when the institution makes a practice of a half-yearly budget review.

If there is sufficient warning it is possible to spend such windfalls wisely. Everyone has, or should have, a "wish list" against such a chance, but it is essential to be able to argue in favor of its use on something much more important, provided that it can be obtained in the time available. At the least it should be possible to obtain agreement to use some of the money for processing costs (e.g., OCLC charges), a position that can be buttressed by the fact that the federal government did at last allow such costs to be a legitimate charge against its Title II programs. Or if a major microform set is to be acquired, the cost of cabinets should be included.

### Final Evaluation

When all perturbations have subsided, the final act of the year, conducted in the next year, is to see how closely expenditures paralleled projection. Minor differences can be overlooked, but major ones should be examined to see why they occurred.

Some relate to external causes—a new union agreement, greatly increased prices for goods and services. Some relate to changed priorities—savings diverted to pay for new equipment. Some may arise from totally unplanned events—added hours imposed by administrative fiat. Others may have arisen by chance, and some items may have been overlooked in setting up the original budget. In each case it is necessary to determine why, so that corrective action can be taken if needed.

Being wise after the event does not change the past, but it can help lead to better control in the future. Budgetary control is a continuous process and requires close attention. Use the information gained from analysis to improve performance in the future and to generate information for use in presenting future budgets.

## REFERENCES

Breivik, Patricia Senn, and E. Burr Gibson, eds. 1979. *Funding Alternatives for Libraries*. Chicago: American Library Association.

Chen, Ching-chih. 1980. *Zero-Base Budgeting in Library Management: A Manual for Librarians*. Phoenix: Oryx Press.

Clark, Charlene. 1986. "Private Support for Public Purposes: Library Fund Raising." *Wilson Library Bulletin* 60: 18–21.

Dowd, Sheila, John H. Whaley, Jr., and Marcia Pankake. 1986. "Reactions to 'Funding Online Services from the Materials Budget.' " *College and Research Libraries* 47: 230–37.

Gherman, Paul. 1982. "Salary Planning." *Journal of Library Administration* 3 (Fall–Winter):87–97.

Ginsburg, Sigmund G. 1985. "Austerity in Higher Education." In *Financing Information Services*, pp. 7–23. *See* Spyers-Duran and Mann 1985.

Harvey, John F., and Peter Spyers-Duran. 1984. "Effects of Inflation on Academic Libraries." In *Austerity Management in Academic Libraries*. Edited by John F. Harvey and Peter Spyers-Duran, pp. 1–42. Metuchen, N.J.: Scarecrow Press.

Hayes, Sherman. 1982. "Budgeting for and Controlling the Cost of the Other in Library Expenditures: The Distant Relative in the Budgetary Process." *Journal of Library Administration* 3 (Fall–Winter):121–31.

————. 1985. "Total Resource Planning for Academic Libraries." In *Financing Information Services*, pp. 109–19. *See* Spyers-Duran and Mann 1985.

Kantor, Paul B. 1985. "The Relation between Costs and Services at Academic Libraries." In *Financing Information Services*, pp. 69–78. *See* Spyers-Duran and Mann 1985.

Lee, Sul H. 1977. *Library Budgeting: Critical Challenges for the Future.* Ann Arbor, Mich.: Pierian Press.

————, ed. 1984. *Library Fund-Raising: Vital Margin for Excellence.* Ann Arbor, Mich.: Pierian Press.

Lynden, Frederick C. 1982. "Financial Planning for Collection Development." *Journal of Library Administration* 3 (Fall–Winter):109–20.

Martin, Murray S. 1977. "Budgetary Strategies: Coping with a Changing Fiscal Environment." *Journal of Academic Librarianship* 2:297–302.

————. 1978. *Budgetary Control in Academic Libraries.* Greenwich, Conn.: JAI Press.

————. 1983. "The Organizational and Budgetary Effects of Automation on Libraries." *Advances in Library Administration and Organization* 2:69–83.

————. 1985. "Financial Planning—New Needs, New Sources, New Styles." In *Financing Information Services*, pp. 91–108. *See* Spyers-Dunn and Mann 1985.

————. 1986. "Financing Library Automation: Selling the Costs and the Benefits." *The Bottom Line* (June):11–16.

Martin, Noelene P. 1982. "Interlibrary Loan and Resource Sharing: New Approaches." *Journal of Library Administration* 3 (Fall–Winter):99–108.

Matthews, Joseph R. 1980. *Choosing an Automated Library System.* Chicago: American Library Association.

Poole, Jay Martin, and Gloriana St. Clair. 1986. "Funding Online Services from the Materials Budget." *College and Research Libraries* 47:225–29.

Riggs, Donald E. 1984. *Strategic Planning for Library Managers.* Phoenix: Oryx Press.

Shirk, G. T. 1986. "Financing New Technologies. Equipment/Furniture Replacement and Building Renovation: A Survey Report." *College and Research Libraries* 45:462–70.

Spyers-Duran, Peter, and Thomas W. Mann, Jr., eds. 1985. *Financing Information Services: Problems, Changing Approaches, and New Opportunities for Academic and Research Libraries.* Westport, Conn.: Greenwood Press.

Talbot, Richard J. 1982. "Financing the Academic Library." In *Priorities for Academic Libraries.* Edited by Thomas J. Galvin and Beverly P. Lynch, pp. 35–44. San Francisco: Jossey-Bass.

Ungarelli, Donald L., and M. M. Grant. 1983. "Fee-Based Model Consideration in an Academic Library." *Drexel Library Quarterly* 19:4–12.

Young, Harold Chester. 1976. *Planning, Programming, Budgeting Systems in Academic Libraries.* Detroit: Gale Research Co.

## SELECTED BIBLIOGRAPHY

Martin, Murray S., ed. 1983. *Financial Planning for Academic Libraries.* New York: Haworth. (A monograph also published as the *Journal of Library Administration* 3, nos. 3/4 [1982].)

# 10

# Staff Management and Budget in Small Academic Libraries

*Floyd C. Hardy*

Academic libraries are an integral part of the intellectual community. One of their primary purposes is to support teaching and research. Access to their resources by both seasoned scholars and inexperienced students is essential. As patterns for seeking information change, the library must respond appropriately. Problems must be addressed in a timely fashion. New ideas must be sought. This overview discusses some of the factors that influence the management of staff and financial resources in the academic library.

## ORGANIZATIONAL CHANGE AND STAFF MOTIVATION

Staff management requires a constant search for ways to motivate the staff, to facilitate change, and to maintain a high level of enthusiasm and zeal for the purpose and mission of the organization. Universities and colleges that are confident in the purpose of their existence are strong enough to absorb new ideas and to attempt fresh approaches to old problems.

Continuity and stability are characteristics of many colleges and universities, which generally seek to project images of long traditions and rich histories. These attitudes may pervade the campus and influence the rate at which changes occur. Although colleges and universities often attempt to adopt procedures that improve efficiency, there is a strong tendency on many campuses to cling to the traditional and the familiar. It is not surprising that academic libraries are not usually in the forefront of adopting the latest trends in management theories and budget procedures.

Technology disrupts routines, but it also creates openings for introducing new procedures and ideas. Technology offers resourceful staff members a chance to acquire new skills. Computer technology, in particular, often dictates changes in the workplace that would otherwise be difficult to achieve.

Changes are sometimes made in response to recommendations or anticipated recommendations by a visiting accreditation team. An unfavorable accreditation report may be required to trigger actions necessary to correct deficiencies. A library that has lost the competitive battle for funds before an accreditation visit may find a significant shift in attitude after it receives an unfavorable rating in the accreditation report. Survival of the institution is at stake when the library is endangered, and most institutions will set aside the resources necessary to meet accreditation requirements.

Vacancies that occur on the staff also provide opportunities for organizational changes. Reassignments may be made at that time that would otherwise encounter resistance.

Communication will always be an important aspect of any organization, because it is the process by which participants exchange ideas and by which the objectives, aims, and ideals of the organization are internalized. Although many aspects of organization management have changed as a result of discoveries about human behavior, the staff meeting remains an essential part of staff management. There is a need for members of a library's staff occasionally to discuss concerns that may on the surface appear trivial but may have a significant impact on the staff's morale and performance. Transactions of staff meetings can often be the basis of change. Decisions that seem routine to the director should in many instances be presented to the staff to inform them about the thinking of the director, even if the director perceives them as strictly administrative decisions. This procedure may slow the decision-making process, but it gives the director confidence that changes will be accepted.

Library staff members, like other workers, are motivated when they believe that their labor will be rewarded by promotions and other financial benefits. Perquisites such as travel funds should be distributed by taking into account the needs of the entire library. Sharing these resources with other departments strengthens staff morale and motivates personnel.

Libraries should not underestimate the motivational aspects of having staff members jointly participate in writing proposals. Certain benefits obtain even for unsuccessful proposals. Invaluable experience in writing is one result. Writing proposals also demonstrates initiative, places the library in a position of leadership in the institution, and builds organizational cohesion.

## Management Trends

Administrative structure determines, to a large extent, staff-management patterns. Participative-management concepts are relatively recent among academic libraries, which traditionally followed hierarchical administrative designs. Although some academic libraries have restructured their management, many of them are still not equipped to respond quickly to changes in their environment.

Academic libraries, like other organizations, are products of history. Rigid pyramidal administrative designs heavily influenced by tradition best describe the management of academic libraries until the 1960s (Holley 1972: 177–78). Early textbooks describe the prevailing operational characteristics, which included span of control, delegation of authority, coordination, and line and staff functions (Joeckel 1939: 5–6). These works also set aside a considerable amount of space for describing clerical and professional positions, defining administrative ability, and recommending the content of professional training. Sick leave, promotion, ratings, and tenure were also cited as areas of importance (Lyle 1945: 252–95).

Clearly, these are relevant topics for discussing the management of any organization and are still found in recent monographs on academic library administration. Changes have occurred, however, in how these matters are discussed. Early texts conveyed a strong belief in immutable administrative principles appropriate for the library environment. Little attention was given to the psychological needs and social context that undergird human behavior. Only in recent studies of academic library management can one find extensive discussions of the dynamics of organizational change, based on psychological and sociological concepts (Evans 1983).

The hierarchical structure of the library has come under particular scrutiny. Studies of participatory management have been undertaken in the academic library (Evans 1983: 54–55). Research has shown a positive relationship between job performance and participation in decision-making (Vroom 1959: 325). Theory X, Theory Y, and management by objectives are concepts that originated in the world of business that are familiar to readers of library literature.

It appears that modern management techniques have been accepted by the library profession without questioning the extent to which these concepts are compatible with the academic milieu. It is conceivable that some management concepts appropriate in the business world might be unsuitable for academic libraries. Management theories are often based on research that takes place in industry, and a substantial portion of the literature has been written with a built-in bias for the corporate culture. Certain human behavioral patterns, which are relevant in business settings, may require different interpretations in the academic world.

If libraries rigorously apply management concepts based on free enterprise and aggressively pursue fee-based services in competition with private industry, librarians may be accused once again of being nonacademic technicians rather than active participants in the teaching and research process.

## Interaction with the Parent Institution

In 1930 a critic cited the failure to teach citizens how to use leisure time as a serious shortcoming of American higher education. He is disapproving of people who spend time at the movies or talkies, "many who attend during one day two or more of these often inane, or even questionable and indecent entertainments" (Schlipp 1930: 209). This critic placed part of the blame on machines that have "taken away much of the former difficulty attending most types of work, and also nearly all of the element of creative endeavor and the consequent interest in completed achievement and the final enjoyment of it'' (Schlipp 1930: 209).

Schlipp's ideas are part of an ongoing debate about the aims of education. Many universities and colleges define their missions in terms of a liberal education, which implies a foundation in skills necessary for productive, satisfying use of leisure time. Whatever the goals and objectives that a college or university defines for itself, the academic library must be prepared to support the institution's efforts to carry out its mission. A technically competent, service-oriented library staff that is excited about learning is prepared to play an important role in the life of a college or university. Effective management is an essential ingredient in helping the staff to channel its energy, clarify its ideas, and shape its attitudes in order to provide the best service possible to the university. Full participation in the academic enterprise is necessary before the library can make a substantial contribution to the world of scholarship. Faculty recognition of the library must take the form of active involvement and support, rather than symbolic gestures of respect.

One could almost conclude from a study of the recent history of higher education that before 1960 most campuses were models of serenity. In these peaceful kingdoms, collegiality—the sense of a close knit community of shared information and values among faculty, administrators, and trustees—prevailed. In this favorable environment, faculty often assumed a prominent role not only in academic matters but also in constructing budgets and selecting academic officers (Karol and Ginsburg 1980: 11). Enrollment changes, financial strains, and collective bargaining have eroded collegiality (Karol and Ginsburg 1980: 11). Although it is probably true that on some campuses there was less conflict when enrollment was smaller and funding was adequate, the idea of collegiality has perhaps been romanticized. Uprisings that occurred in the 1960s are evidence of long-standing, repressed grievances on the part of students and faculty.

In one academic setting, a collegial structure has resulted in librarians functioning ''as equals with a rotating chairperson position'' (Bechtel 1985: 553). Participation by all professional librarians in the decision-making process has served to create an atmosphere in which ''librarians now work as partners rather than competitors'' (Bechtel 1985: 553). Management structures capable of stimulating high performance without undue emphasis on competition would certainly be attractive to some academic libraries.

Some academic librarians have established peer-review procedures and collegial processes comparable to those practiced by their teaching faculty colleagues. Previously existing hierarchical management structures in these libraries have not been totally dismantled and function alongside a collegial structure (Brown 1985: 478). To what extent this arrangement interferes with the performance of the academic library has not been determined, but it has caused some to speculate that the library may not be able to respond effectively ''to a university environment which itself may be in a state of retrenchment, rapid change and technological innovation'' (Brown 1985: 478). Problems related to organizational flexibility, accountability, and communication have also been attributed to the existence of parallel functioning hierarchical and collegial management structures (Brown 1985: 480).

Library managers have traditionally received higher salaries than librarians without managerial responsibilities. In a collegial environment, scholarly pursuits are generally held in higher esteem than managerial skills. Nonmanagerial positions in collegial situations may tend to be more attractive to some librarians than nonmanagerial positions in noncollegial environments (Brown 1985: 480).

Because the library is an integral part of the university, it cannot escape pressures exerted on the institution it serves. Competition for funds may have a chilling effect on the relationships between the library and other departments. Similarly, when there is keen competition for tenure tracks among faculty, efforts by librarians to gain or retain faculty status may encounter a cool reception if not open opposition.

Effective management is essential in preparing the staff to respond constructively to changes within the college or university. One possible response for the library is to seek to combine some of its resources with compatible resources of other units on campus in an effort to strengthen the entire institution. One result may be a revival of some of the elements of collegiality.

## Staff Management and Technology

Because computers are expensive and versatile, libraries with limited budgets may find it necessary to choose between hiring new staff members or buying a computer. Among the potential effects of automation are shifts from data generated by people to data generated by machines and "from personnel to equipment and contracted services" (Martin 1983: 74–5).

Because computers are a recent tool in most organizations, their impact on the workplace has not been comprehensively assessed. Computers used to streamline procedures in one department may produce backlogs in another area. Libraries do not always have the resources required to enlarge or reduce their staff sizes instantly according to need. Personnel reassignments may be necessary to deal with backlogs in a specific department and may be negatively perceived by the persons being transferred. Staff members may believe that their usefulness to the organization is marginal or perhaps dispensable (Watson 1983: 90–1). To minimize the possibility of an adverse impact on morale, efforts should be made to use reassignments as opportunities to enrich the working environment by assigning tasks that require new skills and expand areas of responsibility.

Because libraries place service high on their list of priorities, the reference department is frequently identified as the logical recipient of personnel who must be moved as a result of automation. Greater weight should be given to transferring staff members on the basis of aptitudes and interests, rather than automatically transferring them to the reference department. As library services diversify, the definition of reference services will encompass new activities.

Some observers predict that computer systems in companies will "exaggerate the problem of inflexibility and difficulty of change that already exists" (Martin 1983: 71). Sometimes when computers are introduced into organizations, certain procedures fall naturally into rigid, routine patterns. Bold, creative, decisions are required to minimize the impact of computer applications that reinforce undesirable organizational characteristics. A library that automates should be prepared for "new procedures, new staffing patterns, new budget and program priorities, shifts in certain kinds of authority and decision-making, and extensive changes in the library's expenditure patterns" (Martin 1983: 73).

Libraries have experienced substantial increases in expenditures for machines without comparable decreases in expenditures for people (Martin 1983: 80). If libraries fail to use the new technology to provide information, they will not survive in this highly competitive environment in which "power will shift significantly towards those who are knowledgeable in automation" (Martin 1983: 81).

Demands for efficient library services will continue to increase as forces that propel the technological revolution intensify. If the academic library fails to provide the services that users expect, "their functions may be at least partially distributed" (Brown 1985: 479). To maintain its status as the major information center on campus, libraries must "use technology to achieve excellence in information access, collections and service" (Brown 1985: 482). Caution in the application of technology, however, is advisable. Automation in libraries "has not brought the savings that were predicted and it is doubtful whether they will eventuate unless the whole process can take a new direction" (Martin 1982: 4).

## BUDGET DECISIONS AND STAFF MANAGEMENT

Academic libraries are looking simultaneously at new staff-management concepts and modern budgetary procedures. Soaring prices, smaller budgets, and revolutionary computer technology have served to accelerate the application of modern financial methods in the college and university environment.

Academic libraries generally construct budgets that fit into the financial accounting system of the institution with which they are affiliated. Like most managers, library administrators tend to adopt budget procedures that they believe will yield the best results. Complex budgets will not be used without assurances that the outcome will be worth the effort. Because of the competition for funds on most campuses, the general approach to budget requests is to seek the largest justifiable amount that has a good chance of being approved.

Budget practices are changing to accommodate computers. Computers also give libraries access to new statistical data, which can be used to support the library's request for new services, such as on-line data searches. Another dimension of computers is reflected in the need to hire personnel knowledgeable about library computer applications. These personnel needs have placed additional strains on the library's budget. Salaries commanded by personnel trained in computers may be beyond the reach of many small academic libraries. Small academic libraries in particular may find it necessary to provide members of the present staff opportunities to acquire computer skills.

A library's budget gives some indication of the direction in which it is moving and presents ''in financial terms its priorities and plans for programs and services'' (White 1984: 170). Like other planning activities, the budgeting process can be effectively enhanced by staff involvement. Staff members who are given the opportunity to express their ideas on budget allocations are likely to educate themselves about the budget process and will be able to ''provide valuable assistance with budget recommendations. Encouraging staff involvement also creates an environment whereby budget decisions are seen as valid and equitable and not viewed as arbitrary and capricious. Involvement in the budget process generates staff support and acceptance of final budget decisions'' (White 1984: 172).

A travel committee can serve to enhance staff participation in the budget process by helping make decisions on how available funds should be distributed (Hendricks 1982: 130). A travel committee could also exercise its judgment in a manner designed to link travel opportunities to staff-development priorities. Workshops, seminars, and so on that offer training in bibliographic instruction or automation are examples of activities a travel committee may focus on in efforts to sharpen the skills and increase the expertise among library staff.

Staff management is particularly difficult in organizations experiencing stressful events, such as significant cuts in personnel and sharp decreases in the budget for resources. Under these circumstances, a library may find it necessary to redefine its mission and restructure its personnel (Behn 1980: 614–16). Libraries may not be able to maintain all of the traditional services and may find it necessary ''to do fewer things well'' (Webster 1982: 19). Money previously spent for resources may have to be redirected to people and machines (Martin 1982: 5).

One cost-cutting strategy some libraries use is to delay filling vacancies in order to ''generate salary savings needed to help balance the library's budget'' (White 1984: 174). If services deteriorate as a result of vacancies, the staff may be temporarily transferred from one department to another to cover an emergency situation (McCabe 1984: 228).

Unlike other successful enterprises, libraries rarely ''manage their budgets to encourage innovation and development as critical components'' (Webster 1982: 19). Libraries may find it necessary to charge fees for service and to seek other funding sources (Webster 1982: 20). They may encounter student resistance to even modest service fees during a period when there is widespread dissatisfaction with the high cost of attending college (Evangelauf 1986: 1).

Contractual services are consuming a larger percentage of the library's budget each year. Innovative high-density formats are among the new products that require contractual funding. Some of these new products are purchased before there are data on which to base an intelligent prediction of the level of usage. Under the pressure and fear of impending obsolescence, libraries often make substantial financial commitments before studying the impact these commitments will have on staffing and service. In modern libraries, the "one-time purchase of an information package for subsequent use is diminishing as the purchase of information on demand is increasing" (Daniels 1986: 362). Trends in service point to the fact that "emphasis on access over possession has already become acceptable as an idea, but it must become an operating philosophy" (Talbot 1982: 43).

Books represent the traditional model that libraries have used in conceptualizing access to printed information. In the new environment of miniature devices, compact documents, and electronic access, an enormous amount of data can be stored in small spaces. As a result, the future library "will probably be a smaller facility functioning as a gateway agency, a node in a comprehensive information network" (Daniels 1986: 361). Smaller library facilities may help contain the costs associated with maintaining a massive collection of printed materials.

It is the view of some librarians that the upper limits have probably been reached with respect to the average percentage of the total institutional budget that will be allocated for library services (Talbot 1982: 43). If the upper limits have been reached, it may be necessary to implement cost-cutting measures that will have an impact on staff management. Flexibility will be needed to shift staff according to demand for service in the library environment.

## SUMMARY AND CONCLUSIONS

Libraries, like other organizations, must respond appropriately to a changing environment. Technology, accreditation requirements, and staff vacancies are among the factors that can influence the rate at which changes occur.

Libraries are relatively slow to adopt new procedures and to apply new technology. In institutions in which tradition and historical continuity are valued above innovation, the library will probably be slow to embrace radical changes.

Some libraries have moved away from pyramidal administrative designs and toward managerial approaches that facilitate staff participation in decision making. Libraries have also sought to create collegial working relationships based on models provided by the teaching faculty. Management techniques should be tested to determine if they are compatible with the environment of the academic library.

Computers have brought into sharp focus the distinction between machine-generated data and people-generated data. Because of budgetary constraints, management is increasingly forced to make highly sensitive choices between machines and people.

Staff participation in how the budget is distributed can broaden the staff's understanding and acceptance of budget decisions. Libraries should not expect a continuation of consistent annual increases in the percentage of the university's budget they receive each year. Future libraries are expected to be smaller units in which the emphasis will be on access to information sources rather than on possession of these sources. Further increases in funds earmarked for contractual services can be expected to result from an emphasis of access over possession.

Decisions pertaining to staff management and budgeting will always be critical elements in library operations. A high level of performance in delivering library services will be easier to attain when these decisions are made with wisdom and foresight.

## REFERENCES

Bechtel, Joan M. 1985. "Rotation Day Reflections." *College and Research Libraries News* 46 (November): 551–55.

Behn, Robert D. 1980. "Leadership for Cut-Back Management: The Use of Corporate Strategy." *Public Administration Review* 40 (November-December): 613–20.

Brown, Nancy A. 1985. "Managing the Coexistence of Hierarchical and Collegial Governance Structures." *College and Research Libraries* 46 (November): 478–82.

Daniels, Evelyn H. 1986. "Educating the Academic Librarian for a New Role as Information Resources Manager." *Journal of Academic Librarianship* 11 (January): 360–64.

Evangelauf, Jean. 1986. "Anticipation of Another Round of Tuition Hikes Sparks Debate Over Why Costs Are Rising So Rapidly." *Chronicle of Higher Education* 33 (December 3): 1, 30.

Evans, G. Edward. 1983. *Management Techniques for Librarians*. 2d ed. New York: Academic Press.

Hendricks, Donald D. 1982. "Faculty Status and Participative Governance in Academic Libraries." In *Advances in Library Administration and Organization*. Edited by Gerard B. McCabe, Bernard Kreissman, and W. Carl Jackson, 1:127–37. Greenwich, Conn.: JAI Press.

Holley, Edward G. 1972. "Organization and Administration of Urban University Libraries." *College and Research Libraries* 33 (May): 175–89.

Joeckel, Carleton, 1939. *Current Issues in Library Administration: Papers Presented before the Library Institute at the University of Chicago, August 1–12, 1938*. Chicago: University of Chicago Press.

Karol, Nathaniel H., and Sigmund G. Ginsburg. 1980. *Managing the Higher Education Enterprise*. New York: Wiley.

Lyle, Guy R. 1945. *The Administration of the College Library*. New York: H. W. Wilson.

Martin, Murray S. 1982. "Financial Planning: Introductory Thoughts." *Journal of Library Administration* 3 (Fall-Winter): 1–9.

———. 1983. "The Organizational and Budgetary Effects of Automation on Libraries." In *Advances in Library Administration and Organization*. Edited by Gerard B. McCabe and Bernard Kreissman, 2:69–83. Greenwich, Conn.: JAI Press.

McCabe, Gerard. 1984. "Austerity Budget Management." In *Austerity Management in Academic Libraries*. Edited by John F. Harvey and Peter Spyers-Duran, pp. 225–235. Metuchen, N.J.: Scarecrow Press.

Schlipp, Paul Arthur. 1930. "The Most Critical Failure of the American College." In *Higher Education Faces the Future: A Symposium on Education in the United States of America*. Edited by Paul Arthur Schlipp, pp. 207–27. New York: Liveright.

Talbot, Richard J. 1982. "Financing the Academic Library." In *Priorities for Academic Libraries*. Edited by Thomas J. Galvin and Beverly P. Lynch, pp. 35–44. San Francisco: Jossey-Bass.

Vroom, Victor Harold. 1959. "Some Personality Determinants of the Effects of Participation." *Journal of Abnormal and Social Psychology* 59 (November): 322–27.

Watson, Tom G. 1983. "The Librarian as Change Agent." In *Advances in Library Administration and Organization*. Edited by Gerard B. McCabe and Bernard Kreissman, 2:85–97. Greenwich, Conn.: JAI Press.

Webster, Duane E. 1982. "Issues in Financial Management of Research Libraries." *Journal of Library Administration* 3 (Fall-Winter): 13–22.

White, Robert L. 1984. "A Library Budget Process: Incorporating Austerity Management." *Journal of Educational Media and Library Sciences* 21 (Winter): 169–79.

## SELECTED BIBLIOGRAPHY

Cheng, Ching-Chih. *Zero-Base Budgeting in Library Management: A Manual for Librarians*. Phoenix: Oryx Press, 1980.

Clark, Philip M. *Microcomputer Spreadsheet Models for Libraries*. Chicago: American Library Association, 1985.

Cowley, John. *Personnel Management in Libraries*. London: Clive Bingley, 1982.

Gross, Bertram M. *Organizations and Their Managing*. New York: Free Press, 1968.

Jones, Noragh, and Peter Jordon. *Staff Management in Library and Information Work*. Lexington, Mass.: D. C. Health, 1982.

Koenig, Michael E. D. "Budgeting and Financial Planning for Scientific and Technical Libraries." *Science and Technology Libraries* 4 (Spring-Summer 1984): 87–104.

Koenig, Michael E. D., and Deidre C. Stam. "Budgeting and Financial Planning for Libraries." In *Advances in Library Administration and Organization*. Edited by Gerard B. McCabe and Bernard Kreissman. 4:77–110. Greenwich, Conn.: JAI Press, 1985.

Lahti, Robert E. *Innovative College Management*. San Francisco: Jossey-Bass, 1973.

Lee, Sul H., ed. *Library Budgeting: Critical Challenges for the Future*. Ann Arbor, Mich.: Pierian Press, 1977.

Martin, Murray S. *Budgetary Controls in Academic Libraries*. Foundations in Library and Information Science, Vol. 5. Greenwich, Conn.: JAI Press, 1978.

Reneker, Maxine. "Funding Levels and Changes in the Process of Scholarly Communication: Critical Issues for Management of Academic Science Libraries." *Science and Technology Libraries* 4 (Spring-Summer 1984): 19–30.

*Report of the Commission on Librarianship at Stanford* (ED108564). Stanford, Calif.: Stanford University Libraries, 1975.

Russell, Lee G. "Staff Adequacy in Corporate Sci-Tech Libraries." *Science and Technology Libraries* 4 (Spring-Summer 1984): 75–86.

Shaughnessy, Thomas W. "Cutback Management in University Libraries: A Case Study." *Show-Me Libraries* 35 (April 1984): 5–10.

Trumpeter, Margo C., and Richard S. Rounds. *Basic Budgeting Practices for Librarians*. Chicago: American Library Association, 1985.

# 11

# The Library's Materials Budget and Its Management

*Kathryn A. Soupiset,*
*Craig S. Likness, and*
*Richard Hume Werking*

The academic library's funds for books, serials, and other materials, usually referred to by faculty, administrators, and librarians as the "book budget," is a very significant portion of the library's overall budget. As noted below, it typically ranks second in size only to salaries and wages, and occasionally it is the largest single budget element.

Partially because of its size, the materials budget and its management merit and receive considerable scrutiny from librarians, the college or university administration, and attentive portions of the faculty. Another reason for this attention has to do with the fact that, unlike the salaries budget, the materials budget seems to be easily available for discretionary purchases—thousands of them. (Although this availability is generally not as great as it seems because of various commitments such as serials, other standing orders, and approval plans, it nevertheless exists in a way unlike that for other parts of the library's expenditures.) A third reason for this scrutiny is that faculty members, usually with good reason, consider themselves the on-campus experts in their fields and hence very familiar with the book and journal output of their colleagues in the various disciplines. Consequently, they are often anxious that the library make the "right" choices and sometimes are most willing to help it do so and even to be responsible for building portions of the collections, thus making some of these many discretionary purchases.

## THE RELATIONSHIP OF THE BUDGET TO
## COLLECTION DEVELOPMENT

The management of the materials budget occurs within the context of the library's collection-development policy. Every library has such a policy, whether it is rationalized, explicit, and clearly articulated or is haphazard, implicit, and even unconscious. As Herman Fussler observed in 1953, "A library's acquisition policy may represent anything, from the purely fortuitous to the most rigorous selection, but these practices *in themselves* constitute a policy of sorts'' (Fussler 1953: 363, emphasis added).

A broad issue that might be addressed by the collection-development policy is the size of the materials budget. How large does that budget need to be to achieve institutional objectives? Since such objectives are rarely articulated with much attention to the library (if they are articulated at all), this question of size of the materials budget is slippery. How much is deemed necessary is the result of a combination of factors, including historical trends (i.e., what the book budget has been at the library in the relatively recent past); what peer institutions spend on materials (both absolutely and relative to number of students, number of faculty, and number and levels of programs); the size of the library collection at peer institutions, possibly including breakdowns by subject as defined by commonly understood classification schemes; and, probably, the current economic climate at the college or university.

Traditionally, at least for research libraries, the 60:30:10 rule has generally prevailed, with about 60 percent of the library's total budget going for staff, 30 percent for acquisitions, and 10 percent for other costs (Talbot 1982: 38). Statistics from the 117 large research libraries belonging to the Association of Research Libraries show a median acquisitions percentage of 33 percent, whereas data from a group of 53 libraries at selected liberal arts colleges and universities reveal a median figure of 37 percent devoted to acquisitions (Association of Research Libraries 1986; Werking 1986a).

At a practical level, those responsible for collection development spend relatively little time attempting to determine the optimum size of the materials budget or even some optimum percentage of the library's total budget. Rather, they seek to make the best possible use of the monies that are allotted for the purchase of materials.

To help optimize this effort, collection-development objectives and processes should be documented in written policies and procedures manuals. Far too often only an oral tradition is maintained. Written documents may describe collecting objectives for a subject area as broad as English literature or, if appropriate, as narrow as Pre-Raphaelite Brotherhood poetry. The collection strengths and weaknesses, as well as collection goals and objectives, should be identified; the research and teaching interests of specific faculty should be noted as well. The collection-development-statement (or policy) literature is voluminous but also very useful. (For a sampling, see American Library Association 1979; Association of Research Libraries 1977; Boyer and Eaton 1971; *Collection Development Policies* 1981; Dowd 1980; Feng 1979; Futas 1981, 1984; Magrill and Hickey 1984: 21–28; and Osburn 1979.) Although collection-development statements and policies have been especially prevalent in larger academic libraries, smaller academic libraries will also find creating them an extremely useful process. It should remain that—a process. As teaching objectives and research interests change, as subject literatures and publishing patterns change, so will collection-development documents. Because they influence decisions over time, collection-development documents often have historical as well as current importance.

One issue that is often addressed explicitly by the collection-development policy, and always implicitly by expenditures for materials, is the budget's division among different formats. The so-called book-budget expenditures normally go not only for books but also for periodicals, newspapers, other serials, microforms, audiovisual materials, government documents, and binding. What proportion of the budget should be expended for each format? There are no hard and fast rules. For members of the Association of Research Libraries (ARL), the proportion of the materials budget devoted to serials is about 56 percent for the median library, which does not include their binding costs (Association of Research Libraries 1986). In the fifty-three liberal arts college libraries mentioned above, that figure is significantly smaller: 42 percent for the median library (Werking 1986a). Most of the nonserials expenditure is for books.

## CONTROL AND ALLOCATION

An important budget issue that only rarely is addressed in collection-development policies is that of control of the materials budget (Gardner 1985: 140–46; Sandler 1984: 63–73). On many smaller campuses, it is still the teaching faculty that plays the largest role in determining what books are purchased and sometimes also what journals are subscribed to (Goehner 1985–1986: 181–84). On many of the larger campuses during the 1950s and 1960s, the primary responsibility for selection shifted from the faculty to subject bibliographers. In the 1970s and 1980s the same trend has had an impact at some medium-sized and smaller colleges and universities, with librarians, often reference librarians, taking on collection-development responsibilities as a part-time function.

Closely related to the issue of who controls the book budget is the question of *how* that budget is allocated among the various subjects. On those campuses where the faculty has the predominant voice on selection matters, allocation "among subjects" becomes relatively synonymous with "among departments," those on-campus organizational embodiments of the various disciplines. But whether local practices find the faculty members selecting on behalf of their departments and their subjects, or librarians selecting on behalf of the subjects for which they have responsibility, some allocation of the budget, however formal or informal, will be made. As William McGrath has noted, "Nearly every librarian allocates in one way or another. Even when he does not *formally* allocate with specific dollar amounts, he may *subjectively* allocate according to his own biases. If his bias is for chemical engineering, close study of the collection may reveal an *unusually* good chemical engineering section" (McGrath, Huntsinger, and Barber 1969: 51, emphasis added).

The issue of budget allocation is not only an important topic but also is the only materials budget issue that has generated significant controversy and attention in the journal literature. (One of us has recently traced the literature on this topic through the present century, and we will not go into it in depth here (Werking 1986b). Sometimes the issue is posed as a dilemma over whether or not to allocate. As noted above, we believe that the issue cast in this fashion is misleading, since allocation occurs and will occur anyway. Hence a much more useful way to pose the question is whether to establish divisions among subjects (or formats, for that matter) in any formal way or to let events run their course. Sometimes librarians mistakenly assume that allocation is tantamount to faculty control over selection (Gardner 1985: 140–46; Bach 1964: 161–65); although these two things can be closely related issues, they are nevertheless separate.

Common in libraries, and in the library literature over the years, has been the practice of making a division of the materials budget on the basis of some set of numbers. Usually, this practice has focused on the budget for books, leaving aside the matter of serials and other continuations, audiovisuals, and so on, but a minority of libraries do include some of these other formats in their allocation deliberations. The most common bases, over the past half century at least, for allocation of dollars to different subjects (and thus in reality on behalf of the various departments, regardless of whether it is the faculty members or the librarians who are ordering the books) are the number of students in a given department, number of faculty, and number of courses (Werking 1986b). A few pieces in the literature have proposed basing allocation on circulation figures—the use of the collection in the various subject areas (see especially McGrath 1975: 356–69)— and fewer still have advocated what we favor as the single best place to begin an allocation scheme: on the basis of the relative size and price of the literature in the various subjects (see Werking and Getchell 1981). In recent years approval plans have made their appearance in a large number of academic libraries, and those libraries with such plans in operation have thus allocated a significant portion of their budget by size and cost of the literature.

A number of libraries have improved the budgetary control they have over their serials, often with the help of a microcomputer. The ongoing nature of serial publications and the resulting larger commitment of the academic institution make it important to identify "responsibility" for serial titles. On behalf of what subject or department is the library receiving a given title? (Many of the titles in any library will be general ones that the library has initiated on behalf of its patrons at large and not because of the teaching or research needs of one or two departments.) Departmental and divisional lists can be generated to get an approximate sense of how large a portion of the serials budget a particular subject or department consumes. If a department disavows its relationship to a given title (whether because it is seeking new subscriptions or for other reasons), that department's faculty members are less likely to be consulted about any prospective cancellation of that title.

## BUDGET FLEXIBILITY

Proper management of the materials budget requires a certain amount of ingenuity and flexibility. It is highly desirable that the college or university administration allow the library to carry encumbrances into the next fiscal year. When that is not allowed, libraries often seek to pay ahead on materials they are certain they will buy fairly early in the next fiscal year, perhaps a portion of their serials invoice covering the subsequent calendar year. If that, too, is prohibited locally, the library usually tries to overencumber by a certain amount, but that requires considerable and time-consuming scrutiny of the order process. All of these strategies are particularly important in those settings where a subsequent year's budget is reduced if the current year's funds are not completely expended. In any case, libraries need to plan well enough to avoid the situation of purchasing marginal materials just to spend all of their budgets. Collection-development librarians also seem more aware than they used to be of the importance of using the materials budget as a means to secure necessary equipment, since funds for library equipment on many campuses are very scarce. How many microforms can be purchased before additional cabinetry will be needed to house them? Or how many more years, or months, of service can one squeeze out of microform readers and reader printers? A number of the microform vendors, though, unfortunately, by no means all, are becoming astute and offering equipment bonuses instead of discounts with the purchase of sizable microform orders.

Budget flexibility could also extend to some of the library's labor costs. In one instance, a number of vendors working with an academic library received copies of the library's microfiche catalog and at the outset identified titles they were offering that were not in the catalog and hence much more likely candidates for purchase. Those libraries with card catalogs could undertake a version of the same process. A distant vendor could, through the library's good offices, hire someone in the local community, pay that person to check the catalog in the same way, and in turn receive the library's business.

It is entirely possible that too much flexibility, in some hands, would be as bad as too little. It is becoming increasingly fashionable to talk about paying for recorded information and for access to that information out of the same library materials budget. That is, various networking costs and costs for on-line bibliographic searching in some libraries come out of the materials budget rather than a supplies or services line. Moreover, some observers advocate subsidizing on-line data-base searching by using the materials budget, apparently because in their opinions operating budgets are already strained to the maximum and also because many books go unused while the results of a data-base search are used. Opponents of this approach point out that the proponents are confusing the library's role as a service organization with its role ''as a long-lived resource'' and that a data-base search benefits only one user whereas a book or journal is added to the collection with the expectation and hope that it will benefit more than one. (For a recent and useful discussion-debate of this issue, see Poole and St. Clair 1986; and Dowd, Whaley, and Pankake 1986.)

Thus far we have focused on the larger issues involving the materials budget and not the logistical matters. Central to these logistics and to the management of that budget in most libraries is the acquisitions department.

## THE ACQUISITIONS DEPARTMENT AND THE BUDGET

Some library directors prefer to separate from the acquisitions or order department some of the functions identified below, frequently by incorporating the bookkeeping functions into their own offices. The description here, we believe, is the most common arrangement, the one with which the three of us are personally most familiar (in several libraries), and the one that, not surprisingly, we consider the best for most situations.

One of the major roles of the acquisitions department is to provide bookkeeping and statistical information for those individuals who have an interest in encumbering and expending the library materials budget; indeed, Thomas Leonhardt described acquisitions as "a service within a service" (Leonhardt 1984: 74). This information is supplied by the acquisitions department to other parts of the library (i.e., library administration and collection development) and to others outside the library (i.e., faculty members, donors of gift funds, book dealers, and the campus business office). The library director and the collection-development librarian are vitally concerned with the allocation and monitoring of the materials budget. Faculty members are eager for the library to purchase those titles that will support their teaching and research. Donors of gift funds are interested in how libraries are using their money. Publishers and vendors are eager for the library to support their businesses by purchasing the materials they handle. The campus business office is concerned with the efficient handling of university funds.

The records that are maintained in acquisitions serve a very important purpose for the library administration. That purpose is to monitor and report on the progress of encumbrances against and expenditures from the materials budget. (For basic information on acquisitions budget issues and procedures, see Evans 1979; Ford 1978; Martin 1978; Melcher 1971; Reid 1984; and Rogers and Weber 1971: 89–111.) The library director can use this information with both the collection-development librarian and the college or university administrators.

It is important that there be a sense of trust between the library director and the acquisitions department. Written procedures and regular reports are an extremely important basis for that trust. Each library develops its own procedures for reporting encumbrances, expenditures, and other pertinent statistics, but all reports should be accurate, as self-explanatory as possible, and easy to follow. (See figure 1 for an example of such a reporting form.) Even when these guidelines are followed, there should also be regular meetings to keep the library administration informed and to discuss progress of the budget.

Within most libraries the acquisitions librarian works closely with the head of collection development. Indeed, in some organizational structures, one person wears both hats. Even in libraries in which collection development and acquisitions are separate, the lines may be either distinct or blurred. In any case, the successful operation of both sections requires close cooperation among all those involved.

**Figure 1**
**Reporting Form**

Tri-State State College
Acquisitions Department
CURRENT BUDGET REPORT
FY 1986/87
From June 1, 1986 thru Date _____

| Account | Target Amount | Currently on Order | Expended to Date | Free Balance | Cash Balance |
|---|---|---|---|---|---|
| APPROVAL | | | | | |
| North American | $ 85,000 | | | | |
| British | 15,000 | | | | |
| French | 5,000 | | | | |
| Spanish | 5,000 | | | | |
| German | 5,000 | | | | |
| Art Catalogs | 5,000 | | | | |
| SUB-TOTALS | $120,000 | | | | |
| | | | | | |
| FIRM ORDERS | | | | | |
| General | $ 32,000 | | | | |
| Reference | 7,500 | | | | |
| Documents | 1,000 | | | | |
| Russian | 500 | | | | |
| Curriculum Lib. | 1,500 | | | | |
| Leisure Reading | 2,500 | | | | |
| Scores | 3,000 | | | | |
| Music Recordings | 7,000 | | | | |
| Microforms | 10,000 | | | | |
| SUB-TOTALS | $ 65,000 | | | | |
| TOTAL BOOKS | $185,000 | | | | |
| SERIALS | $150,000 | | | | |
| BINDING | $ 15,000 | | | | |
| GRAND TOTALS | $350,000 | | | | |

There is much information that the acquisitions department can supply to the collection-development librarian to assist in making budget decisions. One good source for budget preparation consists of bookkeeping histories from previous fiscal years, which facilitate comparisons, help to chart trends, and aid in identifying areas that may have received too much or too little of the budget. By keeping records on the number of volumes received each year, particularly in categories important to the individual library, the acquisitions librarian can determine the average price per volume for material actually purchased for the library. This information can be compared with price indexes or price statistics compiled outside the library and available from several sources, such as *The Bowker Annual of Library and Book Trade Information*, *Library Journal*, *Publisher's Weekly*, and *Choice*.

Another area of mutual concern to acquisitions and collection development is vendor selection and vendor performance. Certainly, one part of this concern is the question of discount versus service. Higher discounts may enable a library to purchase more books with the money it has, but most acquisitions librarians will agree that discount without service is not worth the price. By keeping careful records of vendor performance, an acquisitions librarian can decide which vendors best suit the library's needs.

In addition to keeping an accurate accounting of financial transactions, it is necessary to maintain good records of outstanding orders. By doing an "on-order" inventory toward the end of the fiscal year, one can gauge which orders are likely to be received and how much money may be available for special purchases. Collection-development librarians often have identified certain "big-ticket" items that are appropriate for their library and can be ordered quickly to spend "surplus" funds.

Thus far, the discussion has focused on the importance of maintaining and providing accurate information for budget preparation and status within the confines of the library; however, there are also those outside the library for whom the acquisitions department supplies financial or statistical information.

Libraries have many different ways of dividing their materials budgets, ranging from no departmental or divisional allocations under complete library control to very detailed allocations of books and serials under substantial faculty control. Depending upon the way the library materials budget is divided or allocated, the faculty usually constitutes a group with a great deal of interest in any budget reports supplied by acquisitions. If departments have been authorized a certain amount of money for materials, they will be interested in the ongoing balance of these funds. In some environments individual faculty members are granted a portion of the department's allocation, and they, too, are often keenly interested in the status of their "accounts" containing a few dollars. The acquisitions librarian in that situation must devise a system for identifying requests and keeping track of expenditures that will be informative and accurate, yet as easy as possible to maintain. The library director must also be kept well informed about the status of departmental allocations and special accounts, because he or she deals with these same issues. Faculty members may deal directly with acquisitions or may receive budget status reports through their liaison librarians or bibliographers.

There is another group outside the library that can have an impact on the library materials budget and for whom the acquisitions department needs to maintain accurate records and supply financial information. Most libraries are the beneficiaries of gift funds, whether from individuals or other sources, such as foundations, corporations, or trust funds. These gift monies may be unrestricted, enabling the library to determine what to purchase, or restricted, requiring the funds to be spent in a certain area or on a special subject. In another situation, a donor might give the library a special collection of books and then maintain funding to continue the collection. Gift funds are appreciated and may enable a library to expand its collection in areas that otherwise would not have been well supported. The problem with gift monies is that their timing and continuation are generally uncertain.

Gift funds usually require additional record keeping for the acquisitions department. Donors sometimes request an accounting of how their funds are spent and in many instances are interested in the individual titles that are purchased. Acquisitions librarians should work closely with the library administration and the campus office that deals with donors and gift accounts to determine restrictions when any new gift fund is established. The librarian can then maintain records that fit into established acquisitions procedures in order to supply information on the account and titles purchased. For libraries with many gift accounts, the bookkeeping may become very time-consuming; it is best to develop systems that function as simply as possible. At times this record keeping may seem burdensome, but if records are well maintained and reports can be made efficiently, the reward may come in the form of additional funds for the library or for the institution in general.

While working with the library materials budget, the acquisitions department must deal with bookdealers. Because acquisitions is a business as well as a bibliographic operation, it is extremely important to maintain accurate records when dealing with these suppliers. A good place to start when working with a vendor is to understand his operations and requirements. This can usually be accomplished satisfactorily during a visit from the vendor's sales representative, who can be very helpful in explaining more detailed procedures. An on-site tour of the vendor's operations can also be very enlightening.

In addition, these suppliers of library materials are a good source of information that can be useful in budget planning. They are in a position to see the larger picture of the publishing industry and to help explain trends to the library staff. They usually have more specific information, such as the average price per volume of the materials they supplied to a library during a certain time (Blackwell North America 1986; Baker & Taylor Company 1986). In particular, subscription agents can be very helpful in supplying information on price projections. They are usually able to answer questions concerning projected inflation figures, the effect of foreign-currency fluctuations, and other factors that might influence subscription prices. They can also provide information on a library's specific titles. For instance, how many of the library's titles, and which ones, increased in price more than the average inflation figure? One of the general managers of a large subscription agency has suggested that this information on inflation factors for subscriptions might be useful if ranked from highest to lowest within the Library of Congress classification number or by discipline (McClendon 1986). These titles may or may not be candidates for cancellation, but they at least could undergo examination by the collection-development librarian or bibliographers.

The vendor's organization (for example, the size of staff) can be directly affected by fluctuations in library materials budgets, especially if those library accounts are sizeable. Thus the vendor is very interested in the status of the library budget and in the status of the library-vendor relationship. The acquisitions librarian should remember that although the vendor can provide many kinds of services to the library, this relationship is indeed a mutually dependent one, and open communication is always important.

Acquisitions librarians realize the importance of accurate record keeping, but the business office is one department on campus for whom accuracy is essential. In dealing with the business office, a new acquisitions librarian should first contact the institution's financial officer, both as a gesture of good will and as a means to understanding the operation of the institution's accounting system. Much can be gained by explaining the acquisitions department's needs and any difficult bookkeeping procedures and then establishing some procedures to work within the institution's system. In any case, the library will need to maintain certain records, as indicated by the business office, which are necessary for audits.

The everyday idiosyncrasies that always arise in bookkeeping are usually best handled by the accounts payable personnel in the business office. Once again, personal contact and a genuine interest in solving problems often smooth over misunderstandings. The acquisitions librarian should be acquainted with personnel in the accounts payable department; but a most important contact within the library is the bookkeeper, whether that person works in acquisitions or is part of the library-administration department. One of the most important qualifications for a library bookkeeper, in addition to ability with bookkeeping matters, is the ability to communicate clearly (both orally and in writing) and to work well with other people. The bookkeeper will work closely with the personnel in the business office and also with personnel in accounting offices of publishers and vendors, diplomatically defending the library's operation or admitting an error and correcting it. The bookkeeper is the person who is most counted upon to make sure not only that the normal invoices and expenditures are handled correctly but also that the same efficiency applies to unusual problems in the library bookkeeping system. A positive working relationship with the accounts payable personnel will help facilitate day-to-day interaction and will certainly help meet the needs of both the library and the business office.

The information that the acquisitions department supplies to the business office is chiefly in the form of invoices approved for payment, statements that have been researched, and budget balances to reconcile with business-office records. It is the responsibility of acquisitions to maintain accurate records in order to provide that information. (A good source of library bookkeeping forms and procedures is Alley and Cargill 1982.) Here, as with book dealers and acquisitions departments, the informational needs of acquisitions and the campus business office are reciprocal and require good channels of communication.

In this era of many new technologies, acquisitions procedures and activities are being streamlined as functions are being automated. Automation can now provide financial and management reports more quickly and easily than before. Automated acquisitions systems include fund accounting as an integral part of the ordering and receiving processes, and some libraries have chosen this management method. Other libraries are able to make use of on-line budget management by linking up with their institution's accounting system. Still others make use of various software packages that are available for a free-standing microcomputer. At the same time, manual systems can also be constructed that are capable of providing the needed information in an efficient manner. Automation will continue to play an important role in data manipulation and report generation, but it is no substitute, and is not intended to be, for the common sense that directs it. Traditional goals of acquisitions departments remain the same: to order and receive library materials and to provide financial information to various groups with which the department interacts.

## CONCLUSION

Administering the library materials budget properly requires a number of elements. It requires cooperation among colleagues within the library, across the campus, and in the wider world between librarians and vendors. It requires attention to detail, good organizational skills, timely and informative reports, and flexibility, all working within the framework of a library's collection-development policy to make available the resources that are most appropriate for that environment. It requires, in sum, the best blend of sound and creative management.

## REFERENCES

Alley, Brian, and Jennifer Cargill. 1982. *Keeping Track of What You Spend: The Librarian's Guide to Simple Bookkeeping*. Phoenix: Oryx Press.

American Library Association, Resources and Technical Services Division, Resources Section, Collection Development Committee. 1979. *Guidelines for Collection Development*. Chicago: American Library Association.

Association of Research Libraries. 1977. *Collection Development Policies SPEC Kit* (SPEC Kit #38). Washington, D.C.

———. 1986. *ARL Statistics, 1984–85*. Compiled by Nicola Daval and Alexander Lichtenstein. Washington, D.C.

Bach, Harry. 1964. "Why Allocate?" *Library Resources and Technical Services* 8 (Spring): 161–65.

Baker & Taylor Company. 1986. *The Approval Program: Management Information Report, Subject Section, 1985–86*. New York.

Blackwell, North America. 1986. *Approval Program: Coverage and Cost Study, 1985/ 86*. Beaverton, Or.

Boyer, Calvin, and Nancy L. Eaton. 1971. *Book Selection Policies in American Libraries*. Austin, Tex.: Armadillo Press.

*Collection Development Policies* (CLIP Notes #2–81). 1981. Chicago: Association of College and Research Libraries.

Dowd, Sheila T. 1980. "The Formulation of a Collection Development Policy Statement." In *Collection Development in Libraries: A Treatise*. Edited by R. D. Stueart and G. B. Miller, pp. 67–87. Greenwich, Conn.: JAI Press.

Dowd, Sheila, John H. Whaley, Jr., and Marcia Pankake. 1986. "Reactions to 'Funding Online Services from the Materials Budget.' " *College and Research Libraries* 47 (May): 230–37.

Evans, G. Edward. 1979. *Developing Library Collections*. Littleton, Colo.: Libraries Unlimited.

Feng, Y. T. 1979. "The Necessity for a Collection Development Policy Statement." *Library Resources and Technical Services* 23 (Winter): 39–44.

Ford, Stephen. 1978. *Acquisition of Library Materials*. Chicago: American Library Association.

Fussler, Herman. 1953. "Acquisition Policy; The Larger University Library." *College and Research Libraries* 14 (October): 363–67.

Futas, Elizabeth. 1981. "Issues in Collection Building: Why Collection Development Policies." *Collection Building* 3 (Spring): 59–60.

———, ed. 1984. *Library Acquisitions Policies and Procedures*. 2d ed. Phoenix: Oryx Press.

Gardner, Charles A. 1985. "Book Selection Policies in the College Library: A Reappraisal." *College and Research Libraries* 46 (March): 140–46.

Goehner, Donna M. 1985–1986. "A Lesson Learned the Hard Way; or, The Cost of Relinquishing Acquisitions Control." *The Serials Librarian* 10 (Fall-Winter): 181–84.

Leonhardt, Thomas W. 1984. "Collection Development and Acquisitions: The Division of Responsibility." *RTSD Newsletter* 9: 74–75.

McClendon, James C. 1986. Ebsco Subscription Services. Dallas Tex. Telephone conversation, May.

McGrath, William. 1975. "A Pragmatic Book Allocation Formula for Academic and Public Libraries with a Test for Its Effectiveness." *Library Resources and Technical Services* 19 (Fall): 356–69.

McGrath, William E., Ralph C. Huntsinger, and Gary R. Barber. 1969. "An Allocation Formula Derived from a Factor Analysis of Academic Departments." *College and Research Libraries* 30 (January): 51–62.

Magrill, Rose Mary, and Doralyn J. Hickey. 1984. *Acquisitions Management and Collection Development in Libraries*. Chicago: American Library Association.

Martin, Murray S. 1978. *Budgetary Control in Academic Libraries*. Greenwich, Conn.: JAI Press.

Melcher, Daniel. 1971. *Melcher on Acquisitions*. Chicago: American Library Association.

Osburn, Charles B. 1979. "Some Practical Observations on the Writing, Implementation, and Revision of Collection Development Policy." *Library Resources and Technical Services* 23 (Winter): 7–15.

Poole, Jay Martin, and Gloriana St. Clair. 1986. "Funding Online Services from the Materials Budget." *College and Research Libraries* 47 (May): 225–29.

Reid, Marion T. 1984. "Acquisitions." In *Library Technical Services: Operations and Management*. Edited by Irene P. Godden, pp. 89–131. Orlando, Fla.: Academic Press.

Rogers, Rutherford D, and David C. Weber. 1971. *University Library Administration*. New York: H. W. Wilson.

Sandler, Mark. 1984. "Organizing Effective Faculty Participation in Collection Development." *Collection Management* 6 (Fall-Winter): 63–73.

Talbot, Richard J. 1982. "Financing the Academic Library." In *Priorities for Academic Libraries*. Edited by Thomas J. Galvin and Beverly P. Lynch, pp. 35–44. San Francisco: Jossey-Bass.

Werking, Richard Hume, and Charles M. Getchell, Jr. 1981. "Using *Choice* as a Mechanism for Allocating Book Funds in an Academic Library." *College and Research Libraries* 42 (March): 134–38.

Werking, Richard Hume. 1986a. Unpublished Data from Fifty-three Liberal Arts College Libraries, Taken from the "Bowdoin List," Compiled by Arthur Monke; and the ACM/GLCA List, Compiled by Dennis Ribbens; both sets for 1984–1985.

———. 1986b. "Budgeting for Collection Development." Based on papers delivered to Collection Management and Development Institutes at Trinity University, May 1985, and The University of North Carolina at Chapel Hill, May 1986.

# 12

# Library Budgeting and Financial Management in the Public Academic Library

*Robert L. White and Allan J. Dyson*

## THE BUDGET AND BUDGETING—WHAT IS IT?

A *budget* is a document (or series of documents) that presents a plan of action in financial terms (Prentice 1983: 90–91; Martin 1978: 14). It has three basic functions: planning, management, and control (Martin 1978: 12; Schultze 1968: 5–9). *Planning* involves establishing goals, setting a time frame for accomplishing them, and determining the level of financial support needed. *Management* is concerned with acquiring and allocating resources to achieve the goals. *Financial control* helps to ensure that funds are used for approved purposes and that there is compliance with authorized spending levels; it requires a system of monitoring expenditures and generating up-to-date financial status reports. *Budgeting* is simply the year-round and continuous process whereby budgets are constructed.

## TYPES OF BUDGETS

Budgets come in different formats. Line item; formula; performance; program; program planning and budgeting system (PPBS); zero-base budgeting (ZBB); lump sum; and mixed models are described here.

### Line-Item Budgeting

The use of the line-item budget is widespread (Evans 1983: 274; Prentice 1983: 93, 121; Chen 1980: 7; Koenig 1980: 3). It emphasizes putting dollars into specific lines (e.g., salaries, books, utilities) rather than how money will be divided within the library or how effectively it will be spent. Broad expenditure categories include personnel (salaries and hourly wages), library materials (books, serials, and other materials), binding, and other expenses (telephones, equipment, travel, and so on). The current budget is accepted as a given, and a new budget is based on increases to it.

The line-item budget is relatively easy to prepare since projected increases are simply added to last year's allocations. However, there is no required mechanism for reviewing the value of existing services.

## Formula Budgeting

Formula budgets use quantitative factors to calculate the level of funding—for example, the number of students or the number of doctoral programs. They are input based and not directly related to the level of service provided. They have been most widely employed in the libraries of publicly supported institutions (Summers 1974: 27). The Clapp-Jordan formula and the Association of College Research Libraries (ACRL) College Library Standards are examples (Chen 1980: 9; Prentice 1983: 118–20; Association of College and Research Libraries 1986: 189–200).

Once agreed upon, the use of formulas makes budgets relatively easy to prepare. There are, however, disadvantages. Formulas have a built-in assumption that there is a relationship between quantitative factors and quality library service. Most formulas are based on a minimum level of support, but the parent institution or funding agency may treat them as maximums (Allen 1972: 29; Koenig and Stam 1985: 85). Also, full funding of a formula may well be determined less by the accuracy of that formula than by prevailing economic and political conditions (Prentice 1983: 120).

## Performance Budgeting

Performance budgeting stresses activities and efficiency (Chen 1980: 10). It looks at how efficiently resources are being used by examining the unit costs for library services. The costs of activities such as answering reference questions, cataloging, processing interlibrary loan (ILL) requests, or circulating books are analyzed. After unit costs have been developed, it is possible to state that it costs X dollars to answer a reference question and Y dollars to order and catalog a book. The budget is calculated based on the projected volume of activities for the year multiplied by the unit costs of those activites (Koenig 1980: 6).

## Program Budgeting

In a program budget, dollar amounts are assigned to separate functions or programs—for example, information services, collection development, materials processing, and administrative support. It makes use of line-item budgeting techniques, since each function is subdivided into line-item categories such as personnel or equipment. A program budget is output oriented since it is possible to view where library resources have been allocated. The construction of a program budget is dependent on accurately determining where funds are allocated within the library. Its advantage is that it provides the library director with a detailed picture of how library money is being spent. It is also an effective method for communicating the library's needs to its parent institution (Koenig 1980: 3; Koenig and Stam 1985: 90, 92). A shortcoming involves the conceptual problem of grouping services into programs. The interrelationships between library functions may make it difficult to divide them into program categories (Martin 1982: 301).

## Program Planning and Budgeting System

The program planning and budgeting system (PPBS) was first established in the Department of Defense in 1961 (Schultze 1968: 1). It adds a planning and evaluation element to budgeting. It includes planning, programming, and budgeting in a single system (Chen 1980: 10).

The elements of a PPBS system have been well documented (Chen 1980: 10–11; Summers 1974: 21–27; Koenig 1980: 9–11; Prentice 1983: 106–109; Schultze 1968: 19–32). Its major benefit is the linkage between planning and budgeting within the context of a multiyear time frame. The major disadvantage is the time required to implement it. The system is complex and requires a great deal of quantification (Young 1976: 85–173). In addition, it may require more information than the decision-maker can obtain or handle. Although elements of PPBS are still used, the enthusiasm for it has decreased, and it has not been widely adopted in libraries (Koenig and Stam 1985: 92–93, 96).

## Zero-Base Budgeting

Zero-base budgeting (ZBB) was first developed by Peter Pyhrr while he was at Texas Instruments (Pyhrr 1970). It acts as if no previous budget existed, with nothing taken for granted (Chen 1980: 12). Existing activities are scrutinized just as closely as new proposals. The basic steps and process in implementing ZBB have been extensively described (Chen 1980; U.S. Office of Management and Budget 1977: 22342–53). Goal and program oriented, it provides a high level of detailed information to management. The major disadvantage is the time needed to implement the system.

## Lump-Sum Budgeting

With a lump-sum budget, a library is allocated an amount of money and instructed to operate with that total during a fiscal period. This allows maximum flexibility since no amount is attached to any one spending category (Chen 1980: 9; Prentice 1983: 120). Because they give the parent institution little control over how funds are used, lump-sum budgets are now uncommon (Summers 1974: 14–15).

## Mixed-Budget Approach

Many libraries use a mix of approaches (Martin 1978: 25). A library may have a line-item budget that has been partially constructed through a formula to determine funding for library materials or staffing. Or a library may receive its funds (and report expenditures) in a line-item format but internally may use a program budget (or other budget system) for planning and allocation.

## THE BUDGET PROCESS

Budgeting should be viewed as a continuous process throughout the year. Many institutions have a fiscal year from July 1 to June 30, whereas others operate with a different or two-year (i.e., biennial) cycle. However one operates, a multiyear approach to budgeting is a practical necessity. Within any given period one will be spending the current budget and resolving problems from the previous year (Evans 1983: 267). The preparation of the next year's budget must begin with an eye toward whether programs started during next fiscal year can be continued thereafter. There are some well-defined elements to a library's budget process (Martin 1978: 7). The following comprise the main components.

### Development of Goals and Objectives

It is important to link budget decisions to library goals, and the budget process should commence with the establishment of these goals (Prentice 1983: 44; White 1984: 173). A clear statement of goals provides a context for making budget decisions. If these goals are internalized through staff participation, a common understanding of what is most important can facilitate the making of budgetary and other major library decisions.

### Information Gathering

It is exceptionally valuable, in preparing the budget, to have information regarding institutional planning and new academic programs. The library needs to participate in academic program planning, but this is not always the situation (Martin 1978: 57). The library staff may have to rely on informal contacts with faculty and administrators to keep in touch with new academic directions.

To prepare a defensible budget document, information relating to the library's services must also be acquired and analyzed. The information required to present a creditable budget request will largely be defined by the requirements of the parent institution (Martin 1978: 54). The best sources of information for budget planning are the library's own records: statistics, previous budgets, cost studies, and so on (Prentice 1983: 66). Well-documented information increases the likelihood that the budget request will be considered seriously.

## Planning

Before the budget is prepared, the library needs to decide on the best way to reach its goals. One way to determine this is program analysis. The following steps outline the methodology (Hatry et al. 1976):

1. Define the problem.
2. Identify the objectives.
3. Select evaluation criteria or measures of effectiveness.
4. Specify client groups served or affected by the program.
5. Identify alternatives.
6. Estimate costs of each alternative.
7. Estimate effectiveness of each alternative.
8. Document and present findings.

As campus resources are stretched, the competition for financial support intensifies. Methods such as program analysis enable the librarian to present the case for the library's budget effectively.

## Preparation of the Budget Calendar

A budget calendar is an essential planning document for the successful operation of the budget process (Prentice 1983: 44; Lynden 1982: 116). The calendar presents a chronology of major dates and milestones of the budget process while making clear to the staff what the steps in that process will be (White 1984: 174).

## Budget Preparation and Presentation

Based on goals and on planning and budgetary information, a preliminary budget is prepared and discussed several months before the start of the fiscal year. It serves as a forecast for personnel, library materials, and other expenses and provides the framework for making final budget decisions later. When constructing the forecast be as accurate as possible, since the closer the fit between the forecast and actual expenditures, the smoother the budget will function during the year (Martin 1978: 15–16).

The construction of a final budget depends on receipt of final information from the academic institution (e.g., budgetary assessments, personnel freezes, inflationary increases for materials). The preliminary budget is revised as required after receipt of firm budget information. In addition, estimates are refined and operating assumptions reviewed before being incorporated into a final budget.

A formal presentation may need to be made of the final budget. When presenting the budget it is best to "play it straight" in making projections since one's credibility will depend on it (Evans 1983: 272; Koenig 1980: 46). Depending on institutional practice, the budget may be presented to the administration of the institution, the library staff, or both. It should be clear, well documented, and packaged in a manner that explains the financial basis of the library's operations.

## Monitoring the Budget

After adoption of the final budget, the library's management has the fiduciary responsibility to see that funds are properly spent and used to further the goals of the library. An accurate library accounting system will ensure that approved budget allocations are recorded and that spending is limited to budgeted amounts. Such a system is indispensable in determining how much money the library has left to spend during the year (Smith 1983: 91, 105). The reporting function is an important part of the budgetary process. Estimates in the budget need to be compared regularly (e.g., monthly) to actual expenditures and expenditures adjusted as needed (Evans 1983: 264; Martin 1978: 165).

A midpoint budget review should be conducted to examine the first six months of the fiscal year. After presentation to and discussion by the senior managers and department heads of the library, midyear budget adjustments should be implemented as required (White 1984: 177). If it is desirable to shift money between budget categories, the library director must be aware of the guidelines for transferring funds. This is the most effective time to administer fiscal "first aid," since near the end of the year, there may be so little money left that covering deficits is impossible.

## Year-End Funds

Academic libraries may find themselves with unexpected year-end funds. Salary savings from unexpected vacancies or from a longer-than-expected recruitment may leave the library with a surplus toward the end of the year, or excess funds may be made available from the parent institution (Martin 1978: 18). In any case, have a plan as to where such windfalls might best be spent (e.g., library materials, equipment replacement).

## Carrying Funds Forward

When an order is placed, the estimated price is usually recorded as an encumbrance to prevent overexpenditure of accounts. Often goods and services ordered during one fiscal year are received or paid for the following year. If the parent institution permits carrying funds forward to cover outstanding orders at year-end, there is no problem. If funds cannot be carried forward, it becomes essential to freeze a portion of the new year's appropriation to meet these obligations before constructing a new budget (Martin 1978: 119–20). This is similar to determining what percentage of the materials budget must be reserved for continuations before allocations for new materials are made. If an academic institution allows neither funds nor encumbrances to be carried forward, all outstanding orders at year-end must be cancelled and reordered the following year.

## Closing Out the Budget

No matter how carefully expenditures are estimated, there will be discrepancies at year-end and the prospect of unexpended funds within some budget categories. In public institutions, government funds usually must be expended (or at least encumbered) within the same fiscal year they were appropriated (Martin 1978: 169).

The library director or budget officer must be aware of the deadline for placing purchase orders and for closing out the budget. The budget calendar is the guide here. At the end of the fiscal year, a final budget report is often necessary (Martin 1978: 171). This report can provide comparative information for checking the next year's preliminary budget and planning for the next year's final budget.

## BUDGET CATEGORIES

An academic library's budget usually has three components: personnel (salaries and wages); library materials (monographs, serials, microforms, maps, and so on) and binding; and supplies and expenses (travel, equipment, supplies, utilities, and so on).

## Personnel

Salaries and wages typically comprise about 60 percent of a library's operating budget (National Center for Education Statistics 1983: 203; Hayes 1982: 125; Evans 1983: 274). The distribution of the staff among service areas may vary widely from library to library; nevertheless, the library director needs to be sensitive to the existing work load and how the staff is assigned within the library. A procedure whereby library units request additional staff should be incorporated into the budget process. When planning the budget and potential sources of funds, salary savings from vacant positions should not be overlooked. Many institutions allow savings from vacancies to be retained by the unit where the vacancy occurs, an important source of funds in helping to meet service obligations. Since the amount can vary substantially from year to year, it is best to use a conservative estimate (Martin 1978: 111). It is particularly important to have a process to review vacant positions as to whether they should be filled and at what staffing level, since vacancies often provide the only time that it is operationally easy to reallocate personnel resources (Prentice 1978: 20).

## Library Materials

Library materials and binding comprise, on an average, about 30–32 percent percent of the total budget (National Center for Education Statistics 1983: 203; Hayes 1982: 125; Evans 1983: 274). In planning the budget for library materials it is important to determine what is presently being expended, to review projected price increases (data usually available from library literature or vendors) and to have accurate information on the institution's academic programs (Martin 1978: 115; Lynden 1982: 109–13).

As noted earlier, many libraries have funds for materials allocated by formula. In most cases, a formula serves as a mechanism for allocating funds based on a library's pro-rata share of the funds available. This is most common among multicampus institutions or where available funds are calculated statewide and then distributed to individual institutions.

In most cases, a library will have to make a case to the administration for financial support. Frederick Lynden summarized a strategy that offers the best chance for persuading academic administrators (1982: 119):

1. Demonstrate the need to provide inflationary increases to maintain current acquisition level.
2. Explain the value of maintaining and increasing library collections to support research and instructional programs.
3. Garner faculty support for the library's budget.
4. Present an honest request based on demonstrated need.
5. Use persuasive comparisons with other institutions.

## Supplies and Expenses

After the personnel (salaries and wages) and library materials categories, the remainder is called by a variety of names: goods and services, supplies and expenses (shortened to S & E), or simply "other." S & E comprises about 8–10 percent of a typical academic library's budget (National Center for Education Statistics 1983: 203; Hayes 1982: 125; Evans 1983: 274). The following are typical of what one would find in this category: travel, staff-development and recruitment expenses, office supplies, computing costs, photocopy expenses, equipment and building maintenance, telephones, and the inevitable "miscellaneous." Compared with other budget categories, S & E is the smallest. However, it is important because these expenditures provide the support for everyday activities that keep the library functioning (Martin 1978: 128; Hayes 1982: 130). This category can present problems for budget planning, because of the variety of items within it. Over time, one can lessen this difficulty by maintaining an accounting system that provides records of past expenditures in order to establish a data base for budget projections.

More financial demands are being placed on this category as academic libraries move increasingly from manual to automated processes and must pay not only for equipment but also for ongoing maintenance and replacement. As libraries become more dependent on automated systems, there will be a growing need to increase the S & E budget significantly (Hayes 1982: 129).

It is important to monitor expenditures for S & E, in order to generate a regular budget report for library management (Smith 1983: 105). Based on the report it may be necessary to adjust specific budgeted amounts, especially as the end of the fiscal year approaches, since it may be much easier to change these amounts than those in the areas of personnel or library materials.

## BUDGETARY TOPICS AND ISSUES

There are a number of additional issues that require some attention when discussing academic library budgeting practices. They include political factors, staff involvement, budget cutting, and library charges.

### Political Factors

A budget is a political document and budgeting is basically a political process (Prentice 1983: 27–28; Evans 1983: 270; Koenig 1980: 53; Chen 1980: 5). In this sense the political process can be viewed as the competition for and allocation of financial resources. If politics is the process that determines "who gets what," with the outcome of that competition for resources reflected in the budget (Wildavsky 1979: 4), it follows that the library director is required to be "politically aware," a leader who must educate the campus regarding the library and its services (Johnson 1982: 35; Lynch 1977: 92–93). The politically aware librarian must have the following skills (Lynden 1982: 115–16): effective communication (to sell the library's budget to the campus administration clearly and briefly), credibility (to be able to convince campus administrators of the worth of the library's budget request), and the ability to rouse broad faculty support (to ensure that the request will not be taken lightly).

The political standing of the library director can be enhanced by demonstrating that as a librarian he or she is also a problem solver, a planner, and a manager. Library management should cultivate good relations with other campus financial and budget officers (Koenig 1980: 53–55; White 1984: 172).

### Staff Involvement

As important as external contacts are to "budgetary success," it is equally important for the director to keep staff involved in all stages of the budget process, to generate understanding and support of budget decisions (Martin 1978: 142; White 1984: 172; Prentice 1983: 56–57). Information sharing and staff participation will create an environment in which budget decisions are seen as

valid and fair, not arbitrary or capricious. A staff that has taken part in determining goals and has had the opportunity to participate in the budgetary process
will be in a much better position to represent the library's services and philosophy
to the campus community (Martin 1978: 22).

## Budget Cutting

At some time each library director faces the unpleasant task of cutting the
budget in response to unexpected cutbacks by the library's parent institution or
state funding agency. A percentage cutback can always be handled by reducing
the budgeted amount for each program by that amount. However, the strategy
of across-the-board cuts does not take into account the goals of the library or
priority among library programs. It is desirable first to assess the library's overall
goals before implementing any major budget cuts. Before cuts are made, there
should be an analysis of what reductions would have the least impact on services.
On the other hand, a director may wish to try the risky course of cutting a highly
visible service (such as library hours) in the hope of overturning the cutback
(Martin 1978: 139–40; Prentice 1983: 39; Webster 1977: 76–78).

If significant cuts are required, the personnel and library materials budgets
must be reduced, since the size of the S & E budget is too small to yield much
money (Hayes 1982: 126). With less money available, the challenge is to continue
to provide satisfactory service. A no-growth or austerity budget environment
can present opportunities for prioritizing library operations and determining
where economics can be realized (Yavarkovsky 1977: 61).

Cutting the budget will have an impact on how the library provides services.
If funds for part-time or student employees are cut, the library's service hours
are bound to be reduced. A reduction in career employees is often accomplished
by attrition and savings generated by the freezing of vacated positions (Prentice
1978: 20). But with such a reduction, those staff members will have more to do
and obviously no additional time to do it. Given this situation, backlogs are
bound to develop, and the response time in meeting library service demands will
surely slow down.

As the second largest budget category, library materials funds may also have
to be cut. Whether or not the faculty is extensively involved in developing the
library's collections, it is important to consult with academic departments regarding acquisitions cutbacks in their disciplines. It is difficult enough dealing
with the cuts themselves, without having to handle complaints from faculty
members that they were not sufficiently involved or informed of the cutbacks.

## Library Charges

A library facing a tight budget may reach the difficult decision that charging
for certain services may mean the difference between continuing or cancelling
them. Examples of library charges include recovering the cost of providing data-

base searching and covering the cost of providing interlibrary loan services (Martin 1978: 89–90; Prentice 1983: 162–64; Bommer 1977: 53–54). The income generated needs to be properly accounted for. It may be necessary to create separate income fund accounts (depending on local circumstances) to keep track of money received. Library income from such charges should not be commingled with other library funds, since at the close of the fiscal year (or perhaps even during the year, if an audit is performed) the library will be requested to account for the income received.

## CONCLUSION

The budget process must be viewed as a continuous and year-long activity, which includes developing goals and objectives, gathering information and planning, preparing and presenting the budget, monitoring the budget, and closing out the budget at the end of the fiscal year. It sets the context for developing and providing library services that support the programs of the college or university.

## REFERENCES

Allen, Kenneth S. 1972. *Current and Emerging Budgeting Techniques in Academic Libraries, including a Critique of the Model Budget Analysis Program of the State of Washington*. Seattle: University of Washington.

Association of College and Research Libraries. 1986. "Standards for College Libraries, 1986." *College and Research Libraries News* 47 (March): 189–200.

Bommer, Michael. 1977. "Decision Models, Performance Measures, and the Budgeting Process." In *Library Budgeting: Critical Challenges for the Future*. Edited by Sul H. Lee, pp. 51–60. Ann Arbor, Mich.: Pierian Press.

Chen, Ching-chih. 1980. *Zero-Base Budgeting in Library Management: A Manual for Librarians*. Phoenix: Oryx Press.

Evans, G. Edward. 1983. *Management Techniques for Librarians*. New York: Academic Press.

Hatry, Harry, et al. 1976. *Program Analysis for State and Local Governments*. Washington, D.C.: Urban Institute.

Hayes, Sherman. 1982. "Budgeting for and Controlling the Cost of the Other in Library Expenditures: The Distant Relative in the Budgetary Process." *Journal of Library Administration* 3 (Fall-Winter): 121–31.

Johnson, Edward R. 1982. "Financial Planning Needs of Publicly Supported Academic Libraries in the 1980's: Politics as Usual." *Journal of Library Administration* 3 (Fall-Winter): 23–36.

Koenig, Michael E. D., 1980. *Budgeting Techniques for Libraries and Information Centers*. New York: Special Libraries Association.

Koenig, Michael E. D., and Deidre C. Stam. 1985. "Budgeting and Financial Planning for Libraries." In *Advances in Library Administration and Organization*. Vol. 4. Edited by Gerard B. McCabe and Bernard Kreissman, pp. 77–110. Greenwich, Conn.: JAI Press.

Lynch, Beverly P. 1977. "The Impact of No-Growth Budgets upon Academic Libraries." In *Library Budgeting: Critical Challenges for the Future*. Edited by Sul H. Lee, pp. 89–96. Ann Arbor, Mich.: Pierian Press.

Lynden, Frederick C. 1982. "Financial Planning for Collection Management." *Journal of Library Administration* 3 (Fall-Winter): 109–20.

Martin, Murray S. 1978. *Budgetary Control in Academic Libraries*. Greenwich, Conn.: JAI Press.

———. 1982. "Budgeting—the Practical Way," *Canadian Library Journal* 39 (October): 299–302.

National Center for Education Statistics. 1983. *Digest of Education Statistics, 1983–84*, by W. Vance Grant and Thomas D. Snyder. Washington, D.C.: Department of Education.

Prentice, Ann E. 1978. *Strategies for Survival: Library Financial Management Today*. New York: R. R. Bowker.

———. 1983. *Financial Planning for Libraries*. Metuchen, N.J.: Scarecrow Press.

Pyhrr, Peter. 1970. "Zero-Base Budgeting," *Harvard Business Review* 48 (November-December): 111–21.

Schultze, Charles L. 1968. *The Politics and Economics of Public Spending*. Washington, D.C.: Brookings Institute.

Smith, G. Stevenson. 1983. *Accounting for Librarians; and Other Not-for-Profit Managers*. Chicago: American Library Association.

Summers, William. 1974. "A Change in Budgetary Thinking." In *Budgeting for Accountability in Libraries: A Selection of Readings*. Edited by Gerald R. Shields and J. Gordon Burke, pp. 11–33. Metuchen, N.J.: Scarecrow Press.

U.S. Office of Management and Budget. 1977. "Zero-Base Budgeting," *Federal Register* 42 (May 2): 22342–54.

Webster, Duane E. 1977. "Choices Facing Academic Libraries in Allocating Scarce Resources." In *Library Budgeting: Critical Challenges for the Future*. Edited by Sul H. Lee, pp. 75–87. Ann Arbor, Mich.: Pierian Press.

White, Robert L. 1984. "A Library Budget Process: Incorporating Austerity Management." *Journal of Educational Media and Library Sciences* 21 (Winter): 169–79.

Wildavsky, Aaron. 1979. *The Politics of the Budgetary Process*. Boston: Little, Brown.

Yavarkovsky, Jerome. 1977. "The No-Growth Budget: Bitter Pill of Opportunity." In *Library Budgeting: Critical Challenges for the Future*. Edited by Sul H. Lee, pp. 61–74. Ann Arbor, Mich.: Pierian Press.

Young, Harold Chester. 1976. *Planning, Programming, Budgeting Systems in Academic Libraries*. Detroit: Gale Research Co.

# PART IV

# Collection

# 13

# Bibliographic Control of Library Collections

## *Eugene R. Hanson*

Bibliographic control of a library collection is a planned and organized activity that systematically identifies, lists, and provides access to its available resources. Essentially, this consists of the preparation of bibliographic citations or entries that serve as surrogates for the items, the selection of appropriate access points, and the listing of these things in a medium such as a catalog. Although the college-library catalog is frequently perceived as *the* bibliographic control device, it has become primarily a means of controlling monographs and selected serials and nonbook items. In addition to the library catalog, bibliographic control is supplemented in varying degrees by other tools such as indexes, abstracts, bibliographies, union catalogs and lists, and on-line data bases.

Bibliographic methods differ, depending upon the purpose of the listing, the potential users, and the experience and expertise of the compiler. Bibliographic description in library catalogs or descriptive cataloging has evolved over a long period and is structured to provide the information that describes the items in terms of their attributes, which usually is reduced ''to what they are 'about' and whom they are by'' (Buckland 1983: 10). Bibliographic control is dependent upon some means of identifying and listing access points including identifiers such as author(s), joint author(s), editor(s), illustrator(s), and title(s), as well as terms or subject headings depicting the content.

Usually, the bibliographic citation contains elements such as main entry; title (available or supplied): person(s) or bodies responsible; bibliographic history; publishing, producing, printing, and distributing information; physical description; and other identifying features that distinguish one from another. The extent and level of inclusion of information varies from one library to another depending upon a number of factors.

Subject access is not a mandatory component of bibliographic control; however, it is an important means for controlling materials when a display of items on a particular topic is sought.

In approaching bibliographic control of the library collection, continuous planning should focus on a number of questions. First, why is it necessary to control items contained in the collection? The answer to this question is found in the objectives of the parent institution since the library collection supports curricular needs and independent learning. As collections grow, the problems involved in identifying, describing, and locating materials become progressively complex. One of the major differences between a university and a college library is the size and contents of the collections. Small-college libraries will have primarily domestic titles that include recognized retrospective and current descriptive, interpretive, and theoretical titles in each curricular field.

Second, what materials should be controlled? They should include all of those collected that will support the stated objectives, regardless of format. Because of their age and less dependence upon tradition, the community colleges have been particularly successful in deemphasizing the format or packaging. Nancy Olson found that 577 of 599 respondents had audiovisual materials either as part of the library or as a separately administered or physically located collection. Forty-one percent reported collections of 1,000–5,000 audiovisual titles, and the percentage of libraries having each type were: sound recording 96 percent, slides 87 percent, filmstrips 86 percent, kits 76 percent, motion pictures 68 percent, video recordings 66 percent, transparencies 59 percent, pictorial works 52 percent, educational games 50 percent, and others 28 percent (1985: 281–82). A 1985 survey of community college learning-resources centers in Illinois found all but one distributed audiovisual equipment, and many were involved in production services, on-line data-base searching, and other instructional based services (Dubin and Bigelow 1986: 599–600). Frequently, the newer media as well as some of the more difficult-to-control items such as government documents, pamphlets, archives, research papers, college catalogs, telephone directories, and annual reports have not been adequately controlled. Every effort should be made to include them in the process.

Third, how should the material be controlled? Libraries have relied most heavily upon some form of catalog including card, sheaf, book, microform, and machine readable. No matter what the form of the catalog is, it has remained essentially the same for the past 100 years. Whoever prepares the catalog determines the degree of identification, description, and listing according to some predetermined set of rules that has been widely discussed and codified during the twentieth century. The composition of the catalog may vary from a simple finding list—which permits a patron to locate a work under the author as named in the work, a title, or a subject—to a complex device designed to assemble related or variant versions, editions, or formats; all items by a single author or others responsible for their creation; and all items dealing with the same subject. Librarians soon recognized that it was costly and repetitive to index periodicals and other less traditional materials in the catalog and promoted first cooperative and later commercial and organizational support for their control. These materials have steadily increased in number, coverage, and variety of formats. Government documents are difficult to control, but the increasing number and the continued improvement of indexes produced by government and commercial efforts have greatly alleviated the situation. Other examples are the development of a wide range of indexes to collections of plays, poetry, short stories, essays, and general literature.

Bibliographic control of the collection in small-college libraries is largely dependent upon a number of existing situations or conditions. The most important factor is undoubtedly financial support since the lack of it can have a devastating impact upon every facet of the process. Surveys by Raymond Carpenter (1981a: 14; 1981b: 412,) and Eileen Dubin and Linda Bigelow (1986: 598) indicate that the small libraries are not receiving the recommended percentage of the overall operating budget suggested by the standards. There are in many cases lacking sufficient funds for materials, personnel, equipment, and the purchase of catalog copy and on-line cataloging services. The most obvious solution is to seek additional funds from normal campus sources. If this is unsuccessful, consider establishing a Friends of the Library group and seek outside grants from government, corporations, and foundations. Many libraries have been successful in developing their automated services or phases of it such as retrospective conversion and equipment purchases as the result of external funding. On-line cataloging services for the fourteen state-supported universities in Pennsylvania began when a Library Services and Construction Act (LSCA) grant provided terminals for each. Another possibility is to support local or regional consortia that promote continuing education, interlibrary loan, cooperative collection development, and the development of union catalogs and lists on a regional and local level that today use the latest compact read-only memory disk (CD-ROM) and a microcomputer with appropriate disk drive. Parent institutions will closely monitor all efforts at fund raising to provide the appropriate office with a number of carefully prepared proposals describing the specific needs of the bibliographic control program.

A second condition is the limited size of the collections in small academic libraries when compared to those in universities. A survey by Raymond Carpenter (1981a: 9–10) indicates that the majority of undergraduate libraries have collections of less than 100,000 and have added less than 5,000 volumes annually, and one-half receive less than 750 periodical subscriptions. Both Carpenter (1981b: 411–14) and Dubin and Bigelow (1986: 599) reported that the majority of the two-year colleges had collections ranging from less than 20,000 to less than 50,000, and a substantial portion received fewer than 300 periodical titles. To estimate the size of a typical small academic library would be difficult in view of the many variables involved. Collection size in itself may not be a key factor because many librarians believe that a working collection of 150,000 may be adequate for most undergraduate programs. No library can possess all of the titles that may be requested, but they should have the resources to locate and to borrow them.

Third, human resources play a key role in the extent and quality of bibliographic control. If materials are to be properly described, analyzed, and listed, adequate professional and paraprofessional personnel must be provided. In the small library, cataloging will probably be done by a part-time librarian who may be involved in other technical services or in the public services. Libraries adding from 3,500 to 5,000 annually will have a full-time cataloger who spends limited time in another area. Carpenter found that "over 40% of the [college] libraries have one staff member for the selection, processing and dissemination of as many as 1,000–2,000 volumes per year," and there was direct correlation between the number of volumes and the amount of personnel (1981b: 13). Forty-three percent of the small two-year colleges had less than one support staff (1981b: 409–10).

These small inadequately staffed departments are in stark contrast to those in large universities, where many librarians and support staff are organized by function, format, language, or subject; where automation is commonplace; and where quantity and complexity of materials reflect research needs. Limited human resources are difficult to compensate for because of negative impact on the final bibliographic products. If campus resources are lacking, several alternatives are possible: implementing labor-saving devices and more simplified methods, reassigning available personnel, and seeking an outside source of workers. Identify and implement simplified procedures and labor-saving devices wherever possible. Although considerable information exists in the literature, these small departments depend heavily upon an objective view of the total process and willingness to consider alternatives and to accept change as a normal solution. Begin by carefully analyzing all of the steps and processes involved. Identify specific reasons or objectives for each and modify or eliminate when possible. Use printed catalog copy, cards or kits, electric erasers, gummed labels, photocopying, duplicators, special typewriters with memories, gluing machines, and micro-computers; several excellent programs are available for producing cards by computer. Consider the reassignment of available personnel. Carefully analyze each of the activities involved, prepare job descriptions, and objectively reassign tasks according to the application of "professional judgment" or simply routines. The support staff is assuming an increasing role in the location and preliminary checking of cataloging copy in printed and machine-readable formats. Use student workers to handle tasks whenever continuity is not as important, using the support staff to revise their work. Try to improve the quality of student work by making the case that academic departments should not get the best qualified or most experienced.

Fourth, physical facilities do influence bibliographic control since cramped, crowded conditions slow down cataloging and processing, hamper the purchase and use of equipment, and frustrate personnel. Once processed, materials must be readily accessible. Study the existing situation and make recommendations for larger quarters, or rearrange furniture and equipment to achieve maximum usage.

## DESCRIPTIVE BIBLIOGRAPHIC CONTROL

Libraries rely heavily upon available cataloging copy in printed, microform, or machine-readable formats. Small libraries find printed catalog cards or bibliographies furnishing copies of catalog cards most economical. The size of the library influences the type of cataloging services used because of available funds and personnel and the number of titles to be cataloged. Because items acquired by small libraries will probably be in-print domestic titles, the full processing services, cards or sets of catalog cards, book cards, and pockets may be readily acquired from book wholesalers. Although not as widely available, a similar approach may be used for audiovisual materials. The Library of Congress, the oldest and largest producer of catalog cards, and other services use a machine-readable data base to produce the cards. Also Cataloging in Publication (CIP), a brief cataloging entry printed in current titles published by many trade and university press publishers, is especially useful in small libraries for quick copy that can be readily duplicated with typewriter or microcomputer and printer. Many bibliographies contain copies of printed catalog entries. The most widely known are issued by the Library of Congress (*National Union Catalog*) and contain comprehensive coverage that may be beyond the needs, budget, and storage capabilities of many small libraries. The *American Book Publishing Record* with its monthly Dewey listing of current titles distributed in the United States is limited but much more economical. It is supplemented by the *Weekly Record*, an alphabetical listing of very recent titles with full cataloging information. Many of the collection-development aids such as *Booklist* broaden the spectrum of cataloging information. Other less selective bibliographies such as the *Monthly Catalog* provide catalog copy for federal documents. Special volumes of the *National Union Catalog* dealing with audiovisual materials including motion pictures, filmstrips, transparencies and slides, video recordings, cartographic materials, and sound recordings have long served as sources of copy for a particularly difficult area of cataloging. The use of cataloging copy may slow the process, since the cataloger must await its publication or if using on-line cataloging may wait for someone else to catalog it. As a last resort, original cataloging may have to be done if all else fails or if speed is essential. Try to avoid duplicate effort and devote additional time to the subject analysis when possible.

Many small-college libraries follow the lead of the universities and have contracted for services from bibliographic utilities such as the Online Computer Library Center (OCLC) and University of Toronto Library Association System (UTLAS), which provide cataloging support including printed catalog cards. There is a direct correlation between the size of the library collection and the use of the OCLC services. A survey of community college learning-resource centers in Illinois found that fewer than 50.0 percent subscribed to the OCLC (Dubin and Bigelow 1986: 600). Another of the four-year colleges found that 64.5 percent used the OCLC; of them 50.0 percent had collections of 60,000 to 79,000, and 87.0 percent had more than 175,000 (Reynolds 1981: 15). Of those using the OCLC, Barbara Moore found that 41.6 percent cataloged fewer than 5,000 titles annually, 63.8 percent had only one terminal, and although all but two used the OCLC to produce cards, 44.8 percent used other production methods (1981: 31–32). Olson found that in addition to using the OCLC-produced cards,

29.0 percent used Library of Congress cards, 9.0 percent purchased from jobbers or independent suppliers, and 62.0 percent used totally or in part locally produced cards (1985: 283). Small libraries must carefully weigh the cost of on-line cataloging with traditional methods. Mary Dagold succinctly compared the advantages and disadvantages of the OCLC cataloging as well as its cost and concluded that libraries adding 3,500 titles annually, which is the number added by more than 50.0 percent of the colleges and universities and most others, would be far wiser and more economical in using printed catalog cards (1983:139–40). Although Dagold strongly believed that funds should not be channeled away from material resources for on-line cataloging, the benefits of access to an extensive on-line union catalog for interlibrary loan and the building of a strong standardized machine-readable data base for the future should not be overlooked.

After printed catalog cards or copy is located, the process of revising it should be done in terms of individual library needs as expressed in policy statements and procedure manuals that strongly influence "the degree of efficiency and the professionalism . . . practiced in the cataloging unit (Burlingame, Fields, and Schulzetenberg 1978: 126). In small libraries, catalogers have greater flexibility in conforming to local needs and are more closely associated with the total bibliographic process than are those in university libraries (Bishop 1981: 169). When inputting to a union catalog, however, all should adhere to the required standards. Most libraries use Anglo-American Cataloging Rules (AACR) II cataloging rules for descriptive cataloging, although in 1981 only 35 percent of the 577 responding libraries used them for audiovisual materials (Olson 1985: 283). Changes in descriptive cataloging on printed cards or cataloging copy should be kept to a minimum in small libraries and every effort made to eliminate nonessential steps. Headings for new personal and corporate bodies should be established in a form recommended by the AACR II if time and personnel permit. Use "see" and "see also" references and information cards to guide users to variant forms. Keep in mind the large amount of time that may be put into the "normalization" of names in order to relate authors, titles, and variant editions so that they can be displayed together. Several studies seriously question the need for extensive bibliographic descriptions. One found that author, title, edition, year of publication, and call-number listings appear to satisfy the needs of most users of a divided computer-output microfilm (COM) (De Bruin 1977: 262). Another suggested:

Much of the information normally included in the catalogue entry is very rarely used by readers, and its inclusion makes catalogues difficult to use with results that some may not be found. If such data were excluded, users would be helped and it would provide an opportunity to consider providing other, more valuable information, particularly subject annotation and access. (Seals 1983: 144)

Recent interviews with users of on-line catalogs indicate that the bibliographic record should be enriched by: "Annotations, summaries, or abstracts of books;

Titles of essays in volumes of collected works or festschriften; Individual musical pieces on sound recordings; Introductions of books; Book jackets materials; Evaluative information, such as book reviews, intended audience(s); Assignment of more subject headings to books'' (Markey 1985: 41).

The inclusion of annotations or summaries is particularly important for audiovisual materials, and abstracts have long been a part of many indexing services. A cooperative effort is needed to eliminate duplication in expanding the patron's knowledge of widely used titles. In addition, a number of minor suggestions that may prove useful in the small-college library should be considered. Tracings for added access points and subject headings should be included on all cards produced for the catalog since they provide further hints for the user about the content of the work. Contents notes should be made for all important collections of literary works and for audiovisual materials consisting of many parts. Analytics, author-title, or title should be made for important works that are not indexed in one of the commercially produced indexes. All indexes, abstracts, and bibliographies should be carefully described in terms of bibliographic attributes and content because of their potential usage by patrons. Use abundant guide cards in the catalog so that desirable access points are easily located. Information and reference cards should be copiously provided to aid in using the catalog and guiding them to related information sources not accorded full bibliographic coverage in the catalog. Reserve the first two drawers of the card catalog for "new books" where catalog cards may be prefiled so that patrons have access to them while awaiting final filing.

The ultimate decision of what level of descriptive cataloging should be used for small-library catalogs must be made in terms of local bibliographic needs and the restraints of personnel, time, and finances. The ready acceptance of Library of Congress cataloging as a standard of high quality by most libraries is logical, but blind adherence to it in every detail is unnecessary and not economical. Frequently, our acceptance of Library of Congress copy becomes more a matter of expediency since it is available and most frequently accepted for the printed catalog cards or copy. The biggest problem with Library of Congress copy for small libraries is not with the descriptive cataloging portion but rather the subject analysis.

## SUBJECT ANALYSIS AND CONTROL

Our discussion now shifts from that part of bibliographic control that is oriented toward the descriptive to one that emphasizes the intellectual content. In the small-college library this component plays a key role since undergraduate students rely heavily upon the subject approach in catalogs, indexes, abstracts, and bibliographies beccause they are unfamiliar with the literature of the field. Karen Markey reported that subject access to the MELVYL on-line catalog appears to be in greater proportion to any other type of research (1985: 37). Although progress has been made in the subject control of materials, many of the early problems persist in our classification schemes and subject-heading lists. The ability to verbalize a particular subject is essential since alphabetical listings provide subject-heading lists and indexes for classification schemes. Early use of random subject words from the title was replaced by standardized lists developed by Sears and the Library of Congress. Although still popular in small-college libraries, *Sears List of Subject Headings* is losing ground to the more comprehensive *Library of Congress Subject Headings*, which is more widely used on printed cataloging copy. Olson (1985: 283) found that 78.0 percent of the libraries, and Edward O'Neill and Rao Aluri (1979: 5) found that 93.7 percent of the records surveyed used Library of Congress subject headings.

Although classification was first used for catalog arrangement, college libraries now use it for subject shelving. The Dewey Decimal Classification scheme is used in approximately 40.0 percent of the college libraries according to surveys cited by Olson (1985: 283) and Helen Tuttle (1976: 439). The problem with classification is its unidimensional capability since an item can be only in one place on the shelf as opposed to the multidimensional ability of subject headings in the catalog. An early study of the effectiveness of library classification found that it identified only a small number of the titles on a single subject (Kelley 1937: 200). The possibility of again using classification in the on-line catalog should be beneficial to users. The present shelf list does provide some subject control since it is basically a unidimensional classified catalog with two indexes, the subject-heading list, and the index to the classification scheme. Students frequently browse shelves, where they can actually examine titles if they are there; however, the shelf list gives an overall picture of the key works available and enables users to become familiar with the literature of subject areas and the pattern of subject headings and call numbers. Another practical use is to produce subject lists by shingling the cards and copying them on a photocopier. One author makes the extreme suggestion that the shelf list be eliminated in an effort to save time and money (Pickering 1974: 11).

Doralyn Hickey pointed out that "the anxieties and confusions associated with subject analysis in the United States stems from the fact that American libraries have no clear philosophy of subject control" (1976: 288). In spite of over a century of experience and study, little has been done to lessen the complexities and improve the use of the subject catalog.

One of the problems is an inability to identify the typical user. Each library should study the question of subject analysis and access in developing policies and procedures. The process is somewhat easier in a small-college library, where subject control directly supports curricular needs of a fairly homogeneous group of students.

Appropriate terminology is a key problem demanding consideration of many variables. The determination of subject headings that are meaningful to patrons for all periods or circumstances is highly unlikely. The problems of selecting the "best" subject heading(s) and an optimum number constantly frustrates catalogers. Every effort should be made to use terms known to the "typical" college-library catalog user. As new terms evolve and old ones become obsolete, make provisions for keeping current. The best solution is to change the old to the new form, but this is too time consuming. A compromise is to change if only a few are present (e.g., six) and to use "see also" references or explanatory notes pointing out the change in usage. Use gummed labels for making corrections. An overreliance upon Library of Congress copy may result in poor subject analysis since one typically tries to select one subject heading to convey the overall content of each work. Edward O'Neill and Rao Aluri found that the average number per OCLC record was 1.41 and that 85 percent used either one or two (1979: 7, 18). The difficulty in applying the principle of the most specific heading is apparent as "how specific is specific?" The situation can be alleviated somewhat by adding scope notes to the catalog, similar to those found in the subject lists or thesauri, and by systematically including "see" and "see also" references to direct users from terms not used to those that are used and from general to more specific or related terms. Student orientation to the catalog should pay particular attention to the subject listing of materials. There are a number of other possible approaches to improving subject control, although they will not be equally effective in all situations.

The development and use of subject lists or thesauri based upon carefully formulated principles, to ensure maximum uniformity, consistency, and logic, are essential. Study the methods used by the indexes for periodicals, documents, and so on to determine if a similar approach might be useful in the catalog. Know which indexes would be most beneficial to your library and make every effort to purchase them since much of the economy in cataloging depends upon the degree to which indexes and catalogs supplement each other. Do not duplicate indexing efforts. Consider increasing the number of subject headings for works that will be of particular value in supporting the curriculum. Use subject analytics to bring out special sections or chapters that may be unknown in spite of the "see" or "see also" references. The cost of the extra cards and their filing is negligible in view of the need to obtain optimum usage for the limited number of available titles. Become aware of the potential of automation for improving subject access by increasing the number and type of subject headings, abstracts, descriptive annotations, and other possible access points. Study the use of the newer indexing such as the Preserved Context Index System (PRECIS), which permits a separate entry for each significant term and supports the addition of many subject terms without the economic burden encountered in the card catalog.

Large subject files become a problem because of the many cards representing works on the same subject. One solution is the use of inverse chronological filing with subject cards interfiled by publication date rather than main entry so that patrons will have first contact with the latest material on the subject. This approach was used by John Crerar Library in Chicago for more than 100 years. Recently, Trinity University rearranged the subject portion of a COM catalog and suggested that it could easily be done in any public on-line catalog (Werking, Miller, and Whaley 1986: 9). Undoubtedly, the time needed to complete such a change in a card catalog would be substantial, but so might the benefits be to users who are not familiar with authors or who simply refuse to go through every card. Chronological filing is not unknown to users who have searched the history subdivisions of the catalog or those approaching periodical and other indexes by years.

Don't try to totally redo the catalog, particularly the subject portion, since the potential for subject control is considerably brighter for the on-line catalog, which will become commonplace by the twenty-first century. Many of the major problems of the old catalog will be eliminated or alleviated because of patron access to many of the Machine Readable Cataloging (MARC) fields. Searching could be done by classification number(s); subject headings; keywords in titles, annotations, and abstracts; and qualifiers such as form or year level of difficulty.

Study the problems and solicit information from students and faculty; become familiar with the newest indexing techniques, subject lists, or thesaurus; read about and observe the public on-line catalogs now being used; consider funding approaches and cooperative ventures; and keep an open mind as you brace yourselves for the next century. In the meantime experiment with the current subject catalog as time permits.

## SOME FUTURE PROSPECTS

Bibliographic control is achieved through a standardized process that is influenced by many internal and external variables. Although combinations of catalogs, indexes, and other bibliographies have been applied, control of small collections has changed little in the past century. Automation presents an excellent medium for the storage and retrieval of citations, but the future is filled with uncertainty. A recent study of student attitudes toward proposed on-line catalogs in two college libraries found that more than one-half preferred the card catalog, which prompted the authors to admonish planners to consider all potential problems (Walton, Williamson, and White 1986: 392–97). Small-college libraries must begin planning and preparing for their role in national, regional, and local bibliographic networks as well as the development of on-line public catalogs. The use of the OCLC or other on-line cataloging service is logical if economically feasible. Sufficient human, financial, and physical resources should permit participation in contributing, using, and sharing bibliographic information. A standardized catalog data base using the MARC format, which ensures compatibility, should be developed. Careful authority control should ensure uniform access points such as terms, names, and subject headings. Networking at all levels should be supported as it continues to develop and is more closely interrelated through linkage systems. Cooperation between bibliographic-control interest groups should be further expanded to monitor vocabulary more closely, to avoid duplication, and to improve methods of indexing and dissemination. The CD-ROM will become a key medium for the distribution of information without the high communication costs.

If technology is to support bibliographic control, librarians must adopt systematic and scientific methods in their attempts to solve problems rather than depend upon tradition and intuition. Change must not be viewed as a threat to the status quo but rather should be considered a normal procedure for improvement.

# REFERENCES

Bishop, Marian. 1981. "The Challenge of Cataloging in the College Environment." In *College Librarianship*. Edited by William Miller and D. Stephen Rockwood, pp. 164–72. Metuchen, N.J.: Scarecrow Press.

Buckland, Michael. 1983. *Library Services in Theory and Context*. New York: Pergamon.

Burlingame, Dwight F., Dennis C. Fields, and Anthony C. Schulzetenberg. 1978. *The College Learning Resource Center*. Littleton, Colo.: Libraries Unlimited.

Carpenter, Ray L. 1981a. "College Libraries: A Comparative Analysis in Terms of the ACRL Standards." *College and Research Libraries* 42 (January): 7–18.

———. 1981b. "Two-Year College Libraries: A Comparative Analysis in Terms of the ACRL Standards." *College and Research Libraries* 42 (September): 407–15.

Dagold, Mary S. 1983. "The Last Frontier: Possibilities for Networking in the Small Academic Library." *Library Resources & Technical Services* 27 (April-June): 132–41.

DeBruin, Valentina. 1977. "Sometimes Dirty Things Are Seen on the Screen: A Mini-Evaluation of the COM Microcatalogue at the University of Toronto Library." *Journal of Academic Librarianship* 3 (November): 256–66.

Dubin, Eileen, and Linda Bigelow. 1986. "Community College Learning Resources Centers at the Crossroad: Illinois, A Case Study." *College and Research Libraries* 47 (November): 596–603.

Hickey, Doralyn J. 1976. "Subject Analysis: An Interpretive Survey." *Library Trends* 25 (July): 273–91.

Kelley, Grace. 1937. *Classification of Books: An Inquiry into Usefulness to the Reader*. New York: H. W. Wilson.

Markey, Karen. 1985. "Subject Searching Experiences and Needs of Online Catalog Users: Implications for Library Classification." *Library Resources & Technical Services* 29 (January-March): 34–51.

Moore, Barbara. 1981. "Patterns in the Use of OCLC by Academic Library Cataloging Departments." *Library Resources & Technical Services* 25 (January-March): 30–39.

Olson, Nancy B. 1985. "Survey of Audiovisual Materials Collections in Academic Libraries." In *Cataloging of Audiovisual Materials: A Manual Based on AACR 2*. 2d ed. Edited by Edward Swanson and Sheila Intner, pp. 281–84. Mankato, Minn.: Minnesota Scholarly Press.

O'Neill, Edward T., and Rao Aluri. 1979. *Research Report on Subject Heading Patterns in OCLC Monographic Records* (Report number OCLC/RDD/RR–7911). Columbus, Ohio: Online Computer Library Center, Research Department and Development Division.

Pickering, James H. 1974. "Why A Shelf List?" *The Unabashed Librarian*, no. 11 (Spring): 11.

Reynolds, Dennis. 1981. "A Survey of Libraries in American Four-Year Colleges." In *College Librarianship*. Edited by William Miller and D. Stephen Rockwood, pp. 7–29. Metuchen, N.J.: Scarecrow Press.

Seals, Alan. 1983. "Experiments with Full and Short Entry Catalogues: A Study of Library Needs." *Library Resources & Technical Services* 27 (April-June): 144–55.

Tuttle, Helen W. 1976. "From Cutter to Computer: Technical Services in Academic and Research Libraries, 1876–1976." *College and Research Libraries* 37 (September): 421–51.

Walton, Carol, Susan Williamson, and Howard D. White. 1986. "Resistance to Online Catalogs: A Comparative Study at Bryn Mawr and Swarthmore Colleges." *Library Resources & Technical Services* 30 (October-December): 388–401.

Werking, Richard, Ruby Miller, and Jay Whaley. 1986. "Rearranging the Subject Catalog at Trinity University." *College and Research Libraries News* 47 (January): 7–9.

# 14

# Archives Administration

## Susan Grigg

Archives pose a special problem for academic libraries. Virtually unknown before the Second World War and rare until the 1970s except in large or privileged institutions, they are in growing demand even in colleges that do not otherwise maintain research collections, although they are still lacking in some major universities. The purpose of this chapter is to help librarians in smaller academic libraries respond reasonably to these rising expectations. Because most librarians have no training in archives administration, it seems more useful to offer a prescriptive survey than to focus on current issues in well-established programs.

The classic function of an archives is to preserve selected records of a government or administration for the continuing use of its officers. This requires a statement of authority from the governing body, a survey of records in files and storage areas, an initial transfer of records of continuing value that are no longer in frequent use, schedules for the future disposition of current files, preservation measures, finding aids, and such good retrieval that offices will clearly benefit from their cooperation. Such a program may also serve independent inquirers, subject to restrictions in law or policy.

These archival responsibilities must be distinguished from the newer administrative service of records management. The purpose of records management is to improve the recording of information and the organization and use of the resulting records so that the information can be readily retrieved and the records can be discarded when they no longer have administrative value. Archives benefit from the better recording of information, but the destruction of records once they have outlived their administrative usefulness may deprive future scholars of important material. Most facilitative or housekeeping records may eventually be discarded, but most substantive or program records should be retained. Archivists protect the historical or archival value of the latter by monitoring the scheduled destruction of managed records just as they incorporate scheduling into their own programs if the institution does not practice records management.

Administrative service is central to any archives, but it is rarely preponderant in college and university programs. This is because academic archives often trace their origins to special college-history collections and have since responded enthusiastically to the increasingly widespread demand for comprehensive information about academic life. In this view, the history of the college or university can be fully recovered only if all segments of the academic community are adequately represented, and this makes it necessary to collect materials produced by faculty members and students, individually and through their independent organizations, as well as those generated by administrative offices. Academic archives that accept this responsibility thus serve as special collections on the theme of institutional history as well as performing the classic records function.

Whether archivists are transferring records from offices or accepting gifts from private donors, they select material according to its expected contribution to the historical record. The classic formulation is that the historical value of records may be evidentiary or informational. Their evidentiary value is that they document the program or activity that produced them. Their informational value derives from the fact that they also contain information that may be useful for purposes other than analysis of that program or activity. For example, admissions-office files not only document the development and application of admissions criteria but also provide information about individual applicants. Evidentiary value can often be preserved by selecting a small portion of an office's files. Informational value is frequently so dispersed that the file must be sampled, weeded, or else saved or discarded as a whole.

Records are appraised in a larger context as well. Many files can be discarded with little or no loss of archival value because the information and sometimes the actual records are available elsewhere. This is more and more often the case as bureaucracies ask the same questions repeatedly, computers accumulate data and present it in different formats, and electrostatic copiers produce many copies of the same record. Hardly any archives saves more than 10 percent of its institution's records, and most archivists would be satisfied if their programs were supported at this level. On the other hand, archivists must keep watch for subjects that are not adequately documented in any institutional record. Some of these gaps can be filled by acquiring material from private donors. Others make it necessary to create documentation by recording current events or conducting oral-history interviews.

Appraisal should be based on a comprehensive survey of the institution's records in offices, storage areas, and the archives itself. The surveyor locates the records, identifies the various filing sequences, and then evaluates them according to the criteria outlined above. The findings take the form of disposition schedules, which declare that some files or parts of files may be discarded after specified intervals, whereas others must be retained permanently. The recommendations are expressed in general terms so that they can be applied to the future growth of the same files as well as the records already present. The analysis must also generate ideas for improving the record-keeping system, but such suggestions should not be mistaken for a full records-management program.

Records should remain in the custody of the office of origin, whether they are kept there or in a separate storage area, until it is time to discard those that are scheduled for destruction. Then the permanent records should be transferred to the archives unless their administrative use remains high. If the office of origin is short of storage space, it is more likely to implement the disposition schedule in a timely way; otherwise, the archivist may need to take the initiative.

Besides acquiring office files and other unpublished records, the archives should function as the library of record for the institution's publications. It is common to retain two copies of every title for security purposes. Backfiles can be assembled through the initial records survey and through donations by professors and alumni. Thereafter offices should be required to furnish their publications automatically by placing the archives on their distribution lists.

Documentation of the faculty is more problematic. The administrative records of most institutions yield only a fragmentary record of professors' activities since teachers, scholars, community leaders, and even the most prominent research institutions are inconsistent in their efforts to compensate for this. A few institutions ask all long-time faculty members for their papers, including things such as syllabuses, lecture notes, professional correspondence, and personal letters and diaries. Others solicit them only from outstanding scholars or wait for them to be offered. Still others do not accept faculty papers at all. Archives that take only a limited interest in faculty papers may be motivated by budgetary constraints or doubts about their research value in relation to their bulk. Some archivists fear that faculty members will be offended if their papers are appraised objectively.

An ambitious collecting program might begin with solicitation of every faculty member at the time of retirement. This also provides an opportunity to request the return of any administrative files that belong to the institution but have remained among the professor's personal papers. Faculty members whose careers are of special interest might receive repeated solicitations if necessary. These efforts are sometimes complicated by competition from other institutions for the papers of outstanding scholars, although more and more, archivists believe that subject-based and geographically defined repositories should not solicit papers of persons who are primarily faculty members of institutions that have their own archives. It is generally irresponsible to fragment the record of a professor's life by encouraging the distribution of papers among several repositories, even if this means retaining papers unrelated to one's own institutional history.

Collecting faculty publications is a separate question. Some professors consider this to be a more basic archival function than the preservation of their papers, but many archivists believe that it should be left to the library except when the publication might be used in conjunction with related papers such as notes or drafts. A middle ground is to take reprints whenever they are offered but accept books only when they support use of the faculty member's papers or are outside the scope of most current library collections. Whatever the policy, it should be coordinated with that of the library.

Faculty members participate in academic life through independent organizations as well as individually and through institutional channels. Any archives that collects faculty papers will thereby acquire many of the files of these organizations, but a separate collecting program is necessary if the records are to be reasonably complete and up to date. When the organization is concerned with tenure or other conditions of employment, it may be difficult to convince its officers that the archivist who is responsible for the institution's own records is also a trustworthy curator for the organization's adversarial files, but there does not seem to be any ethical obstacle to this dual role if the institution is willing to respect it.

The activities of students, like those of professors, can be documented thoroughly only by gifts of materials to which the institution has no legal claim. These materials might include records and publications of student organizations, audiovisual recordings of student activities, and personal papers and reminiscences of individual students. A sampling of such materials can be acquired simply by accepting them selectively when they are offered by students or alumni. It may be very time consuming to solicit them systematically from such a large and transient population, and there is the recurring nightmare of being offered a thousand sets of notes from Art 101, but some special effort is justified because records of student activities hold the loyalty of alumni and provide excellent opportunities for undergraduate research.

It is important to distinguish between papers made by students and papers made by alumni after graduation. Some archives occasionally acquire the papers of an outstanding graduate in the interest of public relations, but this is a doubtful practice from a professional viewpoint. The papers are not likely to be of great value to the institution's own faculty and students if there are no other collections in the same field, and outside scholars will be inconvenienced for the same reason. If an institution wants to collect personal papers, it should establish a separate program with an appropriate theme (such as local history, a professional field in which the institution is outstanding, or a population of special relevance such as Hispanics or women). Such a program may share staff and facilities with the institutional archives as long as the additional costs are acknowledged in budgeting, but it should have a separate identity. It may give special attention to qualifying alumni but should not exclude others.

Acquiring unpublished materials from independent sources has legal and financial implications. Transfer of ownership should be accomplished with a special form called a donor agreement or deed of gift. Some institutions design these forms to discourage or even prohibit any limitations on the donation, but others allow qualifications such as restrictions on use, withholding of copyright, and return of unwanted items to the donor. The creators and inheritors of the sorts of personal papers that are appropriate for institutional archives usually accept the convention that such materials should be donated rather than sold, and some archives make it a policy not to purchase such materials. Older institutions may have the opportunity to spend several hundred dollars a year on memorabilia offered by dealers, and occasionally, it may be necessary to choose between raising money for the papers of a prominent faculty member and losing them to a manuscript repository with a large endowment.

Office files are maintained in an order that reflects their origin rather than their contents. When a file or a selection of folders from it is transferred to the archives, neither the folders nor the items in them are reordered except to correct conspicuous filing errors. This is the principle of original order. The folders may be recombined with others taken from the same file at different times but should never be mixed with items from other sources. This is the principle of provenance. Materials that arrive with no recognizable order are grouped according to the activities that produced them.

All files arising from a particular administrative unit and most other records from the same source are considered to be part of a single record group, and each group is subdivided into series and subseries reflecting the subdivisions of the unit and its record-keeping system. Folder lists or other segmented descriptions from the various transfers of records are combined in inventories to represent the organization of the record group, and lists from later transfers are inserted as they are produced. The inventory for each record group includes an administrative history of the unit that produced the records and a brief description of their organization and contents. There may also be a guide to give researchers an overview of the record groups and other holdings of the archives.

Institutional publications fall outside the record-group system, but the record copies should be organized according to provenance and presented in the same order. If space permits, additional copies of the most frequently used titles may be kept in the reading area for the convenience of readers, browsers, and staff members. The library's bibliographers may want to select some institutional publications for the library's collections so that they will be handy for reference and available for circulation, but the risk of readers' depending on these few titles instead of discovering better sources in the archives is even greater than when government documents are cataloged as ordinary monographs and serials. It is out of the question to catalog all institutional publications individually because of the loss of provenance.

Miscellaneous items acquired independent of the regular transfer of files, and publications are often placed in a separate subject arrangement that may partially recapitulate the record-group system but lacks consistent provenance and order. It may include things such as clippings, letters, notebooks, and printed ephemera that have been donated by individuals, sent casually by college officers, or inherited from an older collecting program. Access is easiest if the items are arranged according to basic components of academic life such as graduating classes, academic departments, buildings, and recurring celebrations. The resulting organization is presented in a list that summarizes the contents of each folder but does not usually describe items individually. Some archives create a corresponding source of information about individuals by consolidating files from various offices that contain uniform data about some class of the community such as professors, students, or alumni. This is defensible as a concession to the fact that such materials are much more often consulted for information than for their evidentiary value, but the loss of the latter must be considered.

Audiovisual materials are also maintained separately in most cases, whether they come from institutional or independent sources. This is because they have special storage requirements and because they are so often used by subject without reference to related materials. Cross-references, annotations, and electrostatic copies (of photographs) can be used to preserve evidentiary links with other records from the same offices of origin. When photographs are available by the thousands, a subject arrangement like the one proposed for miscellaneous items is the obvious means of access, but it is often difficult to assign an item to a single subject category. The photograph files of the yearbook, newspaper, or public relations office may be kept in their original order or incorporated in a master file.

The papers of each faculty member should be treated as a separate manuscript group. There may be some usable order in the professional files, but the archivist must usually arrange most of the items to reflect the professor's diverse activities. The arrangement is presented in a finding aid called a register, which usually consists of a biographical sketch, a note on provenance, a note on scope and content or other descriptive essay, and a folder list. The registers for all collections of faculty papers may be brought together in a separate section of the finding aid system, but papers originally belonging to faculty members themselves should not be mixed with the institution's own records about the same individuals.

Independent faculty and student organizations may be offered the same scheduling service as the institution's own offices, but most are too small and informal to make this worthwhile. A more reliable procedure may be to acquire records annually from the outgoing officers. Each such accession may be arranged in the same order, or the components may be interfiled with earlier accessions according to physical type such as minutes or officers' reports. The inventories for the records of all of these independent organizations may be placed in a separate category of the finding-aid system.

The classic archives depends entirely on inventories for access to its holdings, but catalogs are common in both backward and advanced programs. Many archives keep any catalogs inherited from college history collections because they provide unparalleled subject access to early items that are too miscellaneous to fit into the record-group system. Others are introducing on-line cataloging as they take advantage of the new Machine-Readable Cataloging (MARC) format for archives and manuscripts, now available in the Online Computer Library Company (OCLC). Some archivists view this as an opportunity to increase efficiency by standardizing finding aids and automating internal control of records. Others see it as a chance to increase use by facilitating subject access and by publicizing holdings through the library's union catalog and even through access points outside the institution. There are also archives software packages for personal computers, but they are more useful for administration than for readers' use as finding aids.

Another means of improving subject access without obscuring provenance or original order is to index basic serials such as the student newspaper and the minutes of the governing body. The indexed passages are useful in themselves and also facilitate subject access to other sources by identifying and dating significant activities. Most archivists believe that the effort would be better expended on improving control of the much greater mass of unpublished records, but indexes begun by an earlier college history program may be of considerable value even if they are no longer kept up.

The most essential service function in any archives is to provide records and information to administrative offices. Each office should have copies of the inventories of its own records so that it can request folders by number, but the archivist must also be ready to use the inventories and the records themselves to find material by subject. When a record is called for, it should be taken to the office of origin rapidly and safely, and the archives should reclaim it after a reasonable time to prevent its loss. Good service is especially important if the goal is to assume control of new records within a few years of their creation. Administrative staff members should rarely need to come to the archives themselves except to select records of such sensitivity that the archives staff does not have item access to them, and such materials are more properly kept in an intermediate storage facility called a records center if there is no room in the office of origin.

Other potential users of the archives include professors, students, local residents, and visiting scholars. Their access is determined first by law. State and federal regulation of institutional records reflects an increasingly complicated interaction of the right to information and the right to privacy. The impact is greater on public than private institutions. Both institutional records and donated manuscripts require a broader understanding of copyright than is necessary for librarians who handle only published materials. It is also advisable to be familiar with the law of libel and able to recognize information that may expose the institution to civil liability.

In many cases access is also limited by the institution or by the donor of independently owned materials. Governing bodies and chief administrative officers sometimes restrict use of their own records for many decades or indefinitely, although usually with exceptions for individually authorized scholars. Such extreme limitations are at odds with the academic commitment to open inquiry, and archivists should argue against them when they are longer than necessary to protect personal privacy and recent policy deliberations. It is often appropriate to accept a temporary restriction on access to donated materials, especially if it is reasonably based on their actual sensitivity, and most archivists call such material to the attention of unwitting donors.

Because few individuals have the experience to anticipate the wide range of information available in a well-developed archives, the level of use may depend as much on outreach programs as on holdings and reference service. Students will become the largest class of users, outnumbering even the institution's own office staff, if they are given enough opportunity. Publicity efforts should begin by taking full advantage of the library's orientation and bibliographic instruction programs, but the archives can also make special appeals through exhibits (ideally in a central library location), proposals to professors for class assignments, leaflets offering general guidance and specific research suggestions, and articles in the student newspaper and alumni magazine. The faculty and students of the history department are the most obvious audience for such overtures, but at least as many potential users can be found in disciplines such as English, political science, and education. However, it is necessary to remember that users of archives are very dependent on individual staff assistance. Heavy demand in the formative years of a program may leave little time for acquiring additional materials and making them ready for use.

Public service hours are a special problem for archives not only because the stacks should be closed but also because most readers require at least initial assistance from a trained staff member. Few archives maintain a schedule much beyond forty weekday hours, and many find even that impossible. If many class assignments require use of the archives, limited evening or weekend hours are important even for full-time residential students. If staffing is insufficient to provide coverage during the many hours when the archivist must work on records at another location, the daytime closings should be regularly scheduled and coincide with the most popular teaching hours.

Preservation is as severe a problem for archives as for libraries. The most universal preservation method is to remove or replace fasteners and containers that are themselves deteriorating or causing the deterioration of the items they touch. Paperclips, rubberbands, ordinary staples, and most other fasteners in regular office use should be removed and then replaced as necessary with rust-proof staples. The folders used in original office filing and the cartons used in temporary storage should be replaced with acid-free boxes and folders.

The second most common method of preservation is to reproduce records in a more enduring medium. Copies of fragile or popular photographs, graphics, and audiovisual recordings should be substituted for the originals in casual use. Newspaper clippings, carbon copies on newsprint, and other visibly deteriorating paper should be copied onto paper of archival quality. Microforms are often mentioned as a more comprehensive solution to deteriorating paper, but it is easy to underestimate the costs. Photography for preservation must be done to national standards, and this usually requires both a costly contract with a discriminating commercial microfilmer and an archivist who is knowledgeable enough to see that the standards are observed. A nonprofit filming facility in a nearby research institution is an excellent but not widely available alternative. Buying a camera for operation by a library staff member is a doubtful economy because good equipment is expensive, because it takes considerable experience to photograph irregular archival materials with consistent clarity at a reasonable speed, and because especially careful processing of the film is essential to its long-term survival.

Other preservation measures may be applied on a smaller scale. Damaged or deteriorating items may be flattened, cleaned, deacidified, mended, or encapsulated if the archivist has been trained for these operations and appropriate equipment and supplies are available. Library and archival preservation programs may be combined if it is recognized that library methods are adequate for archival materials only if they confront the ultimate cause of deterioration. Exceptional documents such as charters or drawings may merit the attention of a professional conservator if they have the character of artifacts or art objects as well as providing information.

The best environment for archival materials is the same as the best environment for books. Ideally, there should be uninterrupted humidity and temperature control, isolation from possible sources of flooding, filtering of natural and fluorescent light, and fire protection through a Halon system and heat or smoke detectors linked to a constantly monitored alarm. If such facilities or the closest thing to them are available only on a limited scale, they should be reserved for vital records, photographs, and audiovisual materials. When a choice must be made from less satisfactory facilities, the stress should be on fire detection, limited and gradual temperature fluctuation, and isolation from flooding. It is tempting to place the archives in the remotest corner of the attic or basement because it attracts fewer users and requires little interaction with other library staff members, but such peripheral locations often have the worst environment.

Like any free-standing library, the archives requires space for storing collections, working on them, and making them available to readers. Separate areas for these functions should be partitioned off if possible because security is especially important for unique materials and because readers are especially entitled to quiet in a noncirculating collection. This is often impractical, however, because space is usually scarce and staff members must often provide security in the reading area while performing other functions. Readers should not be allowed in the stacks even if there is no physical obstruction, but duplicate copies of frequently used publications may be kept in the reading area to facilitate ready reference and browsing. Each full-time staff member should have at least two large tables with adjacent shelving to use without interruption for work on the collections. If it is occasionally necessary to spread out onto the tables used by readers, special care should be taken so that they do not feel they are less important than the preparatory work. Basic equipment should include a word processor for preparing inventories, shared time on an electrostatic copying machine with excellent quality of image, and preservation equipment appropriate to staff members' training.

Archives boxes are usually stored on steel shelving that is most distinctive for its proportions. The shelves should be wider than those used for books so that the boxes do not extend so far beyond them as to be unstable, and both shelves and supports should be spaced permanently to accommodate their folder-sized dimensions with minimum clearance. The units may reach as close to the ceiling as light fixtures and fire-control devices permit, so long as rolling stairs enable all staff members to handle boxes on the highest shelves. Maps, posters, and other oversized items are easier to retrieve from map cases than from folios. Pamphlets, photographs, publications, and other undersized items can sometimes be stored in spaces that are too shallow for archives boxes. It may be necessary to place especially sensitive materials in a locked cage if student workers are to have unsupervised access to the remaining shelving. Because the boxes need not be shelved in the inventory order, empty space may be consolidated in the least convenient locations with no need to reshelve older accessions as new materials are received. Materials may also be shelved in remote storage areas if they have adequate climate control and security and there is daily paging service. Regardless of the site, an engineer should confirm that the floor will support the extraordinary weight of fully utilized archival shelving.

The volume of holdings and hence the space required for storage depend more on the vigor of the previous two decades' collecting program than on any greater antiquity of the institution. This is because the most recent records are the most bulky and because most of them come into the archives only as the result of continuing effort by the archivist. An institution that has been enrolling several thousand students for several decades may have holdings extending several thousand linear feet and growing more than 100 feet a year, but the national average is 2,000 feet for all academic archives and 1,000 feet for smaller institutions. Microphotography is sometimes mentioned as a means of conserving space, but filming of archival quality is too expensive for any purpose but preservation, and it may be impolitic to discard the originals until they are absolutely unusable.

Adequate staffing begins with the selection of a well-qualified professional archivist, but there is no consensus on qualifications and no easy means of evaluating applicants' credentials. The Society of American Archivists (SAA) does not accredit archives training programs, and its educational guidelines are not easy to apply to any particular program. The SAA recently decided to establish a certification program for experienced practitioners, but there will be easy access to grandfathering before an examination is required.

Notwithstanding this continuing vagueness in professional self-definition, there is enough consistency in current practice to provide some guidelines for hiring. Regular graduate training in archives administration ranges from one to five or more courses, beginning with an introductory course and adding a practicum, a seminar or thesis, and specialized training in fields such as records management, cataloging, oral history, and preservation. These courses may be taken individually or as a special field within a master's program in history or library science, and completion of a specified group of courses may result in a certificate or diploma separate from an advanced degree. The academic archivist who has completed many specialized courses will find uses for most of the resulting capabilities, but employers may wish to remain flexible about the amount of graduate training required to ensure a good selection of otherwise promising applicants. Some of the most extensive and best publicized public history curricula have been developed only in the past few years, and their archives instructors and related degree programs are not necessarily as good as those in universities with older but more limited offerings. Libraries are more likely than historical societies or government archives to require the MLS degree, and many archivists protest that this requirement is based on administrative rather than professional needs.

Preparation below the level of regular course work is less satisfactory but still defensible in certain circumstances. Two-week institutes are a reasonable alternative for those who lack access to regular graduate programs or wish to develop some understanding of archives as an adjunct to a career in library science. Workshops lasting one or two days give exposure to basic skills and provide continuing education.

Finally, it must be acknowledged that many archivists continue to be accepted as professionals despite their lack of specific training. Half of all academic archivists employed in 1982 had neither a course nor an institute nor a workshop in archives administration, and this is also true of some current leaders of the profession. Training is more and more often required, but it is still possible to qualify for a professional position with only a graduate assistantship or other paraprofessional employment in addition to a master's degree.

Without paraprofessional assistance, the archivist will not be able to sustain both the development and the use of the collection. A college graduate with historical and library interests can learn within a few months to carry out many of the operations in the transfer and care of records and give elementary reference service in the archivist's absence. With adequate training and supervision, student assistants may become competent workers on nonconfidential materials and spread the word about the archives among their fellow students. If there is an archives training program nearby, it is often possible to add an intern to the effective staff, but supervision during the practicum and completion or correction of the work afterward may take as much time as the work itself, and the projects that are most suitable for training may not be those with highest priority for the institution. Archives sometimes receive offers of assistance from emeritus faculty and local alumni, and special projects can sometimes be found that put their interest and intelligence to good use without requiring extensive training or creating dangerous dependence on their efforts.

The archives must be funded mainly out of the library budget, but it has more opportunities for external funding than most other departments. It may be eligible for grants from state or federal historical and cultural agencies, especially if it is beginning or modernizing its program or seeking support for preservation. It is also an attractive object of fund-raising among alumni. Finally, there is some chance that it will draw additional support from the central administration because of its contributions to records management.

Very few archives have collections and services as comprehensive as those described in this chapter. An institution that takes a great interest in its history, has a strong liberal arts program with emphasis on student research experience, and has enrolled several thousand students for several decades might well employ three full-time regular staff members without quite fulfilling this ideal, and most archives in smaller institutions employ only one or two staff members or even make do with the part-time efforts of a reference librarian or a curator of special collections. When choices must be made, most archivists try to acquire publications and major record series, accept other records and faculty and student materials when they are especially attractive, meet urgent preservation needs, and provide solid reference service based on modest outreach. Such a program keeps a healthy balance among the development, maintenance, and growth of the holdings. As faculty members, students, and alumni become more aware of the uses and interest of local historical knowledge, they will develop needs that cannot be met without large and diverse collections; both internally and globally, an increasing supply of archives generates increasing demand. Some archivists nonetheless stress administrative service as the primary archival function and suggest that it will lead to increased support, but a program that exists largely to serve the offices that produced the records has little reason for being in the library.

The Society of American Archivists (SAA) is the major source of guidance in archives administration and an important focus of activity in the curatorship of personal and family papers. Its journal, *The American Archivist*, has carried dozens of articles on academic archives in its fifty years of publication, and many of the most important have been collected in *College and University Archives: Selected Readings* (1979). There is no textbook on the management of academic archives, but the SAA intends to publish a manual in 1988. Other useful SAA publications include its packet of job descriptions for college and university archivists, its *Guidelines for College & University Archives*, and its two manuals and other specialized titles on virtually all aspects of archives administration. The College and University Archives section matches experienced archivists with newcomers to the profession in its Adopt-an-Archivist program. The SAA education officer can provide information about the organization's own workshops and the training programs of universities. For a list of publications or more information about any program or service, write or call the SAA, Suite 504, 600 South Federal Street, Chicago, IL 60605 (312–922–0140).

The major works on archives administration in general are Theodore R. Schellenberg's *Management of Archives* (New York, 1965) and *Modern Archives Principles and Techniques* (Chicago, 1965). Articles on various aspects of archives management can be found in recently established archives journals such as *Provenance*, *The Midwestern Archivist*, and *Archivaria* as well as in library journals such as *College and Research Libraries*. For an introduction to the literature of records management, write to the Association of Records Managers and Administrators (ARMA), Suite 215, 4200 Somerset, Prairie Village, KS 66208.

## NOTE

The author is indebted to Margery N. Sly, Smith College archivist, for her thoughtful reading of the manuscript version of this chapter.

# 15

# Periodicals Management

## *Donald K. Tribit*

It is important for the individual managing a periodicals department to maintain a broad perspective of the function and role in that area. In most instances, the volume of work is overwhelming and ever beckons the assiduous librarian to work harder and accomplish.

It is very easy to spend too much time nobly striving in routine activities, with each day's shipment of journals being the major form of attention. It is important to create a schedule allowing time for planning and organization. Resolve to step back periodically and view the operation of the department and observe the patterns of patron utilization.

Organizational structure varies from library to library. Some libraries are strictly compartmentalized with technical and public departments having very separate and distinct functions. In the smaller academic library, this type of organization is not common. Out of necessity, librarians learn to perform in both spheres. Through this involvement they have the benefit of developing a broader view of the interrelationships of public and technical services. This is valuable to the librarian with serials responsibility. It is essential that the supervisor have an understanding of the methodology of selection, acquisition, processing, and control of serials. Central to this is an awareness of academic needs and a clear view of the place of serials as a vital component of the library collection.

There are problems that are common to periodicals librarians that should be viewed with the goal of developing a comprehensive program designed to mitigate their impact. Due consideration should be given to solving prolems that are most directly inhibiting services or adversely affecting operational functions.

## SPACE SAVING

Space is finite. Periodicals librarians must make decisions or recommendations about the use of space in their area. Two methods allow more information to be stored in a given amount of space: microform and compact shelving.

## Microform

Microform processes are a great space saver with the potential of saving 85 percent or more in filing area compared to the traditional method of storing hard copy. However, a required element in a program designed to meet user needs properly is the provision for reading the reproduction of hard copy from microform. Too often decisions are made to go to microform without adequate attention being paid to the development of a quality program using equipment specifically chosen to meet the requirements of the resources to be selected. Decisions must be made regarding microform format and polarity. As much as possible, it is best to keep the number of types of microformats in your library to the minimum that need dictates. The traditional library microfilm format is 35mm, allowing enough width to accommodate adequately the newspapers and journals. It is available in either a positive or negative mode. Opinions differ in regard to which configuration is more comfortable to the reader. Some users think the dark (negative) background is easier on the eyes, and others prefer the black on white (positive) microfilm, which presents an image like that of the printed page. It is also necessary to make a decision on the type of microfilm to purchase. The industry standard continues to be silver halide film, which is considered archival when it is preserved in pristine condition in a controlled environment. Much has been written in recent years concerning the relative merits of silver, vesicular, and diazo film with specific reference to the merits of the use of each respective type on a day-to-day basis by a variety of users. Opinion continues to vary, and we can be assured that considering the variables, it is doubtful that a consensus will be reached in the foreseeable future. In the article "Microfilm—Which Film Type, Which Application?" Suzanne Dodson brought together diverse thoughts of industry leaders on this subject. She stated, "one would think that an increase in information would have simplified the task but instead, we seem to be inundated with conflicting lists of information" (Dodson 1985: 88).

Some libraries are opting to use microfiche as an alternative or supplement to 35mm or 16mm microfilm. Prime vendors are now supplying subscriptions on microfiche on a quarterly basis. Vendors focus upon the advantage of quarterly distribution with microfiche as opposed to an annual or a semiannual shipment of film to subscribers.

A third option available is the use of 16mm microfilm either in open-reel or cartridge format. Cartridges provide ease in threading. Readers and reader printers, however, must be compatible with the cartridges being employed. Also, there is the additional overriding cost of the cartridge, which will impact on the library budget. Some space saving is an advantage of using 16mm film. The typical eleven-drawer microfilm cabinet can accommodate 35mm or 16mm reels. But 16mm is not generally suitable for newspapers, and opting for the use of both 16mm and 35mm will necessitate education and direction of the user to proper reading equipment. It is necessary to have 16mm take-up reels on readers when using 16mm film, and the level of magnification should be appropriate.

Patrons will be frustrated if they are using 16mm film on a reader with a lens designed to accommodate 35mm film. A postage-size image on the screen will result when users are viewing 16mm screen on a reader with a lens configuration designed for 35mm.

It is essential to have appropriate and well-maintained equipment. Instructions should be clear and understandable, and the staff must be available to assist patrons who need assistance. Readers and reader printers should be located in an area that is sufficiently close to staff stations that are manned during all hours that departmental services are provided. Student workers or other appropriate employees should be actively involved with care and maintenance. It is foolhardy to enter into a microform program without making a commitment to keeping the equipment in optimum working condition. "The primary emphasis is keeping dust, grit, and other foreign particles removed from the critical parts of the machine, such as the glass, flats, objective lenses, condenser lenses and the guide rods" (Hall and Michaels 1985: 26).

It is essential to have a selection policy that inhibits the proliferation of microfilm formats. Build the collection in a systematic fashion and purchase readers and reader printers compatible with these needs. Limiting the proliferation of formats will be less frustrating to the user, will make storage less complex, will require less space for readers and reader printers, and will make your operation more streamlined and cost effective.

## Compact Shelving

Compact shelving can dramatically increase the storage capacity in a given area. It is an alternative that is much less expensive than expanding the building. Through the use of tracks on the floor, ranges of stacks can be compressed with the elimination of a majority of the aisle space. Ranges are glided laterally by hand with surprising ease. Only in installations with exceptionally long ranges is motor drive necessary.

Flexibility in design is achievable, enabling one to develop installations for areas from several thousand square feet on up. Vendors can plan cost-effective installations to assemble the needs of smaller libraries. It is beneficial to have vendors come on site and work up alternative patterns of shelving and placement for a given area so that a determination can be made on the design that best suits your needs. Storage capacity, patterns of access, control view, and esthetics are all elements of consideration that need to be applied with evaluating alternative compact-shelving arrangements. It will be necessary to determine floor-load capacity to ensure that the area can accommodate the added weight load of compact-shelving ranges. Pillars, ceiling height, and existing lighting are features that must be taken into consideration in the development of compact-shelving plans. During initial vendor on-site visits, it is advisable for a library staff member to stay with the vendor as he makes notes on the physical layout.

It is most helpful for the librarian to supply the representative with blueprints that can be used at the vendor's facility when the drawings are formulated.

At Purdue University, compact shelving was installed in a new undergraduate library storage facility. A report said that "the mobile system will require 22,300 square feet as contrasted with 80,900 square feet that conventional shelving would have required to provide for 1.1 million volumes" ("Purdue Purchases Mobile Book Stacks," 1981: 330).

California State University at Long Beach used another vendor to supply a compact-shelving need. They indicated that "15,000 square feet of new library space would be needed for conventional stacks to hold 150,000 volumes in 3,800 square feet of space" ("Compact Shelving Helps Delay Need for Construction at CSU," 1983: 412).

It is important to take an overall view of your library and, if space is a problem, to develop a strategic plan to accommodate current and future needs. Visit libraries with compact installations and obtain their views. Libraries of various sizes are using compact shelving in open- and closed-stack configurations. Consider the demand level for the materials to be housed in compact shelving. Is it feasible to separate lesser used serial collections and designate them for compact shelving? An analysis should be made of the total collection with a view toward creating space most suitable for overall needs. A Pennsylvania liberal arts college is using compact shelving for bound volumes that are directly accessed by patrons.

## KEEPING ABREAST OF CHANGING TECHNOLOGY, EQUIPMENT, AND METHODS

### Organizing Literature

In general, company representatives can be most helpful to the librarian in developing and refining the programs. It is most beneficial to keep up-to-date catalogs from vendors; they can be kept in appropriately labeled file folders. It is also advisable to date materials upon receipt. Vendors often do not date promotional literature and other valuable mailings they distribute. This is especially common with literature on equipment. Manufacturers, for example, frequently do not want to have a microform reader identified with a particular year.

### Convention Exhibits

Serials librarians will find the exhibits at conventions to be an excellent source of valuable information. It is advisable to visit booths in a systematic fashion with specific intent to compare services and new product lines. Serials agents, automation specialists, marketers of indexes, microform vendors, and shelving companies exhibit products at national level shows. It is profitable to begin your exhibit visits early in the day when vendor representatives are generally less busy and have more time to answer your questions. Whenever possible, establish contacts ahead of time so that vendors can program individual attention to your needs.

Serials agents frequently have on exhibit samples of journals that you may peruse and examine. Librarians can obtain lists that can be checked to indicate the specific issues they would like to receive. The agents use the lists and contact vendors who then mail sample issues to the attention of the requestor. There is no pressure to subscribe and librarians are under no obligation to the subscription agents. This is a valuable service that is time saving and productive.

Manufacturers use national level conventions to introduce new equipment to libraries. New-generation microform readers and reader printers are appearing on the scene, and it is beneficial to compare the features of competing lines. The recent emergence of bond-paper microform copiers is a significant break-through that has positive benefits for libraries and their users. Bond paper is cheaper than coated paper and has an appearance and feel that appeals to the user. With these new-generation copiers, we have achieved a psychological breakthrough that is most beneficial. Faculty members who have been critical are praising the quality of copy that they are now receiving. Many just cannot believe that the bond-paper copies produced for them are actually from micro-forms.

Adequate preparation is the key to getting the most out of your exhibit visits. When analyzing and reviewing microform equipment, it is worthwhile to bring along samples of the types of microforms that are found in your library. Vendors tend to keep on hand for demonstration purposes microform samples that are best suited for use on their equipment. How well does the copier handle various formats? Can it accommodate both 16mm and 35mm film? Can the reader printer readily be switched to accept microfiche?

## Agent Utilization

Personal contacts made with vendors can be of inestimable value for serials librarians who are striving to keep abreast of the evolutionary world of serials librarianship. Agents have constant personal contacts with academic libraries and are a source to draw upon in determining where counterpart serials librarians have discovered unique ways of handling problems. They can help in establishing contacts for the serials librarian with other librarians with common interests and concerns. It is valuable to converse with other serials librarians on the topic of serials agent services they are receiving.

Serials agents can provide a spectrum of reports supplying worthwhile infor-mation relating to subscriptions. These reports can be tailored to specific need and are valuable to the user when doing serials collection analysis and review. Alphabetically arranged title listings can be generated including specific data designed to meet individual need. Helpful information might include indexing sources and respective columns showing the subscription costs for the past few years. The data are more inclusive than those found in the current-year invoice and can be arranged to suit individual preference.

It is worthwhile to request that the vendor print a listing to your specifications in the spring to use as a reviewing aid in doing an analysis of the serials on the current-year subscription list. It becomes a work sheet that can be used for systematic review of titles with adequate leave time for decision-making before the renewal date for the forthcoming year. In addition to this basic list, vendors can also print out subject lists that are generated using a Dewey or Library of Congress subject coder or based upon a unique or modified system that can be supplied to meet the specific needs of an individual library.

## COLLECTION DEVELOPMENT

### Library Faculty Relationships

It is beneficial to make use of the vendors' generated lists when interacting with academic departments. They contain requisite data that are needed in the in-depth review of titles and can serve as a work sheet for making decisions on retention or deletion of titles. There are many positive aspects that can be derived from an ongoing review. A basic positive is the fostering of a professional relationship with member(s) of academic departments. Through this process the faculty develops a knowledge of the collection and the budgetary process. Involvement generates interest and concern that can be directed to support the library and its budget. It is imperative that allies of the library budget be found wherever possible across the college campus. Individuals with more than superficial knowledge are the type of advocates needed to develop the clarion call required to maintain an adequate budget in the face of competition for resources from other campus constituencies.

Interaction with the faculty should be conducted with specific knowledge that ultimate decision-making on selection and deselection rests with the library. It is essential that the faculty outside the library has a clear understanding that its role is advisory. During interaction with the faculty, it is beneficial to make statements reinforcing the concept that librarians are charged with the responsibility of maintaining a balanced collection that supports the needs of a diverse constituency. Wholesale cutting of titles supporting lower division undergraduate research should not be done in favor of purchasing more esoteric journals favored by an academic specialist.

Serious consequences can occur when control of the budget devolves from the library. Donna Goehner painted a graphic picture of the imbalances that have occurred through the faculty controlling a major portion of an academic library budget.

Since 1981 we have been operating under a system where more than 60% of the funds available for literary materials are allocated to the academic departments. The departmental members serving as representatives make all the selection decisions and can purchase whatever materials they deem most important for the collection. Having been given the responsibility for collection development, many of the academic faculty decided to reinstate periodical subscriptions previously cancelled by the library. (Goehner 1985–1986: 182)

## Maintaining a Balanced Collection

It is imperative that collection development be geared to the needs of student research, faculty, and administration with a mix that provides support across the board. We as librarians need to extend an extra effort to ensure that resources are purchased to undergird all academic areas with appropriate measure to department when the faculty is less interested in participating in the selection process. Each library must, to a greater or lesser degree, fill in the gaps when the faculty is not willing to participate. For various reasons some institutions will achieve more cooperation than others. At Duke University there is a trend away from faculty participation in selection. "The majority of the present generation of faculty . . . do not consider the selection of materials to be their responsibility and find themselves too busy with other duties to recommend materials for library purchase on a regular basis" (Ezzell 1985: 23).

Review and analysis are key aspects of selection. View requests for new journal subscriptions in relationship to current holdings. Balance is important in the creation and maintenance of a viable collection. It is our vital concern that resources are expanded so that there is the diversity necessary to support all departmental areas and programs.

"A well-planned budget requires more than just the correct allocation of dollars; it must also include a well-developed plan of action that can be quickly implemented should unexpected events occur" (Almagro 1985–1986: 173). These prophetic words constitute an axiom that should be heeded by serials librarians in all types of settings. Contingency planning is necessary so that a well conceived pattern of action can be employed to face the expected as well as the unexpected. How should a librarian respond to the reality of having the next year's budget cut in half? Perhaps you will never have to face this drastic situation. A great many more libraries are facing the challenge of static budgets juxtapositioned with an inflationary rate that is constantly eroding the value of the dollar.

## Selection and Deselection

Libraries should develop selection policies that outline procedures for selection and deselection of serials. Faculty can be asked to rank titles based upon the value of a given title in support of departmental courses and programs. Individual lists can be used, or a composite departmental list can be developed. Whenever possible, the serials librarian should include on a title-by-title basis an actual or calculated figure on use. This calculation becomes more meaningful when a librarian is able to provide use statistics over a number of years. The spectrum of use statistics will give data on titles that basically support courses that might be offered only biannually or on some other pattern of irregular offering.

Use statistics may be gathered using a random checking of loose, bound, and microform items before reshelving. This system of checking can be used in parallel with a core group of journals that is monitored on a continuing basis. This core group could be the most expensive 10 percent of the titles on the subscription list or any other combination by which a specific benefit would be achieved through monitoring.

While doing subject-area title assessment, an analysis can be made of titles that cover the same general subject area. Use and departmental ranking are two factors that can be taken into consideration in evaluating respective titles that overlap in subject coverage. All other things being equal, the weaker journals could be targeted for deacquisition in the near or distant future. It might be appropriate to delete parallel coverage titles in conjunction with the addition of new titles in a given department subject area. The faculty generally adapts to a system when there is a pattern of flexibility and a discernible pattern to the serials acquisition process. Developing a system of give and take allows for titles that appear noteworthy to be added and at the same time provides an ongoing process of pruning within the given subject area.

Vendors can include indexing information for applicable titles appearing on general or specialized listings. To save space, vendors frequently abbreviate the names of indexes using a twin letter code or some other appropriate abbreviations to signify a specific index. Indexing data is valuable to the librarian providing reference service and should be included in listings passed on to faculty and patrons. Indexes and abstracts are the keys to unlocking the knowledge in the journals that serials librarians so assiduously acquire and access for patrons. It is incumbent on practitioners to follow the logical step of tying together journal titles with the appropriate indexes. Notations on indexes can be added to the Kardex cards for individual titles enabling employees to provide patrons with the spectrum of indexing services accessing any given title. Thus patrons learn of applicable indices from a single title or subject-list-searching approach. Consideration can be given to including on-line services that access a given title in bibliographies and the Kardex card adjacent to the index or abstract listing.

## RESOURCE UTILIZATION

### Enhancing User Skills

It is essential that patrons be given direction and assistance in accessing information. Undergraduates need to have the opportunity to give an awareness of the value of indexing services as an integral part of their learning experience. There is no substitute for hands-on knowledge that naturally evolves during the process of getting familiar with the basic search tools in a given area. Librarians should avail themselves of the opportunity to provide instructional sessions to classes at a time when an assignment is being made where use of an index or abstract service will be most appropriate. Introductory classes in psychology, for example, can come to the library and receive an introduction to the use of *Psychological Abstracts*. This can be offered with an overview presented by the librarian followed by a hands-on session for the remainder of the period by which the students can explore their topic with assistance and guidance provided by the librarian and the psychology professor. The librarian should prepare a bibliography or pathfinder sheet that will be helpful to students as they proceed with the assignments.

The organizational structure of the library should be patterned to facilitate instruction in a systematic and coordinated manner. Ideally, a bibliographic instruction librarian provides user instruction with the serials librarian supplying backup and logistical support. Reference and serials librarians should function synergistically with the objective of nurturing and sustaining the bipartite challenges of maximizing resource use and creating confident patron clientele.

Students who have a positive experience with an abstract or indexing service are less reluctant to venture out and use indexing tools in other subject areas. During the introduction of an indexing service, it is beneficial to point out the similarities of serial-accessing tools in related areas. Annotated bibliographies that list alternates and parallel sources are helpful to patrons and provide a framework that they can employ as they branch out and explore. It is essential that patrons become self-directed in using the library. Sometimes, immediate introduction to a data-base service deprives the individual of the opportunity to experience the excitement of the unfolding of knowledge that can be achieved through exploration and use of paper volumes of an abstract or indexing service. "A potential danger lies . . . in a wholesale reliance on the online search as a substitute for the index table. Undergraduates by and large lack the in-depth subject knowledge and associative terminology to rely solely on Boolean matches as the basis for the construction of initial bibliographies" (Gordon 1985–1986: 170).

It is not my intent to downgrade data bases whether they are of the controlled-vocabulary or the text variety. They provide an opportunity to correlate terms and bring together citations in a fashion that cannot be achieved through traditional searching of manual paper indexes. The librarian must provide support and direction in the use of data-base services. A user-need profile is essential before each search to ensure that proper parameter limitations are in place and to determine that the search strategy is geared to specific patron need. This involves time, effort, and expense that impacts on the library. It is apparent that traditional paper-formatted indexes and data-base services both have a place in academic libraries. Librarians need to look at the total picture of service and work with patrons in using the tools that best meet their individual needs.

## COLLECTION MAINTENANCE

### Subscription Agents

Almost universally, academic libraries employ subscription agents as an intermediary in the serials ordering process. Discounts from publishers to agencies have virtually disappeared, and the costs of agency handling have been passed on to the purchasing library through the application of a service charge over and above the basic subscription costs. The prevailing view has been that the library still gains because the cost of the service charge has been viewed as being less than the equivalent cost in labor that would be expended if libraries entered their subscriptions directly with the publishers. This thesis has been challenged by a serials librarian at a university library receiving approximately 17,000 subscriptions (Paul 1982: 31). Other authors herald the concept that serials agents continue to provide a service that is cost effective.

It is worthwhile to examine procedures and keep abreast of the cost of contracted services. The value of a given service to the library must be viewed in its totality with consideration given to the total spectrum of derived benefits. It is most important to analyze costs on a regular basis and to let the vendor know that cost is under review. Probe to determine ways of mitigating service charges. Investigate the possibility of receiving discounts for paying the basic subscription invoice in advance. Try paying in July, for example, rather than September if it is possible to achieve significant savings. Additionally, some vendors supply a discount to libraries that pay the invoice within thirty days of receipt. If feasible, establish this arrangement and take the discount off the invoice before payment. It is up to the serials librarian to take the lead in working with fulfillment agencies. Review invoices on a continuing basis to ensure that there is a smooth and sustained flow with attention directed to the avoidance of bottlenecks. The best formulated system needs supervision and monitoring. It is easy, in a serials department with myriad competing commitments, to batch work and in the process neglect to submit invoices within the prescribed discount period.

### Filling the Gaps

Maintaining the integrity of the collection is a challenge. Patrons invariably request the issue that is missing. It is incumbent upon serials librarians to have diverse and systematized methods in place to fill the chinks in the collection. Claiming must be continual and ongoing. Publishers have shortened the time in which they will accept claims. To protect your rights, it is better to claim early rather than to assume that there has been a publishing delay. Use the forms and services of agents in the process of fulfillment. Pay close attention to notes in agents' newsletters regarding the status of titles. It is valuable to call or write agents to obtain up-to-date information on the status of individual titles. Use the

800 line with the agent to ascertain status whenever expedient. If there is no 800 line it is worthwhile to establish a policy of calling collect. Patrons should be provided with specific information regarding titles in question. Messages can be placed in the Kardex pocket for a given title so that an answer is available at the point of subsequent inquiry.

It is essential to maintain a group of active sources for replacement issues. Check with your serials jobber or binder to determine whether either one maintains copies of recent issues on file as a service to customers. EBSCO, for example, maintains two years or more of duplicates, which are available free to its customers upon request. Another valuable source is the American Library Association, Resources and Technical Services Division's Duplicates Exchange Union. The only obligation of membership is for each institution belonging to circulate at least once each year a list of duplicates to each of the other more than 600 libraries participating. Lists are reviewed and returned to the issuing library. Postage charges of one dollar or more are reimbursed.

There are a number of dealers across the country that maintain back files of serial publications. It is wise to develop a relationship with some of these agencies. It is possible to develop a credit account with some dealers. Using this arrangement, a given library's duplicates are purchased and credit is developed with the understanding that issues needed can be supplied when available through expenditure of credit. This is especially beneficial in filling gaps in titles that are not available in microform or in dealing with cases where for esthetic reasons paper back files are being maintained.

In many instances, the purchase of a volume unit in microform is the most expedient way of closing that elusive gap of one or more issues. Serialists should be mindful of the fact that there is a potential for creating user frustration when in a given title there is a pattern of shifting repetitively from paper to microform in situations in which there is a sustained pattern of intermittent gaps. This practice provides a pattern of continuity that allows the user to function efficiently and concurrently eliminates the necessity for maintaining complex listings in holdings files.

It is worthwhile to have a battery of sources at your disposal for use as complementary sources for replacement issues. It is most exhilarating to have completed the quest of replacing the last of a series of missing issues needed to round out a volume that can then be dispatched to the bindery.

Claiming of foreign titles is an area that can be most trying and arduous. The vagaries of respective postal systems further complicate the process. Publishers abroad are paralleling the North American practice of shortening the time in which claims will be honored. To facilitate continuity of receipt, at least one European jobber is providing check-in services in the country of origin. The jobber, for a set fee, checks in the titles in a Kardex in the agency office and makes claims for issues not dispatched by the publishers. Issues of various titles are then bundled and sent air freight across the Atlantic to the receiving agent.

They are then mailed to the subscribing library. Some added charges for the foregoing services are offset because certain titles are charged at the issuing country rate rather than the North American rate.

The Universal Serials Book Exchange (USBE) in Washington, D.C., is another valuable source that may be drawn upon to obtain the elusive issues that are needed to complete gaps or missing issues in a serials collection. This is a vast storehouse containing a plethora of issues that are supplied on a first-come first-serve basis. This organization is nonprofit and its purpose and function is to provide needed resources to libraries across the globe. It has recently revamped the membership structure to allow library consortia to join with a significant savings evolving to individual institutional members. Despite the higher per-issue rate to nonmembers, it might be advantageous to begin a relationship with USBE by sending a list of perhaps twenty-five missing issues to get a feeling of how it functions in support of library needs. Charges are on a per-issue or per-volume basis geared to defray overhead costs with no correlation to the original cost of the material. This allows an institution to obtain fill-in issues that are prohibitively priced from the publisher as other back-issue sources.

A corresponding service provided by USBE is the supplying of issues to fulfill interlibrary loan needs. Issues are supplied to the requesting library with the intent that they may be used in place of a photocopy. This allows an institution to satisfy user demand in special situations where there are calls that exceed the per-year copyright restriction on borrowing a given title. This provides a safety valve that obviates the need to place a subscription when there is a significant short-term demand for a particular title. It allows the serials librarian to meet a need in a flexible and nonbinding way.

## Cost Consciousness

It is incumbent upon serials librarians to focus upon and expose inequities that develop in handling acquisitions. Maintaining an awareness of pricing structure is necessary so that we can take appropriate steps when warranted. A cursory review of serials invoices over the past few years would bring to light the dramatic increases that have been imposed by many British publishers upon North American customers. North American customers, in many cases, are paying on the highest level in a triple-tiered pricing structure. This tripartite system includes an inland price, an increased price to the majority of countries outside the United Kingdom, and an additional arbitrarily inflated charge to libraries in North America. It is imperative that librarians face this issue head on and do everything in their power to bring pressure upon discriminating publishers. Articles have appeared in the literature, and this issue is being addressed at conferences. "It has been difficult to circumvent this unfair practice for periodicals from Britain. The only alternative has been to cancel some subscriptions" (Ruschin 1985: 8).

The academic faculty needs to become aware of cost as a factor in decisions relating to acquisition or deacquisition of journals. Substitutes in many cases can be found that will allow for the servicing of patron needs in a most cost-effective fashion. The faculty can become a vocal ally in the campaign to thwart discriminatory price structures.

Cost containment is especially necessary in the serials world. Cost containment must be ongoing, and it is necessary to have a policy to keep rising costs in check. According to a recent study, U.S. periodicals for 1985

show an average increase of 8.6 percent over 1984 prices, with an average subscription price of $56.70; last year's (1984) average subscription price was $54.97, which was an increase of 9.4 percent over 1983. Despite this continuing trend of lower percentage increases, the U.S. Periodicals Index (USPI) is increasing at a far faster rate than the Consumer Price Index (CPI). (Horn and Lenzini 1985: 53)

## LIBRARY COOPERATION

In facing the challenge of escalating costs, librarians must use a variety of options. Cooperation is an essential feature of any well-planned and executed program that is designed to provide for user needs and at the same time remain cost effective and efficient. Smaller libraries need more than ever to extend themselves to meet the needs of their patrons. "The growing number of serials titles, the high cost of currently published titles, and the declining population which so strongly affects library budgets, have all set the stage for libraries to depend on one another more heavily for serials they lack" (Bloss 1985–1986: 142). It is important to reiterate that serials librarians must unite in a concerted effort to enhance services.

Is there a library cooperative group already functioning in your area? If so, do not be hesitant about contacting the group. Serials librarians make a valuable contribution to cooperative groups. Invariably, one of the most beneficial and cohesive elements of library cooperation is an up-to-date union list of serials. It is not self-serving to state that the union list serves as a wellspring both of service and inspiration in the development of cooperation within a group of academic libraries. It provides the skeletal framework that supports interaction among members of the group. Through this continuing contact, true cooperation is fostered, librarians learn to work together, and ancillary patterns of sharing germinate within the group. This is especially beneficial to libraries in rural areas where distances have been perceived as an insurmountable barrier. It is helpful, especially in the formative stages, to have cooperative meetings at an institution that is more or less centrally located. This would allow, in most cases, for institutions from an approximate radius of 300 miles to attend a single-day meeting. Amazingly, as cooperation is fostered and creative juices begin to flow, distances become less of a burden.

Through cooperation, libraries can have the flexibility to enhance individual strengths. Sharing of resources is mutually beneficial and provides the latitude and flexibility that are necessary in the development of collections that are both cost effective and supportive of academic need. Modern technology is our ally and is contributing to facilitating cooperation on a number of fronts. Institutions can use on-campus computers or the facilities of bibliographic networks in the development and updating of union lists. Improvements in reprography have allowed for quick and facile production of photocopies from paper or microform that can be readily shared. Telefacsimile has become a more cost-effective and efficient communication device and is being adopted as a functioning component of seasoned library cooperatives.

## REFERENCES

Almagro, Bertha R. 1985–1986. "Budgeting and Planning: A Tandem Approach." *Serials Librarian* 10, nos. 1–2 (Fall-Winter): 173.

Bloss, Marjorie E. 1985–1986. "And In Hindsight...The Past 10 Years of Union Listing." *Serials Librarian* 10, nos. 1–2 (Fall-Winter): 141–48.

"Compact Shelving Helps Delay Need for Construction at CSU." 1983. *Library Journal* 108 (August): 412.

Dodson, Suzanne C. 1985. "Microfilm—Which Film Type, Which Application?" Charts. *Microform Review* 14 (Spring): 88.

Ezzell, Joline R. 1985. "Building a Serials Collection in an Academic Library." *North Carolina Libraries* 43 (Spring): 23.

Goehner, Donna M. 1985–1986. "A Lesson Learned the Hard Way; or, The Cost of Relinquishing Acquisitions Control." *Serials Librarian* 10, nos. 1–2 (Fall-Winter): 182.

Gordon, Martin. 1985–1986. "Article Access—Too Easy?" *Serials Librarian* 10, nos. 1–2 (Fall-Winter): 170.

Hall, Hal W., and George H. Michaels, 1985. "Microform Reader Maintenance." Charts. *Microform Review* 14 (Winter): 24–34.

Horn, Judith G., and Rebecca T. Lenzini. 1985. "Price Indexes for 1985: U.S. Periodicals." Charts. *Library Journal* 110 (August): 53–59.

Paul, Huibert. 1982. "Are Subscription Agents Worth Their Keep?" *Serials Librarian* 7, no. 1 (Fall): 31–41.

"Purdue Purchases Mobile Book Stacks." 1981. *Wilson Library Bulletin* 55 (January): 330.

Ruschin, Siegfried. 1985. "Why Are Foreign Subscription Rates Higher for American Libraries Than They Are for Subscribers Elsewhere?" Charts. *Serials Librarian* 9 (Spring): 7–17.

# 16

# Collection-Size Management

## *Frederick E. Smith*

Evidence from the library literature shows that library collections grow at an alarming rate:

Most libraries now have a space problem to solve or soon will. Historically, libraries have exhausted book storage space long before they were designed to. . . . the general causes are clear: volume of publication has reached astronomic proportions and shows no signs of receding; the . . . urge to keep pace with that volume, combined with a reluctance to weed heavily, has led inevitably to prematurely overloaded libraries. (Schorrig 1976: 6)

Furthermore, "For several decades now, academic library collections have been doubling every fifteen years or so" (Gore 1976: 164).

The usual way that libraries have dealt with this problem is to provide more space, either in the form of a completely new building or at least a new wing. Although more space could not always be provided as soon as it was needed, this has been the eventual solution to the problem in most cases. But several factors suggest that this may no longer be the best solution. First, between 1967 and 1974 there took place "the biggest building boom in library history. But it failed to solve the space problem. Although new space was created for 163 million more volumes, 166 million were added to collections in the boom years, thus making the space problem . . . a little worse than when the boom began" (Gore 1976: 165). Second, a difficult combination is at work in many small academic institutions, which is to the detriment of the libraries at these institutions. This combination consists of two parts: the increasing expense of new buildings or wings and the problem of paying for them. Third, bibliographic materials, collections, and data banks are becoming increasingly available in machine-readable form. Given the rate at which this is taking place, libraries will soon have millions of citations and even full-text documents readily available electronically, which will make it unnecessary to acquire and store many materials locally.

In view of these factors, an alternative to a new building or wing suggests itself. The alternative is to manage the space currently available so as to enable the collection to remain, or largely remain, within this space. At this point, it would be clearly stated that this alternative does not apply to major university libraries, which must continue to be responsible for preserving the human record that smaller academic libraries may draw upon as needed. Depending upon the extent to which this suggested alternative is adopted by smaller academic libraries, it may result in implementation of the static-capacity concept, that is, one withdrawal to match each new acquisition, or some degree short of this. But before a decision can be made about adoption of this concept, the question that must be raised is: what are the means of managing the space available so that the collection can essentially remain within this space?

## MEANS OF MANAGING AVAILABLE SPACE

There are several means of managing currently available space. They are use of remaining space and shoe-horning, microform, compact shelving, remote storage, withdrawal, and automation.

### Microform

Microform cannot help as a space-saving device for books. Most books are not available in microform because they would be too long to read in this format. But microform can significantly reduce the shelf space needed for periodicals.

There are a number of factors that must be taken into consideration when evaluating whether a hard copy subscription can be converted to microform. First, it is obvious that the periodicals identified for conversion must be published in microform. Consideration must also be given to the amount of space saved. Hard-copy subscriptions consume considerably more space for some periodicals than for others. It may be worth saving space for some periodicals but not for others. The trade-off of space saved by converting materials to microform versus the extra space required for more readers and storage cabinets must also be evaluated. Although at one time publishers required that hard-copy subscriptions be purchased along with microform subscriptions, this situation seems to be changing. However, the trade-off of the cost of two subscriptions, one hard copy and one microform, compared to the savings in the cost of binding must still be evaluated for some journals. The microform must be of high quality so that the readability of the materials is not sacrificed for savings in space. Quality also has another dimension, which speaks well for microform. "One of the strongest arguments made in favor of microform products is their lasting quality in comparison with paper products" (Lynden 1974: 19). Microform products do not deteriorate as quickly or become damaged as easily as paper products.

More important than any of these factors is that material in microform is simply not as convenient to use as hard-copy material, and for this reason "many people dislike using microforms" (Salmon 1974: 194). The primary problems are the necessity of using reading equipment, restriction of material to one location, and eye strain. This situation has improved over the years and should continue to improve. Microform will always require reading equipment, but portable readers are available on the market, although they are not widely used. Reading equipment has been and will continue to be improved, resulting in less eye strain. One report has summarized the situation by stating that "there is still a substantial amount of user resistance to microforms . . . but this resistance appears to be lessening" (Office of the Executive Director of University-Wide Library Planning 1977: 161). However, microform has been available long enough to predict safely that it is not likely that this medium will be as popular as materials published in hard copy.

In view of the latter, it seems advisable to convert subscriptions from hard copy to microform only for those periodicals that receive a relatively low amount of use. To convert high-demand materials to microform could very well discourage use of the materials. This would run counter to the objective of the library and is, therefore, too high a price to pay. Limiting the use of microform to low-use materials would help to save space in the library but not be a detriment to the mission of the library.

## Compact Shelving

Compact shelving is a mechanical or electrical shelving that runs on a track. It can significantly increase the book capacity of an area where it is located by eliminating space for all but one aisle, which is moved from place to place within the compact shelving as needed. "It is possible to obtain an actual increase in shelving capacity ranging from 75% to 100% by the use of compact bookstacks instead of standard bookstacks" (Poole 1978: 49).

With double, or almost double, the capacity and weight of normal bookstacks, it is probable that the only place where compact shelving can be located is the ground floor. Regular bookstacks must be able to handle a live load of 125–150 pounds (Kaser 1979: 9). For compact shelving, "It has been generally accepted in practice that a floor-loading factor of 250 pounds per square foot is adequate" (Poole 1978: 53). Because it is mechanized or electrical, it also seems advisable to place compact shelving only in a closed stack or remote storage area. A few libraries have placed compact shelving in open-stack areas, but this is the exception rather than the rule.

Compact shelving is considerably more expensive than standard shelving. Most libraries will, therefore, be able to afford it only for selected locations. Compact shelving, in whatever amount it can be provided, is a very effective method of saving space.

## Remote Storage

*Remote storage* is defined as an area separate from the library that consists of less expensive space than the library building provides and that is used to house lesser-used materials. Although for most libraries this is not space that is currently available, which may seem to violate the principle of collection-size management, it is not at all equivalent to a new building or wing either in terms of the amount of space or cost. A remote storage area can serve two purposes. It can serve as a permanent storage area for less-used materials or as a testing-staging area for the ultimate withdrawal of materials.

The former concept serves as a direct extension of the regular library collection. If it were possible to build a bigger library building, this would be done instead, and all materials would continue to be housed in the main library. The only reason a remote storage area is established under these circumstances is because a new building or wing cannot be afforded. Since all materials cannot be housed in the main collection, those designed for remote storage must be lesser used. Without going any farther, it is clear that although this concept of remote storage is of value in terms of providing an alternative to a new building or wing, it is of no value in terms of managing the size of the collection.

It is the latter concept of remote storage that is of value in terms of collection-size management. According to the latter concept, the use of materials, while in remote storage, would serve as the measure to whether they should be withdrawn, remain in remote storage a little longer, or even conceivably be returned to the main collection if they receive an unanticipated amount of use. This concept permits the process of withdrawing materials from the collection to be cautious and deliberate. Books and periodicals are not summarily withdrawn but are instead relocated in the remote storage area where they remain for the number of years stipulated by the given library. After the designated number of years, a decision must be made as to what to do with the item, and it is likely that the great majority would be withdrawn based upon lack of use. In fact, the great majority must be withdrawn if the size of the collection is to be controlled to any significant extent. "The major drawback to remote storage is limited user service and access to materials. Browsing usually is impossible, and users often must wait up to a day to receive materials. However, because of the nature of its collection, a typical storage facility circulates only about 5% of its holdings, as compared to normal figures of 40% or more" (Systems and Procedures Exchange Center 1977: 1).

Clearly, the best location for remote storage would be on campus. Although the storage area would not be open for general use, there should be no more than a twenty-four hour delay in making materials from remote storage available to those who need them. A library staff member should retrieve the materials at a designated time each day. By following these procedures, access to the materials in remote storage would be provided on a frequent and regular basis.

Remote storage may also be located off campus. However, to make materials available to users in twenty-four hours, reliable transportation must be provided. Furthermore, off-campus space may not be owned by the institution, and this would have drawbacks. The institution would have to pay for the space and the possibility would exist that the owner might want to use the space for another purpose thus forcing the library to find new space.

Storage space shared with other libraries off campus may also play a role in the library's future. If an effective system can be developed, cooperative storage space would be more cost effective than space on campus because the campus space could be used for other purposes, and it would also be more cost effective than off-campus space used by only one library because the cost would be shared. It would actually be possible but unlikely for a library to use more than one type or even all three types of remote storage: on campus, off campus for just one library, and shared off-campus space.

There are three criteria that storage space must meet. It must be on the ground floor or on an upper floor with extra strength because of the weight of the materials and especially since these materials will be stored more densely than materials in the main collection. It must also be in a location with a suitable temperature, although this is not to say that temperature controls are required. To be more specific, it is not a matter of concern if storage space is cold, but such space must not be too hot. A low temperature would not damage materials, but a high temperature would cause the pages to become brittle and crack. Storage space must also have a suitable humidity level. On the one hand, there must not be too much humidity or the materials will become mildewed. On the other hand, there must be sufficient humidity or the effect on the materials will be the same as too much heat; that is, they will become dry and brittle. As with temperature, an acceptable humidity level may be obtained without special controls. But if controls are needed, inexpensive stand-alone floor humidifiers and dehumidifiers will get the job done.

Beyond these general requirements, the specific arrangements of a remote storage area may include regular shelving with narrow aisles, compact shelving of regular height, higher-than-normal shelving, or arrangement of the books by call number, size, or either of these options within the year the materials are placed in storage. Regarding the width of the aisles, "In a storage stack for less-used books, 26 in. will do, but less than 24 in. should not be tolerated" (Metcalf 1965: 161).

To summarize, remote storage is important to a collection-size management program in two ways: it provides additional space beyond the library's present four walls at a very low cost, and it is the stepping-stone to withdrawal, which is the key to collection-size management.

## Withdrawal

The most significant factor in collection-size management is an effective weeding program for the two-level purpose of relocating lesser used materials into a remote storage area and then later withdrawing from the collection those materials that have not been used while housed in remote storage.

### Books

Decisions about the storage and withdrawal of books involve three factors. Clearly, the primary criterion is the amount the books have been used. This must be the primary criterion since the primary objective of building a library collection is to have the materials in the collection used. Another criterion is the age of the material as reflected by publication date. The third criterion is the importance of a book to the literature of its discipline regardless of use and age.

*Use of materials*. Library studies have concluded "that a very small proportion of an academic library's collection accounts for nearly all the use" (Gore 1976: 173). For example, 15 percent of the collection accounts for 75 percent of the circulation (Trueswell 1976: 75), or 20 percent of the collection accounts for 80 percent of the circulation (Trueswell 1976: 76).

According to the classic study performed by the University of Chicago, "Past use, where sufficient data are available, was found to be the best single predictor of the future use of a book" (Fussler and Simon 1969: 15). Trueswell agreed with this conclusion and was even more specific when he said that "the last circulation date for books currently being charged was considered to be indicative of the future use of the book" (Trueswell 1976: 80). Using the last circulation date (LCD), he performed studies to determine how many years back this date had to be to satisfy a given percentage of circulation. He concluded that "the over 99 percent figure for circulation satisfaction was comprised of books having LCD within the past eight years" (Trueswell 1976: 83).

In summary, this approach centers around the use of the cumulative distribution function of the previous circulation date. Assuming that this distribution function represents typical circulation for the given library, the 99 percentile position is then determined, and this point in time is considered to be the cutting point for thinning the stacks. Such a cutting point should, if the system works properly, provide a collection that will satisfy over 99 percent of the current circulation requirements. (Trueswell 1976: 85)

What about books that are used in-house and, therefore, have no record of being circulated? The study performed at the University of Chicago and studies done at the Universities of California and Pittsburgh address this question. According to the Chicago study, which was published in 1969, "Books that develop little recorded use develop little browsing" (Fussler and Simon 1969: 115). This study goes on to state that "this means that storing the books with the least recorded use will also minimize the amount of nonrecorded use lost" (Fussler and Simon 1969: 115). The California study, done more than ten years later in 1980, draws the same conclusion. "It is evident from the finds of this study and previous research that the least-recently circulated library materials are the least-frequently used library materials, even given a very broad definition of the term 'use' " (Lawrence and Oja 1980: 55). The University of Pittsburgh study supports the other two studies and provides specific figures.

In summary, these data show that 75–78 percent of those books and monographs that circulate in-house also have circulated externally. Furthermore, based on this analysis, this percentage is increasing with time. Thus we conclude that in terms of whether or not a book or monograph is ever used, it is sufficient to examine the external patron circulation data (Kent et al. 1979: 29).

It is to the advantage of a library to gather both circulation and in-house-use data from its own collection before establishing an active withdrawal program. Referring again to the Chicago study, "our results also suggest the wisdom of postponing storage for perhaps five years and collecting records of use during that time" (Fussler and Simon 1969: 31).

*Age of materials.* The age of materials can in some cases provide information that is useful as to whether a book should remain in the main collection or be stored or withdrawn. In many cases, the age of an item is simply reflected in the amount it is used and would, therefore, be a subset of the usage criterion noted above. The reason that age is usually a subset of usage is that, generally, current materials are used more frequently than older materials because they contain more recent information. At Yale "an analysis of loans by date of publication showed that there was a fairly regular decline in the use of older books among all classes of users" (Totten 1971: 345). If age is considered a subset of usage, recent materials would generally be retained in the main collection because they are more heavily used, and older materials would generally be candidates for storage or withdrawal because they are used very little.

In some cases, however, age should not be a subset of usage. It is possible that older materials may be but should not be used. This could happen if the materials were no longer up to date, and it was to the disadvantage of students to use these materials as opposed to more recent materials. It would be in these cases that age should be the factor that determines whether a book should remain in the collection or be stored or withdrawn. Actually, items that fall into this category should probably not be stored but instead should probably be immediately withdrawn.

*Importance of book to literature of discipline.* Although the history of the use of a book and the related factor of age are the most important considerations in determining whether it should remain in the main collection, be placed in remote storage, or be withdrawn, it would be irresponsible to store or withdraw books based solely upon these criteria. There may be books that are very important to the collection that should never be stored or withdrawn even if they never circulate. Classics in the literature of the various disciplines are examples of such books.

This point of view is well stated as follows: "Any book which was good once may be important for somebody to read again twenty, fifty, or a hundred years from now. That no one has consulted the book for any particular period of time

... is not a reliable measure of the book's real or potential value'' (Heffner 1975: 5). Furthermore:

An academic library is a center for learning, not just a support for the educational activity that takes place in the classroom. From exposure to a good and not too selective library, a student may get an independent and quite different view of his subject from that promulgated as orthodoxy by the faculty. A library rigorously selected for its current utility puts blinders on the student and diminishes the opportunity for him to strike out on his own. (Heffner 1975: 5)

By no means should every decision about the retention, storage, or withdrawal of books be based strictly on usage or the related factor of age. Consideration of these factors must be tempered by consideration of the importance of a book to the literature of the discipline.

### Periodicals

The same three criteria that are used for books are also used to evaluate periodicals for retention in the main collection, placement in storage, or withdrawal.

*Use of materials.* Reflecting the findings of the book-use studies noted earlier, the University of Pittsburgh study found that with periodicals "a high percent of usage was provided by a small percent of the collection" (Kent 1979: 67). However, most libraries operate according to the policy that periodicals do not circulate, which means that periodicals are used only in house in most libraries. Therefore, the conclusion drawn earlier for books that in-house circulation for a given book may be predicted by its out-of-house circulation does not apply to periodicals in most libraries. But there are other methods that are useful. Three such methods are presented here as examples of what can be done. According to one library:

To decide what titles, or portions of titles, can be substituted by microforms, or even disposed of, we have tried to keep track of use by title and, within title, by decade. . . . we can only estimate use by recording the volumes reshelved, assuming on the basis of other studies, that about one volume is left unshelved for every three or four used. While rough, this count still gives us some basis for saying to a faculty member: "Look, none of the first fifty volumes of the *American Journal of International Law* has been used in two years. Why can't we just keep the last ten years and depend on interlibrary loan for the others? Or do we really need to subscribe to it all?" (Farber 1976: 38)

At another library, "the use data are generated by simply applying a small, pressure-sensitive label to the spine of a volume the first time it is reshelved by library personnel. . . . thus at any given time the tagged volumes represent those that have been used at least once since the study began" (Shaw 1978: 480). "Unused items represent a substantial resource from the viewpoint of identifying candidates for cancellation, storage, conversion to microform, or redistribution within a consortium'' (Shaw 1978: 482).

Although not associated with any one library, another method is to gather detailed use statistics for bound volumes and unbound issues that have been removed from the shelves. Unlike the first example, which kept only a title count by decade, this process would record title, volume number and/or issue number, and year. In one respect, it would be best to record all periodical usage because the data gathered would then be comprehensive. But in another respect, it may not be best because it would result in disservice to library users if the data could not be recorded every day, due to individual schedules or other reasons, since volumes and issues that had been used would remain unshelved for two or more days until they could be counted. This would become even more of a disservice during the latter part of a term when these materials are heavily used. In view of these problems, it may be preferable to gather data for materials used just a few days each week, perhaps three. If using this approach would result in incomplete data, this shortcoming would probably be adequately addressed if the recommendation made in the Chicago study that data be gathered for books for five years were also followed for periodicals. Five years worth of data would go a long way toward accounting for any gaps in information that may result from only gathering data a few days each week.

*Age of materials.* With books, the age of materials is not a really significant evaluative factor since this factor is, for the most part, a subset of the usage factor. Although also a subset of the usage factor with periodicals, the age factor will probably be more useful when making decisions about the retention, storage, or withdrawal of these materials. The reason it will probably be more useful is because of the lack of circulation data for periodicals.

Given the need to assess the use of periodicals based upon in-house circulation only, it is helpful to know that periodical usage is significantly greater for recent materials than for older materials. To be specific, the conclusion of two researchers working independently is that ''80 percent of all requests were published within the last five years. The first six years (current and previous five) contributed to almost 84 percent of all requests'' (Totten 1971: 342). Particularly when dealing with long runs of periodicals, age could definitely be a determining factor in deciding which volumes should be placed in remote storage or withdrawn.

*Importance of periodical to literature of discipline.* As with books, this factor must play a role in decisions about whether or not a periodical should remain in the main collection or be stored or withdrawn. ''While zero use must be considered a significant factor, it cannot serve as the exclusive justification for subscription cancellation or other access-limiting decisions. . . . Internal approval of the associated faculty, collection development staff, and reference staff should also be sought in order to ensure that the intellectual integrity of the collection is preserved'' (Shaw 1978: 482).

In short, consideration of the importance of a periodical to the literature of the discipline must provide some balance to the usage and age factors.

## Processes and Effects of Storage and Withdrawal

There are a number of processes involved with and effects of the storage and withdrawal of library materials.

*Storage and withdrawal decisions.* Whether working with books or periodicals, it is recommended that the librarians do the preliminary identification of potential items for storage or withdrawal but that the faculty decide which materials should be stored and withdrawn. Librarians generally are not subject specialists. However, these processes would be most effective if the librarians were to do the initial work and then call upon faculty members, who are the subject specialists, to review their work and make the final decisions.

There are various ways of doing this, and this paragraph suggests one of them. Working both with the materials in the main collection in the library and in the remote storage area, the librarians should identify items that they think should be stored or withdrawn, mark them on the shelves in some manner, and then invite faculty members in the particular discipline(s) and the faculty at large to review these preliminary judgments. A list of the materials that are candidates for storage or withdrawal should then be sent to the library liaison in each department. At the same time, a note should be sent to all other faculty members stating that the list is available from the library liaison in their department, and a personal list should be sent to any faculty member who requests one. By following these procedures, every attempt would be made to keep the faculty informed and to give it the opportunity to provide input into the process.

Those items that the faculty agrees should be stored will be sent from the main collection to remote storage. Those that have been in remote storage for the number of years stipulated by the particular library and that the faculty agrees should be withdrawn will be removed from storage and discarded. Those that the faculty thinks should not be stored or withdrawn would remain in the main collection or remote storage, although the latter should be kept to a minimum since the primary purpose of storage is to serve as a testing or staging area to see if an item should be withdrawn. In fact, items in storage that have been used may be returned to the main collection, although such decisions should be clearly justified. If the faculty does not review the work of the librarians by a certain date established well beforehand, the items should be automatically sent to remote storage or withdrawn, whichever is applicable.

Although a volume will not be stored or withdrawn if any faculty member does not think it should be, this should not be interpreted as carte blanche for the faculty to not agree to having materials stored and withdrawn. What is needed is a positive working relationship between the faculty and the librarians.

By following these suggested procedures, a satisfactory medium would be achieved. Both the librarians and the faculty would be involved in the decision-making process regarding the retention or removal of materials first from the main collection and then from remote storage. The librarians would set the process in motion at each stage, but the faculty would make the final decisions.

*Timetable of storage and withdrawal process.* Storage and withdrawal must be done on a continuing, systematic basis. With manual processes, because of the sheer amount of work involved, it would be difficult to review all materials in the collection each year to identify which items should be sent to remote storage. It would probably be best to review a few disciplines one year, a few more the next year, and so on. Once the entire collection is covered, the cycle would begin again. However, it should be possible to evaluate each year all of the materials that have been in remote storage for the maximum period stipulated by the library because the number to be reviewed would be relatively small. This would be a new group of materials each year.

If the library has an automated circulation system, there is a chance that it will be possible to review the entire collection, both main and storage, each year in order to identify potential items for storage and withdrawal. The computer can easily provide information about the number of times a book has circulated over a given period, which would be a very helpful starting point for the review process. At the very least, the availability of an automated circulation system would make the process faster than manual review and, therefore, allow for more of the collection to be reviewed each year. The role of automated circulation in collection-size management is discussed in more detail in a later section.

*Impact of storage and withdrawal processes on different parts of collection.* "Some departments will no doubt find selection for withdrawal easier to accomplish than others" (Kaser 1979: 4). Speaking in terms of groupings of disciplines, the literature of the sciences usually changes more rapidly than the literature of the social sciences and the literature of the social sciences usually changes more rapidly than the literature of the humanities.

This information refers to the criteria used for storing and withdrawing books and periodicals, discussed earlier, and gives us some insights as to how these criteria should be applied. Again, the use of materials must be the primary criterion in evaluating them for the purpose of retention in the main collection, storage, or withdrawal. However, the information in the preceding paragraph about the comparative rate of change of the literature in the specified subject groupings assists us in understanding the role and effect of the other two criteria, namely, age of materials and importance of materials to the literature of the discipline.

First, it tells us that more items will be considered obsolete because of age in the sciences, fewer in the social sciences, and fewest in the humanities. This criterion particularly applies to decisions about periodicals since there is no circulation information to serve as a guide in making decisions about these materials. Second, it tells us that the consideration of the importance of materials, both books and periodicals, to the literature of the discipline will impact the three groupings in reverse order. It is likely that there will be more items judged to be important to the literature regardless of their use in the humanities, fewer in the social sciences, and fewest in the sciences.

In general, the science collection can be weeded more frequently and extensively than the social science collection, and the social science collection can be weeded more frequently and extensively than the humanities collection. However, this generalization does not apply to every item within these groupings.

*Effect of storage and withdrawal processes on library work load.* An active and widespread storage and withdrawal program will have a definite effect on the work load of the library staff. The increased work load will have three dimensions: (1) the identification of items for storage and withdrawal, (2) the alteration or removal of the records of these materials depending upon whether they are being sent to remote storage or withdrawn, and (3) the actual transfer of materials into or out of remote storage and the retrieval of those materials requested from remote storage. The first will be the responsibility of the librarians, the second will involve clerical personnel, and the third will be done by student employees.

The effects of the first dimension have already been discussed. Each volume will be reviewed in due time for storage or withdrawal in terms of the three evaluative criteria and some version of the procedures noted earlier. The effects of the third dimension require little explanation. Materials must be physically transferred into and removed from remote storage, and materials requested by students and faculty must be retrieved from remote storage on a daily basis (Monday-Friday).

However, the effects of the second dimension—that is, alteration or removal of the records of these items—is less evident and should be explained more fully. With a storage and withdrawal program, catalog maintenance is a three-part process: records must be added for new acquisitions, records for items sent to remote storage must have their locations changed, and records must be removed for items withdrawn. Libraries without a storage and withdrawal program only do the first of the three to any significant extent. It is the adoption of a storage and withdrawal program that makes the latter two necessary on a large scale.

With an active storage and withdrawal program, the work load should at least double. Combining the extra effort required to alter the location of the records of materials sent to remote storage and to remove the records of materials withdrawn, there should be at least twice as much work for a library that is really serious about storage and withdrawal. By going even farther and adopting the static-capacity concept, the work load will triple. Implementation of the static-capacity concept requires that the number of new volumes acquired be matched by the number of volumes stored and that the number stored be matched by the number withdrawn. Therefore, if this concept is adopted, the maintenance process will involve three steps instead of one with each one requiring the same amount of work as the other two. This means that the work load will increase threefold.

An automated catalog would make a dramatic difference in the catalog-maintenance processes. In fact, an automated catalog can be the difference between a storage and withdrawal program working and not working. This will be discussed more in the next section.

## Automation

Automation of certain of the library's services is another way of managing the size of the collection. In fact, the two are natural allies. Automation can play both a short-term and long-term role in collection-size management.

In the short term, the computer can provide information that is very helpful in making decisions about what materials should be stored and withdrawn or conversely which materials require more copies, and it can make the process of altering or removing bibliographic records considerably more manageable than it is as a manual process. The former information is provided by an automated circulation system, and the latter process is facilitated by an automated catalog. Each of these types requires more discussion.

The computer can play a positive role in terms of providing useful information about the circulation of books. An automated circulation system provides a very easy means of determining the level of circulation or lack of circulation of books. It would take several years before the computer could provide a multiyear history of a book's circulation, which is one reason why it is desirable to have as much lead time as possible before having to make decisions about storage and withdrawal. Manual circulation records could provide the required information, but the gathering of the information in this way would be far more cumbersome than if an automated system were used.

The possibilities for use of circulation data from an automated system are far-reaching. These data are . . . the basic information needed to control library growth and maintain collections for the most effective uses. . . . Several studies have examined the data derivable from automated circulation systems and have applied these data to developing policies and decision points concerning . . . duplication and retirement of materials. (Corya and Buckland 1976: 138)

The computer can also provide very positive assistance in maintaining the library's bibliographic records. It would be possible to maintain bibliographic records manually as part of a storage and withdrawal program, but it would be clumsy and would require such an increase in staff that it would not be cost-effective.

With manual systems, it is so costly and time-consuming to change or remove records of discarded materials, many libraries avoid weeding altogether. . . . With a computer-based system, this task becomes relatively easy and cost-effective since, once the change in the master record has been made, all listings, indexes, catalogs, and the like can be changed automatically. The ease with which an automated system can be utilized to discard and retire materials to other less expensive locations can help control library growth by permitting the librarian to be less hesitant about changing the location of materials. (Corya and Buckland 1976: 135)

In the long term, computerization can also help with collection-size manage-ment by providing access to materials available in other libraries so that many need not be duplicated in the local collection. Referring specifically to the static-capacity concept, one observer has said that " 'static-capacity' college library buildings are becoming possible through the imminent advent of electronic library networks that will alter radically in the next couple of decades the extent and configuration of materials necessary for local libraries to hold on their own shelves'' (Kaser 1979: 2). Electronic networks already exist in the form of the Online Computer Library Center (OCLC) and bibliographic data services such as Lockheed/DIALOG. But many other networks will develop over the next several years. Examples of other networks already being developed or projected are a variety of regional networks and the on-line availability of journals and encyclopedias. For the purpose of collection-size management, the ultimate au-tomated tool will be the availability of some form of efficient and cost-effective long-distance, full-text transmission available on a widespread basis among li-braries.

## COST

When discussing the cost of a new building or wing compared with the cost of implementing a collection-size management program, one consultant con-cluded ''that the net effect of pursuing the second option, through its several measures, will be vastly cheaper than the first'' (Kaser 1979: 7).

However, none of these measures, it should be noted is free. Shoehorning and compact shelving accrue costs to the equipment budgets. Greater use of microfilm has conversion costs and requires a larger number of microfilm reading machines. Remote storage . . . requires college space elsewhere. The very process of weeding and requisite record changing that accompanies withdrawal, conversion of format, or change of location, all require more library staff members. More library staff members will be needed also to aid . . . students and faculty members in maximizing their effective use of a changing kind of library and in accessing collections in other libraries first through conventional interlibrary loan but soon also through more advanced technological and electronic sys-tems. (Kaser 1979: 6)

Automation involves costs in terms of hardware, software, conversion of records to machine-readable form, hardware and software maintenance, and miscella-neous expenses such as site preparation (e.g., stringing cable) and desks or tables for terminals. Although the cost of implementing a collection-size management program is not insignificant, it is considerably less than even the cost of a new wing, much less a new building, when taking into account not only the initial cost of the building but also the annual cost of building maintenance over a multiyear period.

## SERVICE

Although the primary motivation behind collection-size management is to control the growth of the collection, this concept also enhances service. A collection-size management program enhances service in two ways. First, the service that a library provides can actually be improved by removing low-use materials and supplementing high-use materials. "Operations research tells us that it is more difficult to find things in a larger collection than a smaller one. In other words, materials never used . . . inhibit the use of material which is used" (White 1981: 35). Furthermore, collection-size management "will result in a pedagogically more effective library. Dead, or dying, wood will be culled from the stacks where it may now obstruct effective library use by undergraduates" (Kaser 1979: 7). Service can be improved even more by purchasing duplicate or multiple copies of books which are in high demand.

Corollary to the proposition that most books in a library are rarely or never used is the proposition that a small percentage of books are always in very heavy demand and thus frequently unavailable when you want to borrow them. Hence, in most libraries you are likely to fail nearly half the time to find the book you want though the library owns it. The demand is too heavy for the supply. (Gore 1976: 173)

Although an estimate of a 50 percent rate of failure may apply more to a university than a college library since the former would have more students seeking the titles in heavy demand than the latter, it certainly is indicative that a problem exists to some degree in a college library and that the purchase of duplicate or multiple copies would help.

The second way in which collection-size management enhances services is by providing access to other collections and data banks. Even libraries that do not manage the size of their collections may improve service in this way. But with these libraries, these services are nice but not necessary and may, therefore, not be provided, whereas a library with a collection-size management program should provide these services both as a substitute for having some materials available locally (this becomes even more pertinent as acquisitions budgets are reduced) and to provide access to materials that would not be available locally under any circumstances (this becomes even more pertinent as service demands increase). As noted earlier, access to materials in machine-readable form is increasing dramatically, and this increase will continue well into the future. This trend has a very positive effect on library service.

## SUMMARY

If not already important to many smaller academic libraries, collection-size management will or should become important in the not-too-distant future. The static-capacity concept will appeal to certain libraries but not to others. However, collection-size management even to a lesser degree is in the best interest of a library. New buildings and wings rarely provide a long-term solution to the space problem, and the usage of the great majority of materials in library collections is very low. These factors coupled with the cost of construction, the limited availability of finances for construction, and the availability of an increasingly large amount of bibliographic data in machine-readable form require any smaller academic library to consider seriously and even practice collection-size management to some extent. Collection-size management should be or become an integral part of the administrative plan for libraries of this size.

## REFERENCES

Corya, William L., and Michael K. Buckland. 1976. "Automation and Collection Control." In *Farewell to Alexandria: Solutions to Space, Growth, and Performance Problems of Libraries.* Edited by Daniel Gore, pp. 131–40. Westport, Conn.: Greenwood Press.

Farber, Evan Ira. 1976. "Limiting College Library Growth: Bane or Boon?" In *Farewell to Alexandria: Solutions to Space, Growth, and Performance Problems of Libraries.* Edited by Daniel Gore, pp. 34–43. Westport, Conn.: Greenwood Press.

Fussler, Herman H., and Julian L. Simon. 1969. *Patterns in the Use of Books in Large Research Libraries.* Chicago: University of Chicago Press.

Gore, Daniel. 1976. "Farewell to Alexandria: The Theory of the No-Growth, High-Performance Library." In *Farewell to Alexandria: Solutions to Space, Growth, and Performance Problems of Libraries.* Edited by Daniel Gore, pp. 164–80. Westport, Conn.: Greenwood Press.

Heffner, Ray L. 1975. "Zero Growth: When Is NOT-Enough Enough? A Symposium." *The Journal of Academic Librarianship* 1 (November): 4–11.

Kaser, David. 1979. "The Westminster College Library." Consultant Report. August 3.

Kent, Allen et al. 1979. *Use of Library Materials: The University of Pittsburgh Study.* New York: Marcel Dekker.

Lawrence, Gary S., and Anne R. Oja. 1980. "The Use of General Collections at the University of California." Research Report RR–80–11 for Office of the Vice-President for Library Plans and Policies at the University of California, January 30.

Lynden, Frederick C. 1974. "Replacement of Hard Copy by Microforms." *Microform Review* 4 (January): 15–24.

Metcalf, Keyes D. 1965. *Planning Academic and Research Library Buildings.* New York: McGraw-Hill.

Office of the Executive Director of University-wide Library Planning. 1977. "The University of California Libraries: A Plan for Development, 1978–1988." University of California Libraries Internal Report, July.

Poole, Frazer G. "Compact Shelving." 1978. In *Running Out of Space—What Are the Alternatives?* Edited by Gloria Novak, pp. 49–57. Chicago: American Library Association.

Salmon, Stephen R. 1974. "User Resistance to Microforms in the Research Library." *Microform Review* 3 (July): 194–99.

Schorrig, Claudia. 1976. "Sizing Up the Space Problem in Academic Libraries." In *Farewell to Alexandria: Solutions to Space, Growth, and Performance Problems of Libraries.* Edited by Daniel Gore, pp. 6–21. Westport, Conn.: Greenwood Press.

Shaw, W. M., Jr. 1978. "A Practical Journal Usage Technique." *College and Research Libraries* 39 (November): 479–84.

Systems and Procedures Exchange Center. 1977. "Remote Storage in ARL Libraries." *Spec Flyer* 39 (December): 1–2.

Totten, Herman L. 1971. "The Selection of Library Materials for Storage: A State of the Art." *Library Trends* 19 (January): 341–51.

Trueswell, Richard W. 1976. "Growing Libraries: Who Needs Them? A Statistical Basis for the No-Growth Collection." In *Farewell to Alexandria: Solutions to Space, Growth, and Performance Problems of Libraries.* Edited by Daniel Gore, pp. 72–104. Westport, Conn.: Greenwood Press.

White, Herbert S. 1981. "Strategies and Alternatives in Dealing with the Serials Management Budget." In *Serials Collection Development: Choices and Strategies.* Edited by Sul H. Lee, pp. 27–42. Ann Arbor, Mich.: Pierian Press.

# PART V

## User Programs and Services

# 17

# Library Instruction for the Small Academic Library: The Total Approach

## *Janet McNeil Hurlbert*

There is no lack of information about library instruction; articles, books, and workshops abound. In recent years, the content of this material has ranged from learning theory and the research process to an array of specific assignment ideas. Also, the Library Orientation-Instruction Exchange (LOEX) can supply examples and models from all types of programs.

Increasingly, there are those who criticize the instruction movement or see it as a fad. Articles such as the one by Donald Davinson (1984) force us to examine hidden cost factors, dilution of reference-desk services, and self-serving attempts to gain faculty status by developing opportunities to teach. Marilyn Lutzker (1981), on the other hand, stressed the values of instruction, especially for undergraduates. Preparation for graduate school, a means of teaching logic and analysis of materials, and a background for using automated systems are all seen as benefits. The real question is, what do we do without instruction? Is it professionally responsible to allow materials to remain unused and for us not to share our knowledge of systematic research? Perhaps we need to examine our definition of library instruction. Instruction must be a program so thoroughly woven into library operations that every aspect of services, physical arrangement, and procedures are directed by this emphasis.

The underlying reason for believing in a need for instruction in small or large settings does not appear to have changed significantly since the Monteith experience in the sixties (Knapp 1966: 11). Librarians view instruction as an assertive and professional way to use their resources and skills to influence a student's ability to perform academic work. In the process, the student becomes better prepared for a profession and life in an information-based society.

In smaller academic libraries, we are often told that ours is the ideal environment for implementing and sustaining a library-instruction program. Certainly, the Earlham College Library serves as an example of what is possible when faculty and librarians share common instructional goals. Yet because of the varying restrictions inherent in smaller institutions, it is necessary to examine instruction as a total library commitment toward giving a clearly defined student body a continuous and personalized service.

## HOW DOES AN INSTRUCTION PROGRAM DIFFER IN A SMALL LIBRARY?

The overall purpose of a good library-instruction program does not vary to any great extent despite the size of an academic library. Approaches to instruction and projects are similar as well, only on a different scale. Methods of enacting and sustaining such programs can vary greatly. Ideas of creating a separate library-instruction department and hiring new support staff, developing professional audiovisual productions, maximizing or experimenting with advanced technology, and performing complex analyses of existing or future programs are unrealistic and in some very small environments are completely unattainable. Even a travel budget for attending workshops or national meetings where information can be shared may be severely restricted.

In the small-college setting, any shift of emphasis within an instructional program will have direct, and probably immediate, repercussions on all other areas of the library. The same librarian or librarians who coordinate interlibrary loan, reference-desk service, and on-line searching must also assume responsibility for bibliographic instruction. Library instruction viewed as an appendage to "regular" duties for a staff cannot be successful. It must be the core of the library's purpose around which other services revolve.

If staff time and money loom as obstacles to an effective instructional situation, why are we viewed as an ideal setting? Obviously, "small" is the key. Knowing and seeing the student body (possibly a homogeneous one) on a routine basis, being familiar with class curricula and assignments in manageable numbers, having a climate of closeness and communication with administrators, coworkers, and fellow faculty members are all prerequisites for a good instructional program. No one would question that such a condition can exist in a small college, but it takes effort and is not a logical result of such an environment. If the above elements are not present to some degree, an instructional program is doomed. Isolationism, stereotypes, and lack of communication can exist in small colleges as well as in large universities.

The intensity of an instructional program presents an interesting dilemma. An aggressive program is hard work. Preparing lectures, meeting varying class schedules, keeping up with technological advances, advising on assignments, and providing the support system for these assignments dominate many months of the school calendar. Once a system is established, the planning function and material preparation will still absorb the slower months. Yet it is usually librarians who suggest such a program knowing the new demands it will place on them and their organizational structure. Seldom are college administrators aware of the range of possibilities within bibliographic instruction. Mere puttering with library instruction might well suffice in meeting the expectations of administrators and even accrediting teams. A small staff is always an acceptable reason for limited activity. Likewise, faculty have different interpretations of library instruction and often underestimate the librarian's potential to engage with them actively in the research-instruction process. In a small-college library, the pressures and expectations placed on librarians may be based more on the college's own traditions than on national standards accepted at larger institutions. Elaborate peer evaluations, a competitive atmosphere, and a demand for research may not be driving forces as they sometimes are in universities. On the negative side, this can encourage lesser output. Positively, it means a certain freedom to direct a program at a pace that matches staffing, resources, and current conditions. Thus a small institution may provide the freedom for striking a balance between the ideal and the possible for each unique situation.

## THERE HAS TO BE A PLAN AND ADMINISTRATIVE SUPPORT

In developing a program, three areas must be considered: the college administration, the needs of the faculty and students as we perceive them, and the flexibility of the library operation itself. Most college libraries will have implemented some library-instruction programs throughout the years. What may not have developed is a consistent, overall plan of action.

College and library administrative understanding and support are essential for the future development of instruction. But we know, in the beginning stages, that individuals must create and sell their programs. A plan is started by "a librarian personally convinced of the value of bibliographic instruction, and personally committed to the program" (Boissé 1978: 10). Problems can arise when that individual fails to translate this somewhat evangelical spirit into sound library practice and to incorporate it into the administration of not only the library but the college (Meyer 1981: 63). Temporary funding, staffing, and grant projects should be viewed cautiously. It is more important to win approval for a program that can be maintained consistently over a long period with resources that the college can reasonably ensure.

Presenting a plan, outlining the stages of this plan, and, especially, detailing the needed responses from college administrators are the best beginning. Although the library must be realistic about the constraints within which a small-college administration operates, there should still be a substantive commitment to the program in comparison to the support given other instructional and campus activities. This support can take the form of goodwill and promotion to the faculty, which costs nothing, to money for end-user searching, computers, and software. A further consideration for continuous funding on a small scale might be alumni financial aid or assistance through a college-development or public relations office for subsidiary items such as publications, on-line systems, interlibrary loan charges, or workshop attendance. In other words, make the campus offices as well as the alumni aware of your instructional outreach goals.

What is this plan that must be presented? We may believe that "at some unidentifiable point several decades ago, academic departments ceased to transmit basic library research methods to students as a standard part of the curriculum" (Beaubien, Hogan, and George 1982: 65). Or, possibly, we are convinced as Carl Hintz (1975: 2) is that professors settle for products that do not make effective use of books and libraries. Do we know what is needed better than our teaching faculty? To impart the knowledge that librarians have to share, we must present a plan consisting of general expectations with a suggested course of action in hopes that, with time, major change will occur not only in assignments but also in attitudes toward the research process as well. The Association of College and Research Libraries (ACRL) in the "Model Objectives for Bibliographic Instruction" provides guidelines that can be used or modified for drawing up unique institutional goals and objectives. In this way, a small library attains a communality with other libraries within the field of instruction.

When formulating a plan, "small" is on our side because librarians with firsthand experience can analyze previous instructional efforts and results, impressions of students' overall abilities, and the way students currently handle assignments. This plan should move away from viewing instruction as a means of survival at times when there is no way for a small staff to answer basic questions repeatedly. Increasingly, we must feel an obligation to communicate our observations to faculty and administrators, and take a lead in the research portion of curriculum planning. Some of these observations include the problems students have in completing traditional term papers: inability to select good topics suitable for a particular library; the last-minute rush that eliminates any sense of research development or process; failure to use a variety of available resources and services; and failure to analyze and evaluate properly the sources that are used. As librarians we want to experiment with more creative assignments or assignments with more check points in terms of the research process. Showing the faculty the other side of an assignment, the side we see as librarians, and sharing ideas about developing new assignments are sensitive issues. However, this is just as much a part of instruction as a classroom lecture.

If more concrete data than personal observations are desired as the planning process continues, several methods can be implemented on a small campus. Whereas a written questionnaire might be seen as pretentious, an informal survey with faculty or student groups, based on personal interviews with a librarian, can be a means for establishing good communications. Other data can be acquired through the use of a pretest on library knowledge during the freshman testing sessions so that over time librarians can gain a statistical basis for judging the incoming classes. This method will also identify those students who because of educational background or English language ability will have an especially difficult time using a college library.

What reorganization within the library will be needed to bring about a total commitment to instruction? First, an attitude must be instilled in all staff members that instruction is the first priority. It is almost impossible for a small-college library to enter into a comprehensive instruction program without commitment from all librarians and staff members and the realization that everyone shares some responsibility for its success. All librarians must bear the teaching load, if not by actually teaching, by delivering certain services such as reference in the absence of those who are teaching. It will also be necessary to examine library operations not only to see where staff and time can be saved but also to make sure that the ways in which library materials are handled and arranged fit with the instructional concept.

What can be changed or eliminated from the services that are now offered? A library must be willing to consider the role that nonprofessionals and student assistants play in supporting library services. As professionals, how much are we willing to relinquish, and what will be the consequences? Individual libraries must weigh their options, experiment, and remain flexible to methods of freeing time.

Also of significance is defining the public that is served by the library. What kinds of services are being given to those outside the college community? If a library, especially in the case of a private institution, is willing to assume a public role as a source for reference and other types of services, direct programs to tuition-paying students have to be reduced when relying on a very small staff. To some libraries, this service may be seen as public relations; to others, a clearer definition of whom to serve, and how, may be an appropriate way of making better use of staff time.

Instruction causes a rippling effect in all aspects of library operations. Initially, we see instruction taking us away from a reference desk that now has increased activity. More use places new demands on equipment, shelving, and general upkeep of materials. Preparation of guides and bibliographies multiplies clerical demands. Eventually, the selection criteria for the types of materials needed may shift or become more sophisticated. There will be more interlibrary loans and on-line data-base searches. A total commitment to creating an instructional environment can change the structure of a library and calls for a complete review of work patterns as well as carefully planned budget projections.

## IMPLEMENTATION OF THE PLAN

With a commitment to library instruction secured and realistic staffing and monetary projections developed, a piecemeal approach is often the only practical way to proceed because of limited staffing and finances. More importantly, it requires time to develop the goodwill and depth of cooperation needed from the teaching faculty. In devising steps to implement our goals, we come to the greatest stumbling block—a successful method of reaching all incoming students in a meaningful way to ensure that they have been instructed on a basic level. Without this first step, advanced orientation and library projects are diluted because of the constant uncertainty about whom we have reached and how. Not only are there a number of methods to consider for reaching all students, but also there is much library literature to read about each technique. A separate course, audiovisual presentations, a completely integrated lecture-assignment with a class, or a programmed instruction approach through workbooks or computers are all alternatives used by various institutions. In choosing what is the most financially feasible and effective means, go back to the initial analysis of what you think the students need, what cooperation can be expected from the faculty, and what the library can provide at a given time. Once again, college size is a major factor. Small colleges stress the value of a personal approach to education, at the same time charging a high price for the experience. The library-instruction program should reflect this personal approach. Audiovisual presentations and programmed instruction are techniques used by large institutions to meet the needs of many students. Computer-assisted instruction accomplishes many of the same objectives but relies on more funding and technological capability. Because of staffing, a small college may have the same conflicts as a large university between the number of people to serve and those to do the basic instruction. Methods to reach many students at the same time should not be discarded as impersonal without proper evaluation of their basic merits. Thomas Surprenant (1978) saw strengths in programmed learning instruments such as their flexibility, immediate required response, and uniformity of presentation. To that list might be added novelty in the case of computer-assisted instruction, which in itself can facilitate learning as well. However, the big advantage to a small college is the fact that no matter what method is used, the same staff will fill a supportive role from the beginning of the assignment to its conclusion. Clearly, instruction is an extension of reference-desk service. The lecture, written unit, or audiovisual presentation does not stand alone if the assignment that follows is designed correctly.

Mary Reichel (1984) emphasized the need for the same librarians to be involved in the passive aspects of reference, meaning desk work, as well as assuming responsibility for bibliographic knowledge through instruction. A small staff has no choice. It will be active at every point in which a student interacts with the library. No matter what instructional approach is used to reach students initially, this first exposure is usually the hardest to implement. Faculty members may resent the deliberate attempt to standardize one aspect of their course. Also, freshman classes such as English involve a diverse number of faculty personalities, and working with such large numbers of students requires expert organizational skill on the part of a small library staff. Certain guidelines should prevail when choosing a method for a small college: (1) What is the most personal and effective method that can be offered with current staffing? (2) Can students see an immediate need for the type of instruction presented? (3) Will the students be able to put the material to use in a way that will involve questions and interaction with librarians? (4) Can more advanced library instruction classes build upon this initial instruction? No matter what method of instruction is used, there will be students who can take the information and use it immediately and creatively. Others will fail to focus on any of the material and will need a step-by-step repeat explanation. Most will fall into a middle category, gaining information that will have to be enforced by individual help as the project progresses. What is important for the student is that the instruction continues, that the format of instruction is varied, and that a majority of the students ultimately reach the desired goals as established in your library's objectives.

There can be too much formal library instruction. A well-designed assignment can often result in indirect instruction. The nature of the assignment, the requirements for the types of materials used, and the procedures mandated for the prewriting process are excellent means of enhancing the formal instruction given at other times. Structuring these tasks not only requires a willingness on the part of the faculty to work closely with librarians in developing assignments, but it also requires mutual creativity in finding alternatives to the traditional, overworked term paper.

## EVALUATION

No system can be successful without a method of evaluation. Collecting quantitative, publishable data is often not only infeasible for the small library but also a misuse of time. The chances to observe, correct, modify, and rework are obvious. Evaluations should be from three directions: the librarian who sees the assignments or tasks from initial instruction to completed project; the student who might well be asked to write a brief statement evaluating certain points of the instruction process; and the faculties' views of the whole procedure collected either informally or at a structured meeting. The key to evaluation is how well upperclass students can handle an information-based project—can they do the things we originally sought to teach them?

The common claim that papers are better when library instruction is given is only partially true. The degree to which they are better relates to the completeness of the instructional process surrounding the assignment. It is also in proportion to how closely faculty and librarians have worked together. Librarians should be involved in evaluating the final bibliographic product of these class assignments to aid them in evaluating their entire instructional program.

## THE FUTURE

Blaise Cronin (1985) presented a thoughtful look at the future of instruction. Our present and future hold user-friendly, do-it-yourself information systems that can, in many ways, circumvent the research process and the library itself. Increasingly, in this sophisticated information age, we are not exactly sure what does prepare a student for the future. Also, the technological differences between what a small institution and library offer compared to a larger one can be in sharp contrast. We should not lose sight of the fact that our immediate goal is to prepare students to meet the challenges of academic work at our own particular institution, and in most cases, this will involve a more traditional approach to instruction for some years to come. However, our graduates cannot compete if we do not make every effort when feasible to introduce at least the basics of modern information access technology.

A library program cannot move faster than its parent institution in implementing technology or, more pointedly, in financing technology. The library, if seen as an authority in disseminating information, may influence the rate at which new advancements are introduced. Something as simple as a word processor will have positive benefits for preparing and changing instructional materials in an efficient manner. The capabilities of computerized searching as well as actual end-user searching should be part of every instruction program and reference service, especially since major vendors now offer pricing options much more suitable to limited budgets.

Often, a small library must wait for technological advances to be tested, perfected, and paid for by larger institutions. The successful experience at the University of Delaware Library (Arnott and Richards 1985) with computer-assisted instruction serves as a useful model for smaller libraries as equipment and software become cheaper and more plentiful. A flexible and diverse instructional program fulfills our professional responsibility to introduce information advances within our capabilities or limitations.

By being aware of new educational trends, library instruction can also find new ways of developing and strengthening its contribution to the college's programs as a whole. Library instruction has had a definite place in college developmental services for many years. Now, the emphasis on writing and writing across the curriculum provides an excellent means of incorporating library instruction into the writing process (Mellon 1984) and certainly encourages us to study research procedures as a learning process as well (Peroni 1981). Also, the teaching methods used in such writing programs may be applied to our own library-instruction techniques. Rather than seeing library instruction itself as a trend, better to incorporate our own instructional goals into the trends occurring in the field of education that surround us. In this way, we direct our own future.

## CONCLUSION

For a library-instruction program to make an impact on its academic environment, it must be the focal point on which library decisions and operations are based. A general, long-range, comprehensive, and realistic plan should be developed. This plan, with goals of developing close working relations with the faculty and establishing a philosophy of instruction, should include methods of organizing library functions so that all library programs and procedures are viewed as support systems for the instructional emphasis. Instruction should reach each incoming student and then proceed to develop students' skills within a discipline so that a certain confidence in handling information will exist by the time of graduation. A variety of instruction methods can be used and should be combined with whatever technology is feasible and affordable. Librarians must continually strive to make research-based assignments a cooperative effort between library and classroom instruction. Administrative support and understanding should be developed and a consistent level of financing established.

There is a discouragement factor built into library instruction. Certain students and faculty will not respond. Just as the future of information retrieval is in constant flux, so are the efforts to establish and maintain relationships with the classroom. Our endeavor is never "finished" but is part of a continuing process.

If the assets of working in a small college are explored fully by librarians, a meaningful program can be not only developed but maintained. It is professionally as well as personally rewarding to be able to work closely with the same students as they grow in the learning experiences associated with college. However, it is vital for a librarian in a small, possibly limited, situation to keep current with the methods and advances in the field of library instruction and education. To this must be added energy, persistence, and patience.

## REFERENCES

Arnott, Patricia D., and Deborah E. Richards. 1985. "Using the IBM Personal Computer for Library Instruction." *Reference Services Review* 13 (Spring): 69–72.

Beaubien, Anne K., Sharon A. Hogan, and Mary W. George. 1982. *Learning the Library: Concepts and Methods for Effective Bibliographic Instruction*. New York: R. R. Bowker.

Boissé, Joseph A. 1978. "Library Instruction and the Administration." In *Putting Library Instruction in Its Place: In the Library and in the Library School*. Edited by Carolyn A. Kirkendall, pp. 1–12. Ann Arbor, Mich.: Pierian Press.

Cronin, Blaise. 1985. "User Education: Getting Our Priorities Right." In *User Education in the Online Age II*. Edited by Nancy Fjallbrant, pp. 55–63. Goteborg, Sweden: International Association of Technological University Libraries (IATUL), Chalmers University of Technology Library.

Davinson, Donald. 1984. "Never Mind the Quality, Feel the Width." *The Reference Librarian*, no. 10 (Spring-Summer): 29–37.

Hintz, Carl W. 1975. "Library Orientation." In *Academic Library Instruction: Objectives, Programs, and Faculty Involvement*. Edited by Hannelore B. Rader, pp. 1–3. Ann Arbor, Mich.: Pierian Press.

Knapp, Patricia B. 1966. *The Monteith College Library Experiment*. New York: Scarecrow Press.

Lutzker, Marilyn. 1981. "Is Knowledge of the Details of Conducting Research Really Necessary for Students Today?" In *Directions for the Decade*. Edited by Carolyn A. Kirkendall, pp. 56–59. Ann Arbor, Mich.: Pierian Press.

Mellon, Constance A. 1984. "Process Not Product in Course-Integrated Instruction: A Generic Model of Library Research." *College and Research Libraries* 45 (November): 471–78.

Meyer, Wayne. 1981. "Will This Innovation, Library Instruction, Be Adopted, By and By?" In *Directions for the Decade: Library Instruction in the 1980's*. Edited by Carolyn A. Kirkendall, pp. 59–64. Ann Arbor, Mich.: Pierian Press.

Peroni, Patricia A. 1981. *The Second Kind of Knowledge: The Role of Library Instruction in Writing Across the Curriculum.* ERIC Document Reproduction Service. ED 217 487.

Reichel, Mary. 1984. "Bibliographic Education and Reference Desk Service—A Continuum." *The Reference Librarian*, no. 10 (Spring-Summer): 191–98.

Surprenant, Thomas T. 1978. "A Comparison of Lecture and Programmed Instruction in the Teaching of Basic Catalog Card and Bibliographic Index Information—Results of a Pretest." In *Proceedings of the Southeastern Conference on Approaches to Bibliographic Instruction.* Edited by Cerise Oberman-Soroka, pp. 54–66. Charleston, S.C.: Continuing Education Office, College of Charleston.

# 18

# Computer-Assisted Library Instruction

## *Terrence F. Mech*

Computer-assisted instruction (CAI) and closely related programmed instruction both boomed in the 1960s with the aid of federal money. When the money dried up, CAI, with its reliance on expensive mainframe computers and programming staff, was out of reach for most libraries. Although libraries had an early interest in CAI, affordable programmed instruction in workbook form caught the attention of libraries. "A workbook meets the definition of programmed instruction by presenting a series of questions, usually accompanied by short descriptive materials, that studenst work through at their own pace" (Adams 1980: 89).

Since the 1970s library workbooks have become recognized as an effective, inexpensive way to reach large numbers of students with some "assurance that they will actually participate in the learning experience. However, like much of programmed instruction, workbooks do not allow for differences in level of student ability; they do not allow students to follow their own interests, and must often depend on the motivation of course requirements to ensure completion" (Adams 1980: 89).

CAI can take the successful library workbook several steps further. However, simply putting a library workbook on a computer is expensive and offers no real advantages because it fails to exploit the computer. The addition of branching programs that direct students to different subprograms based on their responses is what good CAI is all about. Based on their responses students move at their own rate and receive the instruction they need.

Computer-assisted library instruction has much to offer. Previously, high development costs and computer hardware limited CAI largely to universities where extensive CAI research was being conducted. With the advent of inexpensive microcomputers, improvements in programming languages, and librarians' increased familiarity with computers, CAI is entering more libraries.

With CAI, students use computers in active teaching-learning situations, computers acting as middlemen between instructor and students. Computers accept and store information from the instructor, producing it upon student demand, guiding students through prescribed learning sequences at their own pace (Culkin 1972: 301).

CAI usually falls into three interactive patterns.

1. Drill and practice programs ask questions of students and provide feedback to their responses. This type of CAI provides practice for skills already learned.

2. Dialogue programs require that students converse with the computer. The computer presents a problem, and students attempt to solve the problem by questioning the computer and testing their solutions. This Socratic method of CAI is perhaps the most dynamic but least developed form of CAI.

3. Tutorial programs require the computer to function as a lecturer or information presentor. In this type of program students are presented with an instructional sequence consisting of presentations, questions, and feedback. CAI's basic principles also guide development of programmed instruction. "These include: no human instructor present; instruction is presented in small steps; learners make responses in a two way interaction which determines the next step; learners proceed at their own rate; and feedback in the form of responses leads students on the correct path and reinforces their learning" (Clark 1974: 336).

## CAI IN LIBRARIES

The most common use of CAI has been for bibliographic instruction. Academic libraries of all sizes face the task of providing repetitive library instruction to hundreds of underclassmen. Few libraries have enough librarians for this strenuous and time-consuming task. CAI has proven an effective means of providing library instruction while freeing librarians for advanced library instruction.

An early use of CAI for library instruction was developed in 1967 at the University of Illinois. A study compared the effectiveness of CAI and conventional lectures in teaching library skills. Results indicated no statistical difference in the amount of knowledge gained by students (Axeen 1967). Other early efforts at CAI for library instruction were made at the University of Denver, Ohio State University, and Dartmouth College.

By 1977 there was widespread interest in computer-assisted library instruction; unfortunately, there was a shortage of successful programs. Less than a handful of the experimental CAI programs were in operation. In 1977 many libraries recognized CAI's potential, but CAI was to be a victim of universal monetary cutbacks in libraries (Amann 1977).

Since then a number of library CAI programs have been developed with positive results. At the University of Illinois, Urbana-Champaign, Biology Library, a CAI program was "highly effective in teaching biology students to use reference and bibliography collections" (Williams and Davis 1979: 14). In 1978 at the University of Nebraska—Lincoln, results showed that CAI and tutorial methods "were somewhat more effective than the traditional tour for teaching card catalog skills, but cost-benefit considerations restricted further development of either method for large-scale use" (Johnson and Plake 1980: 154). The University of Nebraska—Lincoln later developed a self-paced library workbook.

More recently, University of Kentucky libraries developed a CAI program to assist students in use of the card catalog and Wilson periodical indexes. University of Kentucky libraries "found the program to be a valuable addition to our instructional services. The response from students, both written and oral has been overwhelmingly positive" (Aken and Olson 1984: 39). In 1985 the University of Delaware developed a mainframe-based CAI program for providing library instruction to freshmen. A microcomputer-based generic-library version of Delaware's successful CAI program is available.

CAI can be used successfully for training student assistants and other library personnel. Student assistants are an important part of any library staff; yet efficient and effective training of student assistants is tedious and time consuming. In 1981–1982 Indiana University libraries developed a CAI program to teach student assistants Library of Congress call numbers and basic elements of the card catalog. The CAI program has been successful, and students have responded favorably ("Automated Staff Training," 1982).

In 1978 the University of Evansville's Clifford Library developed a mainframe-based CAI training program for circulation student assistants. This CAI program produced results equal or superior to traditional methods of training student assistants, freeing staff for advanced training of student assistants and other projects. Student response was favorable (Rawlins 1982). Evansville's CAI training program was later rewritten for microcomputers and expanded to include other service areas. No single training method is always best for every situation, and microcomputers have not changed that fundamental piece of educational wisdom (Guilfoyle 1985: 334). At Evansville, computer-assisted training is followed by close personal supervision.

With increased use of technology in library operations, training library personnel becomes more important if not more time consuming. Because there is never enough time to train individuals, supervisors are seeking alternative methods. University of Florida catalogers developed a CAI program, "How to Search OCLC," designed to improve the quality of the Online Computer Library Center (OCLC) search training, to conserve the trainer's time, and to reduce on-line time. This microcomputer-based program developed by catalogers was programmed by an honors student in computer and information science. The program, designed to teach student assistants, paraprofessionals, and others how to search the OCLC, generated very favorable responses even from experienced searchers (Shaw 1984).

Use of CAI to train and assist users of on-line public access catalogs will increase as on-line catalogs become more prevalent. CAI is being used to develop the bibliographic retrieval skills of on-line searchers, to teach and refresh skills, and to test new strategies on a simulated data base before making "real" searches in DIALOG (Caruso 1981). CAI may also be effective in training students how to conduct their own searches of on-line bibliographic data bases (Renford and Hendrickson 1980: 152).

Until recently, most library CAI programs were run on mainframe computers at large universities with appropriately trained computer and CAI personnel. However, CAI even in its earliest development was not limited to large universities. In 1975 a mainframe-based CAI program on using the card catalog was developed at Slippery Rock State College (Wood 1975). The program was written in BASIC and designed for easy adaptation by other libraries in an attempt to spread the use of CAI.

To develop a program that reviews basic skills, arouses student interest, and instills a positive attitude, Newberry College developed a library-instruction computer game that operated on a minicomputer outside of the library (Koelewyn and Corby 1982: 171). Now, with inexpensive microcomputers it is even easier for smaller academic libraries to develop computer-assisted library-instruction programs. In 1982 Mansfield University libraries successfully developed a microcomputer-based library-orientation program.

## CAI TRADE-OFFS

Although CAI is effective it is not without its disadvantages. In developing CAI programs, librarians move from familiar methods of instruction to a computer-based method with which most have little experience. Early CAI suffered from its association with computers. Computers can generate a lot of fear and anxiety in people. Early CAI programs were primitive by today's comparison, and their early reputation cooled ardor for CAI. Early undocumented CAI programs were not easy to adapt from one computer to another and the lack of CAI experts to guide individuals through the morass of authoring languages and technical requirements slowed CAI development. Expensive costs of early computers and programming staffs did not encourage widespread CAI development.

The current availability of microcomputers and improved programming languages have removed large obstacles in the way of expanding CAI. As a result, many individuals are beginning to understand and use computers for educational purposes. Good CAI programs are still scarce. Librarians experienced in using CAI are not plentiful. However, the growing number of library-produced CAI programs indicates that librarians are willing to overcome obstacles to exploit the potential of CAI.

Perhaps the biggest obstacle to developing good CAI programs is the time involved in designing, writing, and revising CAI programs. Complications in developing CAI often show up only when the program has been entered into the computer and is staring at you in a way you never intended. CAI programs, to be effective, must be revised in light of criticism and student feedback. For these and other reasons a team approach is an efficient and effective way to develop CAI.

Although there are obstacles, smaller academic libraries can develop CAI programs. CAI allows smaller academic libraries to provide uniform levels of library instruction to large numbers of students. It frees librarians from the repetitive drudgery of tours and lectures, conserving them for advanced instruction. CAI has many other advantages. It actively involves individuals in the learning process. Students cannot be totally passive using CAI. Student involvement and the ability to proceed at their own pace facilitates learning. Reinforcement of learning is immediate and systematized, theoretically resulting in more effective learning (Chambers and Sprecher 1980: 333). CAI permits students to learn material in significantly less time than traditional lecture methods (Axeen 1967: 11).

Computers have infinite patience. CAI programs are versatile and very flexible and can present a variety of material in a more interesting manner to a variety of learners. CAI programs are easily modified without disturbing the entire program.

Libraries wishing to use CAI for library instruction do not have to develop their own CAI programs. CAI programs prepared by outside agencies may teach generic principles of library research. However, they cannot orient users to your particular library. Previously, most CAI library-skills programs were developed for elementary and secondary schools, leaving college librarians with few CAI alternatives but to develop their own.

## DEVELOPING CAI PROGRAMS

Many individuals assume that you must be a computer programmer to develop a good CAI program. The most important elements in developing a good CAI program are the author's subject knowledge, the ability to develop a sound instructional design, and knowledge of programmed instruction such as library workbooks. Understanding programmed instruction enables CAI authors to use the instruction advantages of the computer effectively. Being able to program a computer is helpful but not necessary to developing an effective CAI program. CAI authors and programmers must be able to understand and communicate what it is they want and what it is the computer or program is capable of doing reasonably.

Choice of a programming language or authoring system greatly affects what the CAI program is capable of doing. A general-purpose computer language like BASIC is a familiar language to nonprofessional programmers. BASIC, the native language of microcomputers, is fairly portable among microcomputers; however, it has limited vocabulary and graphics capability. Programming with a specialized CAI programming language like PILOT is faster. But learning PILOT or other specialized programming languages is time consuming. Another alternative is a CAI authoring system that walks an individual through the authoring process step by step (Eng 1984). A CAI authoring system enables individuals with no programming experience to write customized CAI programs.

CAI authoring systems appear to be the easiest way for individuals to develop CAI programs.

Programming is the most time-consuming phase of CAI development and is not where an author's efforts should go. The author's efforts should go toward preparation of the lesson itself. Authors should identify their goals; specify the behavioral objectives they seek in students; develop an outline of their lesson, content, and instructional strategy; and identify the steps that lead toward their objective (Clark 1974: 342).

Developers of library CAI programs should do what they do best, teach library skills, and leave programming to programmers. CAI authors should concentrate their energies on preparation and revision of their instructional design and text.

## THE MANSFIELD UNIVERSITY EXPERIENCE

Mansfield University of Pennsylvania's experience with computer-assisted library instruction demonstrates that quality CAI programs can be developed by librarians in smaller academic libraries under less than ideal conditions. The competencies needed for production of a computer-assisted library-instruction program can be developed within existing library personnel. In 1982 Mansfield developed a microcomputer-based library-instruction program. The following description of those efforts was adapted from materials produced by the program's author, Deanna Nipp (1984), and is presented here with her permission.

When microcomputers became available, Mansfield librarians began to discuss the need to make microcomputers available to students. As a result they decided to use microcomputers for the repetitive work of library orientations for entering students, conserving staff for advanced library instruction. There was also some expectation that using a medium students enjoyed, like computers, would foster learning. Mansfield chose to produce its own program rather than acquire a commercially produced program because it wanted a program that would introduce students to the organization and services specific to campus libraries.

A librarian was given a one-semester sabbatical leave to learn BASIC (a programming language), educational design and to write a library-orientation program. The librarian spent six weeks learning BASIC from a self-teaching guide, nine weeks designing and coding the program, and another two weeks preparing program documentation. Upon reflection, the program author thought that the skills needed to develop the CAI program could have been developed without a sabbatical (Nipp 1985).

Mansfield's CAI program, designed primarily to transfer skills, is organized into nine units of instruction with interactive questions. The program includes instruction, exercises, and evaluation of a student's understanding of library services (emphasizing reference) and the Library of Congress call-number system and call-number location in the main library, recognition of elements of a magazine-article citation, use of *Reader's Guide* and the libraries' serials holding list, and awareness of the collections and services of the two branch libraries. Successful completion of the program required students to locate a book and article on an assigned topic. A printout of student scores is produced at the end of the program. In addition to using the computer software, Mansfield's program required directions for loading the software into the computer, five cards in the card catalog, shelf dummies scattered throughout the library, and laminated pages from *Reader's Guide to Periodical Literature*.

The original program designed for Apple microcomputers was first used by students in January 1983. Student response was enthusiastic. Program evaluations were positive. Because of an institutional decision to acquire and locate numerous IBM PCs in the library and because students took two hours to complete the program, the program was completely revised during the fall of 1983 for use on IBM microcomputers. In the revised version, educational design improved, writing was tightened, sequencing was more interactive, and graphic rewards to correct answers were added. Total revision of the original program's design and script involved 100 hours (by a now experienced librarian CAI author) and 100 hours for programming by an undergraduate computer-science student. It took the undergraduate student approximately 50 hours to learn a new programming language, PILOT, before the revised programming could begin. Use of a student programmer and the more powerful program language allowed the CAI author to concentrate on teaching library skills by improving instructional design and text of the computer-assisted library program. While Mansfield's Academic Computer Services Department was not staffed to the level that made it possible for them to design and program the library's software, it was a valuable resource in the library's attempt to understand the capabilities of available equipment and commercial programming software.

## THE PRODUCTION PROCESS

The following outline of Mansfield's CAI production process was developed by Deanna Nipp (Nipp 1984) and is presented here in adapted form with her permission. The steps, with some overlap, are listed in the order that seems most appropriate for a library undertaking its first production.

1. Make an assessment of resources that will be needed and plan for funding. Needed resources will include: microcomputers; any special production software, like an authoring language or a graphics tablet; diskettes for the writing and programming process; diskettes for final copies of the program; materials for packaging the diskettes and documentation (documentation includes description of the software, instructions for use, and any peripheral materials to be used with the diskettes); materials for evaluation of the program (most common would be pretests and posttests); staff time for learning needed competencies in educational design (using computers as an instructional medium) and perhaps programming; and staff time for designing, writing, programming, evaluating, and revising.

2. Develop educational design competencies. Learn how to use screen space and computer logic and memory in order to teach. There are several ways to do this.

   A. Read textbooks and published research on computer-assisted instruction. A good place to start is Robert L. Burke's *CAI Sourcebook* (Englewood Cliffs, N.J.: Prentice-Hall, 1982), a complete look at production for beginners.

   B. Review other software. There is no substitute for this. One begins to understand the interactive nature of CAI through this process and develops ideas for organizing a program and using screen space effectively.

   C. Take a course in educational design. Look for one with ample coverage of CAI.

3. Provide for programming competencies. There may be a staff person who can program or who is willing to learn. One good source of potential programmers is students in computer and information science.

4. Design the program.

   A. Write the instructional goals. This step is essential for later evaluation, and it also focuses on the scripting process to follow.

   B. Select the kind of program (i.e., tutorial, drill, practice, and so on) that is most appropriate for the instructional goals.

   C. Organize the program, based on decisions such as whether it is appropriate for all students to be presented the same information in the same order (linear program) or whether students who show higher comprehension can be branched to a more advanced presentation. Experience has shown that "the best results come from accurately matching difficulty against performance so that students never become bored by a succession of easy tasks or overwhelmed by a succession of incomprehensibly difficult ones" (Pask 1982: 152).

   D. Write or script the screens. This is most easily done on graph paper with the same number of spaces across and lines down as on the screen. Script a graph for each screen, avoiding too much text on a screen. Use the side of the graph paper next to the scripted screen display for notes to the programmer. These notes communicate how the program should respond to any input from students—that is, what changes are to be made on this screen and where the program should go when student work on the screen is completed. The designing and scripting process will be facilitated by some awareness of the system's capabilities. What kind of graphics are possible? What's the easiest device for getting input for going to the next screen? Working closely with the programmer during the initial scripting will make it possible to finish most of the scripting without having to go back and make a lot of changes.

5. Program the scripted material, and watch it come to life.

6. Write the documentation, make copies of the program for use, and package them together. Documentation should include title and credits, description of content, notation of equipment necessary to run the program, and other necessary material. Keep user documentation short and simple.

7. Evaluate on the basis of educational goals. A formal system of pretesting and post-testing can be used for content mastery. It is also important to ask for student feedback and actually watch student use to see where the problems are.

8. Revise. Evaluation will show where the program fell short in reaching goals. During initial use, lots of ideas for improvements will also come to mind.

9. Maintain. Make master copies of diskettes and documentation to store in a safe place. Make extra copies of diskettes to replace those damaged in use. If library materials are part of the documentation, check them regularly during times of heavy use to see that they are in the right place and not damaged.

## THE FUTURE OF CAI IN LIBRARIES

Use of computer-assisted library instruction in small academic libraries will increase. Training library staff and teaching of library skills consumes large amounts of staff time. CAI offers smaller academic libraries a very effective solution to training and instruction problems. Microcomputers can be obtained far easier than additional staff. The increased availability of librarian-produced generic library instruction and training programs will further the use of CAI in small academic libraries. For those libraries that wish to develop library specific CAI programs, it is becoming easier to do so. Improved languages and a growing number of librarians and educators willing to share their CAI experiences make it easier for individual librarians to create a meaningful and effective computer-assisted library-instruction program.

## REFERENCES

Adams, Mignon. 1980. "Individual Approach to Learning Library Skills." *Library Trends* 29 (Summer): 83–84.

Aken, Rob, and Laura Olson. 1984. "CAI in Libraries: Creating in-House Programs." *Teaching and Learning Technologies* (June): 36–39.

Amann, Cynthia. 1977. "A Survey of Computer-Assisted Instruction in Academic Library Instruction." In *State-of-the-Art of Academic Library Instruction*, pp. 73–78. Arlington, Va.: ERIC Document Reproduction Service, ED 171 272.

"Automated Staff Training." 1982. *College and Research Libraries News* 43 (November): 356.

Axeen, Marina. 1967. *Teaching Library Use to Undergraduates—Comparison of Computer-Based Instruction and the Conventional Lecture*. Arlington, Va.: ERIC Document Reproduction Service, ED 014 316.

Caruso, Elaine. 1981. "Trainer." *Online* (January): 36–38.

Chambers, Jack A., and Jerry Sprecher. 1980. "Computer-Assisted Instruction: Current Trends and Critical Issues." *Communications of the ACM* 26 (June): 332–42.

Clark, Alice S. 1974. "Computer-Assisted Library Instruction." In *Educating the Library User*. Edited by John Lubans, Jr., pp. 336–49. New York: R. R. Bowker.

Culkin, Patricia B. 1972. "Computer-Assisted Instruction in Library Use." *Drexel Library Quarterly* 8 (July): 301–11.

Eng, Sidney. 1984. "CAI and the Future of Bibliographic Instruction." *Catholic Library World* 55 (May-June): 441–44.

Guilfoyle, Marvin C. 1985. "Computer-Assisted Training for Student Library Assistants." *The Journal of Academic Librarianship* 10 (January): 333–36.

Johnson, Kathleen A., and Barbara S. Plake. 1980. "Evaluation of PLATO Library Instructional Lessons: Another View." *The Journal of Academic Librarianship* 6 (July): 154–58.

Koelewyn, Arie C., and Katherine Corby. 1982. "Citation: A Library Instruction Computer Game." *RQ* 22 (Winter): 171–74.

Nipp, Deanna. 1984. "In-House Production of Microcomputer Software for Library Orientation." Mansfield, Pa.: Mansfield University, Fall.

———. 1985. Mansfield University Libraries, Mansfield, Pa. Interview, June 6.

Pask, Gordon. 1982. *Micro Man*. New York: Macmillan.

Rawlins, Susan M. 1982. "Technology and the Personal Touch: Computer-Assisted Instruction for Library Student Workers." *The Journal of Academic Librarianship* 8 (March): 26–29.

Renford, Beverly, and Linnea Hendrickson. 1980. *Bibliographic Instruction: A Handbook*. New York: Neal-Schuman.

Shaw, Suzanne J. 1984. "Additional Information about 'How to Search OCLC' Software." Gainesville, Fla.: University of Florida Libraries.

Williams, Mitsuko, and Elisabeth B. Davis. 1979. "Evaluation of PLATO Library Instruction Lessons." *The Journal of Academic Librarianship* 5 (March): 14–19.

Wood, Richard J. 1975. "A Computer-Assisted Instruction Program on How to Use a Library Card Catalog: Description, Program, and Evaluation." Arlington, Va.: ERIC Document Reproduction Service, ED 167 156.

## SELECTED BIBLIOGRAPHY

Nipp, Deanna. 1984. "Microcomputers for Library Instruction: The Mansfield University Experience." *Learning Resources* 1 (April): 3.

———. 1984. "Production of a Microcomputer Program for Library Orientation." Mansfield, Pa.: Mansfield University, Spring.

Williams, Mitsuko, and Elisabeth B. Davis. "Computer-Assisted Instruction: An Overview." In *Theories of Bibliographic Education: Designs for Teaching*, Edited by Cerise Oberman and Katina Shauch, pp. 171–91. New York: R. R. Bowker, 1982.

# 19

# It's the Little Things That Count: Methods of Improving Reference Services

*Deborah Pawlik*

Technology may change, books may go out of print, but one thing remains the same—patrons continue to ask reference questions. Questions range from the directional—"Where's the photo copier?"—to the more involved—"What was the price of a mule in 1932?" Recent articles (Hernon and McClure 1986 and Miller 1984) indicate that the quality of reference service offered in all libraries is mediocre at best. This chapter discusses the problems associated with reference work in a small academic library and offers the library administrator a variety of ways to improve service.

Overworked staff, limited resources, and demanding patrons all contribute to the problems of reference work. In many small libraries the reference librarian must assume other professional duties including circulation, interlibrary loan, bibliographic instruction, and supervision of student workers. An unending stream of reference questions is soon viewed as an unending stream of interruptions, and the patience and ability of the finest librarian can be taxed. If the reference librarian is not available, questions are handled by a paraprofessional, clerical, or student staff. Although these employees often deliver excellent service, they cannot replace the professional. An overworked and limited staff gives the small academic library very inconsistent reference service.

Is there a library in the country that has the funding to purchase every book it needs? Small academic libraries generally have budgets that do not permit extensive development of the collection. Updated titles and multivolume reference sets are luxuries that often are pushed aside when more immediate needs arise. A library may have access to an information retrieval system, but finding a staff proficient in searching or finding the time and funds to permit the staff to become proficient in searching is a difficult task.

The 1980s college student is not a knowledgeable library user. Students are unclear about what they need and formulate vague, broad questions. They are also part of the "prepackaged, fast-food" generation. They want information *now*. A librarian who cannot provide an immediate answer is viewed as uncaring and incompetent.

The obvious answer to these problems is to hire more staff, buy more books, and make every student library literate. The financial climate on most small-college campuses makes such solutions impractical. The director must find new, low-cost ways to solve the problem of poor reference service. The following are some suggestions.

## MANAGERIAL CONCERNS

What are your patrons really asking? How do they pose their questions? How long does it take to answer a question? A manager cannot direct a reference department without experiencing it in person. Spend some time answering questions and helping patrons. Have the staff write down the questions they answer. Circulate the questions to the staff. The acquisitions staff will be better able to select material if it knows what the students are researching.

Encourage the reference staff to ask other staff members for help. The cataloging librarian knows the latest material added to the collection. The periodicals librarian may know of a current article on the subject.

## PHYSICAL LOCATIONS

Watch your patrons. How far do they have to walk between the parts of the collection? Where do they leave their books, backpacks, and purses? If you notice your patrons spending more of their time walking, rather than researching, perhaps you need to move things.

Consider creating an information desk, similar to those found in large offices and stores. Directional questions and referrals could be handled there.

Don't take parts of the collection out of numerical sequence. No one will find it. If you absolutely must do so, however, have clear signs. Consider using colored tape on the floor to lead patrons to the proper location.

Arrange things logically. Are the indexes near the magazines? Is the microfilm reader near the microfilm? Are the chairs or benches in the aisles of the reference section so that the heavy books do not have to be carried too far?

Where do the reference librarians sit? Are they behind closed doors? Put them out in the library so that they are highly visible.

## THE STAFF

Hire a reference librarian who likes to work with people and solve puzzles and enjoys the thrill of the search. Applicants for library positions come with grades, references, and resumes, but they lack substantial evidence of their working qualifications. What they really need is a portfolio showing the pathfinders, bibliographies, handouts, and guides they have created. Few librarians have portfolios, but it never hurts to ask. If the position includes teaching library skills, require the applicant to prepare a lecture. Plan to have an audience of staff and students and ask the students their opinions.

Have the staff members brush up on questioning and listening skills. The social work or psychology departments may agree to give a workshop for the staff on interviewing methods.

Train all members of the staff to answer routine questions, such as "Do you have X magazine?" and "Where's the *World Almanac*?" These questions can be answered by anyone.

Require the new employee to spend a certain portion of each day "discovering" the collection and learning the unique qualities of each reference book.

Get to know the instructors, the courses offered, and especially the assignments. Many hours of duplicated effort can be eliminated if the staff knows ahead of time that thirty students will be looking for statistics on education in Latin America.

Begin a program of bibliographic instruction. This may seem like an overwhelming task, but it's the first step in making students library literate.

Have a student act as a library tutor. The tutor can assist students with research and can help students formulate their research into term-paper format.

Be approachable and highly visible. How is a patron to know the staff? If you abhor the thought of name tags, at least try to appear visible and approachable.

## COLLECTION AND RESOURCES

Acquire an information-retrieval system. It may not solve all problems, but it can expand the resources of the collection.

Use the general encyclopedias and almanacs. Librarians and patrons may feel compelled to use more sophisticated sources, but these resources can quickly answer many questions.

Exchange periodical holdings lists with all organizations within driving distance of your library.

Know your neighbors. What organizations in your area have libraries? Do they accept questions from the public? Hospitals, historical societies, and large companies all have resources that can be shared. Get to know the strengths of their collections.

Call other libraries for help.

## METHODS

Create a series of "HELP" posters (similar to "help" screens on a computer) to answer common questions. The "HELP" posters could follow the same color and format, so that they are easily identified by patrons.

Put signs everywhere. Try to remember your first visit to your library. See your library with unknowing eyes and identify areas that need explanation.

Create an information sheet with the answers to the most commonly asked questions. Give the sheet to student workers, staff members and patrons.

Avoid "libraryese." Most patrons understand the meaning of "r" above a call number but "q," "quarto," "f," "folio," "bound periodical," "hanging file," and so on are mysterious terms.

If a question takes more than five minutes to research, take the patron's name and number and call them later in the day or have them return the next day. Librarians do a better job if they are not pressured to provide a quick answer. The secret to this suggestion is really to call them back.

Decide how far to go and when to stop. There's a fine line between answering questions and doing the research for a patron. Librarians can also become so involved in the excitement of the search that they can give more information than the patron wants. This is especially true in an academic library, where teaching students *how* to use the resources is a primary objective.

## MISCELLANEOUS

Keep up to date with current topics. Killer bees, laughter therapy, and designer jeans are all topics that interest students and can be difficult to research when they just become popular.

Be creative. Listen to what a patron says and avoid the temptation to match the request immediately with a book.

Answering questions and helping patrons is the heart of library work. Reference service is not simply a matter of matching a question to a book. It is a dynamic interchange between the patron and librarian. Reference work is not an exact science but the art of helping patrons. By watching patrons and listening to their questions, we can identify many small ways that reference services can be improved in the small-college library.

## REFERENCES

Hernon, Peter, and Charles R. McClure. 1986. "Unobtrusive Reference Testing: The 55 Percent Rule." *Library Journal* 111 (April 15): 37–41.
Miller, William. 1984. "What's Wrong with Reference Coping with Success and Failure at the Reference Desk." *American Libraries* 15 (May): 303–6ff.

# 20

# Off-Campus Library Services and the Smaller Academic Library

*Jean S. Johnson*

Off-campus library services require flexibility and adaptability that may not be possible if constrained by the usual services and resources provided by an academic library. Off-campus students may or may not have access to adequate resources necessary for their course work, and determining ways to make the necessary support available to them is a major challenge.

A college or university may provide off-campus credit and noncredit courses, workshops, institutes, and degree programs in addition to correspondence courses. Except for correspondence, courses may be provided at a distant learning site, in local schools, in libraries, or in community centers, through teleconferencing, or by a combination thereof. Depending on the scope of an institution's program, whether large or small, a variety of means for generating programs may be used. In urban areas courses may be taught across town; in rural areas they may be taught several hundred miles away.

When planning an off-campus library-services program, it is important to know and understand the mission of the institution with regard to extension and how it expects the library to participate. If extension includes just an occasional course emanating from a particular curriculum, there may be few demands placed on the library. If, however, off-campus programming is a major priority of the institution, the library must consider making a parallel commitment to support such programs.

During the development or enhancement of a program in off-campus library services, the Association of College and Research Libraries (ACRL) "Guidelines for Extended Campus Library Services" are very useful ("Guidelines for Extended Campus Library Services," 1982). They can be used to determine how best to proceed. Reading and learning what other institutions are doing is also helpful, and follow-up telephone calls are helpful in getting the latest insights and information. There is a good base of information in the literature, including the proceedings from off-campus library-services conferences sponsored by Central Michigan University in 1982, 1985, and 1986 (Off-Campus Library Services Conference 1982, 1985, 1986).

## PLANNING

It is extremely important to know the nature and scope of the extension program of the institution for which off-campus library services are being planned. Depending on the institution, there could be a department of continuing education, a college of extended studies, or some other organizational entity. It might be run by a department head or a dean with one or more associates responsible for various parts of the programs, such as credit classes, institutes and workshops, correspondence study, or public service. Identify and make contact with the key people and become acquainted with their programs and goals.

The contacts made with extension personnel can be useful in several ways. When they know that the library is willing to provide support and assistance for off-campus students, they can share this information with students and faculty teaching the courses. An extension office may also coordinate with the library when planning for courses and working with new faculty.

If possible, arrangements should be made for the library to be notified in advance of when a course will be offered off campus, where it will be taught, how long it will be taught, and the name, address, and phone number of the instructor. Such information enables one to notify the instructor in advance of how the library can support the instructional process, with contact made through a letter, telephone call, or office visit. Form letters, generated from a word processor or microcomputer, are useful, but personal contact is the most effective means of getting a positive response from an instructor.

The ideal situation, when planning library services for an off-campus course, is to be directly involved when a course is being planned. Depending on whether a course has been taught off campus before and if continuing-education personnel are amenable, it might be possible to sit in on the discussions that occur during the design and development of a course.

As mentioned earlier, courses may be taught in a variety of locations. Unless permanent college or university learning centers with libraries are located in each community, the local public, school, hospital, community college, or even college or university library may be looked to for library services for off-campus students. Contact should be made with appropriate libraries, and in some cases legal and monetary agreements may be needed between the two institutions if effective support is expected.

## FINANCES

Financing off-campus library services can be a sensitive matter for a college or university library. No longer are libraries receiving large sums of money for acquisitions and other support. In many libraries each department believes that its work is extremely important, that it does not receive enough support, and that it must compete with other departments for all possible funds. Many think that the needs of the on-campus students should take priority over off-campus needs. If the institution has determined that extension programs are of equal importance with campus programs, the same rationale may be used to obtain support for off-campus library services.

If extension is not a high priority, it may be more difficult to finance an off-campus library-services program; however, it might be possible to find other sources of funding. It could be that the continuing-education program may be willing to provide some funds for the support of library-extension programs. Cooperation with other state agencies or communities may lead to support in kind. Or grants from private and governmental sources may be acquired.

## PERSONNEL

Minimal staffing of one or more full-time people, including a librarian, should be assigned to off-campus library services. If the program is not too large, a librarian and ten to thirty hours a week of student help may work well. A librarian in the program is very important because of the necessary professional contacts with continuing-education personnel, instructors, and other librarians. A person who is in frequent contact with people outside the library, someone who can analyze the extension programs as they develop and recognize the needs of the students as they become apparent, is better able to plan the development of off-campus library-services programs.

Student assistants can very ably fill requests for resources from off-campus students. However, if the number of requests becomes so great that many student assistants are needed to fill them, other problems arise. The librarian may need to spend too much time supervising the students and training new ones, thus allowing less time for planning and making the necessary outside contacts. At that time it becomes necessary also to employ a benefited full-time or part-time clerk to train and supervise the students.

Another factor to consider when planning the personnel needs of such a program is the quiet times versus the very busy times. Like the activity in the reference, circulation, and interlibrary loan functions, there will be times when student and faculty information and resource requests will arrive in large quantities; at other times there will be little demand. Employment of students generally coincides with the high and low demand times, but when a clerk is employed, it becomes necessary to prepare for other projects that cannot be completed during the busy times of the year. These projects might include research support, resource-guide development, inventories, annual statistical analyses, and program evaluations.

## FACILITIES

It is assumed that office and workroom space is provided for the personnel involved in off-campus library services. Housing the librarian and clerical assistants in the same room can work well until the operation becomes so large that the librarian has no quiet time for writing, planning, and meeting with people from outside the library. Occupying the same room, however, enables the librarian more easily to supervise the work of the students and to keep abreast of program needs of off-campus students.

Facilities located off campus are another matter. The ideal situation is to have library facilities located at each learning center. In most cases, however, courses are not taught at a specially designed learning center but, rather, in schools, community centers, and other locations. If courses are taught in libraries or community colleges, library facilities may be nearby, but if they are taught in schools or community sites, libraries may be some distance away. If libraries are far removed from course sites, the students and faculty must be informed of what resources there are and where they are available. In rural areas local public libraries may be so small that there is little relationship between library resources and the academic requirements the students are trying to meet, and special arrangements to deliver resources must be made. Alternative plans are often necessary and are discussed later in the chapter.

Communication is an important factor in planning for off-campus library services. Students in rural areas several hundred miles from the college or university campus may not be able to afford frequent trips to the campus or even make long-distance calls to the campus library. A toll-free number that they can call for assistance can be very valuable, and a wide-area telephone system (WATS) line can enable them to approach a research project with more confidence.

## RESOURCES

Adequate resources must be made available to off-campus students and faculty. If they are not available in the communities where the courses are being taught, the institution must provide them, such as by pulling books and other materials from the general collection or purchasing them specifically for off-campus use.

There are pros and cons to either of these two arrangements, and a review and analysis should be made for the best way to proceed. Based on a scattering theory, 20 percent of most library books are used 80 percent of the time, and 80 percent are used 20 percent of the time (Davis and Rush 1979: 119). Some books are never used once they have been purchased. A little experimentation may show that some books in a general collection can easily be used for off-campus programs, whereas others are used too heavily on campus. Books that are requested by individual students may be sent to them using the normal circulation procedures of the library with the loan period being considered from the time that the student receives the books. In the long run this may mean that the book is away from the library about one week longer than if it were checked out in person. Any renewal and recall policies should be handled in the normal circulation manner.

Reserve materials may need to be handled differently. Since they are provided for longer periods of time—semester, academic year, or longer—it might not be possible to pull them from the general collection. Reserve materials on campus are still available for other students and faculty even if there are circulation restrictions placed upon them; when materials are sent off campus, they are available only to the students and faculty at a specific site. Depending on the potential demand, it may be necessary to special purchase materials for reserve.

If the library is going to spend money to purchase materials for off-campus use, there should be some guarantee that the materials will have a certain amount of use. Criteria should be developed to be used when considering materials for purchase. Some questions that might be asked include: How many students are expected to be enrolled in the course? How will the material be used? Are there alternative materials available? What is the demand for the material on campus? Will the course be taught on campus at the same time? How long is the material needed? Will the course be taught off campus again so that the material will be used more than once? How soon will it be taught again and how often? Such an analysis of the needs for reserve materials and their potential repeated use should help to make the purchase of materials for off-campus use more justifiable.

To support such purchases, an allocation within the library-acquisitions budget should be made for off-campus library services. What that amount should be is best determined by the appropriate people within the library, including, for example, the extension librarian, acquisitions or collection-development person-nel, possibly the director, and other people as needed. It may take a few years of experimentation to determine what a reasonable allocation might be.

Once materials, including nonprint materials, monographs, and serials, have been purchased for off-campus use, the question of whether or not to catalog them arises. In most cases, the materials will be duplicates of items already in the general collection. Also, many of the materials may need to be rush ordered because an instructor has allowed very little time before a class begins. If this occurs, is it necessary to send items through the time-consuming cataloging process? Probably not. It may be adequate to keep an acquisitions record of all materials purchased and to indicate in some way on the material that it belongs to the library. As long as the collection remains small it can be housed in a closed room or restricted area and be made available for delivery for off-campus use as needed.

A procedure for routine evaluation and weeding of the collection is important so that it does not become stagnant. It is up to the library and the institution to decide if it wants a small, active collection or a large extension library that may be housed separately in the library or at another location on campus. If a separate library is selected, it becomes necessary to determine the purpose and scope of the library. Is it a branch of the main library and can it be used by all students and faculty, both on and off campus, or is it more of a storage facility where the materials within are held until needed for delivery to off-campus sites?

## SERVICES

The opportunities for services to off-campus students can be as broad and varied as the imagination and time available to the librarian responsible for the program. Two of the most obvious services have already been mentioned, reserve materials and filling direct requests from students. Depending on the extent and type of courses offered off campus, filling requests and responding to reference inquiries will probably require the most time of library personnel. Providing reserve materials tends to come in spurts and may cause the staff to be very busy for short periods. Most requests for reserves are received before and early in a semester. The return of reserve materials usually occurs toward the end of a semester.

Filling individual requests from students poses a challenge. Some type of request form, including a copyright statement, should be developed for use by students. Once designed, an abbreviated adaptation of the form may be used when taking student requests over the phone. Even though a request form properly completed by a student is preferred, there should not be a strict rule that only forms will be accepted. It may be that some students will not have access to the forms, but they may have the name and address of the librarian. A letter with a list of the resources needed should be accepted. Some method of cutting and pasting from the list will make the requests as searchable as the precise form. Students off campus do not have the easy access to information that students on campus do, and they should be allowed as much flexibility as possible.

Once requests have been recorded or logged, they can then be searched. A chronological log of requests is useful in maintaining a record of requests filled, those still being searched, or those unable to fill for whatever reason, as well as those not owned by the library and referred to interlibrary loan. Once an article has been photocopied or a book found, either can be mailed directly to the student.

As mentioned earlier, depending on the distances between the library and the instructional sites, it may be necessary to provide a toll-free number to give students easy access to the library extension office. Students in off-campus programs that are across a large city may not need to make a toll call to ask for help, but a student who is hundreds of miles away may hesitate to call long distance.

A toll-free number gives students more freedom to ask questions and seek help. It is also very useful for renewing books; however, restrictions are probably necessary when students need many items. Two or three requests by phone and the remainder by mail is recommended.

Whether the library has an outgoing toll-free number may be an administrative-policy question as well as a fiscal concern. A comparative analysis should be made to determine if the toll-free number is actually cheaper than direct dialing. An institution may have an arrangement with the telephone company whereby all outgoing calls are made at a reduced rate, or a special appropriation in the budget may be necessary.

Microcomputer use in libraries is burgeoning, and a computer in extension is desirable. Record keeping and statistical evaluation are much easier on a computer, but a machine for telecommunications is even more invaluable. By using electronic mail, a student who has access to a compatible computer can input any number of requests, send them to the library, and receive status reports about when the material was mailed and if there are any delays.

Microcomputers at selected locations away from the library can also make possible access to on-line catalogs available on campus. Dial access to an on-line system allows for finger-tip access to the library's holdings. Once it is determined that the library owns an item, a request can immediately be sent to extension.

Alongside computers and telecommunications is telefacsimile transmission of information. A learning site or local library could receive for the student telefaxed photocopied articles from campus. Telefax is labor intensive and does not solve the problem of sending books, but it is a means of making information access and retrieval very rapid. The emerging optical scanning and digital transmission systems will further enhance information delivery.

Bibliographic data-base searches can be a very important service to students who do not have access to the necessary indexes and other bibliographies that may be needed for their research. Searches can be done either by the librarian or by whoever has that responsibility in the library.

Library instruction is a useful tool in working with students who may not have used academic libraries. On-site instruction is the most beneficial to students but may not always be possible. A videocassette presentation made available at a learning site or to an individual who has a videocassette recorder can provide basic information on how to do research, what services are available from extension, and how to prepare requests. Such presentations can be specific to a course or general. Television services within the institution may provide production support for a videotape at little or no cost to the library. The major cost involved would be the staff time needed to plan and prepare the presentation.

Students enrolled in extension courses are usually very committed to learning. The off-campus library services provided to them should help to make their classes rewarding. The library's goal in providing such service should be flexibility and imagination.

## REFERENCES

Davis, Charles H., and James E. Rush. 1979. *Guide to Information Science*. Westport, Conn.: Greenwood Press.

"Guidelines for Extended Campus Library Services." 1982. *College and Research Libraries News* 43 (March): 86–88.

Off-Campus Library Services Conference. 1982. Proceedings. St. Louis 1982, Knoxville 1985, Reno 1986. For information, write to Barton M. Lessin, Assistant Director for Library Off-Campus and Administrative Services, 206 Park Library, Central Michigan University, Mt. Pleasant, MI 48859.

# 21

# Students in the Library

## J. Daniel Vann III

The library has been described as the heart of the college or university. It can be asserted just as readily that the student is the heartbeat of the academic library. Without students there would be no library; with students the criteria, development, and evaluation of library collections and services can be effectively focused.

The smaller academic library affords the potential to participate in the educational process in ways not generally possible in larger academic libraries. It is easier for the librarian to be a member of the educational teaching team, easier for the librarian to participate in the teaching program, easier for the librarian to concentrate collections in limited curricular areas. The smaller academic library may find it more difficult to provide a cultural center for its students, but it can more adequately serve as a social center in which students may mature as an academic as well as a social community.

## THE LIBRARY AS EDUCATOR

In any academic setting the library is above all an educator. Regardless of the magnitude of the collections or the number of librarians engaged in bibliographic instruction or on-line searching, the purpose of the library is to be an educational center of the institution alongside the other two common centers of higher education, the classroom and the laboratory. Every decision in the library should be based primarily on the effective use of funds and personnel to further the institution's educational mission to its students.

The smaller academic library is well situated to participate in determining the evolving educational mission of its institution and in effecting its implementation throughout the institution as well as in the library. Close relationships within the decision-making process are possible as librarians, faculty, administrators, students, and even trustees continually come into contact with one another. Librarians are able to contribute informally to developing plans long before they become formal presentations. Teaching faculty are more apt to consult with librarians before plunging into new programs or even offering new courses.

In this situation it is imperative that the librarian be an educator by background, experience, attitude, and temperament. Textbook answers for developing educational plans to meet student needs are not proper because they are generally not relevant; rather, study, the development of alternatives, compromise, and teamwork are necessary. The educational plan is the institution's, and the library is a central part of that plan. The guidance of the library within such a plan is the challenge of the librarians.

## THE LIBRARY AS INSTRUCTOR

A second function of the library is instruction. More limited in concept than education, instruction is the practical feature of the modern college and university. Effectiveness of instruction is a prime element in student recruitment, student success within the educational programs, and student satisfaction and success in the workplace after the baccalaureate. The smaller institution has generally been more successful in breeding and offering quality instruction, and it is to be expected that the library will be responsible in positioning itself centrally in the instructional process.

As with its role of educator, the smaller academic library is particularly well poised to be involved effectively in instruction. The librarian is in constant contact with students and faculty and often participates in multiple functions like reference and reserves and collection development with the same constituents. Instructional needs are more visible and the opportunity to work with individual students and faculty to address these needs is more available than in larger institutions. More students tend to be known individually by librarians, and the faculty's assessment of individual students and their needs is more likely to be heard by librarians in a smaller institution. By dealing with the same student again and again, the librarians can discern and inculcate development, which is after all the primary aim of the faculty as instructors.

Thus the librarian must be an effective teacher as well as a knowledgeable educator. Beyond being a master of the reference interview and the location of information and materials, the librarian must have pedagogical skills to make presentations in the classroom and to teach "one on one" in a wide array of areas: research methods, bibliographical searching, writing term papers. The skills must be so well hewn that faculty of the disciplines may themselves readily and willingly become students in the library arena without fear of embarrassment.

## THE LIBRARY AS RESOURCE CENTER

The third function of the library is to provide the resources required by students for their academic programs and related endeavors. The library is the extension of the student's bookshelf, record rack, videotape collection, and personal computer software. When the material desired is not in the dormitory room, the family room at home, or the public library branch down the street, it is expected to be available at the academic library. Because the collections here are larger and services like interlibrary loan and on-line searching are more complex than in the dorm or at home, the student expects guidance to quick and easy access when seeking resources in the academic library. This means that all tools to library access are an integral part of the materials themselves: the on-line or card catalog, the serials guide, the indexes and abstracts, the arrangement of stacks and location of collections, the accessibility of on-line searching. It also means that the research and study tools of the dorm room or home must be available for the student in the library: not just the dictionary and course syllabus but also a typewriter and a computer. Even services unavailable at ''home''—such as a photocopier and the helpfulness of a reference librarian—are expected to be available.

The magnitude of students' demand for resources requires the majority of the library's energies in the vast range of areas in which the librarian is the expert: collection development, acquisitions, cataloging, processing, preservation, stack maintenance, circulation and reserves, reference, on-line searching, and the provision of space and equipment. These are the internal mechanics of librarianship but also the art of the librarian. The validity of decisions regarding how to deploy librarians' time and how to budget for materials and services in providing resources will determine the basic effectiveness of an academic library.

The smaller academic library can provide collections, access, and facilities that are custom tailored to its student clientele. Unlike the larger library, its fields of coverage are smaller and more clearly defined, its collections can be developed selectively by acquiring individual items rather than by purchasing en masse, its collections can be more easily cared for, and the spaces for students can be planned with a more intimate knowledge of student-use patterns. The lack of adequate funding is often an advantage because it offers the challenge to develop excellence through innovation and requires wise fiscal decisions.

The provision of resources requires the library to plan carefully, keep in constant touch with faculty and students, maintain a keen awareness of developments in information technologies, become accustomed to adopting technologies only after they are proven rather than when they are new and exciting, and find the best ways of delivering the best possible mix of resources to students with the library's limited financial resources. Evaluation of collections and effective access through interlibrary loan and on-line data bases can be continuous because adjustments in acquisitions and services must be performed with dispatch. The librarian must be a multispecialist and share specializations with other librarians and paraprofessionals so that library operations can be maintained with a limited staff.

## THE LIBRARY AS CULTURAL CENTER

A fourth function of the academic library is to serve as a cultural center of the institution and often also of a town or neighborhood. Providing access to resources may be the library's duty, but the cultural "extras" establish the place of the library within the students' life-styles. A sparkling exhibit, a film showing, a room with music in the air, an appearance by an author or film maker are events that cause students to view the library as a place to go for its own merits rather than a place that must be visited only for fulfilling course requirements.

Especially in the smaller library, this cultural influence is important. Larger libraries are usually on campuses with art museums, lecture and concert series, foreign-film theaters, and political and religious events of many types. Unless the smaller library is in the midst of a bustling city where the institution's students customarily swarm to the community's cultural events, the opportunity for the library to foster cultural events is great. The library is a logical place, because the resources supporting humankind's cultural experience are themselves in the library.

Provision of broad cultural opportunities often not otherwise available on a campus requires librarians that are alert to students' interests. It requires the knack of the entertainer as well as the educator and dilettante in each librarian. It requires a sense of adventure that can be shared with students in planning and producing events as well as experiencing them.

## THE LIBRARY AS SOCIAL CENTER

The function of an academic library that has been least developed and that is most disquieting to libraries is its place as a social center for students. The "sssh" of the scholar and public librarians in times past has overshadowed the visual evidence in any well-used library that students are social beings wherever they are. Academic libraries must recognize this and provide the spaces where differing degrees of expression of student social behavior may occur. A smaller academic library has more need to satisfy the social needs because the campus may be isolated and adequate social centers may not be available on or off campus. The opportunity to work with students to help them plan with librarians for facilities arranged to promote socialization in a proper environment is a yet unmet challenge for academic libraries.

This cursory view of the functions of an academic library illustrates the truism that the student is the central figure in the academic library. Serving the student, satisfying the student, satiating the student, and at times solacing the student become the primary aims of the library. The small academic library can succeed in placing the student at its center.

## IDEAS FOR THE EDUCATOR

An academic library's primary responsibility, along with functioning as a resource center, is to serve as an educator for students. This means, first, the planning of an educational program that will attract students' interests and effectively prepare students with knowledge and skills that will be useful in a career or personally satisfying. Often librarians can launch or participate in an undergraduate library-science program, especially one that prepares students in elementary and secondary education for school librarianship. Other academic programs related to library skills can be developed, such as records management and archives management.

Responsibility for academic programs may not be possible in all smaller academic libraries, but certainly, the development of specific courses can be pursued. Credit courses can be taught in research methods, reference resources, information retrieval, bibliographic searching of on-line data bases, preservation, and the history of the codex. Noncredit seminars, workshops, and clinics can be offered within the community on these topics and also practical office skills like records management and data-base search techniques. Although these courses will usually be offered as library or library-science courses, other courses in research methodology and materials in specific disciplines and professions can be offered through the several academic departments. When the librarians have subject master's degrees or doctorates in these fields, they may well teach courses of a subject nature in a department, thus cementing a mentor relationship with students as well as a colleague relationship with that faculty.

Approaching the student and student needs as paramount, the library will often determine that opportunities should be available for bibliographic and research training on an informal basis. From this perspective come term-paper clinics, how-to publications like guides to research, bibliographies of reference materials supporting each academic program, videos explaining how to use the library's resources, and computer-assisted-instruction (CAI) programs for bibliographic and research strategies. Such educational services make available to students the fundamental knowledge and skills they need to develop.

As an educator, the library may become a center for self-paced instruction, either independently or serving the academic programs. Such instruction is usually multimedia, using a combination of slides, films, videos, print materials, and CAI. Television courses developed within the institution or purchased from outside are often used. Testing and grading are sometimes effected by the library, sometimes by a continuing-education office or the academic departments. Another opportunity in education is training programs for student workers within the library. Formal training with manuals, audiovisual kits, and continuing supervision has been evaluated by many graduates as practical training for future careers.

Keys to planning educational opportunities within an institution are an understanding of the mission and program of the college or university, knowledge of student needs and the academic offerings and opportunities on campus, a desire to make library and information skills available to students, and the arrangement for resources to make the needed educational services readily available. Often students, faculty, and administrators are not aware of students' educational needs in these areas, but it is evident that once programs and services are begun, the demand for more and better services is almost immediate. A library's educational program is the key to the library becoming a focal point within the institution. The representation of the library's director as a dean or chairperson participating in an institution's decision-making on educational matters is essential. Representation of other librarians on principal academic committees is highly desirable.

## IDEAS FOR THE INSTRUCTOR

In its role as instructor, the library is dedicated to presenting its educational programs effectively to students and, as appropriate, to faculty and the community. Using proven and popular methods of pedagogy, librarians trained in teaching skills transmit the knowledge and training established in the library's educational program or plan. Instruction takes five primary formats in today's academic libraries: the lecture, print resources, audiovisual presentations, computer workshops, and the reference interview.

The lecture, which will normally integrate print and audiovisual materials with the spoken word, is still the standard for credit courses, seminars and workshops, and bibliographic instruction (BI) presentations. Whereas courses, seminars, and workshops are usually "packaged" so that they can be repeated again and again, sometimes by different librarians using the same notes, BI has taken a peculiar approach. Although the same lecture is sometimes given for orientation sessions and repeated sessions of the same course, such as freshman English classes, the general practice is to fabricate each lecture to treat the specialized topic and a specific assignment for a credit class. The librarian has conferred carefully with the faculty teaching the classes so that the lecture can prepare the students to perform a library-related assignment. It is expected that the librarian making the presentation will be available to the students at specific times in the library to give tutorial assistance as needed.

Print resources are probably the most used instructional format offered by a library. Whether a guide to reference materials in a subject field or a sheet with current citations to a topic of current concern, the publication tends to be picked up, perused, tucked away to be taken with the student, and later used in locating materials for classroom assignments, assigned papers, or personal interest. Libraries that provide publications that are carefully selected, attractively printed, and prominently displayed provide a major instructional tool. Incidentally, unattractive or poorly processed publications suggest that the librarians who produced them are shoddy in their workmanship.

Audiovisual presentations can be especially helpful to students, save countless hours of librarians' time, and serve as a crowning glory to an academic library. Used primarily as an embellishment to the lecture—and an important one—the audiovisual presentation can also have a primary effect on student instruction when used as a stand-alone medium. Examples of this use include audio explanations of the use of reference sources (dictionaries, indexes, 10K reports) through a telephone-type receiver with a printed example of an entry from the source posted at the receiver; videotapes showing how to use an on-line catalog, certain reference materials, or the facilities and collections of a specific area of a library; and an audio tour of the library building or piece-by-piece description of an exhibit. When it is possible to obtain audio and video productions from other libraries that can be augmented for a given academic library, countless planning and production hours can be saved. Many students learn primarily through hearing or seeing rather than through reading. Libraries must furnish materials in all primary learning formats if they are to be expert and successful in instruction.

Computer workshops, a recent instructional mode of academic libraries, serve two major library instructional purposes. First, they are used to teach on-line search techniques to campus, regional, and national data bases so that students can use these services directly, often at night when rates are cheaper. Second, computer workshops are effective means of training students to use the on-line catalog. With the introduction of the compact-disk–read-only-memory (CD-ROM) format for indexes and data of many kinds, the computer laboratory regularly used for training within library facilities is a distinct benefit to students. If the computer laboratory is equipped with personal computers with a selection of programs (like WordPerfect and Lotus 1–2–3) on hard disks, students can use the laboratory for their classroom assignments when formal presentations are not in progress.

There still remains the function that was the beginning of library instruction— the reference interview. Despite the emphasis on formal or BI teaching by reference librarians, the instruction of students in bibliographic retrieval at the reference desk—whether general, government documents, or periodicals—is still fundamental. The function of the academic librarian is to teach bibliographic-search techniques whenever possible in answering students' questions. Although success in this strategy will inculcate more advanced questions, that will be a true indication of success at the reference desks of academic libraries.

Although the library is the students' instructor, it is also the advisor of students' instructors. Effective librarianship finds means to give feedback to classroom faculty regarding students' performance of assignments requiring library skills. Effective librarians are effective colleagues.

## IDEAS FOR THE RESOURCE CENTER

The academic library began as a resource center for students, and it is this role that must remain paramount despite the incursions of low budgets and the ambitions of some professionals to champion other functions to the detriment of student access to materials and information. In providing access to its resources, the smaller academic library focuses its services on students' needs and demands: access to collections, access to the means of using collections, access to information, access to working space and supportive services, and access to library facilities.

Access to resources requires careful selection of materials in a variety of standardized formats in a single facility. The student studying Beethoven's composition of the Ninth Symphony should be able to sit in one place with an edition of the score, standard music reference works, relevant books and articles, several recordings by different maestros and orchestras, films or videos of performances, and critical studies of the composer. Books and journals alone are not sufficient.

The selection of materials should reflect not only the academic programs but also the interests of students and the subjects that are naturally highlighted by location, politics, economics, and even religion. Student governments have been known to provide special funds to libraries for the establishment of browsing collections, circulating video movies, and even framed art collections that can be borrowed to decorate dormitory rooms.

As skillful as the choice of resources may be, they are of limited use to students without access tools that are timely, standardized, and complete. Uncataloged collections are generally unusable collections. An on-line catalog is essential with multiple-access files including key-word, Boolean search capability, and a number of other indexed files. Within the next few years on-line serials records will also be essential. Students can expect to have access to these bibliographical files through computer terminals or personal computers with telephone modems from dormitories or private residences even when the library facilities are closed.

Programs for access to materials must include the proper selection, ordering, and care for collections, including cataloging, binding, specialized preservation, and proper shelving and handling of materials. They must also include access to other collections, not only through interlibrary loan (twenty-four- to forty-eight-hour delivery is essential) but through student access to national bibliographic data bases (like the Online Computer Library Company [OCLC] and the Research Libraries Information Network [RLIN]). If a student cannot readily and easily find materials that appear in the on-line catalog, the materials are effectively not available. Access to materials also requires the technical means of using media: microform readers and plain-paper printers, video and audio players, and CD-ROM players and monitors. Formats that cannot be easily used and reproduced (like microcards) should not be purchased.

The reference librarian remains the primary information factor in the library. This professional skill in organizing reference and research materials and assisting students in finding information in a systematic manner determines whether a library will be considered an effective information center for students. National bibliographic data bases available through on-line computer searching have become standard. But they are being replaced by indexes on CD-ROM that can be used directly by students, who can immediately walk away with a printed copy of the entries they retrieve. Still it is the guidance of the librarian that is essential. The new data bases, although generally more economical to the library as well as more convenient, have serious flaws relating to completeness, consistency of indexing, and timeliness. Older years of some CD-ROM indexes disappear as new years are added. Thus at this transitional stage in the development of on-line indexing technology librarians must weigh the advantages of each format of indexes and other reference sources on the basis of both the present needs of students and their anticipated needs twenty years hence. Choices are easier when there are sufficient funds to purchase reference sources in multiple formats. Information sources should also include access to the campus' instructional computing capabilities with workstations for student use.

Fundamental to the student is the provision of sufficient and efficient working space and related services. Students working independently, yet bumping arms and jockeying for space for books on the same table, cannot work effectively. Usually, fewer than half of the chairs at a given table for four or more are filled. Supporting services include inexpensive copiers (5 cents a copy is usually possible), rental typewriters, and personal computers with appropriate software.

A final key to the academic library as a resource center is access to facilities themselves or the hours of service. Schedules must be programmed to satisfy typical student patterns in using the library. Often demands for additional hours are really requests for a place to study when residences are noisy or a place to meet friends. Late evening studies can answer many supposed needs for longer library hours.

## IDEAS FOR THE CULTURAL CENTER

The library's role as a cultural center for students begins as an extension of its role as a resource center. The experience of learning that is enhanced and expanded through library resources can be further advanced through the flaunting of available resources. Exhibits of library materials on subjects of current interest, cultural events within the institution or community, and the academic areas provide visible incentives for students to use the library's resources. Film and video showings—perhaps allowing brown-bag lunches—can be offered during the noon hour. Film classics are popular for evening viewing.

Beyond the library's resources, attention can be focused on cultural events within the institution and community. A lecture on music to be played in a concert, an exhibit supporting a campus lecture, and bibliographic and background data on issues being debated on campus can make the library a part of the proverbial "action" or, in other words, "the place to be."

Long-range plans for a library should include a cultural program sponsored by the library itself. Visiting exhibits of books, artifacts, and art will attract student attention. A reception featuring persons related to the exhibits heightens interest. Recitals featuring students, readings by a poet, and lectures by speakers known to students will prove popular.

The availability of a public functions room within the library that can be used by student, faculty, and community groups to offer programs that students can attend is a primary asset. A small grand piano, projection room, pullman kitchen, and comfortable seating can make the room attractive for public programs of interest to students.

Probably the ultimate in programming combines students, library, and other campus resources with high community interest. One example was an afternoon presentation on the *Commedia dell'arte*. Opening with a formal exhibition and refreshments in the fine-arts area of the library, the festival proceeded to an amphitheater where the art librarian spoke on this art form in the printed book, professors of modern languages and art explained the effect of the form on their disciplines, and students performed first an operatic scene from *Pagliacci* and then an adaptation of this art in contemporary mime. Each guest received a published exhibition catalog.

## IDEAS FOR THE SOCIAL CENTER

The role of the smaller academic library as a social center requires contact and insight into each student generation, informed alliance with student-services officers, and sharing of ideas and concerns with student government leaders. A student-advisory committee reporting to the library director can open informal conversations into students' needs and desires. Student behavior at the service and reference desks should be discussed regularly by librarians and support staff.

Four types of services to provide for students' social proclivities are popular. First, smoking and nonsmoking snack areas with concession machines offering sandwiches, fruits, candies, and nonalcoholic drinks can be located within the controlled library area or, preferably, outside library space but convenient enough so that a wrap will not be necessary to reach them. Students who come to evening classes directly from work with a sandwich and an apple in the briefcase or coat pocket need a place where they can eat legitimately. Crumbs and liquids should not reach the reading or stack areas of the library because of the potential harm to collections.

A second service is an area with lounge furniture where students may have some materials available—perhaps newspapers, popular magazines, a browsing collection, or music tapes and video programs. Although student lounging and napping sometimes disturb patrons and library staff, this behavior is a fact of life for traditional college students.

A third controversial but effective service is enclosed outdoor spaces where students can study during warm weather. A sculpture garden, reading deck, or glassed-in portico that is constructed to safeguard collections while offering space for shared study and conversation will become a student favorite as well as a place where loudly conversant students can be directed.

A fourth service is the group study room, preferably walled by glass from open reading areas. When students can study together in visible privacy, there will be more silence for the students who wish to study solo.

A final word. The excitement of the smaller academic library, akin to the hearty intellectual ferment of the classroom, is experienced as librarians participate in the development of students. The success of libraries can be measured by the response of students to finding successfully the collections and services they need and taking pleasure in using them. Successful libraries and successful students are inseparable.

# 22

# Audiovisual Services

## Douglas A. Green

The great impetus for educational use of machines came from the manufacturers of the machines. Quality machines (hardware) have been supplied, but there has been a short supply of quality material (software) for use with the machines. Nonetheless, library managers should maintain an attitude of open-mindedness in studying the advantages that can be obtained from selective use of that which is available and affordable. The challenge is to develop discriminating judgment for selection of equipment (and trained personnel) that in a cost-effective frame can enhance the learning processes within a particular institution.

An appropriate first step always is the assessment of resources on hand. An indispensable tool is a log for recording not only the amount of usage but also for identifying participation (i.e., instructional department). Not to be overlooked is the prime importance of communication with the faculty and students who are using nonprint material to support course-work study. A written record of user response makes an appropriate guide for purchase (and weeding) of nonprint material. Specific questions may be needed to procure the desired information: whether searches were rewarded (i.e., the expected information was found) and whether additional information would be helpful. Ideally, the library manager serves on curriculum committees that strive to correlate the library resources with course-work content. At any rate, the library manager must be acquainted with the curriculum scope and must keep abreast of any alterations that occur in course offerings from year to year.

The logical second step in a plan to improve audiovisual service is the formulation of criteria for weeding items no longer useful as well as items found to be inherently unsuitable for curriculum support. First, it must be determined whether disuse of a given item is actually due to unsuitability of the item or simply due to circumstances that can be changed. It may be that (1) the items are not sufficiently accessible (i.e., stored where students are not permitted to browse); (2) the instructors or students do not know the material is available; (3) an instructor is not making course assignments that require use of collateral material; or (4) students lack orientation in the use of technical facilities. There will always be certain unquestionable items that can be weeded to make more storage space. This includes material that (1) is outdated, such as (a) career-guidance material prepared before the economy was geared to advanced technology or (b) superseded findings in the changing fields of science, technology, sociology, and so on; (2) is irrelevant to the curriculum of the institution; (3) is too technical for correlation with the level of instruction in the institution; or (4) is of poor quality and therefore not worthy of the time required for use. When an item has been checked out only once, and by an instructor, it may be that the instructor requisitioned this item in expectation of finding it useful but after preview decided that it was not suitable for the use intended. It would be safer, however, not to weed out on a basis of presumption but rather to consult the instructor about the item in question.

Accessibility is a major factor in the quality of library service on any material, as much so with nonprint as with print material. Many libraries classify audiovisual materials and shelve them in the stacks along with print materials so that the public catalog will enable a user to find in one location all items on a given subject, regardless of format. The ultimate in accessibility can be achieved with a classed catalog of nonprint media arranged by title, subject, and type of material (cassettes, filmstrips, 16mm films, and so on). It is not difficult to collect the cataloging data necessary for development of this facility, data now being available from a number of bibliographic sources, most conveniently secured through services of the laser disk technologies.

Fundamental to the posture in future role planning for small academic libraries is an acceptance of reality that the term *audiovisual services* would elicit many different associative responses when presented to professionals in different categories of involvement with the various functions: to the library directors, educational technologists, media specialists, and instructors charged with instructional programs. Good economy dictates that administrators avert any confusion or conflict stemming from misinterpretations of the common goal within an institution that operates on limited budget. Insightful teamwork will provide the most convenient and extensive assistance to the total instructional program. One plus for teamwork is that it precludes repetition of costly services. The point of economy cannot be overemphasized, because libraries nationwide are presently in dire economic straits; each new issue of *Library Journal* confirms a decline of library monies.

The advent of technology gave rise to a general expectation, within library circles, that the library would soon be transformed into a facility for integrated learning resources. It did not, in many cases, become the center as anticipated. The implementation of audiovisual services was marked by a dichotomy separating ''book people'' from ''media people.'' This was due, on the one hand, to the prevalent antibook hostility imparted to media students in many schools of education, a matter described at length by Reginald Damerell (1985). It was due, on the other hand, to the prevalent resistance from librarians faced with an array of apparatus demanding new expertise. Although there has been some excessive aggression from educational technologists who strove to build empires with generous allocations, there has been, simultaneously, a considerable degree of passivity demonstrated by librarians willing—or even eager—to cede the area of technology, thus allowing audiovisual services to be managed by departments independent from library supervision and in some cases isolated altogether from the library services. Herbert S. White dwelt on this point in his article, "Library Turf" (White 1985: 54–55).

Unfortunately, there developed, in time, a breach not altogether congenial; tensions grew from competition for funds, which were increasingly channeled to the support of separate media centers, almost always at the expense of the library budget (i.e., as compared to previous allocations). From a standpoint of overall economy and quality of service rendered, the priority of attention must be to heal, or at least to minimize, any breach that exerts a negative influence on morale and productivity throughout the total operation. Role structure places on the library director an accountability for apprisal to the immediately superior administrative official, who may be unaware that significant problems can arise in an audiovisual program executed with divided leadership that lacks objectivity in vision. The message needs to be presented in a comprehensive written report that would permit review and reference. Ultimately, the audiovisual program plan is controlled by the administrative officials who set (or endorse) policies and make assignments to various management roles distributed on campus. Moreover, a total program, set in motion with initial funding, must depend on the vital support of continuing allocations adequate to finance the program growth in terms of resource material, equipment (including service on equipment) and capable personnel for guidance duty.

Among the difficulties that often result from distribution of audiovisual services to departments other than the library, there are several outstanding matters that warrant a serious consideration: (1) The placement of audiovisual facilities in departments outside the library does restrict availability to a limited schedule of hours that the respective buildings are open, this always being shorter than the library schedule (which incorporates evening and weekend hours). (2) The separation of nonprint from print materials could cause inconvenience when, in many cases, the two need to be integrated for a successful program of balanced study. (3) The organization of audiovisual materials outside the library may be inadequate for ready accessibility such as would be provided by routine library-cataloging preparation. (4) The decentralization of resources (and collateral personnel) introduces the risk of inadequate assistance from personnel who, though specifically oriented to the operation of machinery, may have a limited background of academic preparation and experience. (5) The channeling of a disproportionate part of available funds to entities apart from the library may diminish the library budget below the level supportive for personnel with expertise to administer the nonprint media already stored in the library.

To comprehend a pattern of so many facets in audiovisual service, it is helpful to review the historical development of interest and activity directed toward nonprint media. Spurred by reports of successful programs using audiovisual media to train military recruits during World War II, many individuals in this country began to think in terms of a new dimension for imparting knowledge. Institutionally, public librarians were the first to take initiative in a direction of machine-assisted teaching. Their enthusiasm was followed by that of public schoolteachers who were introduced, by colleges of education, to the "innovative" technique of instruction. Interested teachers became organized in a group later called the Association for Educational Communications and Technology (AECT); this group was guided by manufacturers of machines designed specifically for use in classrooms or in laboratories supporting classroom instruction. Manufacturers worked with other groups also, and with colleges of education, during a period when formulation of some guiding concepts was necessary for collective understanding in the new field: educational technology. Federal funding was distributed generously during the 1960s and early 1970s. Within this period the public schools set up instructional materials centers (IMCs), and many community colleges changed the name "library" to "learning resource center" (and often used the title "instructional designer" for a media specialist working with faculty and students).

There are two commonly held concepts of educational technology, as identified by Paul Saettler: (1) the physical science concept, comparatively simple, which "usually means the application of physical science and engineering technology, such as motion picture projectors, tape recorders, television, teaching machines, for group presentation of instructional materials"; and (2) the behavioral science concept, more complex, which is "dependent on the methods of science as developed by behavioral scientists in the broad areas of psychology, anthropology, sociology, and in the more specialized areas of learning, group processes, language and linguistics, communications, administration, cybernetics, perception, and psychometrics" (1968: 2). The Association for Educational Communications and Technology assigned a committee to study the two concepts and then formulate one comprehensive definition that could be used as a frame of reference. The product of this group effort was stated thus: "A complex, integrated process involving people, procedures, ideas, devices and organizations, for analyzing problems, and devising, implementing, evaluating and managing solutions to those problems involved in all aspects of human learning" (Association for Educational Communications and Technology 1977: 164). The juxtaposition of concepts (i.e., physical science and behavioral science) brought about the usage of a new term, *systems approach*, to describe the educational technology field in general. In practice, the systems approach consists of application, to the problems of teaching and learning, of all elements of theory expressed in the AECT definition. The underlying assumption is that a revision of the entire instructional process can be effected, innovating a complete educational system: beginning with learner analysis and statement of needs, proceeding through the development of instructional strategies, and culminating in evaluation of instructional results. Is it not to be expected that such a complexity of ideas would give rise to many differences of interpretation by individuals participating in the program, these differences determined in great measure by the individual's particular bent of understanding, interest, or activity? For example, an instructional designer (as commonly titled) might think of "audiovisual services" as being in essence whatever the instructional designer knows how to do, or has interest in doing, or is doing. The same is true for the librarian and others.

Informed attention is basic for the planning in any department and especially so with regard to the audiovisual area in which much expenditure can take place in a relatively short time. Priority should be given to an assessment of the better location for any given facility, that is, whether it would serve best in the library or whether for one or more reasons it would serve better in another building. An obvious example of a facility that would be misplaced in the library is the hardware and software for demonstration of welding technique. Only one group of students (i.e., in the technology department) would need this demonstration, and they would need to make immediate application by practice; therefore, the instructional aids need to be on hand. An obvious example of a facility that would be misplaced in any department outside the library is the hardware and software for showing full-length motion picture films on subjects that pertain to the course work in more than one department. Specifically, a film (i.e., a drama) graphically portraying the impact of the Civil War or the Great Depression in America might relate to course work in literature, drama, history, sociology, psychology, or economics; therefore, it would be better to have centralized accessibility in the library. Not all distinctions are clear-cut, but before decisions are reached on fine-line distinctions, the advantages and disadvantages should be weighed thoughtfully.

A recent study conducted by the American Library Association reveals three significant trends in the practice of interlibrary loans for audiovisual material: (1) Many libraries are negative in response to other libraries requesting any kind of audiovisual material. (2) Some libraries are restrictive in policy for loan of audiovisual material. That is, there are specified types of material that, by policy, are not to be shared with other libraries. (3) A few libraries are unable to respond at all, because audiovisual materials are not under any authority of the library. That is, the institution maintains a media department entirely separated from the library department (Morris and Brautigam 1984). Even though there may exist a cooperative spirit between the library department and a separate media department, there is yet no feasible system for the institution to share audiovisual material with other institutions. The current practice of interloan is negotiated principally by libraries, and the material that is subject for loan service is, by librarians, prepared appropriately for distribution (the same as print material). Conditions as indicated in the three trends (stated above) give stimulus to thought for planning alternatives, or at least supplements, to the present system of interinstitutional loan service. Worthy of consideration is the possibility for establishment of a centralized, state-serving dispensary that could loan many audiovisual materials not essential or needing to be stored immediately at hand as well as materials that might be needed for use only one time. An adjunctive centralized arrangement should be especially suited to the needs of states in which the rate of revenue decline is alarming and funds for building expansion cannot be supplied at once to several institutions petitioning assistance for an increase of storage space. Proposals for such a facility might profitably be presented to the state governor, who could direct a study by his appointed board, or council, for higher education.

To sum up the points that the manager of a small academic library might do well to observe in regard to audiovisual services: (1) Develop a discriminating judgment for selection of items to be purchased. (2) Keep a careful log of usage to serve as a purchase and weeding guide. (3) Maintain communication with faculty and students for suggestions addressed to the improvement of service. (4) Formulate criteria for systematic weeding of the collection. (5) Arrange materials to be as accessible as possible for faculty and students. (6) Acquaint faculty and students with the scope and nature of material available in the library. (7) Report to administrative officials any problems existent in a divided leadership of audiovisual service on campus. (8) Emphasize to the administrative officials that sufficient staffing of trained personnel is essential for guidance in the use of audiovisual resources. (9) Tailor an overall plan for meeting the needs of a particular library in the setting of a particular institution. (10) Remain flexible to try new approaches when a method is not serving to the optimum advantage for users of the resources.

## REFERENCES

Association for Educational Communications and Technology. 1977. *Educational Technology: Definition and Glossary of Terms.* Vol. 1. Washington, D.C.

Damerell, Reginald G. 1985. *Education's Smoking Gun.* New York: Freundlich Books.

Morris, Leslie R., and Patsy Fowler Brautigam. 1984. *Interlibrary Loan Policies Directory.* 2d ed. Chicago: American Library Association.

Saettler, Paul. 1968. *A History of Educational Technology.* New York: McGraw-Hill.

White, Herbert S. 1985. "Library Turf." *Library Journal* (April 15): 54–55.

# 23

# Satellite Transmission for Voice, Text Data, and Video

## David M. Lawrence

Approximately 2,500 active space satellites are in orbit above the earth. More than 6,000 satellites have been launched since the first Sputnik shocked the world in 1957, and some 3,500 have since fallen out of orbit, burning up upon reentering the earth's atmosphere.

Above the earth's equator is an imaginary belt, 22,300 miles high, known as the Clarke belt, after Arthur C. Clarke, who in 1944 conceived of an imaginary belt high enough above the equator so that if a retransmitter was placed at 22,300 miles above the earth in an orbit equal to the earth's rotation, it would remain there in an apparent stationary orbit; that is, it would not fall to earth or fly off to some distant planet. Such satellites placed in this belt are called geostationary or geosynchronous. Extremely fragile, satellites in a windless environment need not be any stronger than the structural equivalent of gossamer.

Satellites in this belt use frequencies on the "C" band; letters of the alphabet are arbitrary denominations given to certain radio frequencies. Of importance to libraries are the "C" band and the more often used "K-U" band. The "C" band frequency is most often received by the home satellite dish or antenna (Television Receive Only [TVRO]). Also, it is the same frequency received and redistributed by cable companies for entertainment and educational programming. As a perfect circle, the Clarke belt has only 360 degrees in its circumference, so satellites of the same frequency can be placed only at a distance of 2 degrees apart. This allows for only 180 satellites on "C" band placed in the Clarke belt. At this writing nearly 100 satellites are in this configuration, and each of them is visible to one-third of the earth. A receiving station in Russia is not going to be able to access American satellites; however, a satellite dish in New York City might access some of the satellites serving Europe, Africa, or the Near East but none above the Orient serving Japan. This is true of not only East-West (in which only one-third is visible) but also of North-South.

A second type of satellite, not in geostationary orbit but in an elliptical orbit, is constantly moving in accord with Kepler's law of planetary motion; this is true of satellites not above the equator. A series of four equally spaced satellites are required, each transmitting six hours to serve a geographic area on earth. The items needed to receive satellite transmissions are simply a dish, an amplifier with a cable to receive linked to a receiver for sorting out the different channels (transponders), and a television set; all are off-the-shelf hardware. Probably, anyone capable of hooking up the components of a modern stereo set could set up a satellite-receiving-system dish. Prices of satellite-receiving systems are dropping in inverse geometric progressions. Some broadcasters are scrambling their signals, but most allow subscribers to buy a descrambler at a fair price. HBO, high priced for entertainment at $12 monthly, is well worth the price for those who watch at least three movies a month. CNN at $25 yearly is well worth the price.

About ten years ago, an amplifier on a satellite-receiving dish cost between $10,000 and $20,000; now one can be purchased for around $100. At today's educational prices, a simple, fully equipped dish can cost as little as $695. A microprocessor-controlled motor for turning the dish from one satellite to another is the most expensive accessory but well worth having.

Current estimates are that nearly 2 million satellite dishes dotted the countryside by 1985, and as many as 10 million will be in use by 1990; they are not as common as telephones but are very exciting.

For the smaller academic library, a satellite-reception facility offers very interesting possibilities, something that will enable the library to further enhance its role in curricular support. A review of the literature will help explain the realities and the great potential of this technology.


## REVIEW OF LITERATURE

The academic library supporting foreign-language programs finds new opportunity for exposing students to native speakers without the expense of importation or overseas visits. Mark Long reported on a gathering of foreign-language teachers at Creighton University in Omaha, Nebraska, and described achievements at that university, especially by an organization based there (1984: 20). This organization is Satellite Communications for Learning Worldwide (SCOLA), developed by Lee Lubbers, a faculty member who now has a national reputation; his system at Creighton offers Spanish, French, Russian, and other programming to university students. Long advocated participation in this group and suggested writing to Lee Lubbers, Creighton University, 2500 California Street, Omaha, NB 68178 (1984: 23).

In a recently issued videotape, SCOLA described its plans for an international live news network with live news broadcasts received from fifteen countries. Receiving dishes will be placed in Omaha, Gloucester, England, Sri Lanka, and Florida. For students in many disciplines, this programming will be invaluable, with simultaneous English translations as part of the broadcasting. Some 400 libraries, colleges, and universities are now SCOLA members. P. V. Haeghen reported on the goal of carrying college-level instruction to off-campus students as now achievable when students cannot be at the campus (1986: 15).

Carol Tenopir and M. M. Jackson discussed the potential for the vast island chains of the Pacific Ocean and cited reasons why this new technology will be of great value even to the most remote of the Pacific Islands (1984: 189ff.). For librarians serving the major island chains of the Pacific, new opportunities for bringing education and cultural programming to their clientele are now a real possibility. The *Library Journal* reported on the cooperative efforts of two companies to provide subscribers with business data service ("Satellite Dish Owners Offered New Service," 1985: 124).

Higher education is providing a leadership role in using this new technology. In a newsletter supplement, the National University Teleconference Network reported on its efforts. This association of 105 members is developing a telecommunications system for libraries and higher education. The opportunities for its members are substantial and include reaching large national audiences, cooperating with the private sector for national educational interests, and improving development opportunities for their faculties and professional staffs (*National University Teleconference Newsletter Supplement*, 1984).

The private at-home user is finding this new technology greatly appealing, and Thomas Surprenant covered this rather well. The Federal Communications Commission has taken steps toward permitting broadcasting via satellite of television and information services to private homes, especially through the medium of the direct broadcast satellite (Surprenant 1984: 7).

Until now this chapter has concerned itself with receiving, but Hartford Gunn as quoted by Surprenant projected that sending is on the horizon (1984). Surprenant predicted that libraries will transmit information via the direct broadcast satellite in the future (1984: 11).

Public libraries are showing significant interest in the use of this satellite technology. S. J. Amdursky reported the trail-blazing efforts of the Bloomington, Illinois, Public Library commencing in 1984 (1985: 49). He recognized the public library as filling an important educational role for its users (1985: 49). His article should be read by all who are interested in this new service for their libraries. The potential is there for public libraries and obviously very much so for the smaller academic library.

H. J. Rosenzweig gave the programming vendor's viewpoint, noting the worldwide audience potential for information distribution and the broadcasting of an event worldwide; he noted the seventeen-hour concert LiveAid, which had an audience potential of more than 2 billion people (1986: 33).

Bill Parkhurst described the benefits for the publishing industry, ranging from teleconferences for on-the-road book-sales staff, eliminating the trip to headquarters for briefing sessions, to full-fledged promotions for celebrity authors. The cost-cutting opportunities are very real, and he backed up his observations with interviews with people in the industry (1986: 35–36).

Mary Diebler, coming closer to home for librarians, advocated developing or joining cooperative groups. She noted how academic libraries can share college-level educational or instructional programs and how the possibility of sharing resources by special libraries can exist (1982: 233). Diebler went further and offered good technical advice, noting the need for some caution and preliminary study before making a purchase (1982: 234). Her advice is useful, and this article is must reading before buying a system.

In a more recent article, Diebler gave cogent reasons for academic and public libraries taking serious interest in adapting satellite technology; again, this is an article that all librarians who have an interest in this field should read. She noted the potential that libraries have as receiving sites for conferences telecast over satellite channels, the reference information potential, and what the librarian must know to convince administrators to fund the purchase of equipment (1984: 84). She went on to describe the flexibility that such equipment should have and its digital capability, thereby allowing for receipt of video, audio, and data transmissions (1984: 84). Turning to national organizations, she focused attention on the American Library Association (ALA) and the potential an ALA satellite network would have for libraries (1984: 85).

The medical professions and medical libraries have long-term experience in the use of satellite technology for continuing education. Continuing Medical Education Satellite (CMESat) is a series of thirty-minute continuing-education programs for health-care professionals. The video format permits broadcast of pertinent information and updates without the delays common to printed materials. Through use of a programmable video-cassette recorder, programs can be captured for later viewing. Now, thanks to recent advances in satellite telecommunications, programming is available to 80 percent of the health-care professionals in this country. Although it is free, a nominal charge makes possible the receipt of continuing medical education credits. Six major topics are covered each month in each medical education category, and each branch of the medical professions has a similar number of high-quality broadcasts each month ranging from RNSat for nurses to VetSat for veterinarians (Raitt: 1985:283).

David I. Raitt wrote of still more advantages for satellite technology. He noted the potential for high quality of transmissions and possible variations in rates of transmission while observing that the great distances involved (from earth to satellite and return) can take time and may affect some protocols for transmitting data (1980: 143–52).

In another article, Raitt especially advocated data transmission and described a Japanese test for building a large digital system. The opportunity for library use is not overlooked as he mentioned an effort to provide digital sending of documents to small receivers, a cooperative project involving some European agencies (1984: 50–52).

## CONCLUSION

Satellite technology for small academic libraries is affordable, offering many opportunities for enhancing information and media resources; it will enable libraries to support educational and cultural programs for their institutions, whether technologically, scientifically, or liberal arts oriented. This exciting medium offers libraries the opportunity for leadership, placing them in an enhanced supportive role in their institutions.

The authors reviewed here are recognized authorities; their words carry a weight and significance that more fully conveys the strong sense of usefulness and versatility this technology has for academic libraries; reading their papers will convey that to you. You can then consider the advantages and challenges presented and how they can be adapted or expanded to meet the service objectives in your library.

## REFERENCES

Amdursky, S. J. 1985. "Dishing It Out: Satellite Services in Public Libraries." *Library Journal* (November 15): 49–51.

Diebler, Mary 1982. "The Library Superstation: A Library Guide to Satellite Earth Stations." *Information Technology and Libraries* (September): 232–37.

———. 1984. "Marion in the Satellite Age." *The Electronic Library* (April): 81–85.

Haeghen, P. V. 1968. "Satellites Stop Beeping and Start Teaching." In *Advances in Instructional Technology* (No. 55). Edited by G. H. Voegel, pp. 13–20. San Francisco: Jossey-Bass, Fall.

Long, Mark 1984. "The Global School." *Satellite ORBIT International* (July): 20–23.

*National University Teleconference Newsletter Supplement*. 1984. Oklahoma: Oklahoma State University, March.

Parkhurst, Bill 1984. "Books and Satellites." *Publisher's Weekly* (October 26): 35–36.

Raitt, David I. 1980. "Information and Satellites—Some European Activities." Proceedings of the 4th International Online Information Meeting (December 9–11), pp. 43–52. London, England: Learned Information.

———. 1984. "Japan's Information Network System." *IEEE Spectrum* (May): 50–52.

———. 1985. "Look—no paper! The Library of Tomorrow." *The Electronic Library* (October): 276–89.

Rosenzweig, H. J. 1986. "The Upside of Downlinking." *EITV* (January): 32–33.

"Satellite Dish Owners Offered New Service." *Library Journal* (September 1): 124.

Surprenant, Thomas 1984. "Direct Broadcast Satellites: An Interview with Hartford Gunn." *Library Hi Tech* (Spring 1984): 7–12.

Tenopir, Carol, and M. M. Jackson. 1984. "Telecommunication and Publishing in the South Pacific." *Electronic Publishing Review* (1984): 189–200.

# PART VI

# Technical Services

# 24

# Managing Library Automation in Smaller Academic Institutions

## Katharina Klemperer

The management of automated systems is one of the major responsibilities of librarianship today. Not only are large sums of money involved, but also a large number of people will have to live for a long time with the decisions made. The automation manager is expected to keep current on developments in library automation and data processing, in addition to having knowledge of traditional library procedures. Since it is unrealistic to expect all vendors and all librarians to be totally conversant in both areas, the automation manager must act as a facilitator and interpreter between the vendors and end users.

This chapter presents an overview of the issues involved in automating library processes and offers approaches for addressing those issues. The emphasis is on issues that apply to the automation of acquisitions, serials control, circulation, and the public access catalog. Cataloging and on-line searching are not addressed directly, since those automated functions have become standard procedures, and decisions in those areas can be made in a fairly straightforward manner based on cost and service.

The planning issues faced by large and small libraries are similar, but the solutions for small institutions tend more toward reliance on outside services than in-house development and research.

After the library has committed itself to automating one or more systems, the overall process follows the general pattern of assessment of the status quo, requirements analysis, investigation of options, vendor selection and contract negotiation (or in-house development), and product acceptance and maintenance. It is important to remember that the process is somewhat circular, that decisions or events down the road will affect previously made decisions, and that it is naive to assume that the installation of automated systems will follow a straight and direct path.

## ASSESSMENT OF THE STATUS QUO

At the outset it is worth assessing the current institutional environment and considering the significance of various conditions. The major influence on the project will be the availability of funding. The amount of financial support that can be expected will affect all subsequent decisions and may in fact require an initial phase of locating support.

Closely related to finances is the availability of staff. Is the library chronically understaffed? Can it spare the staff needed for pursuing automation projects? Does the staff already include an automation expert? Are there plans to hire one and, if so, on a temporary or permanent basis?

A third question to ask early on is whether or not the library already belongs to a library consortium or whether an administrative mechanism exists for establishing a consortium for automation purposes. An automation consortium presents numerous opportunities for the smaller library: staff expertise can be shared, costs can be shared, influence over vendors is increased. These consortial arrangements also create opportunities for sharing other public and technical services. However, multiple institutions complicate the decision-making process and make it more difficult to reach consensus. Also, depending on the nature of the consortium, remote access and telecommunications issues may need to be addressed in greater complexity.

The library needs to consider the present state of its automated systems as a baseline. Existing systems set up expectations that need to be fulfilled or abandoned. They also often limit choices, particularly if the library already owns hardware that it wants to continue using. If the staff has no experience with automated systems, the period of implementation will be extended, especially if the staff is resistant to the very idea of automation.

The library should be aware of the adaptability of its physical plant. The existing physical conditions will have an impact on the the cost of installing various systems. Older buildings, particularly those of historical significance, will require a far greater expense in wiring than do new ones that already have cabling channels. If a computer is to be housed in the building, there needs to be an adequate power supply and climate control. Depending on the type of system purchased, it may even be necessary to build a computer room. If either the technical or public services of the library are physically decentralized, attention needs to be paid to telecommunications channels and local networks.

Finally, the library should assess the state of general computing services on campus. Is the institution committed to any particular brand of hardware? The library can expect savings if the college has a mass purchase agreement with a particular hardware provider but may then find itself restricted in its choice of software. Will the campus computer center provide facilities management; that is, will it provide operator coverage, hardware and operating-system maintenance, and troubleshooting for the library's equipment? Such an arrangement can be highly beneficial to the library if the computer center is reliable and committed. This arrangement enables the library to consider purchasing customized software independently of hardware, without acquiring its own systems programmer. Is the library under pressure to share a computer with another department on campus? Sharing a computer is usually not the happiest of arrangements, although it may appear on the surface to be cost-effective for smaller institutions. Not only does it restrict the choice of software to that which will run on particular equipment and under the same operating system, but the resulting competition for machine resources inevitably leads to conflict.

## BASIC DECISIONS

After a general assessment of the library's situation, an early decision is whether to purchase a system or to develop one in-house. At this state in the history of library automation, there are very few reasons for a small library to develop a system in-house. Among the valid reasons are that the library already owns equipment running an inadequate system, and no vendor can be found to duplicate the services already provided, or that the library is happy with its own system and wants to add on other functions but cannot locate a packaged system that will integrate with it. A further reason might be that the library or an academic department is pursuing research that it would like to put into practice. Any small library that embarks on in-house development must be prepared to hire a library systems analyst and programming staff and should be prepared to spend many months and years on the development of its own product, which will require improvement and debugging long after it is implemented. The results, however, can be far superior to those obtainable in the marketplace.

A word should be said regarding the advantages of microcomputers versus minicomputers or mainframes. To some extent the differences are semantic. Distinctions have been made on the basis of amount of memory, portability, processing speed, size of disks that can be supported, and number of users that can be supported; and the definitions change continually as more powerful machines are produced. While smaller libraries are more likely to be able to use a micro-based system, it is better to examine all available systems and judge them on the basis of their fulfillment of the library's criteria rather than the size of the computer on which they run.

At this point, assuming the library intends to buy one or more systems, the library should consider engaging the services of a library automation consultant. Unless the library staff already includes a highly qualified automation specialist, investment in a consultant's services is the wisest money that can be spent. The consultant is in a position to assist the library in assessing its needs and is thoroughly familiar with the automated systems on the market, making it possible to guide the library in its decisions without following needless dead ends. The consultant can be selected using some of the same criteria that are used in selecting automated systems: reputation, number of previous clients with the same conditions, and personality. A starting list of consultants may be found in *Consultants and Consulting Organizations Directory* (see Annotated Bibliography).

## REQUIREMENTS ANALYSIS

The library, with the aid of the consultant, now embarks on an intense re-quirements analysis to determine exactly what its needs are. The library needs to develop a clear idea of which systems are to be automated and, of them, which should be addressed first. The view should be long range, and no decision should preclude the eventual automation of any function.

The goal of the requirements-analysis phase is a checklist of required functions and features. It is important to distinguish between absolute requirements and desirable features, since vendor selection will most likely take place on the basis of fulfilling all requirements and the largest number of desirable features, rather than absolute conformance to rigid specifications. These checklists will grow and change as more systems are observed. In small libraries it is possible to involve a fair number of staff members, including both librarians and support staff, in committees whose business is to enumerate the functionality and features that they desire. Examples of possible requirements for a circulation system are:

- The loan period shall be determined as a function of the type of material, type of borrower, and owning branch.
- The system must be able to use barcode labels, not optical character reader (OCR) labels.
- The operator must be able to add barcode labels to items at the point of checkout. The entire collection need not be barcoded in advance.

The library will be considering several broader issues as it develops detailed requirements for the desired system or systems. At some point, the question of the degree of integration should be addressed. Many vendors are now offering integrated packages. Basically, the integrated system provides all automated functions—acquisitions, serials control, circulation, public access catalog, and sometimes cataloging—from a single vendor using a single computer and, most important, using a single data base. The advantages of this are several: only one machine needs maintaining, only one vendor needs to be dealt with, the user interfaces for all systems are likely to be compatible, and, most significantly, the various systems are always in synchronization with one another, because they use the same data base. For example, the on-line catalog can present up-to-date circulation information because circulation status is maintained in the same record that is used for on-line public catalog access. Unfortunately, the company that excels in one area is unlikely to excel in all, so choosing an integrated system may result in some components that are less than ideal. Still, for the small institution, an integrated system is an attractive choice. A small library is actually more likely than a large one to find an acceptable integrated system, because many of the currently available systems have data-base size constraints that are likely to be exceeded only by larger libraries. This gives the small library a wider field from which to select.

The opposite approach is to purchase several independent components from separate vendors. Small libraries should be particularly wary of this approach and should not count on integrating the components after the fact, because such attempts require a great deal of systems expertise, especially if each component resides on its own stand-alone machine. A middle ground receiving a great deal of attention today is the purchase of distinct components that include an interface to another vendor's system. For example, a given acquisitions system vendor may offer an interface to a different vendor's on-line catalog, so that acquisitions information can be transferred to the on-line catalog and searched there by the public. Recognizing that integrated systems often contain a weak link, vendors are now starting to offer a number of these vendor-specific interfaces, and efforts are under way to standardize the interfaces so that they can be generalized to many different vendors' products. This particular approach is probably the most expensive of the three, but is likely to satisfy the largest number of departments in the library.

A related question is how customized the systems should be. The marketplace today contains the entire range, from off-the-shelf "turnkey" packages consisting of software and hardware that can simply be plugged in and run to software products that must be mounted and maintained on the library's own machinery. In the middle are products that are self-contained but enable the client to customize the functionality and user interface to varying degrees and "supported software" that runs on the library's hardware but is maintained by the vendor. Again, the smaller library, particularly one with little data-processing expertise available, will be wise to consider the more off-the-shelf packages, although the cost will be in flexibility and customization. An important consideration is that a vendor who supplies a complete package of hardware and software is responsible for maintaining the whole package. There is great temptation to shift the blame when software and hardware come from separate vendors or when two software products interface with each other.

## VENDOR SELECTION

The actual selection of vendors will be a result of an extended process. Traditionally, a request for information (RFI) asking for general product information was distributed to a large number of vendors to establish a pool from which the finalists could be selected. The information gathered from the RFI was used to identify a smaller number of vendors who would receive a detailed request for proposal (RFP) and a request for quotation (RFQ). Vendors respond to the RFP with a specific proposal for implementing a system and to the RFQ with a price quotation. Previously, the RFP process was necessary and useful. It was through study of many RFPs that vendors, as well as libraries, learned what functions and features were necessary and desirable, and since systems differed widely in their functionality, there was good reason to specify each feature to a large number of vendors. Now that a large body of RFP literature exists and there is consensus as to the general functional requirements of various systems, this lengthy and rigorous procedure has fallen into some disfavor for several reasons (Taylor 1986). First, it is extremely time consuming and expensive, particularly for the vendor, who has no guarantee of any return on his efforts. Unfortunately, this causes many vendors simply not to respond to many RFPs, with the consequence that the library does not necessarily find the vendor best suited to its needs. In addition, the impersonal nature of the process often obscures some of the more important features of the vendor-client relationship, namely, the personalities of the individuals involved and the ability of vendor and client to work together productively.

Many libraries are bound to use rigorous formal procedures specified by their institution or governing body. But if this is not the case, the smaller library, which often does not have funds to spend on a lengthy formal procedure, might be well advised to pursue, with the aid of a consultant, a path of "enlightened decision-making," based on its own observations. Such observations should come as the result of a number of actions: examination of the library literature, observations of systems at trade shows and exhibits, consultation with colleagues who have had experience with the systems under consideration, perusal of literature distributed by vendors, demonstrations by vendors at the library, site visits by library staff to installed sites of prospective vendors, and extensive telephone conversation with the vendors. The RFP can still be used but in a more general form stating the general functional requirements. The field of possible vendors will tend to narrow very quickly, with the final choice made using the detailed requirements list prepared earlier by the library. Such a procedure will also uncover some of the less-easily quantified requirements, such as the quality of the user interface, the quality of customer service, and the responsiveness of the vendor to client needs.

Further vendor selection criteria, beyond those defined in the requirements analysis, should also be applied. What kind of hardware is used, and how easy is it to get emergency and routine maintenance? Is it possible to get equipment on loan while one's own equipment is being repaired? Is a third party involved, and if so is it reliable? What method of troubleshooting does the vendor use? Many vendors are able to dial into the client's system remotely and perform diagnostics and make modifications without a site visit. Are the manuals clear and accurate? Does the system provide security against unauthorized use? Does the purchase price include training? Where is the training given? Are there adequate provisions for backing up data and restoring the data base in case of catastrophe?

Does the vendor supply a source code, that is, the version of the program that can be read and modified by humans? Some vendors, usually of installed software packages, supply a source code at a substantial price; many will not supply it under any circumstance. Usually, a copy of the source code is placed in escrow and given to the purchaser if the vendor goes out of business. The client should be sure that it is always the latest version of the source code that is in escrow.

Purchasing the source code should be considered if the library is planning to write interfaces to the purchased package, in order to determine exactly how the purchased software operates. It is unwise to make modifications to the vendor's program itself, because then the vendor can no longer be expected to assume responsibility for the proper functioning of its software.

In making its final selection, the library must not neglect the hidden and future costs. The cost of preparing the site for installation will depend on both the vendor's requirements and current conditions at the site. Likewise, the cost of data preparation depends on the state of the library's data and the services offered or not offered by the vendor. The ongoing maintenance fees for both software and hardware should be taken into consideration, as should the costs for new releases of the software. It is especially important to be able to upgrade to larger versions of the system with a minimum of expense.

The vendor's reputation is also important. How long has it been in business, and how many installed sites are there? Is anyone successfully using the same configuration that the library is planning to purchase, particularly one of the same size? What are other libraries' experiences with software bugs, and how responsive is the vendor in correcting them? How long is the installation backlog? Is the company so successful that it is overextended, and will customer support suffer? If possible it is wise to obtain a confidential corporate assessment to determine the company's financial robustness.

## CONTRACT NEGOTIATION

Once a vendor has been selected, considerable attention should be given to contract negotiation, preferably with the assistance of legal counsel. Most vendors supply a standard contract, which should be modified to include protection for the customer.

Under no circumstance should the entire payment be made before installation. If at all possible, the installation should be divided into phases, with payment for each phase dependent upon acceptance tests for that phase. A general phasing might consist of a small percentage of the entire payment turned over at the time of contract signing, another after the system has been installed and has passed its benchmark tests, and a final payment after the system has been in place and running under full load, with a specified worst-case response time and minimum downtime. If the purchase consists of several components, each might be considered a phase. The purchaser should test all functions, even if they are not to be used immediately. Any custom development to be done by the vendor must be fully specified in advance and tested with particular scrutiny, since it is not only performance but functionality that is being measured.

Because few installations are identical, benchmark testing is becoming an acceptable way to measure performance. The client library must project what its maximum load will be in precise terms, such as circulation checkout transactions per hour, simultaneous on-line catalog users, or number of retrievals per user per hour. Benchmark tests are simulations of reality under controlled conditions: the staff is assembled to generate the required conditions, which the system must pass. Care must be taken, however, not to generate conditions that are in fact unrealistic. A classic case is attempting to simulate fifty simultaneous users by asking fifty users to formulate a complex search and then all press RETURN at the same moment. It would be reasonable for a perfectly robust system to slow down under such treatment. Benchmark tests can be performed after system installation, or even better, on an identical installed system before contract signing.

With painstaking preparation and a carefully worked out contract, both the vendor and the purchaser will be satisfied at the conclusion of the installation.

## REFERENCE

Taylor, James B. 1986. "The Objective Request-for-Proposal." *Library Hi Tech* 4, no. 1: 37–39.

## ANNOTATED BIBLIOGRAPHY

Background reading and research must concentrate more on journals than monographs, since the field changes very rapidly and the most useful information is the most recent. A number of handbooks and automation overviews are available, but only the most recent are recommended, since they generally become obsolete after a few years. Many of the journals below will suggest useful handbooks.

*Consultants and Consulting Organizations Directory*. Detroit: Gale Research Co. Published every three years, with semiannual supplements called *New Consultants*. This directory is useful in selecting a consultant. It is divided both geographically and by subject, and there is a substantial listing for library consultants. Each entry is annotated as to the precise services offered.

Genaway, David C. *Integrated Online Library Systems: Principles, Planning, and Implementation*. White Plains, N.Y., and London: Knowledge Industry Publications, 1984. This handbook is geared toward integrated systems rather than automated library systems in general, but most of the planning, evaluation, and implementation issues apply to any library-automation project. The book is practical and detailed and gives many specific and concrete examples as well as a survey of existing integrated systems, a directory of suppliers, and an excellent bibliography.

*Information Technology and Libraries* (formerly *Journal of Library Automation*). Official publication of the Library and Information Technology Association, a division of the American Library Association. The articles themselves are generally scholarly and detailed and, occasionally, technical. They are probably more useful to system designers and others who need to keep up with the latest developments than to system purchasers. The critical book reviews in each issue, however, are most valuable in directing the reader to the most recent publications in the field.

*Library Hi Tech*. Ann Arbor: Pierian Press. Sponsored by The Information Society. This journal is probably the single most useful source of practical information and advice for library-automation managers with all degrees of experience. The articles are generally geared to system users and consumers rather than designers and systems analysts. Two regular columns, "The Vendors' Corner" and "The Consultants' Corner," address issues critical to those installing library systems, such as "Funding Library Automation" and "Projecting Library Automation Costs." Each issue usually reviews one or more products or systems in depth, but the user should bear in mind that the presentation is written by a representative of the producer of the product.

*Library Systems Newsletter.* Published monthly by Library Technology Reports, American Library Association. This short (usually eight pages) but highly informative newsletter covers late-breaking developments in the library-automation world, including new-product announcements, financial status of companies, and progress of national committees, as well as brief, thought-provoking articles on topics relevant to automation management, such as sharing a computer, requiring performance bonds from vendors, and using RFIs and RFPs. The newsletter compiles annual surveys of automated systems, which are valuable in the early stages of vendor selection.

*Library Technology Reports.* Published bimonthly by the American Library Association. This report is subtitled "Authoritative Information on Library Systems, Equipment, and Supplies." Each issue presents in-depth analyses written by disinterested expert observers. Past topics have included telecommunications for libraries, circulation-control systems, on-line catalog, serials control systems, and interfacing automated systems. There is usually an introduction containing background information and guidance in evaluating and selecting systems. The reviews compare and evaluate actual products.

# 25

# Networking for the Small Academic Library

## *Dennis E. Robison*

Networking among all types of libraries is not a recent development but dates from the early recognition that libraries are interdependent. Although there have been (and continue to be) many efforts to define what networking is (Markuson 1980), libraries are now recognizing that treating cooperative agreements informally is not sufficient. Rather, formal agreements are necessary, particularly when faced with the need to adopt automation as a part of the network process. Interacting successfully with other libraries involves a clear understanding of the issues of networking as well as leadership and management skills.

## WHY NETWORK?

Networking is based on the commonly held belief that no library can stand alone in meeting the demands of its patrons. In today's college and university library setting, this is even more evident. The academic library is challenged by:

- The increase in knowledge available in a variety of formats growing at an exponential rate
- The changing curricular needs of students—needs that the most adequately funded college library is often not able to meet—and research demands being made on faculty (''publish or perish'' often looms as large on the small-college level as it does in major research universities)
- Library budgets almost, without exception, falling short of the cost of materials, particularly during a period of double-digit inflation
- Changing ways in which information is accessed, especially with the use of automation technology
- The need of librarians and the library staff to share common concerns and seek solutions to problems

For the college library there are basic benefits from networking and cooperative efforts that are common among all types—as sophisticated as shared automated systems or as simple as two libraries sharing resources on a limited basis. Library networks, regardless of level and size, have the potential of (1) gaining access to a wider range of materials and services for students and the faculty than an individual library can ever provide, (2) positioning members to experience economies of scale through shared costs and volume discount arrangements, (3) preparing for or enhancing existing automation activities, and (4) providing formal and informal continuing-education opportunities for librarians and staff (Griffiths 1985a).

There are many instances of networking and cooperative activities among college libraries that are not necessarily an "automated" activity, for example, sharing of periodical lists and interinstitutional borrowing privileges for faculty and students. Library networking at all levels, however, is being dramatically changed by the use of technology, especially the computer. Two decades ago, only the large research libraries were taking seriously the need to automate their activities. With the rise of the bibliographic utilities—Online Computer Library Center (OCLC), Research Libraries Information Network (RLIN), and Washington Library Network (WLN)—and the participation of all sizes of libraries in shared cataloging and on-line interlibrary loan transactions, the networking scene has changed dramatically. Furthermore, the cost of technology has fallen due to the development of new systems and formats by which information is stored. For example, the Virginia State Library's CAVILIR—a computer-output microfilm (COM) union catalog of 1.9 million unique records of nearly all of Virginia's academic and public libraries' holdings in the Machine Readable Cataloging (MARC) format—consists of hundreds of fiche. A recent King Research study (Griffiths 1985c) anticipates that this will be reproduced in future editions in a compact-disk–read-only-memory (CD-ROM) format consisting of no more than two compact disks. In this format, the user will be able to interact with the data base as though it were an on-line catalog. With the purchase of a microcomputer equipped to use CD-ROM technology, a college library of even modest means can provide significant access to bibliographic information for its users.

The goal of distributive processing—placing library-automation activities as close to the user as possible—has benefited from the new technological developments. It is now within the financial means of many state and local library cooperatives to take advantage of the benefits of networking through automated systems. For many years the Hampshire Interlibrary Center (HILC) was an example of traditional networking. Through the cooperative efforts of five Massachusetts colleges, the HILC created a storage center for infrequently used materials, developed shared acquisitions and cooperative purchases, and provided ready access to all collections for its faculty and students. Yet it was not always easy to maintain. Member institutions changed direction, those individuals primarily responsible for the cooperative left the area, and rising costs of higher education caused financial cutbacks for networking activities. Space for the central storage area became critical, and the HILC administrative staff vacancies became difficult to fill (Edmunds and Bridegam 1981). After a serious review of their future, the HILC "decided to evaluate the benefits of merging some of their bibliographic records through various automated systems" (Edmunds and Bridegam 1981). As a result, the HILC members are now using the OCLC's LS 2000 integrated library system, which will form a common automation base. The HILC, by demonstrating the advantages of having bibliographic records in machine-readable form and by working together to achieve common goals, continues to serve as a possible model for college libraries and networking.

In an automated environment, difficulties with basic issues such as bibliographic access to collections, shared acquisitions, and open borrowing privileges are often easier to address than without automation. Technological development and economies of scale have also enabled smaller academic libraries to participate in information retrieval for their users, which was not even imagined a decade ago. On-line literature searching in the early 1970s was commonly understood to be a service offered only by the major research and well-funded special libraries. It would be safe to assume that most college libraries are either offering these services or plan to do so in the near future. Membership in bibliographic utilities or their state and regional brokers can often result in substantial savings in on-line literature costs.

Interlibrary lending is another traditional service that has been significantly improved through automation. Using the OCLC on-line interlibrary loan (ILL) system, for example, a negative request is forwarded automatically to another library, resulting in significant savings in clerical typing as well as a much faster response time. Furthermore, because of the richness of this national data base, the chances of getting the material are considerably better since there is little need for "requesting in the dark," hoping that a library has the item (Tallman 1980). Another benefit from using the ILL subsystem is the automatic keeping of statistical data that is available, albeit for an additional charge.

## DIFFICULTIES OF NETWORKING

Unfortunately, networking—automated or not—has its darker side. It has been a part of the library scene for so long that it has developed its own mythology—"Cooperation is one of those plus words, like Motherhood and the Flag. It is grandiose. It crackles with nobility. It conveys self satisfaction, generosity of spirit, the conferring of benefits. But it is not always wealth that is being shared" (Edmunds and Bridegam 1981). Indeed, one of the consistent concerns expressed in surveys of networking activities is that college libraries tend to buy the same books, subscribe to the same periodicals, and generally do not have much to share (Richardson 1969–1970). Because of the mythology, libraries have often entered into networking activities without the benefit of close and careful analysis. It is often done in small, seemingly innocuous increments that grow into large commitments often difficult to control. Open borrowing privileges, which begin without great difficulty among a few libraries, may result in massive raids of a collection by users from a member library whose college has begun a significant program without adequately funding its library. Tempers become frayed, and commitments are broken. The network suddenly appears not to be such a grand idea.

Membership in bibliographic utilities for purposes of shared cataloging has, in many cases, caused dysfunction among college libraries once they decided to participate in the interlibrary loan system. First there was the euphoria—"Wow, Yale has discovered us—they've just requested a book and sent coupons!" Within a relatively short time, the requests roll in from libraries large and small, known and unknown, requesting items that have just been cataloged as well as everything else under the sun. The clerk who used to handle interlibrary lending part time is suddenly doing it full time and requesting additional staff. The library has gone from net borrower to net lender. The college librarian is faced with (a) requesting additional staff to loan the collections off campus (not a very popular request with most college administrators), (b) pulling the plug on the terminal (but getting materials for one's students and faculty is so much more efficient), or (c) placing restrictions on what materials will be lent and to whom (What, and be considered uncooperative?).

## SEEKING SOLUTIONS

Most of these and other tensions within networking can be dealt with by imaginative leadership and management by college librarians. They must be, for networking on balance is not really a choice—it is a necessity for survival. Some of the issues are (1) preparing the staff for networking activities and the changes that will come, (2) working with other networking libraries to set goals and prepare ongoing evaluation and assessment of these goals, and (3) obtaining support for networking from the local college administration. Obviously, many of these things are interrelated; for example, participating in networking without adequate funding and support will probably cause a problem in staff morale.

### The Library Staff and Networking

One of the major benefits of networking is the opportunity for librarians and the staff of member libraries to share common concerns and to participate in meeting the objectives of the network. "One of the very best investments any library director can make toward greater interlibrary cooperation is in allowing time for staff members to get to know those with whom they will be cooperating" (George 1977). This takes time, one of the hidden costs of networking, but it is essential (De Gennaro 1980). It can help clarify policies and procedures that have been set at the network directors' level but may not have filtered down to the operational level. It also enables the sensitive manager to adjust these policies and procedures if provisions are made for feedback from the staff to the front office.

A networking library needs to have its house in order. If a staff member has caused internal problems due to weak interpersonal skills and no corrective action has ever been taken, this same person under networking conditions is not likely to become a paragon of joy. A study on attitudes and opinions on networking found that "people were also identified as significant hindrances. The reluctant staff member or the personality problem were frequently named as factors having a negative influence on cooperative efforts" (Offerman 1981). Networking is a commitment that must be enthusiastically shared at all levels if it is to be successful.

Networking, particularly if automation is involved, is a powerful change agent. A library manager will need to address this in order to encourage innovation and reduce the fear of change. Planning will need to take place well in advance of instituting any significant new patterns into the work flow. Whenever possible, the staff, which will be participating in new procedures, should be involved in the design and implementation of these changes.

## Network Goals, Assessment, and Evaluation

Networking goals should be established and its purposes made clear to all participants. Cooperative efforts are critically dependent upon the good faith and efforts of all involved. However, librarians are inclined to move to other opportunities. Without goals, the network that is heavily dependent upon the good efforts of a few key people will find itself floundering.

Thomas Ballard (1985), although a critic of most networking activities in the public library sector, suggested that the following steps be taken before entering networking. These steps are also valuable in assessing current networking activities:

- Estimate the benefits—is it merely the "spirit of cooperation" or are there truly materials to share? Are the collections within the member libraries rich enough to add diversity, or is it poverty that is being redistributed?

- Build in evaluation—how many users from other libraries actually took advantage of the network? What kinds of materials were borrowed and by whom? What was the unit cost per item lent? Were items provided within an acceptable period (very important when a faculty member has been told the library will not take his favorite but esoteric journal because "it's available on loan in the cooperative")?

- Support estimates of benefits—this is important before undertaking major automation projects, for example, developing an on-line or COM system for network serial holdings. Does the cost of the project really match the estimated benefits or can one continue to consult three or four printed serial lists from member libraries?

- Seek cheaper alternatives—do the bibliographic records need to be on line or can a computer-output-microfilm (COM) fiche file meet the objective?

An example of not planning or anticipating networking expenditures is the current dilemma over costs recovery for net lenders. Although it may now be considered hindsight, one wonders that if the real costs of interlibrary lending had been known by many college librarians, would they have been so generous? King Research has reported, in a study completed for the Commonwealth of Pennsylvania, that "the average cost of processing interlibrary loan requests for loans that are filled" is "$6.52 for monographs," "$6.93 for serials," and "$6.87 for other items" (Griffiths 1985b).

If the college library is not a participant in one of the bibliographic utilities, another dimension needs to be considered. Some have chosen not to become involved because of the disproportionate costs of joining when compared to the number of items purchased to be cataloged (Dagold 1983). Although it is not directly within the bounds of this discussion on networking to get into the myriad of details concerning shared cataloging through OCLC, WLN, and so on, some comment needs to be made. Most libraries do not join bibliographic utilities exclusively for the purposes of interlibrary lending but rather wish to participate in shared cataloging. In so doing, they have incurred significant "hidden" costs along with deriving great benefits.

The costs involved, beyond those easily identified, such as first time use, terminal purchases, telecommunications, and membership fees, have been organizational change, active participation in committees of the automated network, professional stress (a college-catalog librarian's records are now available for national scrutiny), and a continual need to keep up with technological change through reading and workshops.

## Support for Networking

Networking is an enhancement—doing better what we have always done— and often the most difficult line in the budget to sell. Most colleges and universities are still reeling from the effects of double-digit inflation and high energy costs. They are looking everywhere they can to cut costs. Without sufficient background about the purposes of library networking, an uninformed college president or dean may interpret this activity as a way in which to reduce library costs. Although it is true that libraries enter into cooperative agreements in order to share resources, they are doing so to survive because the materials budgets have suffered mightily during the past decade. In most cases, there is nothing to reduce. If three member libraries are subscribing to the same relatively unused journal, one copy in the cooperative may be adequate. Therefore, two libraries save, and one continues to have the commitment. If there is some *quid pro quo,* recovered funds will be put back into other journals, which will enrich the cooperative. The result will be an overall gain for the network but no reduction in expenditures for the individual members. Furthermore, as suggested, networking takes time and staff—resources that are usually an add-on cost to the operating budget.

## THE NETWORKING FUTURE

Networking has had a long, if not illustrious, history. Because of technology, especially the almost universal adoption of the computer in all types of libraries, the future of cooperative efforts looks very bright. Barbara Markuson, executive director of INCOLSA, Indiana's statewide network, suggested that:

Perhaps the overriding theme is that, as professionals, librarians have failed to grasp that linking libraries together via telecommunications and computers is not just another good instance of how cooperative librarians are. Rather, that networking provides unparalleled opportunities for a dramatic restructuring of the library as an operational unit and for an astounding array of new information services better designed to meet the needs of an increasingly complex user community. (Markuson 1980)

What are the trends for the future, and how will they affect the smaller college library? Library leaders and network executives have been involved in lively discussion about this in recent years. Because of the constant change in technology, automation among libraries and networks is far from stable, but some consensus seems to have been reached.

### State and Local Networks

While they are still operating with informal regions of cooperation and promoting resource sharing, several states are installing integrated systems, and several more are looking into networking plans (Griffiths 1985a). This is, in part, the result of active participation of libraries within a given state in the OCLC system and less expensive data storage and retrieval technology. Distributive processing is now reaching the end user. Because of this, there is serious doubt that a "national" network, centrally organized and governed, will ever exist. Rather, the state and local networks will, providing that linking of systems is ever accomplished, become the de facto national network (Luquire 1983).

### Networking for Everyone?

Because of the anticipated development of state and local networking and its influence on all libraries, there will be considerable pressure on *all* libraries to become a part of the system. There will be cost incentives (grants to acquire the necessary hardware, software, and reconversion expense) that will encourage participation. This is in recognition that the smaller library does indeed have something to contribute to the data base as well as the need to spread out the interlibrary loan load more evenly among the network members. It is also probable that net lending libraries will be partially reimbursed for their efforts. However, the prudent library manager will need to find ways of funding continuing participation in network activities.

## Network Costs

The start-up costs for state and local networks using automation will remain formidable in spite of relatively inexpensive technology. Funding agencies will give close scrutiny to how librarians will approach resource sharing in order to recover some of the costs. Richard De Gennaro's caution that "there is the ever-present danger that overselling the benefits of network membership may raise the expectations of academic administrators for unrealistically high cost savings, and thus provide them with a rationale for reducing budgetary support for libraries" (1980) is valid. Networking needs to be sold on the basis of enhanced service to users as well as a possible cost-savings strategy. What may be true for research libraries may also have some relevance for smaller academic libraries.

Computerized libraries in a network environment will be more effective because they will provide new and more useful services, but those services will supplement, rather than replace, existing services. Consequently, the automated network libraries of the future, to the extent they are successful, will actually cost more to operate than today's autonomous libraries. But that cost will be considerably less than that which a single library would have to bear in order to sustain the usual exponential growth patterns of traditional research libraries. (De Gennaro 1981)

## Delivery of Materials

Statewide systems now under study, as well as those that are successful, have stressed the need for an effective delivery system to back up interlibrary lending. Although one may debate how quickly a patron wants an item, delays of several days will not be sufficient if the network is to be acceptable to faculty and students. A business student, under the weekly pressure of a course taught by case study, is done a disservice by being told that the article he wants will take ten days, and if he wants it, his only option is to drive fifty miles to the lending library. Future networking will permit libraries finally to reach that level of service that brings materials to people, rather than sending people to materials. Telefacsimile, that dismal failure of fifteen years ago, may yet become a cost-effective method of transmitting information.

## Resource Sharing and Collection Development

Librarians must take the initiative in developing networkwide collection-development policies because (1) it is a professional responsibility to be good stewards of the resources available; (2) if librarians don't, someone else is going to do it; and (3) networking will enable librarians to expand their vision beyond local collections and look toward the development of a network resource. With rapid retrieval of bibliographic data of member libraries, efficient transmittal of interlibrary loan requests, and a satisfactory delivery system, librarians will be in a much stronger position to use scarce resources to support their institutional needs rather than some vocal faculty wish list.

## Regional Networks and the Small Library

The regional networks have long recognized that networking should involve all types and sizes of libraries. For the small library, technologies "are often inappropriate due to the cost, the training required to achieve proficiency and the training required to keep abreast of enhancements" (Luquire 1983). With the newer, less costly technology such as microcomputers, regional networks see an active role they can play in assisting smaller libraries in achieving the benefits of automation. Frank Grisham, executive director of SOLINET, predicted that "distributive processing will inevitably become the concept that shall bring a most dramatic change in our current relationships. The old theory, that we must push as much as possible out toward the user, will prevail. A key element in this process will be service to small libraries" (Luquire 1983). Louella Wetherbee of AMIGOS said, in regard to future members of the network, "It is certainly true that the type and kind of library that approaches us for services is changing. There are more special libraries. There are more small libraries" (Wetherbee 1984). College libraries that have not been able to see their way clear to participate in their regional or state network may now have an opportunity to do so.

In summary, the outlook for networking for the college library is very encouraging. It is not, however, the most comfortable place in which to be for a library director who is unwilling to take risks, whose goal it is to maintain the status quo. The dramatic changes that larger libraries have been facing are now before the smaller academic library. It is important that the staff is well prepared for these changes and does not perceive them as a threat. Instead, they must realize that the services offered to meet the information needs of faculty and students will be infinitely better than in the past.

## REFERENCES

Ballard, Thomas H. 1985. "Dogma Clouds the Facts." *American Libraries* 16:288–89.
Dagold, Mary S. 1983. "The Last Frontier: Possibilities for Networking in the Small Academic Library." *Library Resources and Technical Services* 27:132–41.
De Gennaro, Richard. 1980. "The Role of the Academic Library in Networking." In *Networks for Networkers*. Edited by Barbara Evans Markuson and Blanche Woolls, pp. 306, 307. New York: Neil Schuman Publishers.
———. 1981. "Libraries and Networks in Transition: Problems and Prospects for the 1980s." *Library Journal* 106:1046.
Edmunds, Anne C., and Willis E. Bridegam. 1981. "Perspectives on Cooperation: The Evaluation of a Consortium." In *New Horizons for Academic Libraries, ACRL*

*1978.* Edited by Robert D. Stueart and Richard D. Johnson, pp. 278, 280, 282. New York: Saur.

George, Melvin. 1977. "Small Academic Libraries." In *Multitype Library Cooperation.* Edited by Beth A. Hamilton and William Ernst, Jr., p. 155. New York: R. R. Bowker.

Griffiths, Jose-Marie. 1985a. *Study to Develop a Long-Range Library Automation and Network Development Plan for the Commonwealth of Virginia—Phase I Report.* Rockville, Md.: King Research, pp. 23–24.

———. 1985b. *Study to Develop a Long-Range Library Automation and Network Development Plan for the Commonwealth of Virginia—Phase II Report.* Rockville, Md.: King Research, p. 37.

———. 1985c. *Study to Develop a Long-Range Library Automation and Network Development Plan for the Commonwealth of Virginia—Final Report.* Rockville, Md.: King Research, pp. 1–2, 5.

Luquire, Wilson, ed. 1983. *Library Networking: Current Problems and Future Prospects.* New York: Haworth Press, pp. 21–23, 31, 41.

Markuson, Barbara Evans. 1980. "Revolution and Evolution: Critical Issues in Library Network Development." In *Networks for Networkers.* Edited by Barbara Evans Markuson and Blanche Woolls, p. 32. New York: Neil Schuman Publishers.

Offerman, Glen W. 1981. "Participants' View of an Academic Library Consortium." In *New Horizons for Academic Libraries, ACRL 1978.* Edited by Robert D. Stueart and Richard D. Johnson, p. 304. New York: Saur.

Richardson, B. E. 1969–1970. "Trends in Cooperative Ventures among College Libraries." *Library Trends* 18:88.

Tallman, Johanna E. 1980. "The Impact of the OCLC Interlibrary Loan Subsystem on a Science Oriented Library." *Science & Technology Libraries* 1:32.

Wetherbee, Louella. 1984. "A Conversation with Louella Wetherbee." *Technicalities* 4:10.

# 26

# Integrating Public and Technical Services: Management Issues for Academic Libraries

*John M. Cohn*

It has been observed that information-organization managers, especially librarians, have shown little published concern for structure as an element in their organizations' effectiveness (McDonald 1981: 47). This may reflect the relative lack of concern for organization design among librarians or the fact that managers in information organizations are often not in positions with sufficient power to effect significant changes in the design of their organizations. Librarians are at best middle managers in larger organizations, such as colleges or universities, and may not be able to restructure their shops at will. Still, library administrators must be aware that structure, although not the only contributing element in organizational effectiveness, is an important factor in how well the library achieves its objectives. Furthermore, administrators do have a significant role in charting the direction taken by their libraries and must understand how prevailing patterns of organization hinder or promote what libraries seek to accomplish.

This chapter examines one recurring question in the literature of library organization: the issue of organizing library functions into separate "public services" and "technical services" departments. This arrangement is common to both larger and smaller academic institutions and, more critically, is the basis for how librarians conceptualize what they do as professionals. Emphasis is placed on how changing circumstances within and around libraries are challenging this particular organizational pattern and the assumptions about library service that it reflects.

## SOME CONCEPTS OF ORGANIZATION AND STRUCTURE

Organization is the formal and informal structure through which decisions are reached and individuals perform job tasks that contribute to the goals of the enterprise. Organization, however, is more than the formal structure of departments. It includes both the external conditions and pressures that create oppor-

tunities and limitations for the enterprise as well as the internal relationships that
affect performance and production—those between administrators, between management and staff, relationships within staff groups, and so forth (Martin 1984:
5, 7).

A holistic view of management practice views organizations as ''systems''—
a series of relationships between interacting, dynamic elements, organized together as an integrated, goal-oriented whole. In this conception, changes in the
external influences or conditions upon an organization directly affect the internal
relationships between and among the organization's component parts (Nitecki,
1983: 47–58). The purpose of organizing is to aid in making objectives meaningful and to contribute to organizational efficiency. An organization is efficient
if it is structured to aid the accomplishment of enterprise objectives with a
minimum of unsought consequences or costs stemming either from internal
relationships or from external pressures.

Management theory holds that the basic cause of an organization structure is
the limitation of the ''span of management.'' This principle holds that in each
managerial position, there is a limit to the number of persons an individual can
effectively manage, the number varying according to underlying circumstances
(Koontz et al. 1982: 301–3). Thus, for example, the inefficiencies of broad spans
of management must be balanced against the inefficiencies of long lines of
communications. The losses from having multiple administrative departments
must be balanced against the gains from expertness and uniformity in delegating
functional authority to centralized staff and service departments.

In practice, the more that provisions are made for building flexibility in an
organizational structure, the more adequately that an organizational structure can
fulfill its purpose. Every enterprise moves toward its goals in a changing environment, both external and internal. To move successfully, the enterprise must
not only be goal oriented but also must strive toward an integrated holistic
structure capable of realizing these goals. The enterprise that develops inflexi-
bilities, whether they are resistance to change, too complicated procedures, or
too firm departmental lines, is risking inability to meet the challenges of economic, technical, biological, political, and social change.

## ORGANIZATION AND ACADEMIC LIBRARIES

Organizational issues confronting academic libraries are many and varied.
Budgeting with anticipated or actually diminished resources, staff development,
collegiality versus bureaucracy in a ''professional'' organization, staffing policies
and strategies, human-resource management, organization design, and job design
or satisfaction are just a few of them. Internally, the major issue appears to be
the role of staff librarians in overall governance (participatory management),
followed by the question of titles for administrative officers and training for
management responsibility (McCabe 1985).

The issue of organizational design, for large university libraries, has been manifested in the need to integrate automated operations successfully into the traditional structure as computerization became a major factor in libraries after the late 1960s (Cline and Sinnott 1983). For learning-resource centers in two-year colleges, on the other hand, the issue has been one of unifying library and media services and now possibly integrating as well nonlibrary campus services such as testing, printing, and word processing (Person 1985). The major organizational design question before the field today confronts libraries of all sizes because it deals with the fundamental structure found almost everywhere: the bifurcation between public (readers, users) services and technical services. The question is: how "differentiated" can our libraries afford to be? What degree of segmentation and departmentalization is feasible or desirable in today's library environment?

## The Separation of Public and Technical Services

Most libraries, despite innumerable permutations of organizational structure, are characterized by a basic division between public service functions and technical service functions. *Technical services* commonly comprise acquisitions, cataloging, and the physical preparation and repair of materials. *Public services* include reference, interlibrary loan, data-base searching, and serials and book selection. Book selection is often a component of a broader department of collection development, which may be in technical services or public services or may be a separate department. Circulation and reserve are sometimes public services, sometimes technical services. This separation is customarily ascribed to historical factors, particularly the growth of specialization in twentieth-century American life and the perceived advantages of such specialization. Another factor has been the massive growth in the size of libraries and in the increasing complexity of their knowledge base and the pattern of service offered to patrons. Finally, all of these elements are viewed as part of the larger movement in this country toward bureaucratization, efficiency, standardization, and the organizing of life through predictable and controlled systems (Stevenson 1984: 31–41).

With the arrival of automation, changes began to occur in the organizational patterns within technical services, the area in the bifurcated structure most affected by the new technology. Pronounced differences occurred only after the Online Computer Library Center (OCLC), when it became clear that traditional organizational arrangements were unable to respond to new operational conditions. There began a gradual consolidation of similar functions into specialized units within the technical services (Kraske 1978: 11–12).

The concept of integration and rationalization, with consequent changes in procedure and work flow, remained limited to technical services. Public services, which were by and large untouched by automation at the start, did not experience these changes. More importantly, "the relationship of those departments whose structure was affected most by automation to other departments remained, in most instances, unchanged" (Kraske 1978: 12). If anything, the appending of system specialists to the technical services side only intensified the separation. Once the impact of automation was felt within the public services, in the forms of machine-assisted searching and use of the on-line public access catalog, the issue of restructuring was raised in earnest. It was argued that the traditional division was too firm and inflexible, that technological and other changes were already modifying and would even further alter both the internal relationships within and the external relationships between these two areas.

## Challenges to the Tradition

Michael Gorman (1982: 82) observed that "the destructive effect of the dichotomy between 'public' and 'technical' services is still not widely recognized." Although this seems to be generally true, it is also clear that more and more writers in the field are calling attention to problems with the traditional separation of functions.

Critics fall into one of two broad categories—those, like Gorman, who see the split as one of entrenched attitudes retarding the "wholeness" of librarianship, and those who question the continued usefulness of an organizational pattern established in a bygone era, long before developments such as automation and networking changed the way we do business. These perspectives are often interrelated, but it is useful to separate them for the purposes of discussion.

*1*. A major challenge to the traditional separation of functions comes from those who believe it reflects a perception that there are first-class (public service) and second-class (technical service) positions within the profession (Bachus 1982). We are familiar with the notion, for example, that technical services librarians "like to work with books" and avoid people, whereas the real professionals are the public service librarians at the reference desks who "like to work with people." On the other hand, there is the view that public service librarians would be helpless without the bibliographic systems maintained by the catalogers. Catalogers work the reference desk, but how often do reference librarians do cataloging? And so on.

Critics charge that these perceptions represent serious misunderstandings, antagonisms, and parochialisms that retard change in our field. Moreover, maintaining the administrative distinction between the two areas only perpetuates the divisions. Michael Gorman has consistently argued that cooperation and progress will be elusive as long as each side claims uniqueness and superiority and that we must begin to see librarianship as complex but integrated. "[A]s long as we accept the implication that librarianship as a profession and library work as a service lack wholeness, we will suffer and our library users will suffer" (Gorman 1982: 82).

*2*. Thomas Shaughnessy (1979: 143) observed that organizational change seems to be more a result of new technologies than anything else. Writing almost twenty years ago, when the new technologies first began to make their presence felt in libraries, Mary Lee Bundy (1968: 324) advised that "automation may well demand a revision of the traditional organizational structure in libraries. Automated processes seem to cross departmental lines. In the long run, may not automation require broader divisions in libraries and fewer departments?"

During the early years of library automation, as previously noted, the traditional bifurcation of library functions was reinforced by virtue of systems specialists being appended to the technical services side. However, in the present era of the on-line public access catalog and on-line systems generally, this may change. The separation of professional tasks—or as Pauline Cochrane (1984: 53) expressed it, "builders of the catalog and the inventory keepers vs. middlemen or customer representatives"—will diminish, eroded by the convergence of bibliographic files and the obsolescence of centralized processing. In essence, as functions become automated, their interrelatedness will cause the collapse of old departmental structures. General access to the same information will allow first technical processes and then both technical and public services to become the interrelated continuum they are—and were—when academic libraries were smaller (Striedieck 1984: 119–20).

*3.* A characteristic of today's library is the blurring of the library's boundaries with external organizations. From the systems perspective cited earlier, external influences must always be considered a key element of the library's environment; libraries are relying more and more on outside agencies for service and expertise, to the point where locally established policies and practices may be seriously affected or determined by these outside agencies (Cline and Sinnott, 1983: 109–10). Examples of such outside organizations include computer centers, consultants, commercial vendors, regional library networks, and bibliographic cooperatives. Libraries have never been completely autonomous, but increased activity involving these organizations has caused the traditional boundaries of libraries to become even less distinct and internal operations to be impacted by these involvements.

The clearest manifestation of this phenomenon, perhaps, is participation in a resource-sharing network. As networking affects major operational components of the library, changes must occur in the organization of the library ("Networking and Library Organization," 1985; Dougherty 1978), some of which relate to the separation of public and technical services. For example, as libraries use network services, imbalances in resource allocations among library activities will occur. Thus as access to bibliographic data improves, demand will grow because information is available quickly. This will affect the distribution of resources between technical services and user services activities. Or since network participation changes the nature of work in collection development, circulation, interlibrary loan, and other areas, people's jobs are affected, sometimes demanding retraining or reallocation of tasks within and between departments.

To sustain this increased interaction with the environment and to cope with the changes that result, most libraries will find it necessary to strengthen internal communications and coordination. Libraries must eliminate communication barriers and reduce unproductive conflict that inhibits effective networking. This may mean having to make structural changes in the organization of the library.

## Prospects for Change

New organizational patterns and shifts in the physical location of staff performing tasks have unquestionably become characteristic features of modern library organization. For example, there is the commonly occurring shift of circulation from public services into technical services, reflecting the need for a single, machine-readable data base for circulation, acquisitions, and cataloging (Manning 1984: 23). Larger academic institutions are decentralizing original cataloging operations because on-line files can be displayed and manipulated through terminals at remote locations (Hudson 1986: 25). These changes only infrequently lead to outright integration of public and technical services departments. It would appear that the form of specialization reflected by the traditional bifurcation of functions is still preferred by librarians and that widespread, radical change is not likely to occur in the near future (Stevenson 1984).

Some evidence of this is contained in a 1984 survey of 117 members of the Association of Research Libraries (ARL). Geared toward organizational change, and particularly the prospect of integrating public and technical services, the survey showed that of the 82 respondents, 46 indicated that they were organized along the traditional lines, whereas 36 reported some form of integration. None reported complete integration. The report reflected the usual blurring of lines: technical services staff spending some time at the reference desk, both public and technical services staff selecting materials. However, the organization charts received with the questionnaires indicated only a modicum of formal integration (Busch 1985).

Some see the old bifurcated structure giving way to a new duality. Referring to Penn State's experience with the on-line catalog, Suzanne Striedieck (1984: 119–20) described a "horizontal structure of specialists cutting across divisions, acting as a counterpart to vertical supervisory structures, which stress similarities of process within each function." By extension, most original catalogers would be dispersed into public service units; public services, collection development, data-base searching, and original cataloging duties would be combined. Gorman (1984: 156–61) foresaw a "professional quotient" and an "automated/clerical quotient," involving all librarians more in direct public services. In Gorman's view, claiming, check-in, clerical acquisitions, circulation, the "information desk," and tours would be the responsibility of nonprofessionals or paraprofessionals; original cataloging, selection, evaluation, reference and bibliographic services, and direct instruction would be handled by the professional staff.

## The Traditional Structure and Small Academic Libraries

Given the more complex organizational structures found in larger academic institutions, most of what one reads in the literature reflects the experiences of larger libraries; however, the issues raised here pertain no less to smaller institutions than to universities. At my learning-resource center (8 full-time equivalent (f.t.e), librarians, 100,000 books and nonprint materials, serving 9,000–10,000 students), formal administrative integration was accomplished in 1983. The previous reader-services and technical services separation was in larger measure responsible for an undercurrent of "our people, their people" and a frequent lack of interdepartmental cooperation. Catalogers did work the reference desk, but formal integration was opposed. Technical service and reader-service librarians alike viewed the former as concerned with "things" and the latter with "service to people." (Moving circulation to technical services was fine since circulation was concerned with things.) Given the heavy commitment to automation in both areas, a coordinated approach to hardware acquisition and placement, data-base management, and terminal scheduling was essential. Today, a network-services librarian—a cataloger with intersecting technical and public service responsibilities—reflects the library resource center's (LRC's) commitment to resource sharing. This position would have been unthinkable before 1983.

Critics look to the small academic library of yesteryear as the model of an integrated structure. This has some validity, but we must not forget that the issue is as much one of mind-set as of structure, and this is a problem for smaller as well as larger libraries. As Doralyn J. Hickey has perceptively noted:

If the public services sector is unable to deliver the material . . . , the technical service sector is likely to receive the blame, whether deserved or not. . . . [T]he fact that a library is small does not seem to assure that the technical services staff will be excused from that blame. Even in a one-person library, there is a tendency to charge the other "self" (the cataloging self) with the responsibility by saying, for example, "Well, I just haven't had time to catalog that yet." (Hickey 1975: 181–82)

Thus the question of retaining the traditional separation of functions needs to be addressed by libraries of all sizes—in fact, by the profession as a whole.

## CONCLUDING REMARKS

We return to the question asked earlier: How differentiated can an organization afford to be? As Michael McCaskey (1983) has pointed out, the greater the differentiation, the harder it is for the organization's units to coordinate, and the heavier the burden on information processing and decision-making in the organization.

The concept of "integrative" management practices in the business sector has received a great deal of attention. One critic argued that there is a definite distinction between "integrative" and "segmentalist" thinking in management. The latter is characterized by a compartmentalization of actions, events, and problems, by defining problems as narrowly as possible, seeking solutions in past decisions and existing structures, and resisting change. The former approach sees problems as wholes, seeks to reduce the inherent conflict among organizational units, and develops mechanisms for transcending differences and finding a common ground for diversities and specializations (Kanter 1983: 17–36).

The degree of commitment to integrative thinking in our libraries depends upon administrative policy, goals, and objectives. It depends first on how important the administration and the staff believe it to be for the library to be one integrated, albeit multifaceted, operation. It is more important than we apparently believe. Hugh Atkinson (1984: 112) has observed that "arbitrary divisions of labor within a library by reference, circulation, cataloging, or acquisitions do not meet patrons' needs. . . . The need for information is not related to the step in the library process at which the information is being handled."

Smaller academic libraries no less than larger ones must begin to make serious inroads into the traditional bifurcation of organization. This has little to do with automation, for although we argue that the on-line catalog demands greater collaboration between public and technical services, this collaboration should have existed all along. Is it any less important in a card-catalog environment?

We need to understand that although automation and networking provide excellent rationale for the integration of these services—to strengthen communication and the work flow—there is a need to reexamine our structures simply to provide better service. The real tragedy of the traditional separation of functions is that it has perpetuated the blurring of professional and nonprofessional tasks, in many ways the bane of librarianship. It behooves us to end the public services-technical services split and concentrate instead on identifying and understanding our role in providing information services to the academic community.

Finally, Lowell Martin (1984), citing the current period of stabilized or reduced enrollments in our colleges, believes that in academic library administration, this is a time not for the builder but for the conservator. I suggest that for the smaller academic library, this is the time for the "organizer," the librarian who can successfully adapt operating structures to changing economic, political, and technological realities. Librarians must develop a stronger sense of organizational coherence within and across functional and structural boundaries. Only then will we make the best and most efficient use of our resources—both human and material.

## REFERENCES

Atkinson, Hugh C. 1984. "The Impact of New Technology on Library Organization," In *The Bowker Annual of Library and Book Trade Information*. 19th ed. New York: R. R. Bowker, pp. 109–14.

Bachus, Edward J. 1982. "I'll Drink to That: The Integration of Technical and Reader Services." *Journal of Academic Librarianship* 8 (September): 227ff.

Bundy, Mary Lee. 1968. "Automation as Innovation." *Drexel Library Quarterly* 4 (January): 317–28.

Busch, B. J. 1985. "Automation and the Integration of Public and Technical Service Functions." *RTSD Newsletter* 10: 25–26.

Cline, Hugh F., and Loraine T. Sinnott. 1983. *The Electronic Library: The Impact of Automation on Academic Libraries.* Lexington, Mass.: D. C. Heath.

Cochrane, Pauline A. 1984. "The Changing Roles and Relationships of Staff in Technical Services and Reference/Readers' Services in the Era of Online Public Access Catalogs." In *Reference Services and Technical Services: Interactions in Library Practice.* Edited by Gordon Stevenson and Sally Stevenson, pp. 45–54. New York: The Haworth Press.

Dougherty, Richard M. 1978. "The Impact of Networking on Library Management." *College and Research Libraries* 39 (January): 15–19.

Gorman, Michael. 1982. "A Good Heart and an Organized Mind: Leadership in Technical Services." In *Library Leadership: Visualizing the Future.* Edited by Donald E. Riggs, pp. 73–83. Phoenix: Oryx Press.

———. 1984. "Online Access and Organization and Administration of Libraries." In *Online Catalogs, Online Reference.* Library and Information Technology Series, No. 2. Edited by Brian Aveney and Brett Butler, pp. 153–64. Chicago: American Library Association.

Hickey, Doralyn J. 1975. "Public and Technical Library Services: A Revised Relationship." In *Essays for Ralph Shaw.* Edited by Norman D. Stevens, pp. 179–189. Metuchen, N.J.: Scarecrow Press.

Hudson, Judith. 1986. "Cataloging for the Local Online System." *Information Technology and Libraries* 5 (March): 5–27.

Kanter, Rosabeth Moss. 1983. *The Change Masters: Innovations for Productivity in the American Corporation.* New York: Simon and Schuster.

Koontz, Harold, et al. 1982. *Essentials of Management.* 3d ed. New York: McGraw-Hill.

Kraske, Gary. 1978. *The Impact of Automation on the Staff and Organization of a Medium-Sized Academic Library: A Case Study* (ED190153). Washington, D.C.: Educational Resources Information Center.

McCabe, Gerard B. 1985. "Contemporary Trends in Academic Library Administration and Organization." In *Issues in Academic Librarianship: Views and Case Studies for the 1980s and 1990s.* New Directions in Librarianship, No. 7. Edited by Peter Spyers-Duran and Thomas W. Mann, Jr., pp. 21–35. Westport, Conn.: Greenwood Press.

McCaskey, Michael B. 1983. "An Introduction to Organizational Design." In *The Management Process: A Selection of Readings for Librarians.* Edited by Ruth J. Person, pp. 183–93. Chicago: American Library Association.

McDonald, Joseph. 1981. "Organization Structure and the Effectiveness of Information Organization." *Drexel Library Quarterly* 27 (Spring): 46–60.

Manning, Leslie A. 1984. "A Technical Services Administration." In *Library Technical Services: Operations and Management.* Edited by Irene P. Godden, pp. 15–42. Orlando Fla.: Academic Press.

Martin, Lowell A. 1984. *Organizational Structure of Libraries*. Scarecrow Library Administration Series, No. 5. Metuchen, N.J.: Scarecrow Press.

"Networking and Library Organization." 1985. *LAMA Newsletter* 11 (January): 20–21 (Cooperative Library Organization Column. Edited by Charles T. Townley).

Nitecki, Joseph Z. 1983. "Conceptual Dimensions of Library Management." In *The Management Process: A Selection of Readings for Librarians*. Edited by Ruth J. Person, pp. 19–30. Chicago: American Library Association.

Person, Ruth J. 1985. "The Organization and Administration of Two-Year College Learning Resources." *Library Trends* 33 (Spring): 441–57.

Shaughnessy, Thomas W. 1979. "Library Administration in Support of Emerging Service Patterns." *Library Trends* 28 (Fall): 139–49.

Stevenson, Gordon. 1984. "The Nature of the Problem if It Is a Problem." In *Reference Services and Technical Services: Interactions in Library Practice*. Edited by Gordon Stevenson and Sally Stevenson, pp. 3–7. New York: Haworth Press.

Striedieck, Suzanne. 1984. "And the Walls Came Tumblin' Down: Distributed Cataloging and the Public/Technical Services Perspective." *Challenges to an Information Society: Proceedings of the 47th ASIS Annual Meeting* 21:117–20. White Plains, N.Y.: Knowledge Industry Publications.

# 27

# Competitive Selection of Domestic Library Booksellers: Developing a Request for Quotation

## *Gerard B. McCabe*

Library booksellers as individuals often are hardworking dedicated people who have special interests or, as companies or firms, are collections of such individuals. So as individuals vary in their interests and approaches to their trade, so also do the companies or firms they represent. The characteristics of the people become the characteristics of the company. The company that excels in supplying the productions of small private presses often has an individual who worked hard to establish good business relationships with the press proprietors and who may have taught that skill to other people in the company. Academic librarians and the libraries they represent are similar to the bookselling firm, but more often the former adapts a skill or interest to the needs of the latter. The art librarian develops the art collection, and the engineering librarian works on the engineering collection; a change of positions would require a change of interest but not of skill in collection development. In seeking to form a business relationship for the objective of building good library collections, librarians attempt to seek out booksellers who can satisfy the needs of their libraries. This chapter discusses a way to finding that relationship, specifically, with companies or firms.

Very often library booksellers are selected for subjective reasons influenced by personal contact. One or more librarians may meet with a representative, listen to a presentation, and decide to offer the library's order business to that firm whether it be for books, periodicals, or other material. A presentation heard at a library-association conference may provide the basis for a decision. Sometimes a librarian has had previous experience with the bookseller in another library. In other instances, a librarian has a sense of dissatisfaction with a bookseller's service, and when another firm's representative visits, the decision to change is made. In all of these cases, the same result occurs: one or more firms obtain the library's business with no solid evidence of performance matching the library's perceived needs. This is hardly fair to booksellers or to libraries. These oral presentations and brief conference encounters are not the best means of beginning an important business relationship. Again, in these situations no convincing statement exists of what the library's actual service needs are from a bookseller. No study by the librarian has been made, so no evidence exists to support these decisions. In this chapter another method of selecting booksellers is proposed.

## IDENTIFYING SERVICE NEEDS

After the fact of selection of a bookseller, librarians may elect to do a performance study (Grant and Perelmuter 1978). When more than one bookseller is employed, performance comparisons are made (Stokley and Reid 1978). Among other articles, one reports on a study of seven booksellers (Bell 1982), and another reports on eleven booksellers (Baumann 1984).

A better way to select library booksellers is to identify through self-study exactly what the library's needs for service are. Librarians should know before seeking a bookseller what service characteristics are being sought. Articles such as those just mentioned and others appearing in library periodicals provide information useful in formulating questions. The study's specific objective is to identify what the library requires from its bookseller(s). Librarians can then identify what requirements they should impose on vendors for (1) the vendor's speed of order fulfillment, (2) the level of coverage of scientific or other subject areas, (3) books from small presses and or other specialized publishers, and (4) any other factors such as reports and billing that may be critical for their library and its institution.

In beginning this process librarians should first identify a few qualifications for their library. First of them is any limitations caused by the size of the available materials budget. With limited funds, an academic library is obligated to purchase only curriculum-supportive materials. Perforce, material selection must follow well-defined guidelines for acquiring current new materials. With better funding, a library may have broader policies allowing for retrospective development of some collection areas, something that may require the services of a specialized bookseller. With a limited small budget, the librarians must consider how reasonable it is to attempt to divide it among several booksellers. For a low volume of annual business, there is no incentive for a bookseller to provide any special service. Costs that are too high cannot be offset from profits on a small account. Any special needs the librarians identify must be reconciled with the raw fact that booksellers, like any business, require incentives for maximum performance. A sense of the number of booksellers with whom the library can expect to negotiate for service can be determined by the size of the materials budget. Proportional distribution of funds among subscriptions, standing orders, and firm orders, allowing for some direct-to-source ordering, will help clarify how many booksellers the librarians can consider fairly. It is in the librarian's best interests to narrow down the number to as few as possible. Assuming that domestic subscriptions will be assigned to one or two firms and that one firm may receive most of the standing-order business, the service needs that were identified, together with the remaining budget, should indicate how many more booksellers may be required to meet objectives while still providing a sufficient incentive to booksellers.

Curriculum determines the second qualification. Is it primarily undergraduate with or without an honor's program, and how many major fields are offered? If there is a graduate program, how many fields are included? The objective is clarifying the academic levels required in materials selection. Useful guidelines for identifying academic collecting levels were prepared by the Collection Development Committee in a division of the American Library Association several years ago. (Collection Development Committee 1977). These guidelines are helpful and are understood by booksellers.

A review of the library's prior experience with the order process will help in identifying the third qualification. What persistent problems exist that should be removed? What other shortcomings prevail? If there has been a significant percentage of unfilled orders annually, what is the real cause?

Through study and literature review, guided by these qualifications, librarians will arrive at an understanding of what they should require from a bookseller for specific needs and what compensations are necessary for any deficiencies of either their own making or that of a bookseller. The goal is to communicate these service requirements in a document to competing booksellers.

## THE REQUEST FOR QUOTATION

The last concern is deciding on a method of selecting a bookseller(s) competitively. This chapter proposes doing so through preparation of a request for quotation. By profiling the library's service needs through questions they want resolved, librarians can identify desired bookseller characteristics. This document can be in either of two forms, a textual statement with questions noted within paragraphs or as a questionnaire. In either case an introduction should identify and describe the institution including the scope of its programs, demographics, and the specific types and levels of the materials the library usually orders and expects to order under the proposed contract. Concerns the librarians have or problems they wish to avoid can be identified also. The text should state clearly that a long-term contract or contracts will be awarded on the basis of the scored responses to the questions. Scores for replies are predetermined but are known only to the librarians preparing the document. Scoring systems can vary. In a different context, evaluating a bookseller's performance, Davis offers a system based on 100 points (Davis 1979: 59). In this chapter a loose system is used.

Time allowed for response once the request for quotation is mailed should be at least thirty days. A cover letter should state this allowance and also clarify the possibility of questions being permissible. If any bookseller should ask a question requiring a detailed answer, the response should be made known by letter to the other participants.

A request for quotation differs significantly from a request for bid or bid solicitation in that it establishes performance criteria that a bookseller must meet. A bid solicitation may state that the library will spend a certain sum in a fiscal year and will award a contract to the firm that bids the best discount or range of discounts. As will be seen, a request for quotation will do more; it will require certain standards to be met for consideration; it will establish time-limited performance guidelines that the bookseller must meet. Discounts, although important, will not take precedence over other critical factors.

This procedure introduces a major difference between this method and the usual way of selecting a bookseller described earlier. With performance guidelines established beforehand, the successful bookseller must meet them in order to retain the contract. The following examination of some questions will illustrate some particulars.

## SAMPLE QUESTIONS

*1.* What specific services does the company offer to academic libraries, including types of publishers and subject specialties? This question offers the bookseller an opportunity to identify areas of expertise. Points are awarded according to the importance of the area noted to the library. Replies that state their firms routinely supply university-press publications could be awarded twenty-five points, association presses fifteen points or more if the issue of such presses is an important collecting factor to the library; each subject specialty mentioned is awarded ten points but only if that subject is in the curriculum. With a predetermined score sheet corresponding to the questions, scoring can be done quickly.

*2.* What percentage of the company's business is attributable to academic libraries? Answers to this question will identify those booksellers that have strong interest or specialization in academic libraries. Some possible scores are for replies indicating 90 percent or more (thirty points), 80–89 percent (twenty points), 70–79 percent (ten points), and so on. Firms scoring in these ranges should have qualified service people with a high degree of competence in serving the order requirements of an academic library. This competence overall should vary only in specific service areas; other questions should produce replies that will identify those companies or that company where the particular specializations will best assist the library.

*3.* How are materials shipped to your library customers? Is freight or postage prepaid? How are items listed on invoices? Please include a sample invoice. Delivery methods are important in some geographic areas. Shipping costs are often a separate budget category. Appropriately scored replies will resolve these potential issues. Sample invoices can be evaluated for clarity, and the predetermined scores should be assigned by degree of clarity. To score sample invoices fairly, a group of librarians and order staff should examine the samples and agree on the appropriate score for each.

*4.* Do you have a warehouse, and if so, what is the size of your inventory of titles? For some libraries, a successful fulfillment rate by a bookseller may depend on no more than the size of the warehouse inventory, assuming other replies score favorably. Scores can be assigned in order by range: 30,000 titles (fifty points), 25,000 titles (forty points), and so on.

5. What is your discount schedule for trade, academic, or other titles? For scoring this question, librarians can use either of two types. Points may be awarded for the simple fact of a discount in each category, for example, trade (ten points), academic (ten points), and so on. Another way is to identify discount ranges and then award points: 20–25 percent (fifteen points), 15–19 percent (ten points) and so on. Discounts are important but should not take precedence over other aspects of service. Daniel Melcher expressed this very well: "High service and high discounts are totally incompatible. Good service costs money, and the supplier who spends money to give good service has to get it back in the prices he charges" (Melcher with Saul 1971: 50).

6. What percentage of a typical academic library's orders do you usually deliver within thirty days of the order date? Within 60 days? Within 90 days? If the librarians prefer, longer times may also be included. Answers to this series of questions are very important. Booksellers know what their average fulfillment rates are. For the library the question is, how long can waiting be safely tolerated? For some curricular areas the answer is probably not very long; for others a longer time may be possible, but academic books are not printed in great numbers, and delays entail risk of loss. Resolving this question during the study is best, not after selecting a bookseller (Bracken and Calhoun 1984). With a preestablished criterion, there should be no need to conduct an afterstudy; it becomes a simple monitoring process.

A library's internal procedures are important here. The selection process directly affects the bookseller's fulfillment rate. With an entirely "review-driven" selection process, meaning nothing is ordered that was not cited in a review, the time factor becomes critical, because late reviews cause late ordering. The item may be in short supply or out of print by the time of ordering.

Librarians must establish good selection procedures and routines expediting the flow of orders. While monitoring a bookseller's fulfillment performance, librarians must evaluate their processes affecting that performance. If a high proportion of orders for items two or more years old consistently have a high nonfulfillment rate, the librarians must resolve the problem, not the bookseller. This applies also to subject areas with high nonfulfillment rates; the fault may very well lie with the internal processes.

Fulfillment time is critical when severe fiscal restraints exist, especially when encumbrances are not freed for expenditure on other items as the fiscal period draws to a close. When overencumbering equates with overspending, the library suffers possible loss of its funds. Slow fulfillment rates can do this. Booksellers offering higher fulfillment averages within the time spans listed in the request for quotation should score higher then those that do not.

Other questioons can cover topics such as unfilled-orders policy, reporting and frequency thereof on out-of-stock and out-of-print items, returns policy, special charges for particular services, and any reports that may be provided.

## CONCLUSION

A carefully planned request for quotation reflects a thorough knowledge of requirements for bookseller service. In initiating this action leading to a contractual relationship, librarians also assume serious obligations. A contract binds both parties and should be for a long term, at least two or three years. Melcher, discussing disadvantages of bidding for booksellers, noted the advantages, however, of long-term contracts of such duration (Melcher with Saul 1971: 51). The institution's attorney can advise on preparation of the contract. Once a signed contract is effective, order procedures should be consistent; that is, orders are placed regularly; orders include source information such as addresses of issuing bodies or publishers; descriptive information is always uniform as are order forms when used. Furthermore, librarians will monitor the bookseller's performance, advising fairly of any shortcomings and allowing a reasonable time for correction. Clear, significant nonperformance results in voidance.

There are a number of advantages to this method. The selection process is objective and competitive. The goals of finding one or more booksellers with service capabilities fitting the library's needs are achieved. There is no need for anyone to remember oral statements made by a sales representative in an office visit of a few minutes duration or even months earlier at a conference of some library association. The booksellers describe services in writing and obviously are prepared to stand by these statements. No personal factors whatsoever are involved. The selection process is competitive based on written questions and answers. All interested booksellers have an opportunity to participate. The library's needs are addressed and fiscal control improved by a high rate of order fulfillment. Although this precise method may not appeal to all librarians, the process can be modified so that the essence of competition is achieved without close resemblance to a bid process. A contract guarantees performance; the bookseller gives certain assurance of that by signing the contract. Melcher's advice noted earlier should be heeded. In the final result, library users receive the best benefit, an especially good collection of library materials, as comprehensive as the selection effort and budget can make it.

## REFERENCES

Baumann, Susan. 1984. "An Application of Davis' Model for a Vendor Study." *Library Acquisitions: Practice and Theory* 8: 83–90.

Bell, JoAnn. 1982. "Methodology for a Comparison of Book Jobber Performance." *Medical Library Association Bulletin* 70:229–31.

Bracken, James K., and John C. Calhoun. 1984. "Profiling Vendor Performance [at Knox College Library]." *Library Resources and Technical Services* 28:120–28.

Collection Development Committee, Resources Section, Resources and Technical Services Division, American Library Association. 1977. "Guidelines for the Formulation of Collection Development Policies." *Library Resources and Technical Services* 21, no. 1:40–47.

Davis, Mary Byrd. 1979. "Model for a Vendor Study in a Manual or Semi-Automated Acquisitions System." *Library Acquisitions: Practice and Theory* 3, 1:53–60.

Grant, Joan, and Susan Perelmuter. 1978. "Vendor Performance Evaluation." *Journal of Academic Librarianship* 4, no. 5:366–67.

Melcher, Daniel, with Margaret Saul. 1971. *Melcher on Acquisition*. Chicago: American Library Association.

Stokley, Sandra L., and Marion P. Reid. 1978. "A Study of Performance of Five Book Dealers Used by Louisiana State University Library." *Library Resources and Technical Services* 22:117–25.

## RECENT LITERATURE

Miller, Ruth H., and Martha W. Niemeier. "Vendor Performance: A Study of Two Libraries." *Library Resources and Technical Services* 31 (1987): 60–68. This study is similar to others mentioned in this chapter. The conclusion is most interesting and the last paragraph particularly so.

# PART VII

# Physical Plant

# 28

# Space Utilization

## Wendell A. Barbour, Catherine Doyle, and Hugh J. Treacy

Today's small-academic-library director is faced with a variety of options when renovating an existing library or designing a new building. Developments in automation, shelving, and microform offer many new alternatives to the traditional arrangement of books on the shelf. However, many of these alternatives cost a substantial amount of money and make demands on buildings designed for the static storage of books. Staff members who work well within methods already in use might be unhappy with the thought of changes in these areas.

Michael Freeman (1982) examined the libraries in Jerrold Orne's 1967 and 1968 surveys of new library construction. He found that interior alterations had been made by 63 percent of the thirty-six libraries. Reasons given were "altered program objectives, the varied formats of library materials, and the need to provide services or house collections not foreseen by the building planners of the 1960s." As these libraries approach middle age, they are rapidly becoming filled to capacity and many have no firm plans to add new space.

## THE PLANNING PROCESS

Before drawing detailed plans for change, the director should assemble the necessary documents to guide the planners in their work. Ruth Fraley and Carol Lee Anderson (1985) suggested compiling a space-data file. Items might include the institutional and library-mission statements, goals and objectives, and long-range plans. Copies of the budgets, past space-utilization reports, equipment inventories, collection measurements, blueprints, outlines of present work flow, and building photographs might also be included, if available.

Aaron Cohen and Elaine Cohen (1979) cautioned against formulating precise standards for space utilization. Standards for square footage, volumes, and seating, for example, are dependent upon individual library and user needs. Before embarking on renovation or building, planning guidelines should be established to analyze library needs and the steps to be taken that will ensure the success of the project. Library administrators should become actively involved in the design process, which will be based on a program of present and projected needs.

Once this material has been gathered, the decision might be made to call in a library consultant. A consultant can provide a wider variety of experiences than may be available to the present staff. Ralph Ellsworth (1982), in his article "The ABCs of Remodeling/Enlarging an Academic Library Building: A Personal Statement," described a typical consulting process to remodel an existing building. Consultants can act as advocates for your plans as well as critiquing the architect's plans.

## EFFECTIVE BUILDING DESIGN

Effective use of space is dependent upon the shape of the existing or planned structure. Square-shaped floor plans require less corridor space and provide more usable space than any other configuration. Any design that departs from the versatile square creates wasted or "nonassignable" space (Cohen and Cohen 1979).

For example, one small academic library is arranged around several long corridors leading to staff offices. At the end of corridors on the first and second floors, large stairwells inhibit stack space, which is arranged in rectangular sections perpendicular to the corridors.

This particular design creates an unappealing separation of service areas and an emphasis on staff space over that of stack and user areas. Priorities for space should be given to the library collection and users, followed by staff areas (Cohen and Cohen 1979).

A successful plan for space utilization in a building addition might include the use of modules. A midwestern library employed square modules to increase its total usable space dramatically. Modular building also allows for changing space requirements as library functions evolve.

As libraries become more crowded, creative ways must be found to fit new services into existing space. At one small library the Reserve Department was housed in a large room on the second floor. The room was larger than needed for reserves and could be remodeled into a small classroom with the addition of glass walls and a door on one side of the room. The Reserves Department was moved to the Periodicals Room and housed in the bindery-preparation area. This reduced available space for preparation of materials for binding, just as the library had increased its periodicals holdings from 700 titles to 1,100. The frequency of the binding shipments has been increased, but since the library can bind periodicals only when classes are not in session, this cannot totally solve the problem. Book carts and study carrels are now used to hold overflow materials during peak binding times. It also resulted in the reserves assistant and the periodicals assistant sharing an office and cross-training in each other's job duties. This could have been a potential source of tension, since both people assumed more job duties as well as lost privacy by sharing an office. However, effective administrative leadership and the personalities of both assistants led to a smooth merger of the departments. Student assistants, who once only covered the reserve area, are now available all hours the library is open to provide information concerning the receipt and location of periodicals.

The move has left the second floor of the library without regular supervision by the library staff. This means that patrons now must come back to the first floor if they encounter any problems in finding books in the main stack area on the second floor. The old Reserves Room was quickly converted to a classroom. The former Reserves Room is currently being used for library instruction and audiovisual screenings. It will seat twenty-five to thirty people for a normal lecture, slightly less if a large amount of audiovisual equipment is required. The room is also lined with shelves storing old *Chemical Abstracts* and *Biological Abstracts*. These materials have little use and shelving them in this room has freed up badly needed space in the Periodicals Room.

The main problem today, since the library does not currently have the money necessary to renovate the new classroom area to make it more soundproof, is the noise leaking from the room to the surrounding quiet study areas. However, this is preferable to the old practice of holding classes in the Reference Room or an open study area in the stacks, which required considerable disruption of patrons using the area when classes were being held. It also gives students a better idea of the full extent of the library, since they must go upstairs to the main stack area to reach the classroom.

## AUTOMATION

Automating library functions enables the staff to perform its functions more efficiently. Using space properly will allow the director to take full advantage of automation by redirecting the work flow to fit the new patterns dictated by computer usage.

Many small libraries might be able to use microcomputers to automate several functions. This will enable the library to take advantage of the benefits of computerization without the additional expense of creating a special room to house a minicomputer. The power supply can be a major problem. The typical library building does not have enough outlets to house a computer on every desk, and the middle of the room might not have any at all. An option to consider is adding a power pole in the middle of the room or along a wall. Wires are run from the ceiling in a thin metal pole to provide additional power outlets. Telephone wiring can also be included, if modems will be used. If an existing outlet does not provide enough capacity, a duplex outlet can be converted to a fourplex. Surge protectors, which will allow up to six plugs, also provide an inexpensive alternative. Modular furniture, with its own outlets, provides a more expensive alternative. This furniture can be configured as necessary and changed easily. Modular furniture can provide a work space tailored to each job's requirements, with stations for computer terminals, typewriters, or microfiche readers. Before buying standard furniture, you should examine modular furniture. With modular furniture, each desk can fit the requirements of the job to be done, not some ideal standard. If modular furniture cannot be purchased, special computer furniture should be, so that operators will be able to work in comfort and safety.

The purchase of a minicomputer-based system will involve a more complicated rearrangement of space. Detailed environmental requirements for housing the computer may lead to a major renovation to create an adequate electrical supply, telephone connections, and air conditioning (Damico and Marks 1986). Additional office space may be needed for new personnel, such as a systems analyst. Two main target areas for this equipment are technical services and circulation. Technical services areas often have an open-space design that would lend itself to partition for the creation of a special computer room. Security is also greater, since the area is not open to the public. The lobby or stack space near the circulation desk might be partitioned off to provide room as well. Vendors can provide information detailing the space and environmental requirements of their systems. These things should be studied carefully so that the time and money necessary to complete the work can be budgeted.

Backup equipment needs must be considered when installing an automated system. One small library had to move a photocopier into the circulation area to copy the necessary book and patron barcode information when the circulation system was down. Since there were no funds available to purchase an additional photocopier, a machine was removed from public use and placed in the circulation area, creating additional crowding. Another common circulation backup system is a microcomputer, which will record transactions on disk to be batch processed when the system is up again. Both microcomputers and photocopiers require additional power and space in a traditionally cramped area. Public Access Catalog backups include computer-output microfilm (COM) and fiche catalogs and readers, which require additional expense in space and equipment.

Multiuser terminals can mean the addition of workstations in a crowded area. This can be especially difficult in the card-catalog area. If room is not available for more workstations, the card-catalog worktables can be used for terminals. A low workstation should be provided for handicapped patrons. If public access catalogs will be housed in different areas of the library, a simple user survey, described in the January 1986 issue of the *Library Systems Newsletter* ("Terminal Requirements for Online Catalogs," 1986), can help determine where the terminals should be placed.

The campus computer center can often provide computer time for a small library's automated system on the college's main computer. If the computer is being upgraded, a library package might be included as part of the costs, resulting, in many cases, in substantial savings over an independent system. This method will also provide more technical support from the computer center than the purchase of a stand-alone library system would. Priority for library applications must be guaranteed, even during peak times such as registration. This solution will lessen considerably the space needed in the library for equipment and staff. For the smaller library the campus computer center offers the only reasonable hope for obtaining an automated system. Financial officers who will not allow the library to buy its own minicomputer will often approve the purchase of a library system to run on the college's new main computer. It may also help make a stronger case for the purchase of the machine. Savings will also result from the use of the computer-center staff to maintain the computer, instead of hiring additional library staff for the job.

## NEW TECHNOLOGY

New technology is producing alternatives that can provide a considerable savings in current and additional space for the library. Innovative new uses of microfilm, such as the magazine collection, offer libraries recent periodical collections at a savings in space and in subscription and binding charges. The latest development, compact-disk–read-only memory (CD-ROM), offers librarians indexes such as ERIC and Psychological Abstracts in an easy-to-use format. The initial investment in equipment is expensive, but the savings in space can be great. Further standardization in the field could lead to one machine, which could be used for the specific index the patron wanted to search.

## CONCLUSION

Many methods are being developed to help the director increase space utilization that will work even in the smallest library. Compact shelving, microform, automation, and renovation can help make today's library function in tomorrow's environment.

## REFERENCES

Cohen, Aaron, and Elaine Cohen. 1979. *Designing and Space Planning for Librarians: A Behavioral Guide*. New York: R. R. Bowker.

Damico, James A., and Kenneth A. Marks. 1986. "Library Environment for Automated Systems: Guidelines." *LAMA Newsletter* 12 (March): 28–32.

Ellsworth, Ralph E. 1982. "The ABCs of Remodeling/Enlarging an Academic Library Building: A Personal Statement." *Journal of Academic Librarianship* 7 (January): 334–43.

Fraley, Ruth A., and Carol Lee Anderson. 1985. *Library Space Planning: How to Assess, Allocate, and Reorganize Collections, Resources, and Physical Facilities*. New York: Neal-Schuman.

Freeman, Michael S. 1982. "College Library Buildings in Transition: A Study of 36 Libraries Built in 1967–68." *College and Research Libraries* 43 (November): 478–80.

"Terminal Requirements for Online Catalogs." 1986. *Library Systems Newsletter* 6 (January): 3–5.

# 29

# Facilities Planning for the Smaller Academic Library

## *Bob Carmack*

Planning academic library buildings in today's fast-paced, rapidly changing environment is no easy task. Changes are occurring at such a rapid pace that it is difficult to keep up with the present, let alone plan for the future. The biggest single agent of change on present and future library buildings is technology. Technological changes are drastically altering the way libraries collect and disseminate information as well as the way people use these resources. Technology is viewed by some as a viable alternative, even a panacea, for new buildings, whereas others still hold that the book will continue to be the prominent form of information storage and dissemination for the foreseeable future. Be that as it may, it is still too early to predict the demise of the library-building project. However, major projects in library construction will probably be renovations or expansions rather than new buildings, particularly in light of new technology and the economic situation. This chapter, though, assumes that new construction as renovation is the subject of another chapter.

Constructing library buildings using modular concepts has become the standard. Such concepts allow considerable flexibility in the design, use, and management of space, and it is very likely that modular construction will continue to be the norm for buildings of the future. Regardless, space that will accommodate faculty, students, library staff, and a variety of information storage and dissemination devices plus provide for a variety of power and communication sources, in configurations that maximize flexibility, will be essential. The planner's tasks in defining these needs are not made any easier in that standards long used in allocating space can no longer be indiscriminately applied. For example, whereas twenty-five square feet at one time may have been adequate for a reader station, new technology, in many cases, makes that area too small. Furthermore, with technology still emerging, new standards may be some time in evolving. Until that time, the planner has to be cognizant of the literature and must not be afraid to ask questions or seek advice. Communication with specialists in the field is essential if buildings are to provide the flexibility necessary to provide quality library space for students, faculty, and library staff. One should always remember that when it comes to construction, remodeling, or expansion, the resulting facilities are going to be around for a long time, and one's mistakes very soon become obvious. As such, there are no dumb questions when it comes to building planning. It's easier to answer a dumb question than to handle a dumb mistake.

In most smaller institutions, with some exceptions, expertise in the planning and management of space for libraries may not exist either in the library itself or within the physical plant office(s) of the institution. As such, it is important that a thorough review of the literature be undertaken before beginning any planning program. The periodical literature and resources such as ERIC contain a number of useful articles dealing with both general and specific aspects of the planning process. There are a number of texts available that provide excellent summaries and guides for planning. The major text is Keyes Metcalf's (1986) *Planning Academic and Research Library Buildings,* recently revised by Philip Leighton and David Weber. The American Library Association's Library Administration and Management Association Division has also published a book of helpful essays on planning library buildings (*Planning Library Buildings,* 1986). Reading the literature, and particularly the work of Metcalf, should enable the planner to understand the processes and methods necessary to quantify needs as well as gain sound, basic advice on planning and design of the space needed to provide optimum library service.

It is essential that librarians be a part of the overall institutional planning process. This does not mean that the librarian has to be a member of any formal institutional planning committee that exists, although it would certainly be beneficial. It does suggest that the librarian must establish reliable lines of communication with institutional decision-makers responsible for planning. Whether through formal or informal processes, the librarian will need to keep abreast of the institution's goals and objectives as they relate to capital construction. Conversely, the librarian needs to keep appropriate individuals aware of the space needs of the library. An occasional cup of coffee with the person responsible for facilities operations and planning on the campus is one effective way to establish and maintain lines of communication. Such a process enables the librarian to find out what is happening institutionally and, at the same time, keep the person informed on the library's space needs. Periodic memos on the subject are also a helpful means of keeping appropriate offices apprised of space needs and concerns. The value of communication in the planning process cannot be overestimated.

Getting a project sold is often a time-consuming process that requires detailed documentation of need. The assessment and presentation of need requires the involvement of a number of constituencies to be successful. Although the value of committees is sometimes questioned, politically, a library building committee, made up of faculty, students, and library staff, is essential. This team may be crucial to the success of your selling effort. The term *team* is used advisedly, because if the team is not properly constituted and the team concept not cultivated, the project will have problems throughout the needs-assessment process, and your chances for success will not be enhanced. Each person on the committee will have some part to play, and all must function cohesively. Having those on the committee with hobbies or who will not follow through on assignments only makes the process more difficult. This is not to suggest that there should not, or will not, be disagreements or that the committee should be solely a group of sycophants. It is meant to indicate that the team should represent a variety of backgrounds and be prepared to discuss, in open dialogue, the needs of the library.

The choice of the team, if possible, should not be left to chance. There should be a judicious blend of experience and points of view. There should be representation from a wide variety of constituencies, specifically graduate and undergraduate faculty and students, administration, physical plant, and the library staff. Depending upon the circumstances, particularly if fund raising may be involved, alumni or friends of the library might be represented on the team. In some cases, the local public librarian may have expertise or be able to add a perspective that could be helpful.

The librarian will not, in most cases, be able to appoint the team formally. However, the librarian should make recommendations or submit a list of nominees for the chief executive officer of the institution to consider in making the appointments. On most campuses there is a faculty library committee that, in some circumstances, may be the appropriate planning team. However, this group is usually concerned with service and operation issues that may impede its bringing a new, fresh perspective to an issue dealing solely with space. Working through the appropriate administrative office responsible for student affairs may be a more productive approach to the appointment of students to the committee than working with the student association. This office may often have a better feel for students who would make good members of the team, in terms of interests and continuity, than the Student Association, which may be caught up in its own political agenda. Local circumstances will dictate, however. The library staff should elect its own representation or be involved, through consultation, in the appointment of the person(s) to be on the committee. Consideration should be given to the inclusion of both professional and nonprofessional staff. Crucial to the team is a representative from the physical plant or whatever department on the campus is responsible for buildings and building planning. At the small academic institution level there may not be a person who has sole responsibility for building planning. If such a person does not exist, you should try to get a person from as high in the building and planning hierarchy as possible so that exchange of information is expedited and decision-making facilitated.

The focal point for making the team work, and indeed for the development of the entire process, is the librarian. It is the librarian who will have convinced appropriate decision-makers that a need exists and that a study needs to be done. It is the librarian who will have read the literature thoroughly enough to have developed a level of expertise for leading the team successfully. It is the librarian who will have to do most of the work, either by design or default. Finally, it is the librarian who will have to live with the project after it is completed. The librarian both represents and provides the local expertise, and this person needs to be at the controls. As can be imagined, this is going to leave little time for the librarian to manage the library and its operations. If possible, the institution should provide some released time or other personnel assistance to the library as it goes through the planning and building process.

The librarian needs to take a leadership role in collecting and disseminating the information for consideration by the committee. To avoid prolonged discussion, to say nothing of minimizing disputes, and to facilitate the deliberations of the committee, it is usually more satisfactory to have the committee respond to information provided by the librarian rather than create its own data. In most cases, there is a lack of knowledge or understanding on the part of the faculty and students of the problems and concerns of space planning for libraries. As such, valuable time can be taken up in education and discussion if all of the information is put together by the planning team. Readings, site visits, and presentations can certainly help to bring the building committee's awareness to a higher level, but these learning activities should be combined with basic information provided by the librarian for the deliberations of the committee. More often than not, the building committee will welcome having the librarian take this approach to the needs-assessment process. The librarian will want to make judicious use of the library staff in the preparation of this information.

The tasks of the team appointed to gather pertinent information include, but may not be limited to, the following:

1. Developing the basic assumptions underlying the assessment process

2. Evaluating existing conditions

3. Examining relationships between the library and other libraries on campus, academic support services, and other libraries within a geographical region, if appropriate

4. Looking at alternatives to building

5. Delineating the objectives to be achieved with the new space

6. Determining space requirements

7. Prioritizing space assignments

8. Preparing a document for presentation to the appropriate administrator (McAdams 1983)

Consideration should also be given to having the building committee serve as the planning and program-development committee after an architect has been hired and the project given a go-ahead.

Basic to the activities of the team will be development of the assumptions that will guide it in its study and deliberations. Consensus of the committee needs to be obtained on at least the following concerns:

1. The time frame or life span of the new space
2. The relationship of print and nonprint resources as they pertain to space needs
3. The impact of new technology both as a service and as a resource
4. New directions, if any, that the institution may be planning, particularly as they relate to academic programs
5. The mix and numbers of the population to be served (McAdams 1983)

Because, typically, no special expertise in the planning and building of libraries exists at smaller institutions, a library consultant should be appointed to assist the institution and the librarian, as well as the planning team, in the development of a program statement that delineates the spatial needs and arrangements of the building. The consultant plays an important role in the entire process and great care should be taken in the selection of this person. The American Library Association has a list of consultants that, although not constituting endorsement, does provide a beginning point in the consideration of prospective consultants. Calling around, obtaining recommendations from librarians who have recently completed building projects, and reviewing the literature are other helpful ways to prepare a list of potential consultants.

One of the consultant's most important services will be to interpret the needs and desires of the librarian, the planning team, and the institution itself to the architect. The consultant will typically do this through the writing of a building program that delineates the purposes, functions, and operations of the library in terms of its space requirements, relationships of operations and services, and environmental concerns. The program covers every aspect of the building in-cluding housing resources, services, operations, aesthetics, atmosphere, and environment. It becomes the official document to be used by the architect in developing the actual plans for the building. The consultant may also serve as the institutional representative in terms of dealing with the architect and seeing that all plans are drawn according to the desires expressed in the building pro-gram. With all of these responsibilities, it is not hard to see the importance of selecting the best consultant that you can.

At the smaller academic institution, an in-house architect will probably not exist. When services of an architect are required, the institution will usually select a firm through its formal or informal networks. The architect's primary role will be to design the building, taking into consideration the needs of the library as described in the building program (the function aspect) as well as considering the aesthetic (the form aspect), that is, how the building will look individually as well as within its surroundings on the campus. The architect, in concert with the consultant, librarian, and other members of the administration, may also propose the site, which is, in and of itself, a crucial decision. The location of the library in relationship to other buildings, particularly when con-sidering future expansion capabilities and traffic patterns will impact significantly the library's role on the campus. Care must be taken in the selection of the site not to isolate the library in any respect. The architect will also be responsible for seeing that the building will be constructed in accordance with industry standards and specifications and that it is built within the budget constraints established for the project.

The building program statement is never a static document. It will undergo changes as the various working groups involved in the planning and building process visit, discuss, and consult with one another. The architect will see things that will need to be changed or should be changed for functional, fiscal, or aesthetic reasons. So will the consultant, the librarian, and the planning team. Choosing an architectural firm that has experience in the design and building of libraries certainly is a plus when it comes to implementing the ideas of the various planning groups. However, even with experienced architects, there will still be areas of concern that are not addressed very well either in the literature that supports the planning and building of libraries or in the architect's own efforts. These considerations include concerns both externally and internally within the library. It will fall to the librarian and the consultant to make sure that these elements are appropriately resolved in the execution of the building plan.

Some issues, if not planned carefully, may cause subsequent users of the building, including the library staff, to question its effectiveness. Furniture is of key importance. One should not skimp on price when it comes to the selection of furniture. The furniture will be around a long time and will be subjected to heavy use and, sometimes, abuse. Hence durability as well as comfort are of major importance. Furthermore, technology is forcing a reevaluation of the size, design, and mix of reader stations and furniture for the staff and services. Ergonomically correct furniture is essential for the comfort of the staff, as well as the readers, particularly where use of technology is concerned. With the furniture industry governing the standards for size and design of furniture, one has to be very careful in choosing furniture. The furniture catalogs are full of good-looking furniture at a variety of prices. However, it may be necessary to resist the "standard" as offered in the furniture catalogs if it does not meet your particular needs or design. Thorough testing and examination of furniture and equipment, through hands-on evaluation if possible, should be done before any specifications are drawn and purchases made. Flexibility needs to be built into each work-reader station as well. Each station should have, or have the capacity to have, sufficient power to accommodate not only existing but potential technology. Providing power sources that enhance flexibility in furniture layouts may cause design concerns that need to be considered carefully. Power poles, floor grids, and location of power outlets in core areas, for example, pillars, are existing alternatives that may provide needed flexibility.

Good lighting is essential. However, what constitutes good lighting is subject to debate. Controversy over artifical versus natural light, foot candles, and styles of lighting, to name only a few, still interject themselves into the planning and implementation of building projects. Because of these concerns, the services of a lighting professional should be actively sought. However, the librarian needs to be prepared to address major issues such as intensity, glare, contrast, and shadow in dealing with lighting concerns. Nonglare surfaces should be standard consideration for all reader-staff workstations.

Color is an important facet of space planning that should not be taken lightly. Effective use of color can, psychologically and aesthetically, contribute significantly to the success of a building. Most small institutions will need the services of an expert to help them plan and implement an effective color scheme. In some institutions there may be expertise available in an art, psychology, or design department. For others, the only alternative may be to seek outside assistance. Regardless of the source of the expertise, color needs to be an integral part of the planning process. Integration of a good signage system into the color scheme will also heighten the effectiveness of the building.

Fire-suppressant systems, which were once somewhat of an anathema, are now commonplace in libraries. Continuing research into the effect of a variety of fire-suppressant systems on library materials, with concomitant improvement in their capabilities, and the revision of fire codes have resulted in much greater use of such units. Planners need to consider carefully the varieties of resources typically housed in a library, as well as their location, condition, and value in determining the best fire-suppressant system. Again, fire codes may have an important impact on the type of system you can select; thus awareness of code provisions are important. Furthermore, planning should provide for ventilation systems that can effectively clean the air in all or part of the building following contamination of the atmosphere or environment. The functional success of a building will depend upon careful consideration and response to environmental concerns such as ventilation, air conditioning, heat, lighting, and acoustics.

Floor coverings are another essential consideration. Whereas carpeting was once thought to be an inappropriate covering for libraries, it is now commonplace in most all areas of a building. Once regarded as expensive and a barrier to the effective moving of book trucks and other library furniture, many now recognize carpeting as an economical way to reduce noise and cleaning costs as well as add a pleasing touch to the aesthetics of the building. Improvements in the design of library-book truck wheels and related furniture and equipment have helped to eliminate the problem of moveability while carpeting's role in the aesthetics of a building are becoming more appreciated. Some states have regulations about location and types of carpeting; thus planners need to be aware of such codes in their planning for floor covering. Quality is important.

Preservation and conservation of library materials are taking on increasing importance in library planning. Even the smallest of institutions must provide some effective method that will prolong the life of its resources. Ongoing research and development are helping to provide economical and effective resolutions for these concerns, and special advice should be sought in providing remedies for these problems. At a minimum, there should be some process that will permit control of pests and vermin. With potential toxic fumes and chemicals being involved in such a process, an isolated room, with more than adequate ventilation, is essential.

Externally, matters of access and egress need special attention. Access for the handicapped is important as is a design that will facilitate entrance and egress for all users. Walkways for pedestrians and handicapped should be at grades that make access to and from the building smooth and easy. Traffic patterns for pedestrians, bicyclists, and motorists should be designed, when possible, so that neither gets in the way of the other. Doors should not be so heavy as to be a problem for users, and particularly the handicapped, or cause continuing maintenance concerns because of weight or construction.

Two-wheeled vehicles are becoming a popular means of transportation and provide a particular challenge for the space planner. The planner must be conscious of traffic patterns, parking, and security in providing for these vehicles. Approaches to the library should not interfere with handicapped, pedestrian, or automobile traffic, and bicycles should not be allowed to become a safety hazard by being permitted to park in front of the library doors. Parking should be in areas adjacent to the library, away from the doors, and in areas reserved solely for these vehicles. Security for bicycles while their riders are in the library also needs to be considered. Facilities that will permit the locking of bicycles are a minimum response, and an ultimate response would be the provision of parking areas overseen by security personnel. Provision of parking areas for two-wheeled vehicles will cause much concern for the urban library when both space and security are problems.

Overall, one of the most important tasks that the librarian will have is to see that everything functions well once the building is open. Typically, there is a period of warranty for all or part of the building, and it will be up to the librarian to see that adjustments are made, as necessary, within the warranty period. This may require some firmness and assertiveness (perhaps even some aggressiveness) in terms of getting problems corrected. Remember, though, that you will be in the building for a long time, and it should be made to function as perfectly as possible.

## REFERENCES

McAdams, Nancy R. 1983. "Suggested Approaches to the Planning Process." Unpublished document.

Metcalf, Keyes D. 1986. *Planning Academic and Research Library Buildings.* 2d ed. Edited by Philip D. Leighton and David C. Weber. Chicago: American Library Association.

*Planning Library Buildings: From Decision to Design.* 1986. Papers from the Library Administration and Management Association Buildings and Equipment Section Preconference at the 1984 American Library Association Annual Conference, Dallas, Texas. Chicago: American Library Association.

# 30

# Expanding and Renovating the College Library

## *T. John Metz*

The current high cost of building, ever increasing competition for funds, and rising operational costs for colleges suggest that many more institutions will be considering renovation or expansion of existing facilities in the foreseeable future than will be planning new library facilities. If you have a modular building that was constructed after 1950, with capability for future expansion built into it in a direction that still makes sense, you are fortunate and your task will be relatively easy. If your building appears impossible to expand and occupies the only logical site for a library on campus, if it is designed for expansion in a direction that no longer makes sense, or if the present site does not appear to allow for expansion, the difficulty of the task can be manyfold that of designing a new library.

This discussion assumes an institution that is primarily an undergraduate teaching institution as opposed to a graduate research institution, that focuses more on the liberal arts than on vocational training, and that has an enrollment in the general range of 1,000 to 5,000. It also assumes that alternatives to building such as those listed by Keyes Metcalf (1965: 347) have been considered and that it appears that some remodeling or expansion will be required to meet the library needs of the campus. The steps that follow may be helpful in determining the needs and problems that should be addressed and in establishing a likely direction to proceed.

## DIFFERENCES BETWEEN COLLEGE AND RESEARCH LIBRARIES

There are some areas of building planning in which the focus of concern and the priorities may differ somewhat between an undergraduate college and a graduate research institution: First, the need for study space for students in an undergraduate college is often of more concern than materials storage needs. A given number of students studying occupies a certain amount of space, whether they are reading books or using a remote data base. Also, there may be more emphasis on group interaction and interdisciplinary relationships than in graduate settings, which further emphasizes the importance of study space appropriate to the educational goals and needs of the institution.

Second, some relationships are less critical to operational efficiency in a smaller setting. If only one truckload of books is processed per day, a technical services layout that requires it to be pushed an extra hundred feet is no big problem. Undesirable relationships of spaces should be considered in the context of their impact upon a particular library, not a theoretical one. Do not forgo options that might improve the overall functioning of a college library simply because they would be unworkable in a larger setting.

Third, changes that may greatly alter the appearance of the campus or the library can provoke greater concern on the part of faculty and alumni in a smaller than in a larger setting. More community involvement and more selling effort may be needed to get a building concept accepted.

Fourth, there may be fewer options for building in a smaller setting and greater pressure to incorporate what exists. For example, there is less likelihood on a small campus that a space large enough to serve as temporary library quarters can be found, that an alternative use for an existing building can be identified, or that an active teaching collection will include substantial material that could go into dead or compact storage.

Fifth, a need for additional library space may reflect a general campus need for more facilities, and there may be a great deal of competition for any funds for expansion. Worse yet, the funds that are available may be divided in such a way that only a portion of what is needed can be built. One should not enlarge a library to meet only space needs for the next five years.

## PRELIMINARY ANALYSIS

The first step in determining the library needs for an institution is to analyze what exists in detail, "but avoid getting sidetracked into diverting but endless studies, statistics and surveys" (Harlow 1951: 234). Obtain the following: (1) exact square footages and quantities—people, activities, materials, equipment— for all areas of the library; these areas should be measured carefully by an experienced person who can produce consistent results, not by the nearest available student assistant; (2) a diagram of existing functional relationships within the library; (3) a site analysis—how the library site fits into existing campus traffic patterns; the present visual impact of the library on the campus; access to major classroom buildings, dormitories, food facilities, parking; and so on; the campus planning or physical plant office can probably provide much of this; and (4) a diagram of patterns of use and levels of activity in the present building.

Review the mission statement of the institution and the purpose statement of the library. Then define what the building must provide to support the purpose of the library in carrying out the mission of the institution.

List and quantify, to the degree possible, major institutional factors that could influence future library needs: (1) projections for future growth of the student body, the faculty, and the library staff; (2) expected future growth of library collections and changes in their focus, physical format, and distribution; (3) components that might be added to a future library or removed from the existing one—branch libraries, language lab, computer center, music listening, art viewing, archives, rare books, nonlibrary functions, and the like; (4) anticipated changes in curricula, teaching styles, study habits, level of offerings, and composition of the student body that might affect library use; (5) plans for major physical changes on campus—extensive dormitory building, closing off some access to foot or motor traffic, moving a graduate school or department off campus; (6) changes that might be brought about by library automation and broader access to information on library holdings around campus and resources off campus; and (7) requirements of an expanded program of library instruction that may be needed to assist users in identifying, retrieving, and organizing information from an increasing variety of sources.

Use the materials that have been gathered to determine what is required to satisfy library needs in terms of spaces, equipment, and functional relationships. A library building consultant can be helpful in this process. There are useful formulas and standards for determining space needs in books by Keyes Metcalf (1965: 387), Ellsworth Mason (1980: 8), and others. The Association of College Research and Libraries' (ACRL's) "Standards for College Libraries" (*College and Research Libraries News* 1986) may also be helpful. Many of the formulas, however, do not allow for the special circumstances and the compromises often required by an expansion or renovation. For example, an office with two doors has to be larger than an office with one door to accommodate an equal quantity of furniture and activities; the same number of books will not fit into the same square footage in a building with 23' 10" spacing between columns as in a building with 24' 2" spacing between columns. Use the formulas as a guide, but take into account the special circumstances and needs of the specific institution. As Neal Harlow said many years ago, " 'Library standards' for buildings ought to be kept conveniently in mind, but they are more suitable to new construction, library literature, 25 year plans, and promotional campaigns. Remodelers need to begin by looking searchingly into present conditions, current operations, and existing services" (1951: 233).

## PRELIMINARY DOCUMENTS

Having quantified the library need, it should now be possible to draft the preliminary building program, which should include a statement of institutional mission, library purpose, and building functions. There should be some indication of special requirements for particular areas, significant functional relationships, and how the building will be occupied or expanded over time—it may be desirable to suggest temporary uses for space not actually needed at the time the library opens. Facility population in terms of materials, users, and staff, with growth rates for each category, should be stated. Most of the plan will be a listing of all library functions and components with the required square footage, a summary of their requirements, and an indication of their relationships to other components. Major equipment needs should be listed, with an indication of existing equipment that is reusable. Finally, there should be a statement of general expectations regarding ventilation, carpeting, fenestration, lighting, and so on that applies to the building as a whole.

From the building program, it should be possible to diagram an ideal plan for the organization of functions within the building. This should be a chart with the various functions indicated in boxes sized approximately to the relative square footage each function will occupy. Since some of these relationships within the actual building will be vertical as well as horizontal, the diagram should not be considered to be a prototype floor plan.

Besides physical spaces and functional relationships, a building has certain aesthetic and subjective qualities. A brief list of planning principles should be developed from all that has gone before that provide a sense of how the building should look and feel. For example, "The library's reason for being should be immediately perceptible to the person approaching its front door" is a statement that has more to do with how the building should feel than with how it should be built. Planning principles should bring out the kind of ambience the building should have and serve as a standard of comparison against which all of the ensuing plans and ideas can be evaluated.

There is now a program, a functional plan, and a set of planning principles against which the existing building can be compared. In the process of making the comparison, a listing of the inadequacies of the present structure should be compiled that indicate what needs to be corrected and where expansion is required. Problems will likely fall into the following categories: (1) physical problems—structural, lighting, ventilating, equipment, and so on; (2) user access problems—kinds of study space, physical arrangement, access to assistance, and so on; (3) service problems—primarily conditions that interfere with staff being able to carry out their duties efficiently; and (4) aesthetic problems—those having to do with the general ambience of the library.

## REVIEWING OPTIONS

Planning is now reaching a point where expert assistance will be needed. If there are plans to use a library-planning consultant throughout the project, this is the time to bring one in. At the least, a consultant should review the work that has been done so far and test the methodology and the conclusions. An architectural consultant will also need to be involved in the planning, although it is not yet necessary to choose an architect for the building.

The options that appear to be possible at this point should be listed. They will usually fall into the following categories, with one or more variations on each:

(1) deferred action—do nothing at this point; (2) remodel what exists to a greater or lesser extent; (3) renovate what exists and add space; and (4) build a new building.

Each of the above options should be tested in turn, listing the pros and cons for each one. We will assume that deferred action is not acceptable. Whether the second or third option is pursued is determined largely by the space required and the space that can be provided in the existing building. What follows, then applies to both remodeling and renovation—it is simply a matter of degree. The help of an architect is essential to testing both of these options, and we will not be able to eliminate fully the option of a new building until the remodeling or renovation option has been thoroughly tested.

First, the site needs to be studied. A set of diagrams should be prepared that show the library in the general campus setting, automobile and pedestrian traffic in the sector of campus that includes the library, parking, landscaping of the site, and the surrounding buildings. Other diagrams, such as elevations of the library and of nearby buildings might be needed to address particular concerns regarding the site. Alternative locations should be considered, and the planning group should satisfy itself that the existing site is acceptable for the library for the foreseeable future. If it is not, an alternative use should be sought for the library. If this can be found, the choices are then to build a new library on a suitable site or to find another building that could be modified or enlarged to meet library needs in a suitable location.

Assuming the location to be satisfactory, the existing building should be reviewed to determine if there are any obvious factors that make it inadvisable to attempt to remodel or enlarge the library. Ralph Ellsworth (1982: 335) provides an excellent checklist. One would normally consider building a new library if the cost is less than that of remodeling or expanding. However, if the existing building occupies the only logical site for a library, if there is no apparent alternate use for the existing building and if the cost of razing and rebuilding exceeds the cost of remodeling, the planners may need to study the existing structure in depth and exhaust every possibility of using it before choosing another alternative. If it appears that the existing building can be used, architectural and engineering studies of the building and the site should be made to confirm the following: (1) The building is sound. (2) There are no physical factors that preclude remodeling or expansion. (3) Needed expansion can be carried out at the site in the direction desired—subsoil structure, major utility tunnels, drainage, and so on do not preclude construction in the direction desired. (4) The building can be brought up to current construction code requirements at reasonable cost. (5) Existing heating, water, and power capacities in the building or on campus can handle the expanded building, and if not, what added utility capacities would be required. (6) Walls, ducts, and mechanical apparatus that cannot be removed or pierced. (7) Anticipated expansion will not conflict with general campus planning. (8) Whether or not the existing structure can support an additional floor or floors. (9) The structure can be made sufficiently energy efficient to meet modern standards. (10) How much of existing mechanical, electrical, and plumbing systems can be retained.

Assuming that none of these studies discovers factors that preclude use of the existing building, planning can proceed. By this time, many of the mechanical and other constraints that could affect the design of the building will be becoming apparent. Other constraints will not appear until construction is actually under way—there is no way of anticipating all of the problems that may be discovered in tearing into an older building. A list of all of the known constraints should be prepared that includes every aspect of the project, such as: (1) Site—There may be only one direction in which expansion is possible or makes sense; a certain massing may be necessary to fit the building into its setting, preserve a major campus vista, or harmonize with adjacent buildings; a main entrance may be possible on only one side. (2) Building—Possibly only one floor has high enough ceilings to serve as a main floor; floor levels may vary across the building; additional floors may be impossible; areas where stairways and elevators can be placed to reach all levels may be limited. (3) Code—Some codes require stairways at specified intervals; placement of exits may be restricted; there may be a maximum distance any point can be from an exit. (4) Functions—Must the building accommodate all-night study space? Classrooms? Audiovisual production facilities? (5) Finances—Is there an absolute limit, and is it reasonable to think the need can be met within that limit? (6) Irrationalities—an influential person or group does not want the exterior changed; a tree of some significance to the alumni stands in the path of expansion; someone insists the library be the highest building on campus or be in the exact center of campus; a certain memorial room must be just inside the front door; there must be classroom space, an office for the president, or some other unrelated function; there must be an open court.

## DEFINING AND SELLING THE CONCEPT

A program, a functional plan, a set of planning principles, an option that appears to be worth pursuing, and a list of constraints are now available. From these documents, the library planners, probably with the help of an architectural consultant, should prepare one or more prototype plans that conform to the planning documents and take into account as many of the constraints as possible. These prototypes should not be detailed floor plans but arrangements of the major functions within the total square footage called for in the building program. The prototypes should show the number of floors contemplated with major library functions laid out in both horizontal and vertical profile. Existing space and contemplated expansion space should be clearly delineated. If more space is needed than currently exists, remodeling plus expansion is required.

We have now identified what it is that is needed, the likely direction the institution must take to satisfy the need, and some possible alternatives. Unless the planners are unusually fortunate, a selling job is the next requirement. It might be advisable to call in a professional planning consultant to put all of the material produced so far together for a presentation to the governing body, or the planning group may want to do this. In either case, the services of a professional cost estimator will be required to project the probable cost of construction proposed, along with any alternatives. What should be sought at this stage is not approval to build but approval to hire an architect and to proceed to develop a detailed plan for the building.

## DEVELOPING THE LIBRARY PLAN

Assuming approval of the general concept, a suitable architect must be found to develop a detailed plan. Renovation requires the closest possible relationship between planners and architect. New problems continually arise as work on the old building progresses, and it is important that the architect be available to resolve them. Ideally, a local architect who has a reputation for designing good buildings and for having a primary concern for meeting the needs of the client can be found. Whether or not the architect has ever built a library is of far less concern than good general design, experience with renovation, relative proximity, and willingness to listen to and work with the client. Prepare a list of likely architects, look at buildings they have designed, and talk to clients who have worked with them. Look not only at the reputation of the firm but also at the work of the member of the firm who will be assigned to the project.

In working with the architect, the librarian should prepare specifications and respond to design; the architect should design and respond to specifications. It is acceptable for the librarian to sketch out ideas, diagram functional relationships, and so on but not to design the spaces. For an office, for example, the architect needs to know what furnishings are needed, what functions take place in it, and how it relates to other areas. The architect will then design a floor plan for the office, to which the librarian will respond. If necessary, revisions will be made until it is agreed that it is acceptable.

The task is to develop a concept that meets all of the requirements of the building program, accommodates the constraints that have been identified and those yet to be discovered, is architecturally pleasing, conforms to engineering and code specifications, and can be heated and cooled at reasonable cost. This task can be several times more difficult than planning a new building, and it can severely tax the patience and the imagination of both library planners and the architect. It is very important that all involved keep at it until they get it right, even if a dozen or more plans get scrapped in the process. Both the librarian and the architect will need to do some compromising in most situations, but neither should compromise too much. If a complete impasse is reached, admit it and seek further assistance. It can be very helpful to bring in another architectural or library consultant to take a fresh look at the situation and to suggest some alternatives. Neither library planners nor the architect should resent this. In one difficult case the library planners and the architect were unable to produce an acceptable concept for a renovation-expansion project after two years of their best efforts. An architectural consultant resolved the problem in a matter of days by suggesting an alternative massing and placement of the building on the site that made sense aesthetically and permitted a workable library floor plan. Neither a bad building nor a bad library floor plan is ever an acceptable solution—do not give up too soon.

As library planning moves from the general to the specific, a vast amount of detail on various library functions and needs will be amassed. Concepts for stack layouts, seating, the main floor, and so on will begin to take shape and to evolve. It might be advisable at some point to gather this information into a revised building program that provides much more detail on all aspects of the library. Such a document can be very helpful in communicating library needs to the architect.

In due course, the library planners and the architect will evolve a concept that everyone approves, one hopes, with enthusiasm. The cost of construction should again be estimated. If it is significantly higher than the earlier estimate, the planning group must decide whether to pare back the cost of the project at this point, to present it to the governing board as is, or present it to the board with some alternatives for cutting back. The latter course is probably the best in most circumstances. Both benefits and consequences of the various alternatives should be clearly stated and illustrated. Usually, the architect makes this presentation. A decision by the governing board at this point is a decision to have the architect prepare working documents and to choose and begin to negotiate with a contractor.

## PREPARING FINAL DRAWINGS

Particularly when a renovation is involved, it is desirable to have the contractor begin working with the planning group at the earliest possible time. Through early involvement, a contractor can often suggest alternative methods of construction and procedures that may substantially reduce the cost of the project, while gaining some concept of what the planners and architect are trying to accomplish. This early input of the contractor is lost if a bidding process must be gone through after all drawings and specifications have been established. A contractor can be chosen in much the same way that an architect is chosen, and a negotiated contract can be worked out at a relatively early stage of planning. The architect will need to prepare the documents necessary to allow contractors to submit proposals for doing the work. A contractor should be sought who does excellent work, who has a reputation for meeting schedules and staying within cost limits, and who has experience both with renovation or expansion projects and with projects that involve keeping a building functioning while construction is under way. When contractors present their proposals, look for evidence that they have taken the trouble to analyze the particular project and to make a proposal tailored to that project—many simply bring along a standard proposal with some blanks filled in. Visit renovation or expansion projects the contractor has completed and talk with the clients involved. Get background sketches of the principle employees of the contractor who will be involved in the project and at least meet the person who will be responsible for overall supervision of the project.

When planning has reached the point where the contractor can make accurate cost estimates and establish a schedule for construction, a contract for construction will be submitted for the approval of the institution's governing body. This is the moment of truth when the final decision to build is made.

For those interested in details on the steps involved in planning and working through the actual construction period, a recently published paper may prove helpful: "Getting from Here to There" (Metz 1986). There are also recent articles on the subject by Jane Conrow (1985) and by George Parks (1985).

## REFERENCES

Association of College and Research Libraries, College Library Standards Committee. 1986. "Standards for College Libraries, 1986." *College and Research Libraries News* 47 (March): 189–200.

Conrow, Jane. 1985. "Remodeling Large Academic Libraries: Survival Hints." *College and Research Libraries News* 46 (December): 600–604.

Ellsworth, Ralph E. 1982. "The ABCs of Remodeling/Enlarging an Academic Library Building: A Personal Statement." *The Journal of Academic Librarianship* 7 (January): 334–43.

Harlow, Neal. 1951. "Remodel While You Work." *College and Research Libraries* 12 (July): 233–36, 252.

Mason, Ellsworth. 1980. *Mason on Library Buildings*. Metuchen, N.J.: Scarecrow Press.

Metcalf, Keyes D. 1965. *Planning Academic and Research Library Buildings*. New York: McGraw-Hill.

Metz, T. John. 1986. "Getting from Here to There: Keeping an Academic Library in Operation during Construction/Renovation." *Advances in Library Administration and Organization* 5: 207–19.

Parks, George R. 1985. "A Funny Thing Happened on the Way to the Addition." *Library Journal* 110 (December): 41–43.

# The Small Academic Library: A Bibliographic Essay

## Rashelle S. Karp

"Second to the faculty, the most important source of knowledge on a college campus is the academic library" (Fife 1984). Its importance is reflected in complexity, conflict, and overwhelming diversity. This book has presented the reader with a series of chapters designed to bring some order to the seemingly chaotic world of academic librarianship particularly as it pertains to smaller institutions. This chapter categorizes and summarizes some of the issues and solutions that have been suggested by the contributors.

## ISSUES IN BOOK SELECTION

Tom Galvin pointed out that academic libraries began at "a time when there was a . . . greater sense of community within institutions of higher education"; when the library "was small and so was the number of its users"; and, therefore, when book selection was a simpler matter of choosing from a "commonality of interest" among the faculty (Schad and Tanis 1974: xix). However, the academic environment has grown to the point that faculty members are isolated not only from one another but from the library staff.

One method used by the academic librarian to mediate professionally between competing disciplines, departments, and faculty groups on campus is through budget-allocation formulas that involve the apportionment of definite sums of money to particular academic departments based upon universitywide statistical information (Schad 1970). Allocation formulas were originally developed to avoid the monopolization of library funds by one department. Although this type of allocation solves the monopolization problem, it comes with its own set of problems including the library staff's loss of book-selection power (Danton 1963) and a potential waste of money on departments that, because of inappropriate statistics, get more allocation than actually needed (Bach 1964). One type of allocation formula that addresses these problems involves correlating the Library of Congress or Dewey classification numbers of specific academic courses with the numbers of materials that circulate within that class number from the library

(McGrath 1967, 1968; Golden 1974). Then, based on the correlations, funds can be more accurately allocated to each department.

Another method often used to appease competing departments is the faculty-selection committee (Wilson and Tauber 1956) or faculty-research groups, which identify problems in library services (Haro 1972). The use of the faculty in selection can help to alleviate conflicts that often develop between the librarian and the faculty member who feels that his interests should be of primary importance to the librarian (Marchant 1969) and should take precedence over student needs (Logsdon 1970).

Other methods include networking with other libraries (Markuson and Woolls 1980) and reliance on resource sharing (Kent and Galvin 1977). We are cautioned, however, that reliance upon interlibrary loan and networking as substitutes for selection can have disastrous consequences for the integrity and utility of the collection as a whole (Ballard 1982).

A combination of allocation formulas and the other methods outlined above do a reasonable job of solving problems involved in dividing financial resources campuswide. But yet another problem that must be dealt with is that of how large the entire collection should be. Library budgets no longer afford the luxury of buying everything through large approval plans (Meyer and Demos 1970). Paradoxically, approval plans are now being used to decrease the volume of selection via more detailed evaluation of materials. However, they, like everything else, entail a great deal of sophisticated contract negotiation, evaluation, and constant renegotiation (S. H. Lee 1984), which may or may not be cost-beneficial. But librarians have to decide how much is enough. Or as Daniel Gore put it, "how much is too much?" His "law of diminishing returns" states that "doubling the number of titles in a [collection] . . . will not add 100 percent to its usefulness, but [rather] . . . one or two percent. On the other hand, keeping size constant while periodically revising stock in response to actual reader demand can have the effect of doubling utility" (Gore, 1975a: 1601). His "zero-growth" philosophy is one that many academic librarians currently embrace.

Verner Clapp and Robert Jordan (1965) propounded a formula for collection size that involves the mathematical manipulation of institutional factors such as number of faculty members, number of undergraduate and graduate students, number of undergraduate honors students, number of undergraduate disciplines, number of master's programs, and number of doctoral programs. Each of these data is multiplied by an appropriate weight (or number of books), to provide a recommended size specifically tailored to a particular academic library. Melvin Voigt (1975) recommended adding acquisitions data to the Clapp-Jordan formula, and Colleen Power and George Bell (1978) advocated using circulation statistics to increase the formula's utility.

The means for determining which materials need to be discarded to make room for the new has been discussed at length by Richard Trueswell (1966, 1969), who advocated charting the last circulation dates for materials in the library as a determination of their future utility and therefore discarded candidacy.

He, along with many other academic librarians, believes that the best predictor of future demand for a particular book is its last recorded circulation date. Bibliometrics, or the study and measurement of publication patterns, is also used to determine optimal weeding patterns. In particular, the determination of a small core of periodicals that will satisfy the majority of reader demand (Vickery 1948; Price 1976; Drott 1981; Goffman and Morris 1970) has been studied. The determination of a small core of total resources that will satisfy the greatest reader demand has also been researched (Line and Sandison 1975; Garfield 1981). The rate at which material obsolesces within different disciplines has been quantified and formularized to allow for more efficient and less time-consuming weeding (Fussler and Simon 1969; Line and Sandison 1974; Kent et al. 1979). We are cautioned, however, to take care when discarding or selecting materials on the basis of ''scientific'' formulas because of the dangers inherent in any quantitative formulas that often do not adequately take into account qualitative data (Farber 1976), which often lead us to be satisfied with minimal standards (McInnis 1972) and which are rigid and sometimes arbitrarily designed (T. Pierce 1978).

Finally, the academic librarian must deal with the issue of space and its efficient allocation. Some solutions to the space problem include building new libraries and library additions (Ellsworth 1973); converting print materials to more compactly stored microform materials (Saffady 1978); converting from standard shelving to compact shelving and other nonconventional shelving formats (Leimkuhler and Cox 1964; Metcalf 1965); and using remote storage facilities (Raffel and Shishko 1969; Buckland et al. 1970). It is, however, noted by all of the cited authors that special attention must be paid to the possible inverse relationships between these solutions and user satisfaction in the library.

## MANAGEMENT

In administering the library, many issues must be addressed and resolved by the academic librarian, not the least of which is the determination of the academic library's role within the institution (C. Walton 1982). Whether or not to organize the library around a centralized or decentralized structure is a difficult decision and has been examined in detail by Jeffrey Raffel and Robert Shishko (Shishko and Raffel 1971; Raffel and Shishko 1972) in terms of cost-benefit ratios, as well as by Helen Howard (1981), who indicated difficulties associated with implementing change in highly centralized, formalized, and stratified libraries. Many academic librarians prefer to ''hold duplication of collections and dispersals of service to a minimum'' through centralized library services, while individual academic departments ''press for decentralized service'' (Association of Research Libraries 1970; 35). Maurice Tauber (''Centralization vs. Decentralization in Academic Libraries,'' 1961) outlined three types of centralization (administrative, physical, and operational), and much of the library literature debates the pros and cons of each.

The academic librarian must also grapple with questions such as whether to organize the library departmentally in terms of function, activity, clientele, geography, subject, or form (Wright 1957), as well as how much departmentalization is reasonable (Dunlap 1976); whether or not subject specialization among the staff is advantageous (Fadrian 1982); whether a system of vertical or horizontal stratification in terms of staff mobility is preferable (Koenig 1984); whether or not to implement nontraditional scheduling procedures (Saunders and Saunders 1985); how to include the support staff and student staff in decision-making to encourage better job performance (Leonard 1985; Kathman and Kathman 1985); how to facilitate effective communication (M. Martin 1981); and how to implement work system designs that will increase staff motivation and satisfaction (Martell 1983).

A major area of concern is the implementation of procedures for staff development. Surveys show that many managers advocate staff development, but most do not practice it (Breitung 1976). Three major components of staff development are identified in the literature: (1) participatory management (Weber 1974), (2) professional advancement within the institution (Drucker 1974), and (3) continuing education (Stone 1970). Each one must be provided for through the commitment of the library administrator, as well as through the commitment of funds (Kaser 1971).

Additionally, dilemmas such as how to plan for change are encountered, while the academic librarian attempts to decide whether a formalized program such as the Management Review and Analysis Program (Webster 1974) is preferable to other, less structured means. Collection of statistics is a prerequisite of planning (Carpenter and Vasu 1978) and a crucial factor in effective management (Machlup 1976; Allen 1985). Here, the academic librarian must be very discerning since it is critical that only those data that will assist in planning and decision-making be collected (Hamburg 1978). Equally important is the attention that the librarian pays to data-collection procedures (Carpenter and Vasu 1978; J. Ratcliffe 1982; American National Standards Institute 1983) and to reporting procedures that are helpful (Simpson 1983).

The director and other administrative staff must institute effective personnel-evaluation procedures that include thorough task analyses of specific positions (Maloney 1977). They must develop managerial styles that are either participative (Marchant 1976), management by objectives (Michalko 1975), collegial (Bechtel 1981), motivational (Maslow 1954), scientific (Taylor 1960), task oriented or relationship oriented (Likert 1976), or a combination. They must determine which one is most suited to their personal feelings about humanity (McGregor 1960), as well as which one is compatible with union rules and regulations. Unionization with concomitant decisions concerning faculty status of academic librarians is a problematic area (Guyton 1975; Weatherford 1976). Difficulties in the academic arena arise in terms of what type of bargaining unit the academic librarian joins (Abell 1976; Schlachter 1976), whether or not unionization benefits the academic librarian (Carmack and Olsgaard 1982), and how unionization affects the relationships between the library director and library personnel (Chamot 1976).

In view of all of these issues, it is not surprising that academic library directors must be a little of everything to everyone (Ellsworth 1961–1963), must be tough (Karr 1984), and must be able to deal with stress, ambiguity, hostility, conflict (S. A. Lee 1977), and overwhelming priority dilemmas in terms of competing internal and external influences (Metz 1979).

## BUDGETING

The library budget has long been, and will continue to be, a focal point for the academic librarian, especially in these days of austerity (Harvey and Spyers-Duran 1984). Unfortunately, institutional administrations frequently view the library as a "bottomless pit," into which a great deal of money is dropped, and from which a small amount is gained (Munn 1968). It is because of this that the academic librarian must often justify budget requests in much more detail than other academic departments. Some of the ways in which this is done include:

1. Library-manpower budget formulas that scientifically manipulate variables such as library holdings, library acquisitions, full-time-equivalent (FTE) users, FTE faculty, and total number of students to substantiate requests for higher budgets (Fairholm 1970)
2. Cost-flow accounting models that manipulate variables such as circulation, holdings, acquisitions, and overhead to allow for accurate budget-needs predictions (Leimkuhler and Cooper 1971)
3. Looking at the library as an economic system where costs can be predicted on the basis of number of staff and volume of acquisitions (Marchant 1975)
4. Program budgeting, which involves cost-benefit analysis to avoid overlooking alternatives for accomplishing objectives, the pursuit of wrong objectives, and the pursuit of objectives beyond a reasonable point, as well as to recognize the costs involved in all alternatives (Keller 1969)
5. Zero-based budgeting, where starting from a budget of nothing, the librarian must evaluate each aspect of library service to justify including it in the annual budget (Hersberger 1969; Pyhrr 1970)
6. Total resource planning, which includes an operating budget, a cash budget, and a remainder budget (Hayes 1985)
7. Formula budgets, which emphasize either input to the library (Clapp and Jordan 1965) or output from the library (Zweizig 1981)
8. Program planning and budgeting system (PPBS), methods of budgeting whereby planning, programming, and budgeting are integrated into a unified procedure that provides a solid tool for management (Novick 1969; Young 1976)
9. Traditional budgeting techniques such as line-item budgeting, whereby expenditures are broken down into categories, and lump-sum budgeting, whereby the librarian makes allocations from a total amount (Durey 1976)

Additionally, fee-based models of library service are often proposed in an attempt to make the library, or at least certain departments with the library, self-supporting (Ungarelli 1983). Usually, these models focus on charges for on-line search services (Knapp and Schmidt 1979) or charges to off-campus clients for all library services (Beeler 1984). Some external funds are made available through federal legislation, if the academic librarian applies for them (Ladenson 1982).

## USERS AND THEIR ACCESS TO INFORMATION

The ultimate goal of the academic librarian is to provide access to information for the library patron. In trying to do this, many areas must be examined, not the least of which is the confusion brought about by individually formed department libraries, unofficial reading rooms maintained by teaching departments, and large personal collections in faculty offices (Dougherty 1971). These "quasi-libraries" (Genaway and Stanford 1977) are not centrally cataloged and, in fact, are often not familiar to the academic library staff. But their collections satisfy a core of users who consequently do not request that materials be purchased for the library. This, in turn, penalizes the entire user community, since it does not have access to needed resources.

Many researchers have examined the problem of access from the standpoint of the card catalog and difficulties in using it (Lipetz 1972; Patterson 1973). They have usually concluded that when failures by the user at the card catalog are combined with failures at the shelves, only 40–50 percent of user searches for information are productive (Tagliacozzo and Kochen 1970).

User failure often leads to user frustration (Saracevic 1977). Studies of user frustration have focused on document delivery within the library (Meier 1963; Buckland 1975), how to measure frustration levels (Hamburg 1974; Kantor 1976), space allocation as a factor in user frustration (Orne 1977), and loan-period lengths to increase access (Bobinski 1963; Urquhart and Schofield 1971).

The issue of whether to provide open or closed stacks is also closely related to user frustration. It has been found by researchers that in an academic environment, users tend to place greater importance on the accessibility of collections than they do on the comprehensiveness of collections (Dougherty and Blomquist 1974). This conclusion sheds serious doubt on the wisdom of those who favor decreased access through closed stacks to minimize theft, disarrangement, inefficiency of reshelving, and the need for multiple reading rooms (F. Ratcliffe, 1968). In an open-access situation, the placement of materials is an important factor (Goldhor 1972), as is ease of use (Lancaster 1974). Additionally, the use of remote storage facilities must be carefully evaluated in terms of cost and in terms of user satisfaction (Raffel and Shishko 1969).

The formation of undergraduate libraries was, at one time, an answer to the frustrations felt by the relatively new college student. Begun in the 1930s as a way to serve the needs of this population more efficiently (Wingate 1978), they have steadily declined in popularity because of various problems. Many believe that this type of division "limits horizons and inhibits exploration of the full range of the library's resources" (Person 1982: 11), rather than expanding the undergraduate's ability to access information. Others cite unnecessary duplication of resources and staff as a major disadvantage.

Another solution propounded by many as a minimizer of user frustration is the library-supported departmental library. This is a geographically distant small library linked to the main academic library but with a great deal of autonomy in terms of its day-to-day operation (Newhall 1966). Once heralded as a convenience for both library staff and patrons, the departmental library has fallen out of favor because it is considered to be too small to support adequate staff or resources (Legg 1965), because it necessitates a tremendous amount of duplication of resources on campus (Bruno 1971), and because too much space is needed to house it (Johnson 1977). Currently, academic librarians' answer to competing claims for specialized attention is to hire subject specialists within the academic library who serve as informed channels of communication to the departments with which they are allied (Byrd 1966; Cole 1974) and who are well-trained to select materials in their subject areas (Danton 1967).

The architecture of the library must be closely monitored to minimize user frustration. Specifically, the academic librarian must constantly plan (Poole 1981) and reassess the library's seating space (Mason 1980; Lieberfeld 1983), future growth potential (Metcalf 1965; Ellsworth, 1973), and comfort (Cohen 1979).

Many express the need for better bibliographic instruction within the library as a minimizer of user frustration, and some go as far as to stress the importance of literacy training as a part of effective bibliographic instruction (Richardson 1981; Person and Phifer 1985). Historically, bibliographic instruction has been viewed as a subfield of librarianship; currently, a great deal of importance is attached to it, and some consider it to be a separate discipline (Hopkins 1982; Rader 1982). Most agree that effective bibliographic instruction is that which involves the faculty (Carlson and Miller 1984), is integrated into the students' course work (Kennedy 1970), is related to a course assignment (B. Pierce 1981), and is actively publicized (Rambler 1982). The mechanics of bibliographic instruction have been extensively covered in the literature (Renford and Hendrickson 1980; Beaubien, Hogan, and George 1982), and numerous techniques are documented (Rader 1974; Oberman and Strauch 1982).

Yet another area of user frustration is at the off-campus center, or extension program (Lessin et al. 1983). The Association of College and Research Libraries has published guidelines ("Guidelines for Extended Campus Library Service," 1982) that specifically state that the main academic library has primary responsibility for service to off-campus centers and that the services provided should be adequate. However, reality indicates that off-campus education is often shabbily supported with the photocopy machine (Reardon and Lasky 1980), and electronic access is supplemented by interlibrary loan (Brown 1985), serving as poor substitutes for "real" library service.

## AUTOMATION

The impact of automation in the academic library is felt by all departments. Some think that improved services and benefits to patrons are secondary to the internal improvements in operational efficiency (Jestes 1980) and statistics gathering (Meier 1961). Regardless of who benefits the most, the advent of automation is associated with many difficult problems:

1. How best to implement on-line searching. Whether to charge for on-line searching (Crawford 1979), as well as how much (Beeler 1984, J. Lee 1984), must be considered. Who should perform on-line searches (faculty, students, or librarians) must also be decided (Droessler 1983, Halperin and Pagell 1985).

2. Who to hire to implement automation. The library will need additional staff members who are qualified in the area of automation, as well as people who will document their actions and plans, implement their plans, stick to deadlines, and be willing to locate physically close to the automated system (Weber 1971).

3. What kind of computer to use. This includes considerations such as type of computer and software as well as ownership or leasing decisions (Hammer 1965; Boss 1984).

4. How, whether, and what to automate (Potter 1980; Bryant 1981; Cline and Sinnott 1983).

5. User response to automation, especially on-line public access catalogs (Moore 1981).

6. Librarians' response to automation (J. Martin 1981; Luquire 1983).

7. How best to integrate microcomputers into the library (R. Walton 1983; Welsch 1985) and how to determine appropriate uses of the library microcomputer by students (Guskin 1986).

8. How to negotiate a contract (Boss and McQueen 1982).

9. How best to allocate and reallocate personnel (Conroy 1981).

10. How to introduce the new technology to the staff (Malinconico 1983).

11. What kinds of machine-readable information need to be made available? For example, should the library buy government-produced data and reports that are available only on computer tape or disk (Isaacson 1982)?

12. How to choose an automated library system (Matthews 1980).

13. The impact of automation on library architecture (Weber 1984).

## THE ACADEMIC LIBRARY COMMUNITY

The community of the academic library comprises students, faculty, administrators, alumni, other supporters, the external intellectual and geographic community in which it is located, and off-campus sites (Covar 1976). The problems in meeting the needs of the faculty, students, and administrators have already been discussed. However, there are several issues that must be addressed within the context of the external library community and off-campus centers. Many believe that a great deal of goodwill is fostered by supplying services to the general community including business and industry (McDonald 1985), alumni and the general public (Skeith 1966), and high school students (Sked 1984; LeClerq 1986). However, these services can get out of hand if the academic library becomes too heavily used by the external community. In 1975 the Association of College and Research Libraries approved guidelines to assist the academic librarian codify policies regarding access by persons other than primary clientele (Association of College Research and Libraries 1975). One solution is to limit use to researchers (Farber 1964). In this way, high school students cannot fill up precious seating space just because the academic library makes a convenient study hall. Additional recommendations include charging for various reference services (Donnellan and Rasmussen 1983) and charging for use by business and industry (Hornbeck 1983).

## SUMMARY

The world of the academic library is indeed complicated, and one in which many issues and problems must be solved. The future will be everything but boring.

## REFERENCES

Abell, Millicent I. 1976. *Collective Bargaining in Higher Education*. Chicago: American Library Association.

Allen, G. G. 1985. "The Management Use of Library Statistics." *IFLA Journal* 11, no. 3: 211–22.

American National Standards Institute. 1983. *American National Standard for Library and Information Sciences and Related Publishing Practices—Library Statistics*. New York.

Association of College Research Libraries, Committee on Community Use of Academic Libraries. 1975. "Access Policy Guidelines." *College & Research Libraries News* 10 (November): 322–23.

Association of Research Libraries. 1970. *Problems in University Management*. Washington, D.C.

Bach, Harry. 1964. "Why Allocate?" *Library Resources and Technical Services* 8 (Spring): 161–65.

Ballard, Tom. 1982. "Public Library Networking: Neat, Plausible, Wrong." *Library Journal* 107 (April 1): 679–83.

Beaubien, Anne K., Sharon A. Hogan, and Mary W. George. 1982. *Learning the Library*. New York: R. R. Bowker.

Bechtel, Joan. 1981. "Collegial Management Breeds Success." *American Libraries* 12 (November): 605–7.

Beeler, Richard J. 1984. "Pricing of Online Services for Nonprimary Clientele." *Journal of Academic Librarianship* 10 (May): 69–72.

Bobinski, George S. 1963. "Survey of Faculty Loan Policies." *College and Research Libraries* 24 (November): 483–86.

Boss, Richard W. 1984. *The Library Manager's Guide to Automation*. New York: Knowledge Industry Publications.

Boss, Richard W., and Judy McQueen. 1982. "Automated Circulation Control Systems." *Library Technology Reports* 18 (March-April 1982): 125–266.

Breitung, Amelia. 1976. "Staff Development in College and University Libraries." *Special Libraries* 67 (July): 305–10.

Brown, Doris R. 1985. "Three Terminals, A Telefax, and One Dictionary." *College and Research Libraries News* 46 (November): 536–38.

Bruno, J. Michael. 1971. "Decentralization in Academic Libraries." *Library Trends* 19 (January): 311–17.

Bryant, Bonita. 1984. "Automating Acquisitions: The Planning Process." *Library Resources and Technical Services* 28 (October): 285–98.

Buckland, Michael K. 1975. *Book Availability and the Library User.* New York: Pergamon Press.

Buckland, Michael K., et al. 1970. *Systems Analysis of a University Library.* Lancaster, Eng.: Lancaster Library.

Byrd, Cecil K. 1966. "Subject Specialists in a University Library." *College and Research Libraries* 27 (May): 191–93.

Carlson, David, and Ruth H. Miller. 1984. "Librarians and Teaching Faculty: Partners in Bibliographic Instruction." *College and Research Libraries* 45 (November): 483–91.

Carmack B., and J. N. Olsgaard. 1982. "Collective Bargaining among Academic Librarians: A Survey of ACRL Members." *College and Research Libraries* 43 (March): 140–45.

Carpenter, Ray L., and Ellen Storey Vasu. 1978. *Statistical Methods for Libraries.* Chicago: American Library Association.

"Centralization vs. Decentralization in Academic Libraries: A Symposium." 1961. *College and Research Libraries* 22 (September): 328–40.

Chamot, D. 1976. "The Effect of Collective Bargaining on the Employee-Management Relationship." *Library Trends* 25 (October): 489–96.

Clapp, Verner W., and Robert T. Jordan. 1965. "Quantitative Criteria for Adequacy of Academic Library Collections." *College and Research Libraries* 26 (September): 371–80.

Cline, Hugh F., and Loraine J. Sinnott. 1983. *Electronic Library: The Impact of Automation on Academic Libraries.* Lexington, Mass.: Lexington Books.

Cohen, Aaron. 1979. *Designing and Space Planning for Libraries.* New York: R. R. Bowker.

Cole, Garold L. 1974. "Subject Reference Librarian and the Academic Departments: A Cooperative Venture." *Special Libraries* 65 (July): 259–62.

Conroy, Barbara. 1981. "The Human Element: Staff Development in the Electronic Library." *Drexel Library Quarterly* 17 (Fall): 91–106.

Covar, J. F. 1976. "Community Analysis in an Academic Environment." *Library Trends* 24 (January): 541–56.

Crawford, Paula J. 1979. "Free Online Searches Are Feasible." *Library Journal* 104 (April): 793–95.

Danton, Perriam. 1963. *Book Selection and Collections: A Comparison of German and American University Libraries.* New York: Columbia University Press.

———. 1967. "Subject Specialist in National and University Libraries, with Special Reference to Book Collection." *Libri* 17, no. 1: 42–58.

Donnellan, Anne M., and Lise Rasmussen. 1983. "Fee-based Services in Academic Libraries: Preliminary Results of a Survey." *Drexel Library Quarterly* 19 (Fall): 68–79.

Dougherty, Richard M. 1971. "Unserved Academic Library Style." *American Libraries* 2 (November): 1055–58.

Dougherty, Richard M., and L. L. Blomquist. 1974. *Improving Access to Library Resources*. Metuchen, N.J.: Scarecrow Press.

Droessler, Judith B. 1983. "Online Services at the Reference Desk." *Online* 7 (November): 79–86.

Drott, Carl. 1981. "Bradford's Law: Theory, Empiricism, and the Gaps Between." *Library Trends* 30 (Summer): 41–52.

Drucker, Peter. 1974. *Management Tasks, Responsibilities, Practices*. New York: Harper and Row.

Dunlap, Connie R. 1976. "Organizational Patterns in Academic Libraries, 1876–1976." *College and Research Libraries* 37 (September): 395–407.

Durey, Peter B. 1976. *Staff Management in University and College Libraries*. New York: Pergamon.

Ellsworth, Ralph E. 1961–1963. "The University in Violent Transition." *University of Tennessee Library Lectures,* nos. 13–15. Knoxville, Tenn.

———. 1973. *Planning Manual for Academic Library Buildings*. Metuchen, N.J.: Scarecrow Press.

Fadrian, D. O. 1982. "Subject Specialization in Academic Libraries." *International Library Review* 14 (January): 41–46.

Fairholm, Gilbert W. 1970. "Essentials of Library Manpower Budgeting." *College and Research Libraries* 31 (September): 332–48.

Farber, Evan. 1964. "High School Students and the College Library." *Library Occurrent* 21 (September): 164–66.

———. 1976. "Limiting College Library Growth: Bane or Boon?" *Journal of Academic Librarianship* 1 (November): 12–15.

Fife, Jonathan D. 1984. "Foreword." In *Academic Libraries: The Changing Knowledge Centers of Colleges and Universities*. Edited by Barbara B. Moran, p. xiii. Washington, D.C.: Association for the Study of Higher Education.

Fussler, Herman H., and Julian L. Simon. 1969. *Patterns in the Use of Books in Large Research Libraries*. Chicago: University of Chicago Press.

Garfield, Eugene. 1981. "What's in a Surname?" *Current Contents* 13 (February 16): 5–9.

Genaway, David C., and E. B. Stanford. 1977. "Quasi-departmental Libraries." *College and Research Libraries* 38 (May): 187–94.

Goffman, William, and Thomas G. Morris. 1970. "Bradford's Law Applied to the Maintenance of Library Collections." In *Introduction to Information Science*. Edited by Tefco Saracevic, pp. 200–203. New York: R. R. Bowker.

Golden, Barbara. 1974. "Method for Quantitatively Evaluating a University Library Collection." *Library Resources and Technical Services* 18 (Summer): 268–74.

Goldhor, Herbert. 1972. "The Effect of Prime Display Location on Public Library Circulation of Selected Adult Titles." *Library Quarterly* 42 (October): 371–89.

Gore, Daniel. 1975. "View from the Tower of Babel." *Library Journal* 100 (September 15): 1599–1605.

"Guidelines for Extended Campus Library Services." 1982. *College and Research Libraries News* 43 (March): 86–88.

Guskin, Alan E. 1986. "Library Future Shock: The Microcomputer Revolution and the New Role of the Library." *College and Research Libraries* 45 (May): 177–83.

Guyton, Theodore L. 1975. *Unionization: The Viewpoint of Librarians*. Chicago: American Library Association.

Halperin, Michael, and Ruth A. Pagell. 1985. "Free Do-it-Yourself Online Searching, What to Expect." *Online* 9 (March): 82–84.

Hamburg, Morris. 1974. *Library Planning and Decision-Making Systems*. Cambridge, Mass.: MIT Press.

———. 1978. "Statistical Methods for Library Management." In *Quantitative Measurement and Dynamic Library Service*. Edited by Ching-chih Chen, pp. 31–43. Phoenix: Oryx Press.

Hammer, Donald P. 1965. "Automated Operations in a University Library: A Summary." *College and Research Libraries* 26 (January): 19–29ff.

Haro, Robert. 1972. "Change in Academic Libraries." *College and Research Libraries* 33 (March): 97–103.

Harvey, John F., and Peter Spyers-Duran. 1984. *Austerity Management in Academic Libraries*. Metuchen, N.J.: Scarecrow Press.

Hayes, Sherman. 1985. "Total Resource Budget Planning for Academic Libraries." In *Financing Information Services*. Edited by Peter Spyers-Duran and Thomas Mann, pp. 109–19. Westport, Conn.: Greenwood Press.

Hersberger, Rodney M. 1969. "Zero-Base Budgeting: A Library Example." *Catholic Library World* 51 (November): 158–61.

Hopkins, F. L. 1982. "Century of Bibliographic Instruction: The Historical Claim to Professional and Academic Legitimacy." *College and Research Libraries* 43 (May): 192–98.

Hornbeck, Julia W. 1983. "An Academic Library's Experience with Fee-based Services." *Drexel Library Quarterly* 19 (Fall): 23–36.

Howard, Helen A. 1981. "Organizational Structure and Innovation in Academic Libraries." *College and Research Libraries* 42 (September): 425–34.

Isaacson, Kathy. 1982. "Machine-Readable Information in the Library." *RQ* 22 (Winter): 164–70.

Jestes, Edward C. 1980. "Manual vs. Automated Circulation: A Comparison of Operating Costs in a University Library." *Journal of Academic Librarianship* 6 (July): 144–50.

Johnson, Edward R. 1977. "Subject Divisional Organization in American Libraries, 1939–1974." *Library Quarterly* 47 (January): 23–42.

Kantor, P. B. 1976. "The Library as an Information Utility in the University Context, Evaluation, and Measurement of Service." *American Society for Information Science Journal* 27 (March-April): 100–112.

Karr, Ronald D. 1984. "Changing Profile of University Library Directors, 1966–1981." *College and Research Libraries* 45 (July): 282–86.

Kaser, David. 1971. "The Training Subsystem." *Library Trends* 20 (July): 71–77.

Kathman, Michael D., and Jane M. Kathman. 1985. "Integrating Student Employees into the Management Structure of Academic Libraries." *Catholic Library World* 56 (March): 328–30.

Keller, John E. 1969. "Program Budgeting and Cost Benefit Analysis in Libraries." *College and Research Libraries* 30 (March): 156–60.

Kennedy, James R. 1970. "Integrated Library Instruction." *Library Journal* 95 (April 15): 1450–53.

Kent, Allen, and Thomas J. Galvin. 1977. *Library Resource Sharing*. New York: Marcel Dekker.

Kent, Allen, et al. 1979. *Use of Library Materials: The University of Pittsburgh Study.* New York: Marcel Dekker.

Knapp, Sara D., and C. Frances Schmidt. 1979. "Budgeting to Provide Computer-Based Reference Services: A Case Study." *Journal of Academic Librarianship* 5 (March): 9–13.

Koenig, Michael E. D. 1984. "Myths, Misconceptions, and Management." *Library Journal* 109 (October 15): 1897–1902.

Ladenson, Alex. 1982. *Library Law and Legislation in the United States.* Metuchen, N.J.: Scarecrow Press.

Lancaster, F. Wilfred. 1974. "A Study of Current Awareness Publications in the Neurosciences." *Journal of Documentation* 30 (September): 255–72.

LeClerq, A. 1986. "The Academic Library/High School Library Connection: Needs Assessment and Proposed Model." *Journal of Academic Librarianship* 12 (March): 12–18.

Lee, Joann H. 1984. *Online Searching.* Littleton, Colo.: Libraries Unlimited.

Lee, Sul H., ed. 1984. *Issues in Acquisitions: Programs and Evaluation.* Ann Arbor, Mich.: Pierian Press.

Lee, Susan A. 1977. "Conflict and Ambiguity in the Role of the Academic Library Director." *College and Research Libraries* 38 (September): 396–403.

Legg, Jean. 1965. "Death of a Departmental Library." *Library Resources and Technical Services* 9 (Summer): 351–55.

Leimkuhler, Ferdinand F., and Michael D. Cooper. 1971. "Cost Accounting and Analysis for University Libraries." *College and Research Libraries* 32 (November): 449–66.

Leimkuhler, Ferdinand F., and J. G. Cox. 1964. "Compact Book Storage in Libraries." *Operations Research* 12: 419–27.

Leonard, W. Patrick. 1985. "The Rest of the Organizational Development Equation." *Journal of Academic Librarianship* 11 (March): 34–35.

Lessin, Barton M., et al. 1983. *Off-Campus Library Services Conference Proceedings.* Mt. Pleasant, Mich.: Central Michigan University Press.

Lieberfeld, Lawrence. 1983. "Curious Case of the Library Building." *College and Research Libraries* 44 (July): 277–82.

Likert, Rensis. 1976. *The Human Organization: Its Management and Value.* New York: McGraw-Hill.

Line, Maurice B., and Alexander Sandison. 1974. "Obsolescence and Changes in the Use of Literature with Time." *Journal of Documentation* 30 (September): 283–350.

———. 1975. "Practical Interpretation of Citation and Library Use Studies." *College and Research Libraries* 36 (September): 393–96.

Lipetz, Ben-Ami. 1972. "Catalog Use in a Large Research Library." *Library Quarterly* 42 (January): 129–39.

Logsdon, Richard H. 1970. "Librarian and the Scholar: Eternal Enemies." *Library Journal* 95 (September 15): 2871–74.

Luquire, Wilson. 1983. "Attitudes toward Automation/Innovation in Academic Libraries." *Journal of Academic Librarianship* 8 (January): 344–51.

McDonald, E. 1985. "University/Industrial Partnerships: Premonitions for Academic Libraries." *Journal of Academic Librarianship* 11 (May): 82–87.

McGrath, William E. 1967. "Determining and Allocating Book Funds for Current Domestic Buying." *College and Research Libraries* 28 (July): 269–72.

———. 1968. "Measuring Classified Circulation According to Curriculum." *College and Research Libraries* 24 (September): 347–50.

McGregor, Douglas. 1960. *Human Side of Enterprise*. New York: McGraw-Hill.

Machlup, Fritz. 1976. "Our Libraries: Can We Measure Their Holdings and Acquisitions." *AAUP Bulletin* 62 (October): 303–7.

McInnis, R. Marvin. 1972. "Formula Approach to Library Size: An Empirical of Its Efficacy in Evaluating Research Libraries." *College and Research Libraries* 33 (May): 190–98.

Malinconico, S. M. 1983. "Technology, Change, and People." *Library Journal* 108 (April 15): 798–800.

Maloney, Kay, ed. 1977. *Personnel Development in Libraries*. New Brunswick, N.J.: Rutgers University Press.

Marchant, Maurice P. 1969. "Faculty-Librarian Conflict." *Library Journal* (September 1): 2886–89.

———. 1975. "University Libraries as Economic Systems." *College and Research Libraries* 36 (November): 449–57.

———. 1976. *Participative Management in Academic Libraries*. Westport, Conn.: Greenwood Press.

Markuson, Barbara E., and Blanch E. Woolls. 1980. *Networks for Networkers*. New York: Neal-Schuman Publishers.

Martell, Charles R. 1983. *Client Centered Academic Library: An Organizational Model*. Westport, Conn.: Greenwood Press.

Martin, James R. 1981. "Automation and the Service Attitudes of ARL Circulation Managers." *Journal of Library Automation* 14 (September): 190–94.

Martin, Murray S. 1981. *Issues in Personnel Management in Academic Libraries*. Greenwich, Conn.: JAI Press.

Maslow, Abraham. 1954. *Motivation and Personality*. New York: Harper.

Mason, Ellsworth. 1980. *Mason on Library Buildings*. Metuchen, N.J.: Scarecrow Press.

Matthews, Joseph. 1980. *Choosing an Automated Library System: A Planning Guide*. Chicago: American Library Association.

Meier, R. L. 1961. "Efficiency Criteria for the Operation of Large Libraries." *Library Quarterly* 31 (July): 215–34.

———. 1963. "Information Input Overload: Features of Growth in Communications Oriented Institutions." *Libri* 13, no. 1: 1–44.

Metcalf, K. D. 1965. *Planning Academic and Research Library Buildings*. New York: McGraw-Hill.

Metz, Paul. 1979. "Role of the Academic Library Director." *Journal of Academic Librarianship* 5 (July): 148–52.

Meyer, Betty J., and John T. Demos. 1970. "Acquisition Policy for University Libraries: Selection or Collection." *Library Resources and Technical Services* 14 (Summer): 395–99.

Michalko, James. 1975. "Management by Objectives and the Academic Library: A Critical Overview." *Library Quarterly* 48 (July): 235–52.

Moore, Carole W. 1981. "User Reactions to Online Catalogs: An Exploratory Study." *College and Research Libraries* 42 (July): 295–302.

Munn, Robert F. 1968. "Bottomless Pit or the Academic Library as Viewed from the Administration Building." *College and Research Libraries* 29 (January): 51–54.

Newhall, Suzanne K. 1966. "Departmental Libraries and the Problem of Autonomy." *ALA Bulletin* 60 (July): 721–22.

Novick, David, ed. 1969. *Program Budgeting, Program Analysis and the Federal Budget.* New York: Holt, Rinehart and Winston.

Oberman, Cerise, and Katina Strauch. 1982. *Theories of Bibliographic Education: Designs for Teaching.* New York: R. R. Bowker.

Orne, Jerold. 1977. "Library Building Trends and Their Meanings." *Library Journal* 102 (October 1): 2397–2401.

Patterson, Kelly. 1973. "Library Think vs. Library User." *RQ.* 12 (Summer 1973): 364–66.

Person, Roland. 1982. "University Undergraduate Libraries: Nearly Extinct or Continuing Examples of Evolution?" *Journal of Academic Librarianship* 8 (March): 4–13.

Person, Ruth J., and Kenneth O. Phifer. 1985. "Support for Literacy Education in Academic Libraries." *College and Research Libraries* 46 (March): 147–52.

Pierce, Beverly A. 1981. "Librarians and Teachers: Where Is the Common Ground?" *Catholic Library World* 53 (November): 164–67.

Pierce, Thomas J. 1978. "Empirical Approach to the Allocation of the Book Budget." *Collection Management* 2 (Spring): 39–58.

Poole, Frazer G. 1981. "Planning the College Library Building: Process and Problems." In *College Librarianship.* Edited by William Miller and D. Stephen Rockwood, pp. 233–82. Metuchen, N.J.: Scarecrow Press.

Potter, William G. 1980. "Automated Acquisitions in Academic Libraries." *Illinois Libraries* 62 (September): 637–39.

Power, Colleen J., and George H. Bell. 1978. "Automated Circulation, Patron Satisfaction, and Collection Evaluation in Academic Libraries—A Circulation Analysis Formula." *Journal of Library Automation* 11 (December): 366–69.

Price, Derek de Solla. 1976. "A General Theory of Bibliometric and Other Cumulative Advantage Processes." *American Society of Information Science Journal* 27 (September-October): 292–306.

Pyhrr, Peter. 1970. "Zero Based Budgeting" *Harvard Business Review* 48 (November-December 1970): 111–21.

Rader, Hannelore B. 1974. *Academic Library Instruction: Objectives, Programs, and Faculty Involvement.* Ypsilanti, Eastern Michigan University.

———. 1982. "Bibliographic Instruction: Is It a Discipline?" *Reference Services Review* 10 (Spring): 65–66.

Raffel, Jeffrey A., and Robert Shishko. 1969. *Systematic Analysis of University Libraries.* Cambridge, Mass.: MIT Press.

———. 1972. "Centralization vs. Decentralization: A Location Analysis for Libraries." *Special Libraries* 63 (March): 135–43.

Rambler, Linda K. 1982. "Syllabus Study: Keep to a Responsive Academic Library." *Journal of Academic Librarianship* 8 (July): 155–59.

Ratcliffe, F. W. 1968. "Problems of Open Access in Large Academic Libraries." *Libri* 18, no. 2: 95–111.

Ratcliffe, John W. 1982. "International Statistics: Pitfalls and Problems." *Reference Services Review* 10 (Fall): 92–95.

Reardon, Phyllis, and Lynette Jane Laskey. 1980. "Library Services Survey of Eastern Illinois University Extension Classes." *Illinois Libraries* 62 (April): 323–28.

Renford, Beverly, and Linnea Hendrickson. *Bibliographic Instruction: A Handbook*. New York: Neal-Schuman.

Richardson, Richard. 1981. *Functional Literacy in the College Setting*. Washington, D.C.: American Association for Higher Education.

Saffady, William. 1978. *Micrographics*. Littleton, Colo.: Libraries Unlimited.

Saracevic, T. 1977. "Causes and Dynamics of User Frustration in an Academic Library." *College and Research Libraries* 38 (January): 7–18.

Saunders, Carol S., and Russell Saunders. 1985. "Effects of Flextime on Sick Leave, Vacation Leave, Anxiety, Performance, and Satisfaction in a Library Setting." *Library Quarterly* 55 (January): 71–88.

Schad, Jasper G. 1970. "Allocating Book Funds: Control or Planning?" *College and Research Libraries* 31 (May): 155–59.

Schad, Jasper G., and Norman E. Tanis. 1974. *Problems in Developing Academic Library Collections*. New York: R. R. Bowker.

Schlachter, Gail A. 1976. "Professionalism vs. Unionism." *Library Trends* 25 (October): 451–74.

Shishko, Robert, and Jeffrey A. Raffel. 1971. *Centralization vs. Decentralization: A Location Analysis Approach for Librarians*. Santa Monica, Calif.: The Rand Corporation.

Simpson, I. S. 1983. *Basic Statistics for Librarians*. London: Clive Bingley.

Sked, Margaret J. 1984. "Tertiary and Secondary: Relationships with Schools." In *College Librarianship*. Edited by Rennie McElroy, pp. 79–96. London: The Library Association.

Skeith, M. Elizabeth. 1966. "Role of the Academic Library in the Community." *Canadian Library Journal* 23 (July): 43–52.

Stone, Elizabeth. 1970. "Continuing Education in Librarianship: Ideas for Action." *American Libraries* 1 (June 1): 543–51.

Tagliacozzo, R., and J. Kochen. 1970. "Information Seeking Behavior of Catalog Users." *Information Storage and Retrieval* 6 (December): 363–81.

Taylor, Frederick W. 1960. "Principles of Scientific Management." In *Classics in Management*. Edited by Harwood G. Merrill, pp. 72–103. New York: American Management Association.

Trueswell, Richard W. 1966. "Determining the Optimal Number of Volumes for a Library's Core Collection." *Libri* 16, no. 1: 49–60.

———. 1969. "User Circulation Satisfaction vs. Size of Holdings at Three Academic Libraries." *College and Research Libraries* 30 (May): 204–13.

Ungarelli, Donald L. 1983. "Fee-based Model: Administrative Concerns in an Academic Library." *Drexel Library Quarterly* 19 (Fall): 4–12.

Urquhart, John A., and J. L. Schofield. 1971. "Measuring Reader's Failure at the Shelf." *Journal of Documentation* 27 (December): 273–76.

Vickery, B. C. 1948. "Bradford's Law of Scattering." *Journal of Documentation* 4 (December): 198–203.

Voigt, Melvin J. 1975. "Acquisition Rates in University Libraries." *College and Research Libraries* 36 (July): 263–71.

Walton, Clyde C. 1982. "The Role of the Academic Library within the Institution." In

*Academic Librarianship: Yesterday, Today, and Tomorrow.* Edited by Robert Stueart, pp. 181–204. New York: Neal-Schuman.

Walton, Robert A. 1983. *Microcomputer: A Planning and Implementation Guide for Librarians and Information Professionals.* Phoenix: Oryx Press.

Weatherford, John W. 1976. *Collective Bargaining and the Academic Librarian.* Metuchen, N.J.: Scarecrow Press.

Weber, David C. 1971. "Personnel Aspects of Library Automation." *Journal of Library Automation* 4 (March): 27–37.

———. 1974. "The Dynamics of the Library Environment for Professional Staff Growth." *College and Research Libraries* 35 (July): 259–67.

———. 1984. "The Impact of Computer Technology on Academic Library Buildings." In *Academic Libraries: Myths and Realities.* Chicago: Association of College and Research Libraries, pp. 200–203.

Webster, Duane E. 1974. "The Management Review and Analysis Program: An Assisted Self Study to Secure Constructive Change in the Management of Research Libraries." *College and Research Libraries* 35 (March): 114–25.

Welsch, Erwin K. 1985. "Microcomputer Use in Collection Development." *Library Resources and Technical Services* 29 (January): 73–79.

Wilson, Louis R., and Maurice F. Tauber. 1956. *The University Library.* New York: Columbia University Press.

Wingate, Henry W. 1978. "Undergraduate Library: Is It Obsolete?" *College and Research Libraries* 39 (January): 29–33.

Wright, Edward A. 1957. "Research in Organization and Administration." *Library Trends* 6 (October): 141–46.

Young, Harold C. 1976. *Planning, Programming, Budgeting Systems in Academic Libraries.* Michigan: Gale Research Co.

Zweizig, Douglas. 1981. *Output Measures for Public Libraries.* Rockville, Md.: King Research.

## SELECTED BIBLIOGRAPHY

Ellsworth, Ralph E. 1973. *Academic Library Buildings.* Boulder, Colo.: Associated University Press.

Gore, Daniel. 1975. "Destruction of the Tower of Babel." *Catholic Library World* 46 (September): 52–54.

Gore, Daniel. 1975. "Zero-Growth: When Is Not-Enough Enough?" *Journal of Academic Librarianship* 1 (November): 4–11.

Huguelot, Eugene. "Faculty vs. Staff Selection: Collection Development in the Academic Library." *North Carolina Libraries* 43 (Spring 1985): 15–16.

Metz, T. John. "Getting from Here to There: Keeping an Academic Library in Operation During Construction/Renovation." *Advances in Library Administration and Organization* 5 (1986): 207–19.

Ranganathan, S. R. "Open Access in the Library." *Annals of Library Science* 3 (1956): 11–15.

Weingand, Darlene E. "Library Support of an External Degree Program." *College and Research Libraries News* 41 (September 1980): 242–43.

# Index

# About the Editor and Contributors

GERARD B. McCABE is director of libraries at Clarion University of Pennsylvania. He is coeditor of *Advances in Library Administration and Organization: A Research Annual* and is a contributor to professional library publications.

JOHN K. AMRHEIN is currently director of the library at California State University, Stanislaus. Before moving to California in 1984, he was university librarian at Kutztown University of Pennsylvania for thirteen years and served in various capacities in the libraries of Kent State University and Pennsylvania State University. Amrhein received a B.A. degree from Duquesne University, an M.L.S. degree from the University of Pittsburgh, and an M.A. degree in philosophy from Pennsylvania State University.

WENDELL A. BARBOUR is library director at the Captain John Smith Library, Christopher Newport College, Newport News, Virginia.

BOB CARMACK is director of library and media resources at the University of Wisconsin—Superior. He is active in the Building and Equipment Section of the Library Administration and Management Association, American Library Association.

JOHN M. COHN is director of the Sherman H. Masten Learning Resource Center, County College of Morris, in Randolph, New Jersey, and is a partner with Ann L. Kelsey in DocuMentors, an information-services consulting firm. He most recently wrote an article for *Infomediary* on contract library services.

DAVID R. DOWELL, director of libraries, Illinois Institute of Technology, previously was library personnel officer at Duke University and Iowa State University. He has chaired the Library Personnel Resources Advisory Committee and the Personnel Administration Section of the American Library Association.

Dowell received library degrees from the University of North Carolina and the University of Illinois.

CATHERINE DOYLE is access services librarian at the Captain John Smith Library, Christopher Newport College, Newport News, Virginia.

ALLAN J. DYSON serves as university librarian at the University of California, Santa Cruz. His interests include budgeting and financial management, library and participative management, organizational theory, automation, and planning.

RONNIE W. FAULKNER, library director and assistant professor of education at Glenville State College (West Virginia) since 1984, was formerly reference librarian and coordinator of public services at Tennessee Technological University. He received a Ph.D. degree in history from the University of South Carolina and an M.S. degree in library science from the University of North Carolina at Chapel Hill. Faulkner has written numerous articles in the fields of librarianship, history, and political science.

DOUGLAS A. GREEN, director of the library at Arkansas State University—Beebe Branch, was formerly director of the library, University of Central Arkansas, Conway. He received an M.L.S. degree from Louisiana State University and earned the Ed.D. degree from East Texas State University.

SUSAN GRIGG has been director of the Sophia Smith Collection and College Archives at Smith College since 1985. She received a Ph.D. degree in history with a minor in archives administration from the University of Wisconsin. Grigg has had work published on archives administration and U.S. social history, and she serves on the editorial board of the Society of American Archivists and the bibliography committee of the American Studies Association.

EUGENE R. HANSON received a Ph.D. degree in library and information science and has had extensive experience in small and medium-sized college libraries as a director, cataloger, and teacher of library science.

FLOYD C. HARDY is director of library services at North Carolina Central University. Previously, he was library director at Cheyney University of Pennsylvania and held positions at New York University and Rutgers University. He received an M.A. degree in library science from the University of Michigan and a Ph.D. degree in administration in higher education from New York University.

FRED M. HEATH is director of libraries at Texas Christian University and formerly was dean of library services at the University of North Alabama. He received a B.A. degree in English literature from Tulane University, an M.A. degree in Russian history from the University of Virginia, an M.S. degree in library science from Florida State University, and an Ed.D. degree from Virginia Polytechnic Institute and State University. He serves on the boards of SOLINET and the Library Management Network, where he also holds the post of president-elect.

JANET McNEIL HURLBERT is assistant professor and instructional services librarian at Lycoming College in Williamsport, Pennsylvania. Previously she was head of the Collection Development Department of the James Branch Cabell Library, and then head of the Collection Management Division of the University Libraries of Virginia Commonwealth University, 1974–1982. From 1971 to 1974 she was an assistant reference librarian in the Cabell Library at Virginia Commonwealth University. She served as a reference librarian at Iowa State University from 1969 to 1971.

JEAN S. JOHNSON, head of Extension and Special Services, University of Wyoming Libraries, Laramie, has been at the university since 1971, after completing work toward an M.L.S. degree at the University of Oregon. She has had a number of positions in the library and has held her current one since 1983.

RASHELLE S. KARP is an assistant professor at the Clarion University College of Library Science. She has worked as a children's librarian, a special librarian, a cataloger, and the state librarian for the blind in Rhode Island. Her special interests include collections development, library services to special groups, special libraries, and library automation.

KATHARINA KLEMPERER is director of library automation, Dartmouth College. She received an M.L.S. degree, a B.A. degree in music, and a B.A. degree in biology.

DAVID M. LAWRENCE received an M.L.S. degree as well as a master's degree and a doctorate, both in educational media. With nineteen years of administrative experience in public and academic libraries, he has taught library science and educational media at the graduate level, and he wrote the Library Services and Construction Act grant to provide an electronic-mail system for libraries in all seventeen community-college campuses in Pennsylvania. Currently, Lawrence is director of learning resources at Reading Area Community College, Reading, Pennsylvania.

GEORGE H. LIBBEY, currently the assistant director for administrative services at the University of Georgia, had been personnel officer in Temple University Libraries since 1981, following seven years in collection development and one year in reference at Temple. He is a member of the American Library Association and is active in the Association of College Research Libraries' committees and discussion groups. His research interests include labor relations and professional recruitment.

CRAIG S. LIKNESS graduated from St. Olaf College in Northfield, Minnesota; obtained an M.A. degree in library science from the University of Wisconsin—Madison; and earned an M.A. degree in English from the University of Illinois—Urbana. He has served as humanities librarian (since 1976) and head bibliographer (since 1983) at Trinity's Maddux Library. He has contributed to the *Dictionary of American Biography* and presently is a member of the advisory committee for *Books for College Libraries,* third edition.

MURRAY S. MARTIN is university librarian at Tufts University. He has held other library positions in New Zealand, Canada, and the United States and has been active in library-association affairs in all three countries. His numerous publications cover automation, collection management, and finance. He is the author of *Budgetary Control in Academic Libraries* and editor of *Financial Planning for Libraries.* Most recently, he contributed "Financing Library Automation" to the charter issue of *Bottom Line.* Avocationally, Martin contributes to Commonwealth literature studies and has published several papers on Australian and New Zealand authors.

TERRENCE F. MECH, director of the library at Kings College, Wilkes-Barre, Pennsylvania, was formerly director of library services at the College of the Ozarks. He writes on library subjects for professional journals.

T. JOHN METZ, college librarian, Carleton College, Northfield, Minnesota, was formerly executive director, Midwest Regional Library Network; director of libraries, University of Wisconsin—Green Bay; and associate librarian, Lawrence University. Major building projects include the Carleton College Library, and the University of Wisconsin—Green Bay Library. He has been a principal designer or consultant for numerous small library-building projects.

DEBORAH PAWLIK is the director of Reeves Memorial Library, Seton Hill College, Greensburg, Pennsylvania. She received a B.A. degree from Carlow College and an M.L.S. degree from the University of Pittsburgh. In 1986 the Seton Hill Library was awarded a John Cotton Dana Library Public Relations Award.

DENNIS E. ROBISON has a B.S. degree in history and an M.S. degree in library science from Florida State University and an M.A. degree in social sciences from the University of South Florida. He was assistant reference librarian, head of reference, and assistant director for public services at the University of South Florida (1962–1974); university librarian at the University of Richmond (1974–1985); and university librarian at James Madison University

(1985–present). Robison was on the Southeastern Library Network board of directors (1975–1978) and since 1980 has been a consultant to the Association of Research Libraries/Office of Management Skills.

HERBERT D. SAFFORD, director of library services, Kutztown University of Pennsylvania Rohrbach Library, is a doctoral student in Columbia University's Library Services Program. Before serving at Kutztown, he was director of the Library of Muskingum College, New Concord, Ohio.

FREDERICK E. SMITH is an associate in library services with the Division of Library Development of the New York State Library. He serves as a program administrator-consultant for New York's statewide library-automation program. Previously, he was the library director at Westminster College, Pennsylvania (1975–1985), and he worked in several capacities in the Michigan State University Library System, East Lansing (1968–1974).

KATHRYN A. SOUPISET graduated from Trinity University with a B.A. degree in French and German. Since 1981 she has been head of the acquisitions department at the Maddux Library, Trinity University. She serves as consultant to the Library Materials Price Index Committee of the Resources Section in the Resources and Technical Services Division of the American Library Association, compiling data from *Choice* to produce a U.S. college-books price index. With Craig Likness, she is coauthor of "Acquisitions," in the forthcoming *English and American Literature: A Guide for Library Selectors*.

HUGH J. TREACY is reference and bibliographic instruction coordinator at the California State University Library, Fullerton.

DONALD K. TRIBIT is responsible for periodicals and microform service at Millersville University of Pennsylvania Library and has been at Millersville since 1961. He holds the rank of associate professor and is the chair of the library department. He received an M.L.S. degree from George Peabody College of Vanderbilt University.

J. DANIEL VANN III is director of libraries at Bloomsburg University of Pennsylvania. He completed work toward the Ph.D. degree at Yale University and held professorships in history and a college-library directorship before studying librarianship at Emory University. A specialist in planning library buildings, automation, and collection development, he has presided over five college and university libraries, championing the needs of students and faculty.

KENNETH G. WALTER, director of library services, Southern Connecticut State University, New Haven, is a doctoral student at the University of Georgia. Formerly, he was director of libraries, Georgia Southern College, Statesboro, and before that was assistant director for technical services at the University of South Carolina.

RICHARD HUME WERKING earned a B.A. degree at the University of Evansville and M.A. and Ph.D. degrees in U.S. history from the University of Wisconsin, as well as an M.A. degree in librarianship from the University of Chicago. He has been director of libraries at Trinity since 1983 and has served as chair of the college libraries section of the Association of College and Research Libraries (1987–1988). He is a member of the Online Computer Library Center's Advisory Council of College and University Librarians and of *The Library Quarterly*'s advisory board.

ROBERT L. WHITE serves as assistant university librarian for planning and budget at the University of California, Santa Cruz. His interests include budgeting and financial management, library and participative management, organizational theory, automation, and planning.